Screening Enlightenment

A VOLUME IN THE SERIES

THE UNITED STATES IN THE WORLD

edited by Mark Philip Bradley and Paul A. Kramer

A list of titles in this series is available at www.cornellpress.cornell.edu.

Screening Enlightenment

Hollywood and the Cultural Reconstruction
of Defeated Japan

Hiroshi Kitamura

Cornell University Press
Ithaca and London

First published 2010 by Cornell University Press

Printed in the United States of America

Library of Congress Cataloging-in-Publication Data

Kitamura, Hiroshi, 1971–
    Screening enlightenment : Hollywood and the cultural reconstruction of defeated Japan / Hiroshi Kitamura.
        p. cm.
    Includes bibliographical references and index.
    ISBN 978-0-8014-4599-6 (cloth : alk. paper)
    1. Motion pictures, American—Japan—Influence. 2. Motion pictures—Social aspects—Japan—History. 3. Japan—History—Allied occupation, 1945–1952. 4. Japan—Civilization—American influences. 5. Japan—Civilization—1945– I. Title.
    PN1993.5.J3K57   2010
    791.43'63585204—dc22   2009044415

Cornell University Press strives to use environmentally responsible suppliers and materials to the fullest extent possible in the publishing of its books. Such materials include vegetable-based, low-VOC inks and acid-free papers that are recycled, totally chlorine-free, or partly composed of nonwood fibers. For further information, visit our website at www.cornellpress.cornell.edu.

Cloth printing   10 9 8 7 6 5 4 3 2 1

To my mother Mitsuyo Kitamura
and my late father Takao Kitamura,
parents extraordinaire

Contents

Preface

The Second World War crushed the hearts and minds of most Japanese. This was true for veteran film critic Hazumi Tsuneo. Shortly after Japan's capitulation to the Allies, Hazumi reflected on his jingoistic wartime activities with anguish and regret. Like many of his contemporaries, Hazumi deplored the "imperialistic" actions of his government and military. In contrast, he extolled the United States, whose ideological foundations produced a "miraculous power" that promoted a blending of diverse lifestyles.[1] What particularly caught Hazumi's fancy was Hollywood. In his 1947 book *Amerika eiga dokuhon* (Readers' guide to American movies), the critic praised U.S. cinema as a "synthesis of culture" (*bunka no sōgōtai*) that chronicled the "development, growth…[and] hardship" of the United States.[2] Hazumi was impressed with the medium's display of Puritan thought, the "frontier spirit" in the American West, antifascism, and, above all, "American democracy," which he evidently studied through cinema. The famous critic encouraged young men and women to acquire a "correct understanding" of Hollywood to attain a greater knowledge of the United States. "To comprehend America," he claimed, "one cannot cast one's eyes away from American movies."[3]

Hazumi was one of the hundreds of thousands in Japan who passionately responded to an expanding cultural phenomenon. During the era of the Allied occupation (1945–52), U.S. film studios launched a large-scale cinematic campaign to spread their movies and values across Japan. Over the six and a half years, Hollywood disseminated over six hundred feature films to theaters nationwide, thereby turning the formerly protectionist state into a lucrative and dependable film market. This cinematic campaign also carried a larger mission. Working in conjunction with Gen. Douglas MacArthur, the Supreme Commander for the Allied Powers (SCAP), Hollywood shed its traditional function to "purely entertain" and actively "reeducated" and "reoriented" the Japanese. During the first year of the operation, one U.S. studio manager boasted that Hollywood cinema was an "enlightening" (keimōteki) product that offered a balance of "entertainment and intellect" (goraku to kyōyō) to the viewing population. As a result of its dual function, American cinema was "appreciated by audiences without exception."[4]

This book is an attempt to understand Hollywood's role in Japan's postwar reconstruction. In it I examine the U.S. film industry's commercial expansion and its political, social, and cultural influence on the war-shattered population. Relying on official correspondence, memoranda, minutes, and letters exchanged between the U.S. government, military, and motion picture industry, I investigate the complex institutional negotiations that developed and furthered Hollywood's transpacific operation. Another aim is to demonstrate how the defeated population responded to American cinematic penetration. To this end, I examine the thoughts and agendas of Japanese publicists, journalists, intellectuals, exhibitors, and mass consumers. The sources I use include Japanese-language newspapers, magazines, flyers, promotional guides, movie programs, posters, and oral histories gathered in the two countries.

One of my main goals in this book is to enrich the understanding of the occupation. Standard works have explored the occupation of Japan as a political and diplomatic experience. Relying on painstaking archival research and policy analysis, these studies have elucidated the U.S. government and military endeavors to demilitarize and "democratize" the former enemy, as well as their shifting decision to prioritize economic and industrial recovery in response to the growing Communist threat in East Asia.[5] Since these books were written, interest has grown in the study of the occupation as a social and cultural phenomenon. Intent on understanding SCAP's broader relationship to everyday citizens, a new body of scholarship has cast attention on such issues as race, gender, education, and popular culture.[6] Perhaps the biggest contribution is the elucidation of Japanese perspectives. In *Embracing Defeat: Japan in the Wake of World War II* John W. Dower explores the widespread impact of the U.S. occupation by highlighting the diverse ways in which the Japanese responded to war and defeat. Dower's work refuses to portray the occupation as an "American interlude" devoid of Japanese will, but instead treats it as a "SCAPanese" story and a "lived *Japanese* experience" that reflected the "voices of people at all levels of society."[7]

Dower and others have ably demonstrated the U.S. occupation government's widespread influence on Japanese society. My goal is to elaborate the story by examining the active involvement of Hollywood, an American business institution.[8] During the early postwar era, MacArthur's headquarters granted unusual privileges to U.S. film studios, allowing the recovery and expansion of their trade in a volatile but controlled marketplace. Hollywood responded by assisting SCAP's political mission. While bombarding consumers with Tinseltown glamour and flare, U.S. companies employed a rigorous "enlightenment campaign" to actively spread American values and ideals to the Japanese public. Although largely neglected by historians, this cultural operation attracted hundreds of thousands of moviegoers and inspired change in their political, social, and cultural orientations. Through its mediation between SCAP and the Japanese public, this U.S. private institution reinforced the occupiers' effort to "uplift" and "reorient" the Japanese. Hollywood was a "chosen instrument" that facilitated Japan's postwar reconstruction.[9]

Screening Enlightenment also sheds light on Hollywood. Experts in visual culture and screen studies have increasingly turned to the empirical study of Hollywood's power and influence on a global scale.[10] Their research, however, has predominantly focused on the industry's business with Europe. This transatlantic (or "Europe first") bias has prevented us from fully comprehending the widespread impact of U.S. cinema in much of the non-Western world. Another shortcoming is the tendency to concentrate solely on Hollywood's formal negotiations with governments and foreign industries. Although this literature has enhanced our understanding of tariffs, quotas, censorship, and the state-level handling of film prints, we are left largely in ignorance concerning the social and cultural ramifications of the movie business on the "ground level." What remains lacking, to a surprising extent, is the study of overseas film *reception*, a practice that involves the "confrontation between the semiotic and the social," according to film scholar Robert C. Allen.[11]

This book, then, looks at a market that has been largely overlooked in film and media scholarship. By presenting a study of Japan, I call attention to a prominent non-Western market that has turned into the largest overseas outlet of American cinema in recent decades.[12] The early postwar era was a pivotal moment that cemented Hollywood's presence and popularity across the Pacific. In order to account for this cross-cultural phenomenon, I investigate the intricate negotiations surrounding trade policy as well as the less-explored avenues of film distribution, promotion, exhibition, and consumption. While initiated by a close alliance of U.S. government, military, and industrial authorities, Hollywood's transpacific expansion relied on a vast array of local intermediaries

and consumers who appropriated, reshaped, and absorbed American film culture from the receiving end. The "Hollywoodization" of postwar Japan was a
joint creation of the producers, brokers, and consumers of U.S. cinema in the
two societies.

Finally, *Screening Enlightenment* examines American cultural influence abroad,
or "Americanization." Early efforts to understand the global flow of U.S. values
focused on the sender's perspective. This began after the war when diplomatic
historians and policymakers celebrated the sprawl of U.S. artifacts and ideas—
from Coca-Cola, jazz music, to *Reader's Digest*—as harbingers of democracy,
liberal capitalism, and modern life. Beginning in the early 1960s, a growing
body of analysts began to adopt a critical tone toward U.S. expansionism as a
form of cultural imperialism. Over the past two decades, a new generation of
experts has looked beyond U.S. perspectives and has closely studied the adaptation and appropriation of "American" values in local arenas. These works
have underscored the diverse manners in which peoples and societies outside
the United States refashioned their identities by internalizing and reinventing
"things American." In these accounts, "foreign" actors were not passive cultural
consumers. They were self-motivated respondents who accepted, adapted, and
rejected American values for their own empowerment.[13]

The literature on Americanization is overall fruitful and illuminating, but
much of it, like the scholarship on Hollywood, concentrates on the transatlantic context. To a considerable degree, Japan experts have resisted the Americanization framework, choosing instead to highlight the limits of and resistance
to U.S. penetration.[14] *Screening Enlightenment* counters this trend by examining the intense "Americanization" of early postwar Japan through a study
of Hollywood. It does not depict the expansion of U.S. values as a unilateral
imposition but, rather, underscores the voluntary involvement of the Japanese
in the creation of an imagined "America." I thus treat Americanization as a
"convergence process" shaped to a great extent by individuals and institutions
of the host (or receiving) society.[15] However, this cultural negotiation was also
a hegemonic practice, one in which U.S. agents capitalized on local initiatives
to reinforce their dominance over the Japanese. Americanization, in this sense,
was a rigorous exercise of U.S. cultural power—one that facilitated the integration of war-torn Japan into a new political, economic, and security system
that increasingly revolved around the United States.[16]

The chapters that follow explore the vital role Hollywood played in Japan's postwar Americanization. I begin by looking at the U.S. film industry's trade campaign before the Second World War. I then examine in turn
Hollywood's collaboration with the U.S. government and military during the

Figure 0.1. Cartoonist Sugiura Yukio makes the connection between the milieu of occupied Japan and one of Hollywood's popular releases. *Eiga sekai,* August 1948, 6. © Sugiura Jun. Image courtesy of Gordon W. Prange Collection, University of Maryland Libraries.

war; the U.S.-led occupation government's tense interplay with Japanese and American film companies; Hollywood's promotion and exhibition of American culture through the movies; and the reaction and response of Japanese moviegoers—particularly the culture elites and young movie fans.

The impact of this cinematic program was considerable. On one level, it reinforced the power of U.S. political, military, and business leaders who took part in "uplifting" and "re-educating" the peoples of the former Axis enemy. On another level, it influenced a variety of Japanese agents who pursued entrepreneurial, recreational, and educational opportunities through Hollywood cinema. The layers of negotiation across the Pacific inspired the creation of an uneven bilateral partnership, one that resurrected Japan as a liberal democratic ally while reinforcing America's dominance over it. The postwar reconstruction of Japan owed to a renewed intimacy that drew together the two societies. Hollywood played a crucial role in shaping these larger developments.

Additionally, the far-reaching penetration of U.S. cinema provides insight on America's deepening ties with Asia after the Second World War. Even though ideological rifts and political disputes have threatened and caused breaks in the relationship, U.S. influence in the Pacific, over the decades, has remained remarkably strong.[17] Building on earlier works that have explored this dynamic experience through the lens of U.S. policymakers, perspectives, and political and economic agendas, my book explores the transpacific sphere through a study of both state and nonstate actors; the intertwinement of political, economic, social, and cultural forces; and the negotiation of "American" and "foreign" agents from the top down and bottom up. America's expansion in Asia was a complex interplay of individuals and institutions on both sides of the Pacific. Hollywood helps us understand the multitude of entwinements that have shaped this transpacific world.

In this book, Japanese names generally appear family name first, as is customary in Japan. However, English-language publications by Japanese authors will appear first name first. I have used macrons (e.g. ō and ū) to indicate long vowel sounds in Japanese, except in the names of cities and other geographical locations. Translations into English are my own unless otherwise noted. Any errors are of course mine alone.

Screening Enlightenment

Chapter 1

Thwarted Ambitions

Hollywood and Japan before the Second World War

For the October 1, 1932, issue of *Kokusai eiga shinbun,* a leading periodical of the film trade, Sahara Kenji contributed an essay titled "An International Aspect of the Mission of the Movies" ("Eiga shimei no kokusaiteki ichimen"). In the two-page opinion piece, the head of the International Travel Bureau of the Ministry of Railroads expressed his astonishment with cinema's "international ability to influence" (*kokusaiteki kankaryoku*). Sahara's best example was Hollywood. He noted that American cinema was a "spearhead of trade" as well as a force of "Americanization" in Japan. To him, Hollywood's cultural power was partly evident in "gang" activities seemingly inspired by crime films, but more astonishingly in "every single movement" of the "modern boy and modern girl strolling on the Ginza," including their "fashion or makeup." The government official made particular note of the "kissing" of couples on the platforms of the railroad station in Tokyo. Such public actions were "utterly astonishing," he wrote.[1]

Sahara's commentary was a response to Hollywood's growing presence in Japan. During the late 1910s and 1920s, a time when American movies began to captivate audiences around the world, U.S. studios established distribution offices in Japan to extend their business across the Pacific. Relying on its "scientifically" organized mode of business, its diverse lineup of films, and its formidable cultural appeal, Hollywood built its patronage around large urban centers where American and Western culture enjoyed wide attention. Throughout much of the interwar era, Hollywood drew many educated and well-to-do consumers who looked on the United States as an emblem of "modern" and "advanced" life.

However, the tidal wave of American movies was at best a limited phenomenon. During the 1920s, Japanese studios contested the "Hollywood menace" by gearing up their own filmmaking. By adjusting their growing business to the changing demands of the marketplace, Japanese moviemakers solidified their command over the trade. This industrial momentum coincided with a surge of policy constraints. During an era of rapid imperial expansion in Asia, the Japanese government regulated the U.S. film business through fiscal and cultural protectionism. As a result, Hollywood's market share declined in the late 1930s until Pearl Harbor shut the doors of the film trade in 1941.

Hollywood's prewar campaign was a sobering experience. As soon as they launched their operations, U.S. companies discovered that Japan had developed a thriving movie culture in which Hollywood cinema could achieve a large and permanent following. Yet local conditions refused to reward this optimism. A pair of obstacles—the Japanese film industry and the Japanese government—effectively undercut Hollywood's operation. Despite much success elsewhere, U.S. film industry's business methods during the interwar era were not good enough to win the Japanese market. American studios would have to await a second chance to test their abilities.

The Rise of Global Hollywood

The United States at the turn of the twentieth century was a nation of rising expectations. In the robust decades following the Civil War, the once-torn republic began to develop a powerful industrialized economy. As big businesses fiercely competed in a fluctuating marketplace, tens of thousands of working people from other countries arrived on American shores, yearning for success in a "land of opportunity." As they welcomed the population influx, cities across the country were transformed into networks of railroads, telephone and telegraph poles, and electric lines. In this era of dynamic change, the United States emerged as a true global power. During the Spanish-American War of 1898, the U.S. Navy, to the world's surprise, crushed the waning Spanish fleet in Cuba, Puerto Rico, and the Philippines. Two decades later, U.S. forces led the Allies to a decisive victory over the Central Powers in Europe. By the end of the First World War, the nation possessed the power to influence the lives and affairs of people far beyond the shores of North America.[2]

Hollywood was a child of this rising nation. Born in the mid-1890s, cinematic entertainment in the United States developed first as a pastime for the expanding working-class and immigrant patrons in the industrializing cities.

The dominant cinemas at the time were European, most notably Pathé Cinematograph, a French company that had managed to gain a head start in the international competition.[3] Yet U.S. companies, led by the Edison Company and the American Mutoscope and Biograph Company, soon began to win a larger following in the domestic market.[4] During the 1910s, American filmmakers developed multireel feature-length narratives with complex plotlines. Filmic storytelling increasingly relied on continuity editing, predictability, and verisimilitude acting. Distributors began to merge their businesses to extend their grip across the nation. Thanks to these developments, U.S. companies were able to recover the domestic market from their European rivals by 1917.[5]

Hollywood's globalization occurred in tandem with its control of the domestic market. The main catalyst was the First World War. The destruction of Europe resulted in plummeting industrial and commercial capabilities, including the output of cinematic entertainment. Not only did this undercut the European companies' influence in the United States, it also enabled U.S. filmmakers to extend their business across the Atlantic. Emboldened by a booming national economy, American companies began to overcome their dependency on foreign intermediaries by spreading their products through their own distribution offices. By the end of the war, American firms had established direct representation in Great Britain and Continental Europe, in addition to South America, Australia, and various parts of Asia.[6] In a country that now reigned as the largest creditor nation of the world, Hollywood was set to gain command of the international film market.

The interwar decades were good times for Hollywood. At home, U.S. studios reinforced their dominance through industrial consolidation and expansive marketing. In the late 1910s and 1920s, U.S. companies vertically integrated their operations to develop a firm grip over the three branches of the business: film production, distribution, and exhibition. This institutional alignment allowed studios to streamline the creation and circulation of narrative products—from *Ben-Hur* (1925), *It* (1927), and *The Gaucho* (1928) to *Tarzan, the Ape Man* (1932).[7] The industry was also able to generate extensive publicity. Aiming to excite consumers with what studio mogul Carl Laemmle once called a "circus method of exploitation," U.S. companies showered consumers with a dizzying array of posters, photos, billboards, parades, premieres, and other eye-catching publicity.[8] Exhibitors mushroomed across the nation. Many downtown theaters turned into opulent "movie palaces" that boasted cutting-edge engineering, interior grandeur, and elegant design.[9]

This entertainment business consolidated its power through horizontal integration. In 1922, U.S. companies got together to establish the Motion Picture Producers and Distributors of America (MPPDA), a powerful umbrella

Figure 1.1. Will H. Hays, president of the Motion Picture Producers and Distributors of America. Courtesy of the Wisconsin Center for Film and Theater Research, Madison, Wisconsin.

organization of Hollywood studios.[10] The head of this organization was Will H. Hays, former Postmaster General during the Harding administration. Intent on salvaging the industry's public image from tabloid scandals and unflattering rumors, Hays, the "movie czar" from Indiana, launched an extensive public relations campaign.[11] In 1934, the MPPDA established the Production Code Administration (PCA), a self-censorship apparatus that imposed strict rules regarding morally and politically questionable representations.[12] Under the leadership of a confident spokesperson, Hollywood transformed into a "mature oligopoly" of the Big Five (Warner Bros., Metro-Goldwyn-Mayer, Paramount, Twentieth Century–Fox, RKO) and the Little Three (Columbia, Universal, United Artists) studios.[13]

The MPPDA's activities were hardly confined to the domestic sphere. While taking pains to consolidate the industry's standing at home, it pushed for an "open door" to gain access to markets abroad.[14] In order to better engage with the international arena, Hays founded a Foreign Department within the MPPDA and appointed Frederick "Ted" Herron, a longtime acquaintance, to lead. During his decade-and-a-half of service, Herron tirelessly labored to represent the industry abroad while balancing the interests of member studios at home.[15] The Hays Office also responded to foreign complaints about on-screen content. In order to finesse and diffuse international critics, the MPPDA regularly consulted with studio heads to forge "appropriate" on-screen content. Internal discussions were often geared toward the elimination of offensive caricatures of the on-screen Other.[16]

The Hays Office's commitment to international trade also brought the industry closer to the U.S. government. Capitalizing on his connections with the Republican establishment, Hays in 1924 requested that the Department of State appoint an official to work specifically with the MPPDA.[17] In response, the State Department agreed to assist Hollywood's negotiations with foreign officials and captains of industry.[18] The Department of Commerce became an ally as well. Acknowledging that Hollywood was of "great importance" to America's world trade, the Motion Picture Division of the Bureau of Foreign and Domestic Commerce handled information on censorship regulations, tariffs and tax policies, copyright rules, and other issues that surfaced in foreign markets.[19] Nathan D. Golden, assistant chief of the division, vowed to extend "every possible assistance in organizing, developing, and maintaining a profitable export business."[20] The Commerce Department enlisted a widely used slogan in support of Hollywood: "trade follows the motion pictures."[21]

The efforts to globalize Hollywood came with high rewards. Studio executives and others commonly noted that 30–40 percent of the industry's earnings came from overseas during the interwar era.[22] Although the demographics of "Hollywoodization" stretched across the world map, the primary focus of U.S. studios was Europe, which regularly generated as much as two-thirds of the industry's foreign returns. Hollywood's success across the Atlantic owed to the high market value of U.S. films and the direct-marketing campaigns of studios, as well as the MPPDA's intervention.[23] The performance of U.S. movies was strong in other regions as well. In Latin America, Hollywood's popularity centered on Brazil and Argentina. The region exceeded Europe in the volume (i.e., footage) of consumption.[24] An estimated 10 percent of the industry's foreign returns came from south of the Rio Grande.[25] Likewise, American movies thrived in Australasia—one of the top consumers of Hollywood as measured by footage.[26] U.S. productions also reached the Middle East and Africa during the interwar years. By 1930, Herron boasted that Hollywood movies had "caught popular fancy the world over."[27]

The Birth of Cinema in Japan

East Asia was not as sizable a market as Europe. Yet since its "opening" to the West in the mid-nineteenth century, American entrepreneurs looked across the Pacific to expand their business opportunities.[28] Hollywood's interest in Asian markets rose during the mid-1910s. An early observer was Tom D. Cochrane, who visited East Asia and South Asia in 1916. On his return to the United States, the Universal studio executive told the *Los Angeles Times* that American movies were "much in demand" across the region.[29] Similar remarks surfaced in the following decade. In 1928, *The Film Daily Yearbook* reported steady increases in film exports to the region. The quantity of exports multiplied from four million feet in 1913 to forty million feet thirteen years later. The trade almanac concluded that the "Far East" was "rapidly rising in importance as a market for American pictures."[30]

The centerpiece of the transpacific film trade was Japan. Since the Meiji Restoration of 1868, the island nation had undergone a dramatic course of "modern" nation-building. Led by a new generation of political elites, the society that had long been ruled by the Tokugawa family adopted a centralized government structure with a bicameral legislature and a Prussian-inspired constitution. Under the emperor's reign as a deity, Japan strengthened its military and won convincingly in wars against China and Russia at the turn of the twentieth century. By time of the First World War, Japan had become an intimidating presence in East Asia—one that the Great Powers of Europe and the United States had to reckon with.[31]

Japan began to emulate the Western powers in ways beyond sheer military might. Thanks to the Meiji state's incessant efforts to bolster the economy, Japan developed a vibrant industrial sector interlaced with railroad and tele-graph lines.[32] The engine of these activities was the *zaibatsu,* the tree-shaped financial combines, which pumped money and resources into the boom-ing textile and steel mills. Economic growth fueled a fast-paced population increase, particularly in the sprawling urban centers—especially Tokyo and Osaka—on the Pacific coast.[33] These hubs of human activity were sustained by a large industrial workforce that made its presence felt through daily labor, union activism, and, at times, violence in the streets.[34]

These expanding urban spaces also gave rise to a lively consumer culture. No longer only for the "fastidious dandies" of the Tokugawa era, goods and leisure consumption were enjoyed by a wide range of urbanites—including residents in "low city" (*shitamachi*) neighborhoods, upscale districts, and indus-trial sectors.[35] While never constrained to a single socioeconomic group, this trend toward consumerism was led by the "new middle class" of profession-als and white-collar workers—men and women who shopped at department stores, lounged at cafes, enjoyed music on phonographs and radio, and savored fashion and lifestyle magazines.[36] These eager consumers increasingly pursued material and psychological fulfillment by adapting American values in fash-ion, architecture, literature, gender norms, and home life.[37] Enthusiastic youth earned notoriety as "modern girls" (*moga*) and "modern boys" (*mobo*)—rebels against tradition—as they strolled the streets of the Ginza in Tokyo or trendy areas in other cities.[38]

Cinema came to life in this changing urban landscape. It originated from a public showing of Thomas A. Edison's Kinetoscope and the Lumière brothers' Cinematograph at the turn of the twentieth century. Soon, Japanese entrepre-neurs began to churn out one-reel narratives, typically based on location shots and real-life events, such as the Russo-Japanese War. The films of Edison and other American distributors were gaining traction as well; however, their prod-ucts were by no means dominant in this nascent era of cinema. The most prom-inent pictures were imports from Great Britain, Germany, France, and Italy.[39] As the film historian Tanaka Junichirō noted, the "more popular [foreign] films before World War I were almost exclusively European products."[40] Films such as *Zigomar* (1911) and *Quo Vadis?* (1914)—a French heist film and an Italian historical epic, respectively—were among the biggest hits during this era.[41]

The movies in early twentieth-century Japan, as in many other societies, had a strongly plebian character. This new medium began by joining the ranks of "things to show" (*misemono*)—a carnivalesque assortment of recreational attractions. The early shows opened at existing playhouses, public halls, and outdoor tents where other pastimes—such as *kabuki* and *yose*—were performed; film distributors toured with their musical bands and projectionists to showcase their new technological marvel.[42] During the era before recorded sound, cinema was assisted by oral accompaniment. The *benshi,* as these orators came to be known, generated clarity and excitement through their exaggerated body movements and voice. They also served as bridge figures who rendered foreign films more accessible to Japanese audiences. Unlike in most other societies, oral presentation became a thriving profession throughout the era of Japanese silent cinema. The *benshi* at times became the central draw of the show.[43]

Cinema's soaring appeal during the 1910s contributed to the growth of film-specific venues across the nation. During the first two decades of the twentieth century, the number of permanent movie houses multiplied in cities around Japan.[44] By 1925 over one thousand theaters were in operation; this number doubled a decade later.[45] The great majority of these new outlets were hastily constructed wooden structures with inferior equipment and facilities. Theaters were crowded and "packed to suffocation," one observer complained. Since many theaters lacked air conditioning or clear ventilation, auditoriums were typically steaming hot during the summer season and ice cold during dreary winter days.[46] Since the theaters, one respected film journalist groused in 1927, "could not lure fans just by their name values, [they] were dependent on the drawing power of the films."[47]

The rapid expansion of the movie business coevolved with a dramatic growth in movie going. Initially seen by some as a children's pastime, movie going soon came to encompass a wide array of consumers, children and adults, students and teachers, women and men, farmers and factory workers, bureaucrats and politicians. By the late 1920s, attendance figures reached over 160 million.[48] Movie going during this era was more common in big cities, not only because of greater accessibility to the movies, but also because "residents in big cities," noted the movie almanac *Nihon eiga jigyō sōran,* "tended to watch movies more frequently than residents in regional areas."[49] In 1927 Ishimaki Yoshio categorized these cultural consumers into four groups: those who visit the theaters to kill time, those who are attracted to the stars, those who follow the plot, and aficionados who take the movies seriously. The fourth group, the astute trade analyst noted, often formed "movie study groups" and "screening meetings" for camaraderie as serious movie fans.[50]

Hollywood Goes to Japan

Japan's growth as a movie market was welcome news to Hollywood. During the first decade of the twentieth century, U.S. companies relied on Japanese companies to purchase the films in London and New York.[51] Soon, U.S. companies began to operate directly in Japan. The breakthrough year was 1916. In a time when European film exports to Japan (and the rest of the world) were declining due to the Great War, the Universal Film Corporation, with the help of a local contact, established a branch office in Tokyo.[52] This American company released a large volume of low-budget brand films, namely Bluebird, Red Feather, and Butterfly. These productions, particularly those on the Bluebird label, created an instant sensation.[53] The success of these exports coincided with the growing prominence of U.S. serials—a constellation of action-packed two-to-four-reel episodes released every week.[54]

Universal's success inspired other U.S. companies to place offices in Japan. Paramount Company (1922), United Artists Corporation (1923), Fox Film Corporation (1923), Warner–First National (1925), MGM (1929), Columbia (1933), and RKO (1934) established their headquarters in Tokyo and founded regional branches in cities such as Osaka, Kobe, Fukuoka, and Aomori.[55] These studio operations were usually run by a manager dispatched from the United States, while exhibition, publicity, and other required tasks on the ground were handled by Japanese employees, who took great pride in their service to American companies.[56] The trade often looked on these corporate employees as "modern boys" (*modan bōi*) of the movie industry.[57]

These U.S. companies brought their competitive energy and business skills to the Japanese market. In determining their agendas for Japan, they each gathered data and information on legal regulations, tax systems, rival companies, media outlets, and national holidays.[58] Employees on the ground stressed that their business was based on "systematic action," "efficiency," and "scientific" research.[59] Studios subsequently geared up their publicity, which spread through two channels. One was direct contact from studio headquarters in the United States. Companies such as Paramount and United Artists would directly ship their press books and still photos to the Japanese media. The other was promotion conducted by the branch offices. These local outposts devised publicity for newspapers, magazines, billboards, and other conspicuous places.[60]

Hollywood companies often connected with consumers through creative means. For example, in releasing *With Byrd at the South Pole* (1930), an expedition tale based on rare firsthand footage of the Antarctic, Paramount rented five planes to sprinkle 250,000 flyers and 4,500 free tickets across Tokyo. According to the publicity manager, this stunt yielded "considerable sensation."[61] The marketing of Harold Lloyd's *The Milky Way* (1936), a comedy about a milkman who gets mixed up in a boxing match, included tie-ins with milk retailers, who promoted the film on containers of their dairy products.[62] To attract consumers to *Follow the Fleet* (1936), a musical comedy starring Ginger Rogers and Fred Astaire, RKO developed sailor caps for use by theater employees, dancers, and customers.[63] In order to draw public attention to *Stagecoach* (1939), John Ford's action-packed western, United Artists hired claqueurs to spread favorable rumors at cafes and on the streets.[64]

In this climate of intense studio competition, the content of publicity was far from uniform. But U.S. companies strove to distinguish their products as "superior movies" (*yūshū eiga*) or "exceptionally crafted movies" (*tokusaku eiga*);[65] the promotion of films was additionally shaped by three ingredients. First, American companies publicized the Hollywood star. The good looks and glamour of Charles Chaplin, Clara Bow, Douglas Fairbanks, and others graced magazine covers, theater marquees, and newspaper ads. These screen celebrities, according to film historian Richard Maltby, were "the commodities that most consistently drew audience to the movies."[66]

Second, U.S. companies associated each film to its genre, which helped create a sense of familiarity for the yet-to-be-seen products.[67] "Action dramas" (*katsugeki*), such as Johnny Weissmuller's *Tarzan, the Ape Man* (1932), stressed nonstop motion and excitement in exotic lands, guaranteeing audiences a "100 percent thrill."[68] "Comedies" (*kigeki*), such as Buster Keaton's *Spite Marriage* (1929), offered laughter to "the young, the old, men, women," and even rewarded them with "good health."[69] Romantic stories (*renaigeki*), especially those produced before the 1934 production code, titillated consumers with sexuality. Publicity material of RKO's *Tanned Legs* (1929), for instance, showcased a "large parade of naked legs" as a celebration of "modern sensibility on the cutting edge."[70]

Finally, these companies marketed their films alongside their company brands. By affixing the company's name and logo to their films, studios, according to one film scholar, could develop a "uniformity of the product manufactured" that enabled consumers to better connect to the forthcoming products.[71] Branding also enabled U.S. studios to differentiate their films from rival products. As a result, Paramount, for example, bragged that their films were "high class" (*kōkyū*), while MGM hyped their star-studded lineups.[72] The rivalry among distributors—foreign or domestic—was fierce during the pre–Second

Figure 1.2. The Shinjuku Musashino-kan during the screening of John Ford's *Stagecoach* (1939). Courtesy of the Kawakita Memorial Film Institute.

World War era. Eleven years after the war, a veteran publicist remarked that U.S. companies in the interwar era were "extremely strict" in assuring that their seals were attached. "The logo was like the...national flag."[73]

The studios' competitive mind-set also played out in the arena of film exhibition. Unlike in the United States, Hollywood companies did not own theaters in Japan. In order to succeed in business across the Pacific, U.S. companies had to buy screen time from exhibitors. Hollywood pursued this by resorting to a system of "free booking," under which companies rented prints to exhibitors by the film.[74] The rates were flexible. According to one account, distributors usually claimed between 15 and 25 percent of the film's total earnings, though rental fees could fluctuate anywhere between 10 and 50 percent.[75] U.S. studios generally targeted prestige and up-market theaters in big urban centers, such as the Musashino-kan (Tokyo), Hibiya eiga gekijō (Tokyo), Yaegaki gekijō (Nagoya), and Sekai-kan (Fukuoka).[76] "It is the best strategy," noted a United Artists representative, "to screen movies in the better quality theaters...even if there is some difference in the rental fees."[77]

Contesting the Hollywood Menace

Hollywood's early efforts produced short-term success and hopes for more. Shortly after Universal arrived in Japan, U.S. companies surpassed European distributors and dominated the share of foreign imports.[78] At one point, American studios led all other nations in the number of films released.[79] Hollywood gossip and fanfare penetrated a wide array of publications, including newspapers, mainstream periodicals such as *Chūō kōron* and *Kingu,* and film magazines of various kinds.[80] U.S. movies enjoyed the patronage of a wide variety of moviegoers, particularly the "intelligentsia" or "high-class fans" who, in the words of one critic, looked on the American way of life as an "advanced level of culture and living environment."[81] Many consumers perceived Hollywood as a window on modern and advanced life—ideals that were often linked to the notion of "Americanism" (*Amerikanizumu*).[82]

But this "Hollywoodization" of Japan was at best a limited phenomenon. Japanese film companies quickly regrouped to counter the flood of American movies. While taken aback by the initial surge of U.S. companies, filmmakers in Japan swiftly merged their resources to develop a studio system of their own. In 1924, only a year after a devastating earthquake struck the greater Kanto region (which includes Tokyo), Japanese companies surpassed the output of foreign imports for the first time. Soon "the popularity of Japanese cinema," as *Kokusai eiga shinbun* noted, "far exceeded that of foreign cinema."[83] U.S. film representatives grew pessimistic. As early as 1925, E. Bruce Johnson of First National Pictures observed that native filmmaking in Japan was "quite an extensive business" with no danger of "any fatal competition" from foreign distributors. "American motion picture production," he lamented, "never will command the hold in Japan like it has gained in some of the foreign countries, like Europe."[84]

The surge of Japanese cinema began in the wake of the Kinetoscope's arrival. Finding promise in cinema's business potential, early production companies such as the Yokota shōkai and the Yoshizawa shōkai began to produce a slew of one-reel narratives, typically filmed on location and about real-life events, such as the Russo-Japanese War. In 1908, when Yoshizawa shōkai developed a glass studio as an anchor for its filmmaking, output increased markedly.[85] Small production companies merged with others to form bigger studios, most notably the Nippon katsudō shashin kabushiki geisha, or Nikkatsu for short (1912) and the Shōchiku kinema kabushiki geisha, or Shōchiku (1921).[86] The movies of this early era largely relied on theatrical conventions (namely *kabuki* and the Western-influenced "new faction" or *shinpa* theater), male actors to perform both female *and* male roles, and popular historical dramas and adaptations.

Hollywood's arrival in the mid- and late-1910s posed a serious threat to Japanese filmmaking, but these companies quickly adapted to the needs of the market. A key strategy was to appropriate Hollywood's practices.[87] Starting in the late 1910s, film director Kaeriyama Norimasa, who was soon hired by the Kokkatsu film company, began the "pure film movement" (*jun eiga undō*). Stimulated by American (and European) filmmaking practices, Kaeriyama advocated using screenplays, female actors instead of female impersonators, as well as complex camera work and editing.[88] Japanese companies also sent their personnel to the United States to study Hollywood's mode of production. Expatriates with work experiences in Hollywood—most famously the actor Thomas Kurihara, cinematographer Henry Kotani, and actor-turned-director Abe Yutaka (aka Jack Abe)—returned to Japan and adapted Hollywood's techniques to their filmmaking.[89]

Filmmaking in Japan also grew through industrial realignment. Major studios adopted a central producer system—another Hollywood practice—to expedite the simultaneous production of multiple film projects. The division of labor within these companies, however, relied on long-standing artisanship units (*kumi*) led by established directors. These units thrived on an apprentice system that usually required training, experience, and patience to rise in the hierarchy. From this institution emerged a cadre of noted directors, including Itō Daisuke, Mizoguchi Kenji, Kinugasa Teinosuke, Gosho Heinosuke, Ozu Yasujirō, and Shimazu Yasujirō.[90] These filmmakers were greatly influenced by Hollywood's techniques, such as the close-up shot and continuity editing. Many of them, most famously Ozu and Mizoguchi, developed their own distinct visual styles that international film aficionados would later find mesmerizing.[91]

Japanese companies, in addition, integrated the star system into their filmmaking. Instead of drawing on acting talent from the theater stage, Japanese companies, in their effort to compete with American and European cinemas, began to train performers specifically for the movies. This led to the formation of actor's schools (in the early 1920s) whose curricula included courses and lectures on film production, pantomime, makeup, choreography, photography, the history of theater, psychology, dance, and even Western mannerisms.[92] The years that followed gave rise to top-bill stars such as Hasegawa Kazuo and Bandō Tsumasaburō. Japanese studios gradually did away with female impersonators in favor of female actresses. New starlets, such as Kurihara Sumiko and Natsukawa Shizue, had their photos in newspapers and magazines as well as on the screen. These celebrities fed into the expanding commodity chains that shaped the wider consumer economy.[93]

The newly aligned Japanese film industry contested Hollywood in at least four important ways. First, it competed with quantity. During much of the 1920s, Japanese companies, according to film scholar David Bordwell, churned out some six hundred to eight hundred movies a year—often far exceeding Hollywood's annual output.[94] Although many of these films were low-budget "quickies" that critics deplored for poor craftsmanship, the quantity of narrative output enabled Japanese firms to offer a steady supply of new products. Between twenty to twenty-five prints were made of each (popular) film.[95] Owing to the modest budget size, Japanese companies could distribute their films at a lower cost than foreign productions. Not only did this attract small-time exhibitors, it also kept admission prices low. Japanese cinema, in this sense, was a "cinema of quantity" that built its constituency through offering an affordable product. It established broad patronage as a "cheap amusement."[96]

Second, Japanese filmmakers delivered variety. In addition to mobilizing an arsenal of stars, filmmakers catered to diverse consumer tastes through an array of genres. Native productions during much of the interwar era were divided into two larger umbrella categories: the *jidaigeki,* or period film, and the *gendaigeki,* or modern film. Each of these megagenres contained a hodge-podge of subgenres that catered to different, if overlapping, tastes. The *jidaigeki,* for example, were usually historical dramas set in the Edo (Tokugawa) period (1600–1868). But there were internal variants, such as "captivity episodes" (*torimonochō*), sword dramas (*kengeki*), and "lone drifter" (*matatabi*) stories.[97] The *gendaigeki* genre offered narratives with Westernized social and cultural settings. The subcategories included sports films (*supōtsu eiga*), middle-class films (*shōshimin eiga*), and child comedies (*jidō kigeki*).[98] The genre system in Japan was intricate and complex. Noted film scholar Mitsuhiro Yoshimoto writes that in Japanese film "there are as many different genres and subgenres as in Hollywood cinema."[99]

Third, Japanese companies ratcheted up promotion efforts. As the output of feature films increased, major companies began to form their own publicity departments to better advertise their products.[100] Because of the modest budget allotted per film, these companies could not allocate large funds for promotion.[101] As late as 1935, *Kokusai eiga shinbun* observed that the promotional efforts of foreign distributors were generally "more advanced...precise...and relied on greater budgets."[102] However, whereas foreign film distributors normally advertised films only during the time of their release, Japanese companies hyped products while they were still in production.[103] By the mid-1930s, leading Japanese productions were enjoying ample publicity. For example,

promotion of Nikkatsu's *Daibosatsu Pass* (*Daibosatsu tōge,* 1935), a popular period film (see chapter 3), utilized 500,000 paper tags (*senjafuda*), 800 banners,
20,000 balloons, 8,000 street posters, 300 entrance curtains for bath houses,
and 100 sandwich-board advertisers, in addition to ads on buses, trains, newspapers, and in the air. Publicity costs amounted to 60,000 yen, over half of the
production budget.[104]

Finally, Japanese companies controlled the arena of film exhibition. As the
industry began to churn out film narratives in large volume, each major company aggressively procured movie houses to showcase its products. By the
mid-1930s, the exhibition business, consisting of over two thousand theaters
nationwide, was largely controlled by Shōchiku (566 theaters), Nikkatsu (537),
and Tōhō (around 400).[105] These chains chose to open some of their prestige
theaters to U.S. products in order to capitalize on their "artistic and entertaining" production quality, in the words of one Shōchiku trustee.[106] However,
the majority of their venues were saved exclusively for their own productions.
These studios typically locked up the screens with month-long block-booking
arrangements, which gave unilateral power to distributors in selecting films to
show. In this way distributors could preserve screen time against foreign encroachment while pressuring filmmakers to maintain a steady output.[107]

These resilient practices severely limited Hollywood's expansion. U.S. companies were able to showcase their finest productions in select prestige houses
in big cities, but in most other spaces, even in the metropolitan centers of
Tokyo and Osaka, they were forced to share screen time with Japanese productions in mixed-entertainment programs.[108] Hollywood struggled outside large
population centers. "The movie world in regional areas," an MGM publicist
lamented in 1936, "is uncultivated territory for foreign film distributors."[109]
This included rural markets where traditional amusements such as *minyō* and
bon odori—songs and dances—were far more popular than Western ones.
In midsize cities, such as Nagoya and Fukuoka, domestic films maintained a
commanding lead.[110] Japan posed unexpected difficulties to the world's most
powerful entertainment industry. As film historian Kristin Thompson notes,
it was "unique in keeping a large portion of its domestic market for native
productions without extensive regulation."[111]

Protecting National Culture

Hollywood's troubles in Japan were not limited to the remarkable upsurge in
Japanese cinema. Things got harder in the 1930s, when government intervention

gained intensity. State regulation in Japan originated in the 1910s, when municipal and prefectural authorities began to enact their own control measures to safeguard the public from the allegedly dangerous influence of the moving image.[112] These local developments became national in 1925. In the same year that the infamous Peace Preservation Law that expanded the "thought police" passed the legislature, the Japanese government enacted the Regulation for Motion Picture Censorship (Katsudō shashin firumu kenetsu kisoku).[113] This new measure allowed the Home Ministry to pass, edit, or ban completed film products based on "decency" (fūzoku), which was applied against representations of cruelty, lust, adultery, nudity, profanity, and blasphemy. The government also prioritized "public safety" (kōan). Films were not allowed to degrade Japan's royalty or national prestige, nor were they to inspire crime and social disorder. The new policy took a hard line against left-wing expressions on the screens, specifically the "tendency films" (keikō eiga) that emerged from Japan's proletarian movement.[114]

The Japanese government exerted greater control over the movies in the following decade. Following the Manchurian Incident of September 18, 1931, the Home Ministry, together with the Education Ministry and the Finance Ministry, took steps to transform cinema into an active instrument of Japan's imperial policy. Political and bureaucratic deliberations first resulted in the birth of a government instructional body, the Committee for Film Regulation (Eiga tōsei iinkai) in 1934. Subsequent meetings among state officials gave rise to the Greater Japan Film Association (Dai nihon eiga kyōkai), a semiprivate organization run by government bureaucrats, intellectuals, and heads of studios. In an effort to strengthen the private sector's ties with state-run agendas, government bureaucrats not only applied pressure to the film industry but also took pains to voluntarily draw the filmmakers into the imperial project. In particular, they actively employed what was called a "consultation system" (kondankai) to instruct the captains of the movie industry through forums and meetings.[115]

The presence of the state grew in the years that followed. In 1939 the Japanese government promulgated the Film Law. Inspired in part by the Nazis' Film Law of 1934, this legislation provided stringent state intervention to achieve a "qualitative improvement" (shitsuteki kōjō) in Japanese films. Filmmakers were required to obtain official permission from the minister in charge to commence movie production and distribution. Studio staff—directors, actors, and cinematographers—needed to pass an aptitude test to enter or remain in the profession. The Film Law also granted the Home Ministry greater power to censor films and demand changes in scripts prior to shooting. The new policy prioritized the selection of "good films" (*yūryō eiga*) while curtailing the screening of "movies with problems."[116]

The Film Law's purpose transcended the sphere of movie making. As noted in its first article, the goal of the legislation was to improve the "culture of the national population" (*kokumin bunka*) through the movies. Put another way, the architects of this law desired to reform the quality of films to improve the standards of "Japanese" collective behavior and, by extension, further the nation's advancement in the global arena.[117] Instead of looking down on their own films as "inferior" or "lowbrow," government bureaucrats treated Japanese cinema as a respectable art form and medium. Eager to capitalize on film's ability to influence the public, the Japanese government protected and supported Japanese filmmaking through increased intervention.[118]

The government's quest to elevate Japan's "national culture" led to rigorous control over filmmaking. Following the promulgation of the Film Law, commercial film production was limited to three companies: Shōchiku, Tōhō, and the newly formed Dai nihon eiga seisaku kabushiki gaisha, Daiei for short. Filmmakers were expected to manufacture "cinema of the national population" (*kokumin eiga*), which represented a mixture of "deep artistic taste" and "high-minded national ideals" that could reinforce the Japanese government's expansionist agendas.[119] With the industry placed under strict state regulation, filmmakers produced narratives that depicted idealized versions of Japan's imperialist practices in Korea (*Kimi to boku*, or *You and I*, 1941), China (*Shina no yoru*, or *Night in China*, 1940), Southeast Asia (*Marai no tora*, or *Tiger in Malaya*, 1943), and the United States (*Hawai Marē oki kaisen*, or *Sea War from Hawaii to Malaya*, 1942).[120]

Likewise, film presentation operated under tighter regulations. Following the passing of the Film Law, the Japanese government limited the length of each screening program to three hours.[121] Each feature presentation required the screening of a "culture film" (*bunka eiga*) alongside it. Produced by a number of small and large companies (often commissioned by the Japanese military), the "culture film" was a broad label that applied to a wide variety of documentaries, science films, and military pictures designed to educate audiences.[122] On April 1, 1942, the Japanese government delegated the responsibility of film distribution to a single company, Shadan hōjin eiga haikyūsha (aka Eihai). This new company broke up the company-based structure of distributor and exhibitor, and divided existing theaters—about 2,400 in number—into two nationwide circuits. This system assured the centralization of film circulation in order to maximize the exposure of the new and forthcoming lineup of "national films."[123]

The End of the Beginning

The growth of government control in Japan in the 1930s came at a bad time for Hollywood. With the crash of the U.S. stock market in 1929, Hollywood had to face the Great Depression, which threatened to put studios out of business in the early 1930s. In dealing with Japan, changes in cinematic technology, namely the introduction of sound, posed new difficulties. Part of the problem was hardware installation; due to the high cost of the new projection equipment, Japanese theaters were slow to change the presentation format. This delayed the mainstreaming of "talkies," contrary to Hollywood's ambitions. The use of intertitles with oral dialogue (in English) also presented new challenges to viewers. Even though U.S. companies decided to make their speaking films accessible by adding Japanese-language subtitles, the "discrepancy of national language" led to diminished audiences, noted the film almanac *Kokusai eiga nenkan* in 1934.[124]

State regulation added three difficulties to the struggling industry. First, film censorship was growing tighter. In the late 1920s, Hollywood companies regarded Japan's censorship policy as "fair and reasonable"; the rules appeared no different than the standards applied in other foreign markets.[125] A decade later, when MGM sought to distribute *The Good Earth,* Japanese censors requested as many as thirteen cuts amounting to a total of 470 feet of celluloid. They also required the addition of a prologue that described the Japanese government's mission in China as being to "punish the outrageous Nanking Government" of Chiang Kai-Shek.[126] The same year, censors rejected *Mutiny on the Bounty* (1935), a thirteen-reeler that depicted a revolt of sailors on board a British naval ship. The film eventually passed the inspection after losing four reels worth of celluloid involving scenes of mutiny.[127] One writer who saw the trimmed outcome sardonically referred to the edited film as the *"Bounty without Mutiny."*[128]

Second, the Japanese government implemented new import restrictions. In the fall of 1937, shortly after the Marco Polo Bridge Incident that provoked the Second Sino-Japanese War, the Japanese Finance Ministry abruptly informed U.S. film companies that import permits would now be required for all foreign products.[129] The Japanese government soon imposed a short-lived ban against incoming films.[130] The Film Law of 1939 allowed the home minister to reduce the number of imports at will. Each exhibitor was permitted to screen no more than fifty foreign titles per year.[131] Following this new legislation, the government dramatically curtailed the number of U.S. imports. The volume of U.S. films, which reached as many as 235 in 1935, plummeted to 81 in 1940 and 41 the following year.[132]

Third, these protectionist policies went hand in hand with an effort to restrict Hollywood's financial transactions. In the mid-1930s, tax agents in Tokyo began to request income tax payments based on estimated figures instead of actual earnings. Hollywood complained that this was an "arbitrary method of taxation."[133] More troubling was the government's effort to block the industry's conversion of earnings into dollars. While the short-term ban on foreign films was in effect in 1937, the Finance Ministry also restricted Hollywood's currency transfer as a way of preventing the drainage of yen from the Japanese market. In February 1939, the Finance Ministry once again began to hinder the transmission of Hollywood's revenue.[134] By spring 1941, the U.S. film industry's frozen funds totaled some 45 million yen.[135]

The Japanese government's get-tough policy forced Hollywood to take a new course of action. Immediately after the Japanese founded the Greater Japan Motion Picture Association, U.S. companies hastily organized the American Motion Picture Association of Japan (AMPA). Chaired by Michael M. Bergher of Columbia Pictures, the AMPA brought together the eight U.S. companies that operated independently in Japan. Its aim was to develop a collective front to retain studio interests in response to changing policy circumstances. Since the MPPDA lacked official representation in Japan, the AMPA essentially carried out the Hays Office's functions on the ground. In their periodic meetings in Tokyo, company representatives discussed problems and devised solutions specific to their business environment. In 1936 the U.S. Commerce Department identified the formation of the AMPA as one of the "two important developments... from the standpoint of American participation in this [Japanese] market."[136]

The AMPA's activities centered on direct and indirect negotiations with the Japanese government. In the wake of the 1937 import ban, the AMPA commenced discussions with the Finance Ministry, and specifically Kubo Hisaji, a lawyer and political insider.[137] Kubo had presented himself as an official representative of the Japanese government to the foreign managers of U.S. companies in New York. He was expected to negotiate favorable arrangements on behalf of U.S. companies. On August 10, 1938, Bergher's organization received a letter from the Finance Ministry that noted a desire to reopen the Japanese market to Hollywood under a limited capacity ($30,000 worth of prints at .01 to .015 per foot, roughly 2 million feet of film footage) while authorizing the remittance of up to 3 million yen to New York on a three-year deferred-payment plan. After completing the negotiation, Kubo received a "gratuity fee" of 30,000 yen, per his request.[138]

This apparent progress raised the hopes of continuing the trade in spite of the unfolding war in China. The members of AMPA began to stockpile their new features for immediate release.[139] Yet U.S. companies soon discovered that the Japanese government was intent on blocking their screen program by refusing to issue import permits. On August 10, 1938, AMPA wrote to the Finance Ministry, complaining that the Japanese government had allowed Hollywood to export only two-thirds of the prints initially promised.[140] Nearly two months later, U.S. company representatives urged the Japanese government once again to honor Kubo's arrangement in the name of "justice and fair-play" as well as "the promotion of friendly relations" between the two societies.[141] Little progress was made in the ensuing months. A year later, AMPA complained that it had "exhausted every possible avenue of approach to speed up the fulfillment of the agreement."[142]

Desperate to turn things around, the AMPA approached the U.S. government for assistance and support. It first met with Ambassador Joseph C. Grew to secure official protection.[143] The AMPA also sought the assistance of the U.S. State Department through the Hays Office. On January 10, 1940, Ted Herron wrote a letter to Raymond MacKay of the U.S. government's Division of Far Eastern Affairs. The MPPDA representative complained that the rise of protectionist legislation was posing a "very severe blow" to the industry's business in Japan. He pleaded that the government issue "as vigorous a protest as possible" to the Japanese government.[144] The State Department was hesitant to launch an all-out protest, since Hollywood's "agreement" with the Finance Ministry appeared to be only an "indication of policy" that Japanese authorities were "expected" to follow.[145] Grew did little beyond asking the Japanese to clarify the barriers imposed on U.S. studios.[146]

Meanwhile, the AMPA struggled to maintain the industry's united front against Japanese authorities. Since branch offices lacked the power to make policy decisions on behalf of the company, the coalition on the ground was unable to act swiftly in response to the changing local circumstances.[147] Communication in this hastily developed mechanism produced confusion and contrary information, often baffling Hollywood representatives in the United States.[148] Frictions emerged over the use of the frozen funds. In figuring out the possible usage of such monies, U.S. companies debated the options at length, only to conclude that the decision ultimately lay in the hands of each member studio.[149] In March 1941, one company, Paramount, decided to invest its unremitted funds in Japanese bonds. This was a decision that the U.S. government had discouraged.[150] After the deal was made, the State Department observer criticized the move for placing other member companies in an "embarrassing position" and for "directly assisting [Japan] to finance her war."[151]

By fall 1941, it was painfully clear that Hollywood's days in Japan were numbered. As a step to prepare for its withdrawal from Japan, U.S. companies began to discuss the methods of compensating its employees. The process only added insult to injury, as Japanese workers flatly rejected the offer of a one-month retirement allowance rather than multiyear packages.[152] Pearl Harbor struck the final blow, rendering Hollywood's last-minute financial activities incomplete. U.S. studios lost their property—office space, film prints, and promotional resources—to Japanese authorities and "bootleggers" who circulated the confiscated celluloid across the sprawling empire.[153] Only part of their assets were successfully transferred to the United States in time; some 10 million yen, equivalent to $2.35 million remained frozen in local banks.[154] Some foreign managers were able to flee to the United States, scrambling across Asia and Australia in haste. Others were captured and detained in places such Manila or Shanghai, while studio personnel in the United States worried helplessly and the war unfolded.[155]

The suspension of the movie trade left Hollywood bitter. The transpacific operations of leading U.S. studios rewarded success early on, as their surfeit of big-budget products generated a strong following in large cities especially among educated movie goers. But in other spaces, Hollywood hopelessly lagged behind Japanese cinema, which overall enjoyed a commanding lead throughout the interwar decades. The Japanese government was also effective in blocking Hollywood's expansion. It enforced tight regulations and curbed the entry of American films, until suspending the trade after the Pearl Harbor attack. In prewar Japan, Hollywood was at best a prominent minority. While dominating the movie business in many other countries, U.S. companies since the mid-1920s were able to control only roughly 20 percent of the market share in Japan.[156]

The prewar trade in Japan exposed the limits of global Hollywood. The failure to take command of the Japanese market delivered a psychological blow to the U.S. film industry. During the height of the Second World War, an MPPDA manager noted that Japan could still become "one of our best foreign markets," but admitted that the situation would remain "hopeless" as long as state and industrial forces continued to resist Hollywood on the other side of the Pacific.[157] Success in this challenging market would require new minds, new strategies, and a new international climate. U.S. studios could only hope for them on the eve of the Second World War.

Chapter 2

Renewed Intimacies

Hollywood, War, and Occupation

February 28, 1946: Tokyo. On a late winter afternoon, crowds of Tokyo-ites packed the movie houses for a much-awaited treat. The rumor had spread widely: Hollywood was returning to town! In a city laid low by the air raids and black market chaos, passionate fans crowded the dingy theater spaces, itching to see the new American releases: *His Butler's Sister* (1943), a light-hearted Deanna Durbin comedy, and *Madame Curie* (1944), a sentimental biopic about the Polish-born scientist.[1] Despite bad weather and high admission fees—three times that for an ordinary Japanese film—these two pictures attracted an impressive 350,000 moviegoers during the first ten days, gathering some 1.2 million yen in the box office. After enjoying a strong debut in Tokyo, the prints were quickly circulated to at least twelve other cities, where they were "solidly booked."[2]

Hollywood's arrival in defeated Japan did not happen overnight. It emerged from a renewed intimacy among the U.S. government, military, and business institutions during the Second World War. As the Axis threat in two continents expanded into a global war, U.S. studios joined forces to support their country's war effort. During the second half of the war, Hollywood developed close ties with the State Department and founded the Motion Picture Export Association (MPEA) in 1945. This legal cartel would spearhead the industry's postwar trade in Japan and many other countries.

At the same time, the U.S. government and military worked relentlessly to defeat the Japanese in the Pacific Theater of Operations. As an Allied victory grew more certain, policymakers, advisers, and military officials came together to plan the postwar occupation of Japan. The responsibility fell on General

Douglas MacArthur, the Supreme Commander for the Allied Powers. His SCAP organization implemented a series of sweeping reforms to turn Japan from a warring militaristic state into a peace-minded, democratic ally. SCAP's desire to inject pro-American values into Japanese consciousness led to a controlled reconstruction of its movie culture. The occupiers assisted Hollywood's commercial program through the formation of the Central Motion Picture Exchange (CMPE), the U.S. film industry's East Asian outpost which spread American movie culture across Japan.

Hollywood's cinematic campaign in postwar Japan originated from a close institutional alliance between the industry, government, and the military. It was what diplomatic historians call a "corporatist" partnership, shaped by a convergence of state and private-sector institutions coming together for mutual gain.[3] The war climate created a new bond between Hollywood and the U.S. government, as peacetime norms were dropped to overcome the Axis threat. The blend of intentions inspired a powerful cultural offensive during the war, as well as long-term planning to restore the U.S. film industry's global market in the ensuing peace. Hollywood's postwar offensive was a collaborative response to the international pressures of the World War II era. Without knowing it, the tens of thousands of Japanese fans who caught the first Hollywood movies after the war were enjoying the fruits of America's corporatist union.

Hollywood Goes to War

Nineteen thirty-nine was a transition year for Hollywood. After successfully recovering from the Great Depression in the mid-1930s, U.S. film companies were celebrating the apex of the studio era with such notable classics as *Gone with the Wind, Stagecoach,* and *The Wizard of Oz.*[4] That memorable year, however, also witnessed the beginning of a seismic shift in the movie industry. For one thing, Hollywood was already facing intense scrutiny from the Justice Department, whose antitrust suit against the vertically integrated Big Eight studios eventually forced the divorcement and divestiture of their theaters at the end of the 1940s.[5] U.S. companies also witnessed the birth of television—a new and formidable entertainment medium. On April 30, 1939, the New York World's Fair, dubbed the "the World of Tomorrow," famously showcased a live telecast of its opening ceremony with a dramatic speech by President Franklin D. Roosevelt. A decade and a half later, some 60 percent of American households owned this media novelty. The "tube of plenty" jeopardized the film industry and inspired large-scale changes in Hollywood's business practices.[6]

The biggest problem, though, was the Second World War. The surge of the Axis powers during the 1930s and early 1940s posed a direct threat to the movie business. Hitler's anti-Semitism outraged Jewish and left-wing film-makers who, in the mid-1930s, formed a "cultural front" to push for U.S. intervention in Europe.[7] Studio executives accurately predicted that the Axis powers would undermine the industry's global operations. As Germany, Italy, and Japan threatened the world with military and ideological force, U.S. companies increasingly confronted protectionist maneuvers that curtailed their business both in and around the Axis states.[8] The Nazi invasion of Poland in September 1, 1939, devastated the European market. The film trade in other regions subsequently veered toward chaos and closure. The U.S. entry into the war precipitated by the Japanese attack on Pearl Harbor in 1941. The *New York Times* estimated that the industry's annual earnings would decline by $6 million.[9] The war eventually led to the closure of fifty-eight film markets.[10]

World War II forced Hollywood to alter its way of life. Facing times of extraordinary duress, U.S. companies made significant readjustments in their mode of operation. Unable to continue their normal global business, they focused their resources on available foreign markets (mostly in the United Kingdom and Latin America). At home, studios specifically cut back the output of B films and increased the number of high-end productions, ramped up publicity, and undertook "scientific" surveys to convert the perceived "25,000,000 non-customers" into loyal film patrons.[11] The movie industry also made greater use of independent and unit production. Companies run by David O. Selznick, Walt Disney, and Samuel Goldwyn—the "elite trio" of Hollywood independents—unleashed hits such as *Pride of the Yankees* (1942), *Bambi* (1942), and *Since You Went Away* (1944), respectively.[12]

The industry also jumped on the interventionist bandwagon. Directors, producers, actors, cinematographers, and others in the movie colony—as many of seven thousand of them—joined the military to assist the Allied cause.[13] Those who remained in the colony rallied around the following slogan: "Win the War Now! Anything Else is Chores."[14] Immediately after Pearl Harbor, studio personnel organized the Hollywood Victory Committee and delivered live entertainment to servicemen and women at home and abroad. A month later, Hays founded the War Activities Committee (WAC), which, in the words of its executive vice chairman Francis S. Harmon, aimed to "assist, with all possible vigor, the United States and its allied nations in the successful prosecution of the war, and the winning of the peace."[15] By encouraging the involvement of all sectors of the industry, the WAC generated a wide range of activities, including the distribution of war-related shorts and documentaries for domestic audiences; the production of training films for men and women in uniform; the selling of war bonds and victory bonds; even the collection of scrap metal.[16]

Hollywood, in addition, patriotized many of its feature-length narratives. Following the breakthrough production of *Confessions of a Nazi Spy* (1939), an anti-Nazi espionage film, U.S. companies began to churn out war-related films that pumped up the Allied cause.[17] Even though isolationist politicians in Washington vehemently attacked the war movie as "interventionist pro-paganda," public sentiment was veering in favor of these politicized productions.[18] The output of war pictures increased dramatically in the early 1940s, encompassing a wide range of (sub)genres from combat films (*Bataan,* 1943) to home-front melodramas (*The Human Comedy,* 1943) to musicals (*This Is the Army,* 1943) to comedies (*Miracle on Morgan's Creek,* 1944) to espionage thrill-ers (*All through the Night,* 1941). These pro-war narratives constituted the most dominant production trend in the first half of the global struggle.[19] Some of them earned high acclaim, such as *Mrs. Miniver* (1942) and *Casablanca* (1943), both of which won an Oscar for Best Picture at the Academy Awards. As late as March 1944, *Variety* boasted that "Grade A war pictures" were "the greatest drawing cards" at the box office.[20]

Hollywood's pro-war turn meshed with the U.S. government's shifting actions in the international arena. As citizens increasingly perceived the Axis surge as a threat to U.S. ideals and interests, the Roosevelt administration took steps to mobilize the public.[21] In October 1941, the president announced the creation of the Office of Facts and Figures (OFF) and appointed the Librarian of Congress, Archibald MacLeish, as chief. This new office aimed to inform the public of the ongoing global conflict without appearing as blatant pro-war propaganda. MacLeish specifically referred to the OFF's information campaign as a "strategy of truth."[22] Efforts to influence the international public grew in tandem with such domestic actions. As early as 1938, the State Department had used the Division of Cultural Relations (DCR) to promote spreading information and artistic and cultural exchange abroad.[23] Although originally created to foster "good neighbor" relations with countries south of the Rio Grande, the DCR soon reached out globally to strengthen cross-national relations with its wartime allies in East Asia, Australia, and the Middle East.[24]

The key agency that led the wartime information campaign was the Office of War Information (OWI). A consolidation of OFF and three other government offices, this federal agency, founded in June 1942 under Roosevelt's executive order, assumed the responsibility of disseminating pro-U.S. information and messages to boost the war effort.[25] The effort to build morale at home was conducted by OWI's Domestic Branch, which made use of newspapers, radio, and other communications media to further the American cause. It also influenced the content of Hollywood's feature films without overtaking the industry.[26] The Domestic Branch soon established an office in Los Angeles for its Bureau of Motion Pictures (BMP) and requested Hollywood's cooperation on a voluntary basis. Relying on its forty-seven-page "Government Information Manual for the Motion Picture Industry," the BMP reviewed scripts, synopses, and film prints, and offered "instructions" and "suggestions" to studio personnel.[27] Even though the BMP's involvement occasionally baffled the movie industry, the relationship between government and industry was overall an obliging one. In June 1943, Will H. Hays went so far as to say that the industry "offered to cooperate completely" with the U.S. government and that the BMP helped render "our cooperation one hundred percent effective."[28]

Meantime, OWI's Overseas Branch spread pro-American messages in the international arena. Determined to boost America's psychological warfare against the Axis powers, this office, led by screenwriter Robert Sherwood, orchestrated cultural offensives outside the United States, excluding the Western Hemisphere.[29] In addition to participating in the war effort, the Overseas Branch aided the political and cultural reconstruction of liberated territories.[30] The mission of building peace gained in importance during the second half of the war; although the OWI on the whole suffered severe budget cuts in 1943, its Overseas Branch enjoyed lucrative financial allocations and was, according to Sherwood, in "excellent shape" to carry out the peace-winning mission.[31] In addition to newspapers, magazines, and radio, this office utilized filmed documentaries, newsreels, and short subjects. Sherwood's office also assisted Hollywood's commercial operation.[32] From this active office emerged the Central Motion Picture Exchange, which served as Hollywood's sole distribution office in Japan through much of the occupation era.

The Little State Department

Hollywood found the U.S. government's active cooperation reassuring, but it knew that this did not promise its long-term prosperity. As an Allied victory was becoming a certainty, the studio heads found it increasingly vital to prepare for the postwar film trade. Although the war boom had rewarded U.S. companies with an unexpected level of financial success, some in the industry worried that the economic surge of the early 1940s would taper off once the war was over. Others feared that the growth of "nationalistic feeling" in the wake of the war would lead to a surge of protectionist legislation abroad.[33] Still others were unsure of how to disperse the backlogged films, which were expected to number between 2,000 and 2,500 the year after the war.[34] So anxiety was high at this time. In July 1943, *Variety* ominously predicted that a "titanic struggle" would take place among filmmakers in different societies, as a result of their "first entry . . . into the post-war world markets."[35] In 1945 the Public Information Committee of the Motion Picture Association of America (MPAA), a public relations office represented by the major studios, reported that "our American industry faces the toughest competition in its history and must fight to maintain its supremacy."[36]

The task of relieving this unease rested in the hands of Will H. Hays and Carl Elias Milliken—the latter a former Republican governor from Maine who had served as MPPDA secretary since 1926.[37] Foreseeing mounting challenges in the international arena, the two men decided to act during the height of the war. On October 21, 1943, Hays submitted a confidential memorandum to Secretary of State Cordell Hull in which he argued that the "supremacy" of American cinema was essentially maintained by the "approximate [*sic*] forty percent of motion picture revenues" that flowed from overseas. The government, thus, had a "duty . . . to preserve world distribution . . . [and] retain a truly free screen."[38] Seven months later, Milliken submitted a twenty-five-page memorandum detailing the various trade restrictions that hindered the industry's activities overseas. Echoing Hays, Milliken concluded that a "greater degree of protection" from the government was necessary to facilitate the industry's "dissemination of sound cultural, social and political thought" around the world.[39]

The State Department's response was sympathetic. In a letter sent to diplomatic officers on February 22, 1944, Under Secretary of State Adolf A. Berle acknowledged the "value of the American motion picture to the national welfare" and vowed to "cooperate fully" in furthering Hollywood's interests abroad.[40] Berle's department specifically assigned this task to the newly founded Telecommunications Division, which took on the responsibility of handling radio, telegraph, cable communications, and motion picture policy for international affairs. The chief of this office was Francis Colt de Wolf, who had intermittently served the State Department on matters pertaining to law and communications during the interwar decades.[41] De Wolf was clear about his willingness to work with Hollywood: "American motion pictures as ambassadors of good will. . . . The Department of State and its representatives in foreign countries desire to cooperate fully in the protection of American motion pictures abroad, especially in a difficult postwar era."[42] Hays lauded de Wolf as "peculiarly qualified" to handling motion picture matters.[43]

In the ensuing months, the foreign managers of the movie business, led by Hays and Milliken, periodically met with de Wolf's team to formulate the blueprint for the postwar film trade.[44] What resulted was a plan to approach the international market with a two-tiered strategy. For countries operating under "manageable" business conditions, American studios decided to operate individually. As in the prewar era, trade in these markets depended primarily on studio initiative, as well as what Hays called a "loose cooperation" with the MPPDA's Foreign Department (renamed the International Department by Hays in 1944) to mediate trade difficulties.[45] For countries protected by stringent state policy, the industry desired to mobilize a new apparatus to spearhead studio activities. In March 1945, Milliken called for the "urgent and prompt development" of a trade organization that represented the interests of the industry.[46] The MPPDA secretary's wishes came true three months later with the founding of the Motion Picture Export Association.[47]

The MPEA was not an ordinary business organization. It was a legal cartel formed under the Webb-Pomerene Export Trade Act (1918), which exempted U.S. exporters from the nation's antitrust laws. Although the Justice Department was moving to break up the vertically integrated studios at home, the U.S. State and Commerce Departments fully supported the MPEA as a means of "fight[ing] monopoly with monopoly" in foreign fields.[48] At its embryonic stage, the MPEA consisted of the Big Five and Little Three—that is, Columbia, Loew's MGM, RKO, Twentieth Century-Fox, Paramount, Universal, Warner Bros., and United Artists—and soon welcomed smaller firms such as Monogram and Allied Artists. The association failed to attract many independent companies, which often complained that the MPEA privileged the interests of the majors. But by March 1951, at least twenty-five independents were releasing their products through the association.[49] Owing to its function, status, and authority, the trade commonly referred to the MPEA as "the little State Department."[50]

The person who oversaw the new trade apparatus was Eric Alva Johnston. Then the head of the U.S. Chamber of Commerce, Johnston ventured to Hollywood in 1945 to replace Hays as "movie czar" of the Motion Picture Producers and Distributors of America organization (he soon renamed it the Motion Picture Association of America). A Republican with broad work experience with the Roosevelt administration, Johnston drew favorable attention as a business leader who, in the words of *Variety,* could "grease the wheels and smooth the road" on the industry's behalf.[51] Johnston was determined to serve the leading entertainment enterprise in the world. In an effort to maintain Hollywood's role as "America's greatest salesmen," the new leader of the movie colony vowed to cultivate a "fair share of foreign markets" through political and diplomatic lobbying.[52] The new movie czar immediately earned the trust of studio executives, who unanimously elected him president of the MPEA.[53] Until his unexpected death in 1963, Johnston promoted studio interests overseas. A Johnston biographer acknowledged that "his big achievement for the industry was to open the foreign market for American films."[54]

Managed by a trusted new leader, the MPEA set out to further studio interests abroad in three important ways. First, it negotiated with foreign governments and industries in countries where individual studios were unable to operate alone. The MPEA acted in the interests of all members by removing unfavorable trade barriers (such as import duties, quotas, remittance taxes, currency regulations) and monopolistic practices.[55] Second, it strengthened ties with the U.S. government. Johnston labored to keep the U.S. State Department and Commerce Department as allies of the film industry. Third, it mediated the interests of member studios. In determining which films to export, the MPEA claimed to act in "good faith" and select the most suitable products from the stockpile of all member companies. The share of each company was not based on the profitability of the individual product. To prevent infighting, the MPEA decided to divide its net profits based on the domestic grosses of each studio. This revenue distribution policy played a key role in sustaining a united front.[56]

To the members of the MPEA, collective action was not an ideal form of business. Rather, it was a temporary arrangement aimed at setting the groundwork for future competition. In the early postwar years, the markets that required the MPEA's assistance included three types. One was the state monopolies that were closing behind the Iron Curtain—namely Hungary, Bulgaria, Czechoslovakia, Poland, Romania, Yugoslavia, and the Soviet Union. Another type of market was what *Variety* labeled a "different type of monopoly." This category specifically applied to Holland, a market sustained through two state-supported cartels (a distributor's and an exhibitor's).[57] Finally, the MPEA dealt with countries administered by the Allied occupation. Four countries fell under this category. Japan—along with Germany, Austria, and Korea—soon became a site of the MPEA's rigorous operation.

From War to Occupation

The plans to create the MPEA were maturing as the Pacific War intensified. The Americans and the Japanese engaged in a dogged military struggle on multiple fronts. The initial advantage went to the Japanese, who stormed across China, the Philippines, and the British and Dutch possessions in Southeast Asia. In the

Pacific, the Imperial Navy advanced its superior arsenal of battleships, cruisers, and fighter planes to the South Pacific islands. The United States initially struggled to compete against the Japanese military, but it quickly redeployed its resources in a powerful counteroffensive. After winning a key battle at the Midway Islands in June 1942, the U.S. forces began to pull ahead with a string of victories in Guadalcanal, Tarawa, and Saipan. By the end of 1944, the U.S.-led Allied forces had breached Japan's outer defenses and were eyeing an attack on the main islands.[58]

The Americans sealed their victory in 1945. The Japanese government continued to manage a "thought war" by mobilizing public and private propagandists, but the trend toward defeat was becoming all too evident in the absence of goods and resources.[59] In the island-hopping campaigns, U.S. forces were defeating the desperate Japanese troops in the Philippines, Iwo Jima, and Okinawa. Simultaneously, incendiary bombings began to turn cities across Japan to ashes; the infamous air raids on March 10 razed the city of Tokyo, killing some eighty thousand civilians overnight. America's "strategy of annihilation" reached new heights on August 6 and 9, when the newly created atomic bombs hit the cities of Hiroshima and Nagasaki, respectively.[60] Six days after the dropping of the second nuclear bomb, Emperor Hirohito delivered his famous radio speech to the Japanese public, announcing Japan's capitulation to the Allies. Japan's imperial ambitions had fallen apart miserably, leaving behind death, poverty, and humiliation. The entire nation seemed to linger in a state of shock and exhaustion—what contemporaries called the *kyodatsu* condition.[61]

During the final destructive battles, plans to administer Japan were being developed by the U.S. Department of State. It enlisted a cluster of East Asia experts to design the blueprint for postwar Japan and the wider region.[62] During the final months of the war, two top-level organizations, the State-War-Navy Coordinating Committee and the Joint Chiefs of Staff, finalized the plans for the occupation.[63] Immediately after Japan capitulated to the Allies, the U.S. Army Forces in the Pacific set up military headquarters in Yokohama (soon moved to Tokyo). On October 2, the Military Government Section of the U.S. Armed Forces became the General Headquarters, Supreme Commander for the Allied Powers (GHQ/SCAP). While its personnel and function often overlapped with the military, SCAP was primarily responsible for managing civilian affairs as they pertained to the occupation. This administrative body directed the six-and-a-half-year reconstruction of Japan.[64]

The occupation government was a hegemonic body that assured U.S. dominance in two ways. First, it provided Americans with central authority over their allies. On paper, SCAP operated under the supervision of the Far Eastern Commission, a Washington-based policymaking body representing eleven nations. The Allied Council for Japan, a Tokyo-based four-power organization consisting of the British Commonwealth, the Republic of China, the Soviet Union, and the United States, also advised SCAP. In practice, however, the United States took charge of the undertaking. Unlike the occupation of Germany, which was governed by four Allied powers (Britain, France, the Soviet Union, and the United States) that each took over a territorial zone, the four main islands of occupied Japan fell under the rule of the United States. An implicit aim was to prevent the Soviet Union from gaining control of the occupation. Skepticism about Stalin's intentions had been mounting at least since the late months of the war.[65]

Second, in addition to trumping the Allies, SCAP wielded overarching power over the Japanese. In facilitating the postwar transformation, the occupiers chose not to break up the existing civil administration but to control it indirectly. In an effort to "reorient" and "uplift" the Japanese, the occupiers circulated directives and memoranda to local leaders and interacted with them in person as well. While doing so, SCAP monitored Japanese plans and practices at all levels (regional, prefectural, and local) and enforced change when they deemed it necessary. At times, General MacArthur's men forced Japanese leaders to comply with their ideas. Even though the indirect governing structure of defeated Japan, on a superficial level, empowered the Japanese, the greater authority always lay in the hands of the conquerors. The occupation was in essence "democracy by intervention."[66]

The chief authority of this American occupation was a single man. Born and raised in a distinguished military family, Douglas MacArthur burst on the military scene as a top graduate at West Point and a field marshal of the Philippine Army. During the Second World War, he commanded the U.S. Army Forces in the Pacific. On August 15, 1945, President Harry S. Truman officially appointed MacArthur as Supreme Commander for the Allied Powers—a title that signified both the man and his administrative body. Landing in Japan two weeks later, General MacArthur oversaw the reconstruction of Japan in furtherance of America's ideological and geopolitical interests.[67] Yet the aging general also approached the occupation with a paternalistic attitude.[68] In a Fourth of July message delivered in 1947, MacArthur vowed to "advance" Japanese society beyond its "physical, mental, and cultural strictures of feudalistic precepts—the very antitheses of American ideals."[69] Four years later, the Supreme Commander infamously characterized the Japanese people as a "boy of twelve" when measured by "the standards of modern civilization."[70]

SCAP's program began with the breakup of the Japanese empire. Immediately following Japan's defeat, the occupation dismantled the nation's colonial holdings outside the four main islands and destroyed the weapons used by the Japanese military. Dissolving the wartime empire also required the identification of responsibility. SCAP pursued this by purging politicians and business leaders from respectable positions. Soldiers and officers faced their fates in Allied military tribunals held in Japan and elsewhere. The biggest stage of this legal procedure was the International Military Tribunal for the Far East, dubbed the "Tokyo trials," which sent seven class A war criminals to the gallows. The most controversial decision was to relieve the emperor from legal prosecution. Despite much Allied sentiment to do otherwise, MacArthur and his aides chose not to send Hirohito to court, fearing that doing so would provoke anger and chaos in Japan. The occupiers forced the emperor to renounce his divinity, but he was able to maintain symbolic power throughout the postwar decades.[71]

While demolishing Japan's imperialistic tendencies, SCAP enacted political reform to spread democratic values. The reform impulse of the occupation was strongest during its first two years, when a core group of New Dealers sought to bring "progressive" change to the ailing nation.[72] In this clout of proactivism, the occupiers enthusiastically promoted civil liberties, social equality, and political dialogue across ideologies. The most significant achievement was the new constitution. Determined to replace the Prussian-inspired Meiji Constitution of 1889 with a democratic alternative, MacArthur turned to his own legal team to formulate a foundational document. SCAP's draft was presented to the Japanese who were requested to craft their own draft proposal. The final text, adopted from the American version with minor revisions, contained Article IX in which Japan renounced waging war and possessing aggressive "land, sea, and air forces." It also freed individual citizens from the will of the emperor and granted them "basic human rights" regardless of race, class, gender, and creed. As citizens of a new democratic nation, the Japanese, among other things, gained the right of free speech, free religious practice, and political participation. An unprecedented number of women were now able to participate in elections as voters and candidates.[73]

SCAP's reform also involved economic reconstruction. Starting at the top of the fiscal ladder, SCAP attempted to dismantle the *zaibatsu,* the financial and industrial combines that appeared to play a key role in the imperial war machine. MacArthur ordered these giant institutions to dismantle their holdings to promote competition and small- and mid-sized businesses. This effort reinforced the early attempts to empower the rank-and-file worker. During its first two years, the occupation actively supported organized labor and workers' action—even as this brought Communist and other left-wing movements to the fore. Farmers in the countryside felt MacArthur's presence through land reform. SCAP parceled out the properties of the landlord class to tenants and small-scale farmers who were exploited under traditional agricultural structures. By 1949 some two million hectares of land were delivered to the hands of independent farmers.[74]

The occupiers, moreover, initiated a series of cultural programs to remold the minds of the Japanese. The aim was to replace the perceived militaristic tendencies with peace-oriented, democratic values. In the field of education, SCAP ordered the elimination of militaristic agendas from textbooks and schools, while developing a new curriculum that underscored respect for individual rights and human dignity.[75] The policy toward religion involved the depoliticization of Shintō practices and the promotion of Christianity (which had limited application). The reform of media and communications also consisted of a dual process. SCAP, on the one hand, allowed publishers, journalists, radio commentators, and others to engage in a greater degree of free speech than they had during the war years. On the other hand, the occupiers employed media censorship to control public opinion.[76] MacArthur later explained the reasons for this contradictory approach. "We could not simply encourage the growth of democracy," the Supreme Commander reminisced in his autobiography. "We had to make sure that it grew."[77]

Remolding Japanese Cinema

SCAP's dealings with motion pictures belonged to a larger effort to install a democracy by intervention. To the occupiers, cinema was an appealing medium for three reasons. First of all, it was a powerful nexus. In an era before the flowering of television and digital culture, cinema was arguably the most influential medium for reaching the general population. Second, it was a leading enterprise in popular recreation. Because of its ability to draw large audiences, the movies could offer release and fulfillment to a population crushed by the war. Finally, cinema appeared an effective tool to promote ideology. The intention was not unlike the Japanese government's during the 1930s, when filmmaking became a cultural instrument of the state. MacArthur's headquarters was intent on diffusing its political and cultural values by way of the screen.

Rebuilding the movies began with Japanese cinema. In the wake of the Pacific War, the once thriving film industry was in shambles. Although the main studios survived the air raids, film production had dwindled as a result of material shortages and equipment deterioration. The Japanese government's regulations also constrained the industry's output. During the final year and a half of the war, the Home Ministry imposed new regulations that reduced screen time, the length of each film, and the number of theaters for commercial screenings. The pressure for cultural control, stemming from the state as well as within the industry, remained strong. Even though the number of war-mongering productions actually diminished toward the end of hostilities, a number of films continued to glorify the Japanese empire.[78] As a result, SCAP approached the depleted industry with skepticism and suspicion. It found a dire need to "eliminate government control" of the movies by instilling a "lawful freedom of expression."[79]

SCAP's first move was to influence Japanese industry personnel. On September 22, 1945, occupation authorities held a special *kondankai* meeting with the top studio representatives. The purpose of the gathering, SCAP insisted, was not to give "orders" but "suggestions."[80] In a tense atmosphere, occupation officials announced three basic objectives: the eradication of militarism, the promotion of "liberal freedoms" (such as freedom of expression, religion, and assembly), and the reconstruction of Japan as a peaceful nation. U.S. officials, then specifically encouraged Japanese movie companies to depict the following ten themes:

1. Show Japanese in all walks of life cooperating to build a peaceful nation.
2. Deal with the resettlement of Japanese soldiers into civilian life.
3. Show Japanese prisoners of war formerly in U.S. hands being restored to favor in the community.
4. Demonstrate individual initiative and enterprise solving the postwar problems of Japan in industry, agriculture, and all phases of the national life.
5. Encourage the peaceful and constructive organization of labor unions.
6. Develop political consciousness and responsibility among the people.
7. Approve free discussion of political issues.
8. Encourage respect for the rights of people as individuals.
9. Promote tolerance and respect among all races and classes.
10. Dramatize figures in Japanese history who have stood for freedom and representative government.[81]

The occupiers also sought to eliminate the presentation of undesirable themes. The "basic problem" of Japanese cinema, U.S. officials asserted, lay in the apparent pervasiveness of "feudalistic patriotism," "personal revenge," and the "justification of treason, murder, and deceit in front of the public." Such tropes had to be replaced with "moral codes" that promoted "respect for the individual . . . and peoples of other countries."[82]

MacArthur's headquarters then moved to disband the structure of the wartime filmic establishment. In a directive issued on October 16, 1945, SCAP ordered the Japanese government to repeal the Film Law of 1939 to "free the Japanese motion picture industry from government domination" and "permit the industry to reflect the democratic aspirations of the Japanese people."[83] A month later, the occupiers banned the screening of films that were "utilized to propagate nationalistic, militaristic and feudalistic concepts." After studying the inventories of Japanese film companies, SCAP identified a total of 236 films that could harm its agenda. These films depicted such themes as "conformity to a feudal code," the "creation of the 'Warrior Spirit'," and the "superiority of the 'Yamato'" race. MacArthur's headquarters immediately confiscated films that contained such themes. Many of these surrendered narratives were burned on the shores of the Tama River.[84]

In the months that followed, SCAP relied on two offices to monitor Japanese filmmaking. One was the Civil Information and Education Section (CIE), a civilian office that conducted an array of reforms in the areas of education, religion, and public information. Assigned to further the "reorientation and reeducation" of Japan, the CIE orchestrated a widespread cultural campaign to promote prodemocratic and pro-American values.[85] The task of reconstructing the motion picture was given to the Motion Picture and Theatrical Branch, a noticeably "progressive group" during its first year of operation.[86] The anchor of this branch was David W. Conde, who had worked for the OWI's Psychological Warfare Branch. Considered by many local filmmakers to be a left-wing ideologue, Conde, in his numerous meetings with directors and studio executives, passionately instructed the Japanese to replace "feudalistic" and "militaristic" themes with the ten recommended ones. One of the biggest challenges, he immediately realized, was to prevent cinema's "decline" into apolitical entertainment. "The great majority of . . . movie companies were trying to render the movies completely into amusement. . . . In order to prevent them from doing so, it was necessary to fight [against them]," he later recalled.[87]

The CIE oversaw the movie industry in an advisory capacity. Technically, it did not possess the authority to enforce changes in film content. But Conde's office relied on a strategy that one SCAP insider referred to as "suggestion control," that is, pressuring local filmmakers with "recommendations" and "instructions" until they made the desired modifications.[88] On November 19, the CIE followed up on the "suggestions" given at the September 22 meeting with a list of thirteen themes that it deemed as problematic. These included projects that:

1. played up militarism;
2. concerned revenge;
3. involved nationalism;
4. were chauvinistic and antiforeign;
5. distorted historical facts;
6. approved racial or religious discrimination;
7. portrayed feudal loyalty or contempt for life as desirable or honorable;
8. approved suicide directly or indirectly;
9. either dealt with or approved of the subordination or degeneration of women;
10. flaunted merciless violence and brutality;
11. opposed democracy;
12. approved the exploitation of children; or
13. that violated the Potsdam Declaration or SCAP directives.[89]

The CIE was determined to remold Japanese cinema in ways that served SCAP's reconstruction efforts. During the initial months of the occupation, it requested Japanese companies to make a weekly report on their "progress" in filmmaking. The CIE also announced it would meet with each major studio on a weekly basis.[90] The CIE's interactions with Japanese companies were frequent in the following months.

The other apparatus was the Civil Censorship Detachment (CCD). A subdivision of MacArthur's Civil Intelligence Section, the CCD was a U.S. Army–run intelligence office that furthered SCAP's objectives through cultural regulation and control. In contrast to the CIE, the CCD, according to one insider, had a "strictly negative" role.[91] In an early planning document dated July 10, 1945, the U.S. Armed Forces in the Pacific regarded the CCD's mission as establishing the "security of military information, counter-espionage, collection of military information and . . . intelligence relating to economic, social, and political matters." This was to be achieved through the "censorship of civilian communications in Japan."[92] Once it officially began its operation on September 3, the CCD carefully monitored telephone calls, telegrams, and personal letters. It also kept an eye on the various media outlets, including newspapers, magazines, theater performances, radio shows, and "paper dramas" (*kamishibai*)—picture cards used for storytelling. Its wide-reaching surveillance activities continued until November 1949, when the office ended.[93]

The section in charge of handling the movies was the Press, Pictorial, and Broadcast Division, which, according to an internal manual printed on September 30, 1945, was designed for the "censorship of all newsreels and movies made by the Japanese."[94] On January 28, 1946, SCAP required all owners and producers of motion pictures to submit a complete list of their films to the CCD. Only films that received an identification number from the CCD were permitted to appear on screens.[95] Two months later, the CCD clarified the categories to be used for censorship: "passed," "passed with deletion," or "suppressed."[96] The criterion for censorship was to be based on its Motion Picture Code, which was in place by May 1.[97] It comprised the following nine points:

1. Motion picture productions shall not contravene the provisions of the Potsdam Declaration, which listed the terms for Japanese surrender, or the announced objectives of the Allied occupation.
2. Films containing material conducive to destructive criticism of the Allied Forces of Occupation or of the Allied Powers are prohibited.
3. Films with a military background are prohibited, except when militarism is shown to be evil.
4. The photographing of Allied Forces or matériel is prohibited, except when express approval has been obtained in writing from the Press, Pictorial, and Broadcast Division, U.S. Army Civil Censorship, beforehand.
5. Films purporting to be factual representations of historical events must be truthful.
6. Portrayal of crimes of any kind is prohibited, except when presented as part of a struggle between good and evil, in which the good triumphs. The forces of evil will not be emphasized.
7. Photography purporting to be news photography shall be authentic.
8. Leads, subtitles, explanations, advertisements, and screen dialogue will conform to the spirit of the above provisions.
9. No pictorial record will be made of subjects capable of disturbing public tranquility.[98]

In addition to evaluating each film, the CCD occasionally opened its screenings to larger audiences—particularly its Japanese employees in other SCAP offices—to gauge popular opinion. The CCD's power as a censorship apparatus was considerable. It possessed final authority to allow or reject the exhibition of any film to be shown to the Japanese.[99]

Privileging Hollywood

Arrangements to screen Hollywood features began to take shape at the same time. During its first six months, SCAP allowed screenings of four Hollywood films, all on an ad hoc basis. In October 1945, Japan Cinema Trade Company (Nippon eiga bōekisha) requested of the CIE to screen a handful of foreign films purchased before the war.[100] Two months later, *Call of the Yukon* (1938), a grim love story set in the Alaskan wilderness, hit the theaters in Tokyo.[101] Fans in the cold December afternoons savored the RKO film. One enthusiast, who saw it on the day of its release, marveled at the "bravery" of Richard Arlen, the gritty protagonist in the film. The moviegoer stayed in the theater for two showings, despite being "pushed and shoved by waves of standees."[102] Subsequent releases of *Tarzan and the Green Goddess* (1938) and Chaplin's *The Gold Rush* (1925) enjoyed an equally strong following. Having discovered such enthusiasm, *Variety* reported in January 1946 that "the Japanese are so anxious to see U.S. films that they are begging for them...even the oldest western would be accepted there."[103]

While these American releases were captivating Japanese fans, SCAP began to institutionalize the foreign-film trade. In January, MacArthur's headquarters started compiling a census of foreign films.[104] Since the right of possession of existing prints was far from clear—one official estimated that around 90 percent of foreign prints in 1946 were illegally owned—the occupiers required film distributors to submit proof of ownership.[105] This directive was a means of gaining control over the circulation of knowledge. It also aimed to bring legitimacy and stability to commerce in movies. MacArthur's policy was of aid to Hollywood. Since a number of Hollywood's prewar prints were illegally seized by Japanese bootleggers, SCAP used its authority to return them to the rightful owners.[106]

SCAP then assisted Hollywood in a more crucial way. It helped set up an outpost of the Motion Picture Export Association. The CIE, which eagerly took charge of this endeavor, looked at U.S. cinema with great interest. On the most basic level, U.S. companies held a large stockpile of unreleased films accumulated during the war. This, the CIE believed, would help satisfy the demands of entertainment-hungry audiences. The CIE also believed that Hollywood's commercial screenings would expand the opportunity to show newsreels and short subjects. Using Hollywood could increase the presentation of educational films. Finally, the CIE appreciated Hollywood's message value. While aware that a portion of the commercial products hyped violence, gangsters, and other undesirable themes, CIE officials ultimately decided that Hollywood "had more to contribute to the furtherance of SCAP objectives than the films of any other country or all other countries combined."[107]

The idea of building Hollywood's distribution office actually predated the occupation. As the planning for the postwar period got under way, the Overseas Branch of the OWI began to discuss postwar trade with Hollywood representatives. In fall 1943, Robert Riskin of the OWI and Carl Milliken of the MPPDA exchanged ideas on the postwar film program. By the end of the year, the OWI agreed to assist Hollywood by way of a trusteeship. Under this arrangement, the Overseas Branch would arrange for the dissemination of U.S. features on a temporary basis until conditions allowed Hollywood to do so on its own.[108] This plan was carried out the following year. Aided by a constellation of foreign offices in Europe, Asia, Africa, and the Middle East, the Overseas Branch analyzed the political and military conditions of each nation and formulated plans for film distribution. By late 1944, OWI representatives in the U.S. were visiting Europe to iron out the logistics.[109] By the end of 1945, American movies were penetrating Europe.

The OWI's plans for postwar Japan emerged in fall 1944 as part of a broader attempt to map a blueprint for Asia. In October, the Overseas Branch began with the idea of building forty OWI outposts across East and Southeast Asia. Although the future power structure of the war-torn region remained uncertain, the planners chose to devote maximum attention to two nations: China, because of its territorial and population size, and Japan, because of its perceived animosity toward the Allies.[110] Two months later, the plan became more concrete. In an operational guide prepared for East Asia, the OWI declared its intent to establish a "central film exchange" in every liberated and occupied country. In order to ease the transfer of responsibility to Hollywood, the Overseas Branch promised to supervise the operation "as closely as possible along commercial lines" until U.S. studios were ready to do business on their own. After calculating the data on theaters and the degree of destruction wrought by the war, the planners decided to allot ten prints for Japan—the highest number for any Asian country.[111]

The selection of films proceeded with care and caution. Based on a list of films submitted by the U.S. film industry, the OWI handpicked a group of narrative products based on their suitability for each country. The choice of titles was based on what insiders called an "equal participation" arrangement.[112] The process required a balanced selection of films from each studio.[113] In the early stages, the plan was called the "40 Programs," with the eight major studios contributing five titles each.[114] The list for Japan eventually included forty-five feature films, five per each studio, which now included Republic. (See appendix for a list of the films and studios.)[115]

The selected films were diverse and eclectic. One body of films, such as *Casablanca* and *Watch on the Rhine* (1943), depicted the European theater of war, celebrating Americans and the Western Allies as liberators against the oppressive Nazi regime. Another group introduced "the lives of people who have accomplished great good for the world," to borrow an ex-OWI official's words, such as *Abe Lincoln in Illinois* (Abraham Lincoln, 1940), *Men of Boys Town* (Father Flanagan, 1941) and *Madame Curie* (Marie Curie, 1943).[116] Benevolent figures appeared in fictional accounts as well: *Going My Way* (1944) and *The Keys of the Kingdom* (1944) showcased the humanitarian service of American missionaries. Other products like *The Southerner* (1945), *Our Town* (1940), *Our Hearts Were Young and Gay* (1944), portrayed small-town life in the United States with humility, harmony, and joy. The list also included action-packed westerns—*Tall in the Saddle* (1944), *In Old Oklahoma* (1943), *The Spoilers* (1942)—and romantic comedies—*Kitty Foyle* (1940), *Sun Valley Serenade* (1941), *I'll Be Seeing You* (1944)—that contained high entertainment value.

The U.S. government carried out its plans to build a "central film exchange" in fall 1945. After the OWI terminated its operation, the State Department worked with MacArthur's headquarters to establish this office on the ground. The person in charge was Michael M. Bergher, a Far Eastern representative of Columbia Pictures who had led the American Motion Picture Association of Japan on the eve of the war. In the months after Pearl Harbor, Bergher worked for the OWI's Overseas Branch. Fluent in Japanese, adapted to local customs (his favorite dish was cooked eel), and knowledgeable of the movie business, Bergher arrived in Japan in early November on the State Department's payroll.[117] As the CIE's film officer, Bergher approached a group of former associates to assemble the nucleus of the distribution outpost.[118] Soon, a handful of experienced men landed a one-room office on the eighth floor of the Osaka Building in Tokyo, where MGM had its Far Eastern office until 1941.[119] On February 20, 1946, Bergher received a U.S. Treasury license to start his operation. A week later, the Central Motion Picture Exchange began with the screening of *His Butler's Sister* and *Madame Curie*.[120]

Bergher's mission did not end after launching the CMPE in Japan. Less than a month after his work in Tokyo, he traveled to Seoul to set up a central picture exchange in the Korean Peninsula. Following a series of conferences with occupation authorities—including Lt. Gen. John R. Hodge, the U.S. occupation commander—Bergher founded a CMPE office as part of the occupation government's Bureau of Public Information. According to his report, the goal was to serve "a total of 96 theaters in Korea below 38 [degrees]."[121] On June 15, the CMPE head returned to the United States to join the Far Eastern Division of Universal Studios.[122] MacArthur's headquarters, reported *Variety*, saluted Bergher for having done a "fine job" in East Asia.[123] During his brief tenure as a government official, Bergher laid the groundwork for Hollywood's future operations. The fate of the distribution office would be left to his successor: Charles Mayer.

The founding of the CMPE completed the institutional endeavors to set up the U.S. film industry's postwar campaign in Japan. This outcome was the result of a corporatist matrix formed in response to the war—an extraordinary moment that brought together the U.S. government, the military, and the film industry. This coalition gave birth to the Motion Picture Export Association, the united front of U.S. studios. It also created a U.S.-led occupation body that worked to remold Japan through cultural and cinematic campaigns. Finally, it enabled Hollywood to create and position the CMPE within SCAP. At its beginning phase, the CMPE functioned as an internal organ of the occupation. A year after Bergher's departure, it turned into a full-fledged private enterprise representing the industry's commercial interests across the main islands. Corporatist intimacies allowed Hollywood to take on a market that it previously failed to control.

Chapter 3

Contested Terrains

Occupation Censorship and Japanese Cinema

On July 28, 1949, a group of men quietly gathered at Shōchiku studio for a closed screening. It was the day to view the rushes of *Murderer* (*Satsujinki*), an extended court story about a man's suspected killing of his wife. Present in the dim room were three company representatives, three legal experts (one Japanese, two American), and two censors from MacArthur's Civil Information and Education Section, which routinely monitored the content of the movies. The CIE censors had taken great interest in this production, as they believed that it could introduce "democratic court procedures" and "enlighten... the public." And much of the film, to their delight, did not disappoint. However, occupation officials found a problem in the final sequence, in which the portrayal of the "Japanese police force... was entirely mishandled." Disappointed with the characterization of local law enforcement, the censors immediately "suggested" that Shōchiku reedit the prints. The following day, the studio hosted a second screening with the changes made. This time, the CIE was pleased. Harry Slott, a section officer, specifically found that its presentation had "greatly improved and would unquestionably make a strong contribution" to the occupation.[1]

The *Murderer* screening exemplifies the tense political climate in which Japanese filmmakers operated during the months after the Second World War. While U.S. studios were setting up their postwar trade apparatus, Japanese movie companies faced the challenge of rebuilding their ruined business in the absence of people, capital, and resources. SCAP was another obstacle to the ailing industry. Eager to utilize the screens to "educate" and "reorient" the Japanese, the occupiers imposed their will on filmmakers, in particular by censoring their products. U.S. censors regularly met with directors and studio executives to provide "suggestions" for desirable themes. After studying the synopses, screenplays, and film prints, they requested deletions and modifications whenever the messages seemed inappropriate. Through these practices, SCAP functioned as a regulator of cultural output.

SCAP's dealing with Japanese cinema was not a story of unwavering thought control. The U.S. occupiers were actually more tolerant than fascist and totalitarian regimes that employed state censorship—such as Nazi Germany, Stalinist Russia, or Imperial Japan at the height of the Pacific War.[2] In this regard, American occupiers, as historian Jessica Gienow-Hecht has aptly noted, were "reluctant propagandists."[3] Yet, while constrained by the system, occupation censors went about changing the culture and content of Japanese filmmaking. Through a mixture of pressure and suasion, SCAP officials influenced the production process and interjected their own values into the movies. Filmmaking in early postwar Japan, thus, revived in a hegemonic structure of cultural and political power. It reveals America's strong influence over local activities.

For Japanese filmmakers, the occupation era involved mixed emotions. Generally pleased with the death of the wartime regime and the birth of a new "democratic" climate, Japanese filmmakers often agreed to incorporate the occupiers' ideas and "suggestions." Yet, at times, they regarded SCAP's intervention as an encroachment on their artistic and cultural sensibilities, as it appeared to reflect cultural arrogance and misunderstanding. Thus, although sometimes noted for their "receptiveness," Japanese filmmakers also displayed tenacity and resilience, even resisting SCAP's impositions on some occasions.[4] The gradual recovery of Japanese cinema was a largely nonviolent experience, but it embodied tense interplays of Japanese and American will. During the MacArthur era, Japanese cinema was a "contact zone" that reflected the uneven power dynamic of the occupation.[5]

An Industry in Trouble

The end of World War II ushered in new developments in Japanese filmmaking. Following its arrival in Japan, SCAP disbanded the Home Ministry and allowed the so-called Big Three studios in Japan—Tōhō, Shōchiku, and Daiei—to resume their business free of bureaucratic intervention from their own state. Filmmakers halted their production of war propaganda and,

according to one film historian, began to plan the creation of "escapist entertainment movies, music, and comedy movies."[6] Moviemakers outside these big
companies discovered new opportunities as well. In a time when the demand
for public amusement was suddenly on the rise, independent companies dived
into the business. By 1950 at least twenty-three new companies were compet-
ing in the market, and thirty others specialized in shorts.[7] The output increased
from 21 films in 1945 to 123 three years later. By 1951 the number of films
produced exceeded 200.[8]

Filmmaking of this era, however, came with grave challenges. For one thing,
resources in Japan were scarce. The war had caused a drainage of manpower
from Japan proper. Directors, actors, and staff members who survived war
fronts in China and Southeast Asia were slow to return to their professions.[9]
Most production facilities had survived the Allied air raids, but Japanese companies had to cope with deteriorated equipment and chronic shortages of
coal and electricity—vital energy sources.[10] Most devastating was the paucity
of raw film.[11] In June 24, 1947, Tōhō announced that it would "not call for
expansion." "The reason," the company explained, was "simply the scarcity of
raw film."[12]

Economic instability cast an ominous shadow over the industry. The early
postwar era witnessed a broken economy struggling to rebound from the war.
With the end of the Japanese government's intense control of goods and supplies, the demand for everyday products soared, while productivity remained
low. The country quickly entered an era of rampant inflation. Market volatility particularly hurt the industry by driving up the costs of film production.[13]
This, noted the almanac *Eiga nenkan* in 1950, forced filmmakers to respond
with "cheap amusement products that catered to the interests of the lowly
masses." Although film output gradually recovered during the occupation, the
quality appeared to many as being low. *Eiga nenkan* admitted that the industry
"has not yet recovered to the standards of the prewar [era]."[14]

The specter of wartime collaboration haunted studios as well. Immediately
after the war, Japanese companies hastily announced replacements at the management level in hopes of relieving their businesses from war responsibility.[15]
But the investigation for accountability commenced in the upcoming months.
In April 1946, the new Japanese government, under SCAP's auspices, began
to examine public officials' role in the war. Subsequently, a group of industry
representatives and culture elites formed a special committee to assess the film
industry's war-era actions.[16] This led to resignations by key industry figures
in anticipation of a forthcoming purge in the trade.[17] In October 1947, the
Japanese government announced the decision to remove four industry leaders.

By the end of the calendar year, twenty-seven others were on the government's "purge list."[18]

In addition, turmoil surfaced from within. During the early months of the occupation, employees in each major studio organized their own unions to lobby for higher wages and improved working conditions. On April 28, 1946, workers across the movie industry formed the Japan Film and Theater Workers' Union (Nihon eiga engeki rōdō kumiai, aka Nichieien) to enhance their bargaining power.[19] The rise of organized labor soon led to tense bargaining sessions at the Big Three studios.[20] Friction intensified at Tōhō, where union and management clashed in three successive sessions. Even though the workers' disputes were eventually settled with compromises made by both sides, the company suffered from a growing deficit and an unfolding "management crisis."[21] Workers and employees struggled to heal the wounds etched deeply in their exhausted minds. Some union members chose to leave the company and form their own production company, the Shin Tōhō Motion Picture company.

Furthermore, Japanese production companies struggled because of their intertwined relationship with film exhibitors. Although the occupation inspired a breakup of old institutional structures, the big film companies clung to their nationwide theater chains. According to the *Eiga nenkan* of 1950, Tōhō directly owned 68 theaters and Shōchiku, 72; both companies also maintained distribution contracts with hundreds of other theaters.[22] The ownership of theater circuits enabled the big studios to flourish during the prewar era, but it hurt them right after the war because of print shortages and a drastic decline in output.[23] The ownership of theaters also subjected studios to antimonopoly investigations. In January 1948, the Japanese government passed a law designed to eliminate the concentration of economic power. In the movie business, Tōhō, Shōchiku, Daiei, and Tōyoko were singled out as possible violators.[24] The scrutiny continued for many months.[25]

Continuing Interventions

SCAP became involved in this volatile cinematic climate in three ways. First, it regulated the content of the movies. Determined to make use of the screen medium to further the "democratization" of Japan, the occupation government continued to tamper with film production and content beyond the initial months of its involvement. Second, it assisted institutional recovery. Aware of the chaos and volatility that marred the Japanese movie enterprise, the occupiers prioritized the reconstruction of large studios for the sake of achieving stability. They did so, most strikingly, by opposing union and worker activities after initially supporting them. Finally, U.S. occupiers promoted cultural autonomy. While directly interfering with the production process, SCAP also took part in developing a self-censorship apparatus for Japanese companies. Through the establishment of this new instrument, U.S. officials urged the Japanese to self-contain "lowbrow" film content.

SCAP's involvement in content regulation involved two offices. The Civil Information and Education Section continued to oversee the activities of Japanese filmmakers. The section underwent key personnel changes at the end of the first year. Brig. Gen. Kermit R. Dyke ended his service in May 1946 and returned to the United States; his replacement was Lt. Col. Donald R. Nugent, a "dyed-in-the-wool conservative" who served until the end of the occupation. David Conde, who headed the Motion Picture and Theater Branch, resigned in July 1946 and gave up the position to George Gercke, a staff member of the Information Division who had worked for the film industry before the war.[26] Under new leadership, the CIE continued to examine the synopses, scenarios, and film prints submitted by Japanese studios. It kept a record of its thinking on the subject and actions in its weekly reports.

The other censorship apparatus, the Civil Censorship Detachment, remained active as well. It usually became involved after the CIE viewed and evaluated films. Relying on the Motion Picture Code, the CCD closely examined prints and interjected the agendas of the military establishment. In its monthly reports, the CCD routinely announced the results of the screenings. For example, in a "special report" dated February 17, 1948, the CCD noted that a total of 102 feature films underwent review. Eighty-one of them "portrayed some elements which were beneficial" to the occupation. Thirty-three of them either "portrayed some democratic propaganda, or propaganda criticizing or exposing some undemocratic practice or custom."[27]

The CCD's intervention did not stop here: in addition to scrutinizing the films, it monitored cultural diffusion in the public arena. Censors did this by regularly visiting theaters to assure that regulations were enforced at the screenings.[28] In June 1947, for example, the CCD pressured a movie house in Tokyo to remove its posters that allegedly underscored "feudal ideals." These posters, the censor charged, were a "misrepresentation of fact" of *Gingorō Fights Naked* (*Gingorō hadaka shōbu*, 1940), the feature presentation, since they "advertise the very elements that were deleted from the film in conformity with censorship regulations."[29] Once CCD's vision even extended to a small toy store in Gunma Prefecture, which had sold short strips of old films that contained "objectionable" war scenes. The CCD forced the retailer to "withdraw and destroy" these celluloid pieces.[30]

While regulating the spread of cultural values in the public arena, SCAP cautiously rebuilt the Japanese movie business. It did so by prioritizing the recovery of big companies. Since its operation began in fall 1945, the CIE regularly visited the leading studios to "discuss various problems confronting motion picture production"—which usually involved matters beyond pure film content.[31] The occupiers also supported the newly founded Motion Picture Producers Association (Eiga seisakusha rengōkai, or Eiren; renamed the Motion Picture Association of Japan on March 1, 1947).[32] Originally formed on November 5, 1945, this industrywide organization led by the Japanese Big Three vowed to achieve a "healthy development" of the movie business through "mutual co-operation" and "fair competition."[33] SCAP would maintain contact with the Motion Picture Producers Association to allocate material resources and help facilitate a stable recovery.[34]

The desire to assist industrial recovery led the occupiers to turn against organized labor. Despite its sympathetic attitude toward unions early on, SCAP soon began to oppose labor and left-wing activism, especially as they inspired turbulence through strikes and other union activities. This "reverse course" soon led to SCAP's Red purges of 1949 and 1950.[35] In the film world, SCAP's hostility to organized labor became evident during the strikes at Tōhō studio. As worker discontent with management intensified in strikes, the First Cavalry Division of the occupation's Eighth Army dispatched tanks and troops to suppress dissent. The end of the Tōhō strikes was followed by SCAP's purge of alleged left-wing employees from the major studios. According to one account, at least 137 individuals were removed from the movie business in 1950.[36] In a move that mirrored Hollywood's response to the House Un-American Activities Committee hearings in the United States, the Big Three in Japan refrained from hiring left-wing filmmakers.[37]

SCAP, in addition, instilled an autonomous method of cultural regulation. While monitoring film content themselves, the occupiers took steps to transfer that authority to the Japanese. On January 13, 1946, the CIE's George Gercke initiated talks with Japanese studios to establish a "motion picture code of ethics" modeled after Hollywood's production code. A branch unit of the Japanese cabinet drafted the text in the summer of 1946.[38] For the next two and a half years, the CIE and industry representatives met repeatedly to discuss the content of the code.[39] On April 14, 1949, a large ceremony took place at the

Piccadilly Theater in Tokyo. The CIE attended the event together with studio and government representatives.[40] The Associated Press referred to this event as a "pretentious gesture at self-censorship."[41]

The inauguration celebrated the founding of the Control Committee for the Motion Picture Code of Ethics, which was made up of various individuals representing film studios, producers, distributors, directors, and other production staff members. The committee's responsibility was to read scripts and view film prints to assure that the content of the films would conform to the code, which comprised seven categories: "Nation and Society," "Law," "Religion," "Education," "Custom," "Sex," and "Distasteful Subjects." The code, for instance, demanded that portrayal of violence be to be limited to "what is essential" in accord with Japan's renouncing of war; vengeance was discouraged; religious leaders, such as ministers and priests, could not be ridiculed or villainized; nudity and gender relations had to be handled "carefully" with respect to the sanctity of marriage and family unity; and cruelty—in the form of torture, lynching, brutality against women and children, for example—could not be depicted in a "stimulating manner."[42]

The Control Committee, however, did not immediately earn full-scale autonomy. During the occupation, it operated through close coordination with SCAP. The CIE directly offered "advise [sic] and guidance to the examining committee."[43] It interfered with the committee's daily protocols and occasionally mounted pressure against "undesirable" subjects. Even in the final months of the occupation, U.S. censors required "consultations" before approving films that had been banned earlier.[44] Moreover, SCAP kept an eye on the political orientation of committee members. In a report dated August 20, 1949—a year after the Tōhō strikes ended—the CCD specifically noted that the committee was largely devoid of "leftist leaning" individuals.[45] In response, the Japan Film and Theater Workers' Union complained that "none of the opinion of the laborers are being represented."[46]

In the Contact Zone

The occupation of Japan instilled a new climate in the world of Japanese filmmaking. In contrast to the war years, when the Home Ministry held a tight grip on the industry, the early postwar era fostered a greater level of intellectual openness and artistic opportunity. The mind-set of Japanese filmmakers began to change. Veteran filmmakers who made films during the war felt guilt and shame for contributing to the propaganda. At the same time, the movie-making community found hope and excitement in pursuing its creative endeavors. Some displayed outright joy during the occupation, expressing appreciation to the occupiers for assisting the recovery of the movie industry.[47]

Yet the actual process of filmmaking involved a great deal of tension. While urging the Japanese to take charge of their own projects, SCAP censors hovered around the entire process, demanding changes and revisions of the plots, dialogues, and screen images. The occupiers' intervention often resulted in drastic modifications of film content. The process baffled and perplexed the filmmakers. Disappointed and at times angry at the censors' apparent lack of understanding of their own values, filmmakers often resisted compromising their original inspirations. The uneasy interplay of occupier and occupied played out in individual film projects. Three case studies explore filmmaking in this larger political and cultural climate.

Drunken Angel

The occupiers believed that the movies must serve a constructive purpose. To them, political films that undermined Japan's postwar reconstruction were simply unacceptable; pure escapism was not enough. Determined to use the movies to promote meaningful lessons, the occupiers pressured filmmakers to address social problems of everyday life. In a meeting with Daiei on October 16, 1947, the CIE's Harry Slott called for "more pictures dealing with social and economic problems as related to the future of the Japanese people."[48] In urging Japanese filmmakers to produce "pictures with a message," occupation authorities cited Hollywood's acclaimed social problem films, such as William Wyler's *The Best Years of Our Lives* (1946, which deals with postwar homecoming) and Jules Dassin's *The Naked City* (1948, a neorealistic urban crime drama), as successful models for the Japanese.[49]

Drunken Angel (*Yoidore tenshi*, 1948) was a film that seemed to meet this objective. The story focused on the black market, "the most popular social problem portrayed in the pictures," according to a CCD report in February 1948.[50] The genesis of this Tōhō production was an artificial set of a black market, created for *New Era of Idiots* (*Shin baka jidai*), a 1947 comedy directed by Yamamoto Kajirō. Intent on making full use of this studio creation, Tōhō summoned Kurosawa Akira and Uekusa Keinosuke to create a new film about the underworld.[51] The long-time friends proposed a project that would expose "the rampages and violence of the *yakuza* in a critical fashion."[52] In its "Intention of Productions," the creators vowed to demonstrate the "evil" of the "world of the so-called *yakuza,* where the foundations of all action were

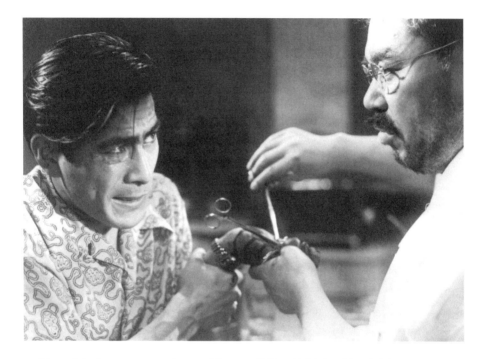

Figure 3.1. A tense encounter between Matsunaga (Mifune Toshirō) and Sanada (Shimura Takashi). "DRUNKEN ANGEL" © 1948 Toho Co. Ltd. All Rights Reserved.

feudalistic duty and obligation, [and where] good and evil was determined by...physical strength." The original title of the film, *City of Bacillus,* implied gang life was a disease.[53] By the time Kurosawa and Uekusa completed the script, the title was changed to *Drunken Angel.*

The story, as detailed in the first script, dated October 30, 1947, revolved around the relationship of two men. One is Sanada (Shimura Takashi), a near-alcoholic doctor who owns a run-down clinic in a raucous neighborhood. His status contrasts with that of a thriving colleague who runs his own hospital and later appears in a chauffeured automobile. The other man is Matsunaga (Mifune Toshirō), a reckless gangster.[54] The two first meet when Matsunaga seeks treatment at Sanada's clinic, claiming that his right arm was hurt by a "nail...sticking out."[55] Sanada actually discovers a bullet in the wounded arm and suspects that Matsunaga, coughing heavily, has tuberculosis. The gangster vehemently rejects the diagnosis, but soon comes to admit to his deteriorating health. The two brusque men quarrel almost every time they meet, but slowly they develop a sense of mutual trust.

The bond of these men is challenged when Okada, a "big brother" of Matsunaga who has spent a few years in jail, quietly returns to the scene. Matsunaga, almost by reflex, pledges allegiance to the elder gangster. The relationship soon turns sour, however, as Okada seizes the junior gangster's money and girl. Okada also intimidates Sanada for having sheltered Miyo, a former patron once sick with venereal disease. Despite threats by the *yakuza,* Sanada holds his ground and calls him a "ghost of feudalism." At one point, Sanada deplores the anachronism in Okada's lifestyle. "Men and women have equal rights, now," the doctor says.[56] Matsunaga is caught between the old and new lifestyles. While refusing to abandon the gangsters' "code of chivalry," he begs Okada not to harm the doctor whom he now trusts.[57]

Sanada tries to salvage Matsunaga from both his TB and his reckless life. Convinced that Matsunaga's illness is rooted in the *yakuza* way of life, the doctor tells the ailing gangster that the only way to cure his lungs is to detach himself from the "rotten and worm-eater [*sic*] people who are just like germs."[58] Matsunaga seems to understand, but he refuses to change his lifestyle. After losing power in his clan, Matsunaga pays a surprise visit to Okada; the scene cuts to a local police station, where the sergeant picks up the phone and learns that Okada has been killed. Matsunaga dies in the hospital due to a lung hemorrhage. Sadly, nobody is willing to claim his corpse. As the gang plans a funeral in Okada's honor, Sanada decides to accept Matsunaga's dead body. Riding in a funeral vehicle, Sanada asks the driver to enter the black market, where Okada's memorial service is about to begin. Staring at the startled gangsters, an angry Sanada, in the final dialogue of the script, tells the driver to make another round "at full speed!"[59]

The CIE found several problems in the story. Part of the trouble had to do with the setting. Censors, for example, questioned the neighborhood's location in a "burned out corner of the city"—which could invoke unpleasant memories of the war.[60] The CIE was also wary about the treatment of the black market. In the submitted script, a censor reacted to the discussions of venereal disease, bootlegging, and alcoholism—common problems known in the underworld. The biggest problem was the ending. Even though the two gangsters die in the end, the script closes ominously with the doctor hauling Matsunaga's corpse around the run-down neighborhood. Tōhō claimed that this ending scene was a form of "protest against the evil world."[61] However, the CIE found it to be "a bit gruesome."[62] The occupiers demanded an upbeat closure to brighten this otherwise dark story.

Following the initial exchange with SCAP, Kurosawa's team, a month later, returned with a revised script. The new version kept the plot largely intact. The co-screenwriters made minor changes in the dialogue involving the first encounters of Sanada and Matsunaga. Okada's lines were also modified. The biggest change came in the ending, which highlights Sanada's conversation with Jin, a nearby bar worker, who, out of her fondness for Matsunaga, decides to hold his funeral service. Sanada, then, is halted by a young schoolgirl, another tuberculosis patient who had visited his office in an earlier scene. The girl hands him an X-ray photo, which shows that she is on the course of recovery. The doctor agrees to buy her a bowl of *anmitsu* sweets to celebrate her reviving health.[63]

Interestingly, this new ending follows a previously absent duel between Okada and Matsunaga. In this scene, the two men, with daggers in hand, pounce on each other to kill. It is an "ugly and brutal fight of two beastly beings" according to the script.[64] Kurosawa and Uekusa end the scene with deep irony: Okada inflicts a fatal wound on Matsunaga and survives the duel. Thus, while Matsunaga soon dies, gangsterism remains alive and well. The revised script also included a bleak dream sequence, in which a white coffin, observed by crows in the sky, is left on the side of a pool of water. Matsunaga, hatchet in hand, breaks open the coffin and finds his own corpse in it. The gangster "screams and runs madly" until the real Matsunaga wakes up.[65]

The actual film adopted the modified ending with Sanada talking to the female student. But the film also kept the duel between Okada and Matsunaga intact. The nightmare scene remained in the film as well, despite the occupiers' complaint that it was "gruesome."[66] In addition, the final product visualized the neighborhood in remarkably dark tones. From the opening scene until the very end, the film introduced what John Dower would call "cultures of defeat"—prostitutes (not included in the original script), a dive bar, and a neon-lit dance hall in which a female singer performs an eerie number titled "Jungle Boogie Woogie."[67] Contrary to the occupiers' desire to show up America as a model for the Japanese, these portraits of urban nightlife, as one film scholar noted, exposed the "pernicious foreign [especially American and Western] influences and the loss of Japanese culture" under MacArthur's presence.[68] The bleakness is further emphasized in the filthy sump at the center of the neighborhood. Bubbling with methane gas and covered with floating garbage, this mosquito-infested pond, according to Kurosawa, was "the symbol of this production," encapsulating the dismal climate of black market society.[69]

As if these were not enough, *Drunken Angel* blurred the lines of good and evil. Instead of portraying this as a Manichaean clash of two antithetical characters, Kurosawa presented both Matsunaga and Sanada as "human beings" with "reason" (*risei*).[70] Matsunaga, a violent and short-tempered gangster, is a "likeable" character who wins the compassion of Sanada and Jin. By contrast,

Sanada is an able doctor who cares for others but is strongly attached to alcohol—a trait associated with the black market. In an early scene, he drinks a bottle of ethanol rationed for medical use, and he does not amend his habits throughout the story. Kurosawa stresses Sanada's flawed attributes by preserving the title, *Drunken Angel,* in spite of repeated criticisms by the occupiers.[71] Unlike a black-and-white Hollywood gangster narrative, *Drunken Angel* is a story of complex morals and mixed messages. In the end, the film does not offer concrete remedies for the Japanese to outgrow the "cultures of defeat."

The U.S. occupiers perceived *Drunken Angel* as a successful production. It was a film in which SCAP identified "both reorientation and entertainment value," thanks to the depiction of an "inglorious end of a thug…who would not reform despite efforts of his sweetheart and doctor."[72] But the film was hardly a product dictated by MacArthur's will. The production process also reveals the determination, persistence, and creative aspirations of Kurosawa's team. To the director, *Drunken Angel* was a ground-breaking film. "In this picture I finally found myself," he later noted. "It was *my* picture. I was doing it and no one else."[73] While subjected to the intervention of occupation censors, Kurosawa, as noted in his autobiography, energetically debated with the occupiers in developing his own film products.[74] A film that helped establish his fame and status as a leading director in Japan, *Drunken Angel* represents Kurosawa's will as much as it reveals the occupiers' presence behind the scenes.

The Bells of Nagasaki

From day one, the occupiers understood that the demilitarization of Japan would be a daunting task. At the very least, it required the disbanding of the military, the elimination of weaponry, and the purging of war-mongers from positions of influence. In addition, the instillation of peace necessitated what one historian called the "psychological disarmament" of the Japanese.[75] In an attempt to ensure long-term peace, the occupation had to convert the minds of the defeated population from war-seeking to peace-loving. To occupation censors, this transition required a scrupulous control over the depiction of war and militarism in Japanese cinema. Fearing that such themes could revive belligerent war-era mentalities, the occupiers employed great rigor to eliminate scenes and stories that involved military songs, symbols, and men in uniform. Censors, notes historian Hirano Kyōko, were "unreasonably meticulous" in their handling of such themes.[76]

The most problematic war theme involved the atomic bomb. During the months immediately following the war, SCAP, for fear of provoking outcry and resentment from the Japanese, imposed heavy restrictions on reportage concerning the bomb, the effects of radioactivity, and the two nuclear-destroyed cities.[77] "Reference to bomb performance or characteristics...official reports of scientific investigations of results of bombing, purported details of manufacture of the bomb or its contents, etc.," a SCAP check sheet cautioned in late 1947, were "not [to] be released."[78] Films about the bomb also came under intense scrutiny. When a film crew from the production company Nippon eigasha landed in Hiroshima in October 1945 to shoot a documentary about the destructive weapon, occupation authorities temporarily halted production. Although the team was allowed to resume its filmmaking, the final product was confiscated by the occupiers. The prints of *The Effects of the Atomic Bomb on Hiroshima and Nagasaki* (1946) were not returned to the Japanese until 1967.[79]

The Bells of Nagasaki (*Nagasaki no kane*) was a biographical picture that confronted the atom. This 1950 Shōchiku production, directed by Ōba Hideo, was based on the actual life story of Dr. Nagai Takashi, a radiologist who lived in Nagasaki for much of his life. His life became tumultuous after the Manchurian Incident of 1931, when Nagai served in the military as a medic and converted to Catholicism on his return. He then worked as an assistant professor at the Nagasaki Medical College, his alma mater, but the years of radiation exposure caused leukemia. Shortly after he was told that he had only three more years to live, the atomic bomb was dropped on Nagasaki. Nagai, who was at the college at the time, survived the blast, but lost his wife. He unselfishly tried to help his patients, friends, and community members, but soon found it impossible to leave his sickbed. From here on, Nagai prayed and wrote his memoirs. With his two healthy children in attendance, Nagai died on May 1, 1951, at the age of forty-three.

Nagai documented his own thoughts and feelings in a handful of books published during the occupation. One was *Leaving These Children* (*Kono ko o nokoshite*), which chronicles his emotional struggles as a dying man about to leave two young children behind. Nagai also expresses anguish over radiation sickness—a subject to which he had ironically devoted much of his professional life. Another of his books was *The Bells of Nagasaki* (*Nagasaki no kane*), which documented first-hand observations of the atomic blast. The book recounts Nagai's efforts to help his students, colleagues, and civilians in the wake of the bomb. The book ends with a denouncement of war, especially the use of atomic weapons. In the final pages, Nagai writes as he hears the bells of a nearby Catholic church ringing over the destroyed city.[80]

Nagai's literary works did not sit well with the occupiers. For example, when *The Bells of Nagasaki* (the book) was first submitted for censorship, Gen.

Charles Willoughby of the CCD suspended its publication for six months, arguing that it would "lead to possibly inflammatory reactions" by the Japanese while "suggest[ing]...that the American was inhuman in using this weapon to expedite the termination of the war."[81] The CCD argued for the suppression of the book "on [the] ground[s] that it would invite resentment against [the] U.S."[82] Shikiba Ryūzaburo, a friend of Dr. Nagai and a trustee of the American Movie Culture Association (AMCA), a Hollywood fan organization run by the culture elites (see chapter 7), attempted to reconcile the differences. In a letter addressed to SCAP, the prominent psychologist supported Nagai's work as it treated the Nagasaki bombing as "the beginning of peace for mankind."[83]

The CCD eventually allowed the publication of Nagai's manuscript, but on the condition that he remind readers of Japanese atrocities. The final publication included SCAP's report of Japanese military brutality in the Philippines titled "The Tragedy of Manila" (*Manira no higeki*). Hastily compiled by MacArthur's Military Intelligence Division, this supplementary text denounced the Japanese military for its "savage acts" (*bankō*) in the Manila Massacre of February 1945. This included the razing of homes and public facilities as well as violence against women, children, and elderly civilians. The occupiers were particularly intent on exposing Japanese atrocities against Catholic institutions and worshippers: "The Japanese," the report stressed, "strove to wipe away the scent of Christianity in the Philippines until the very last bit" was gone.[84] The text also offered a timeline and a set of testimonies by Catholic priests and American military officers who discussed the horrifying experience.

The film version of *The Bells of Nagasaki* originated from Shindō Kaneto, a rising filmmaker who worked for the Shinkō kinema production company before the war. During the occupation era, Shindō joined Shōchiku as a screenwriter and left to work as an independent filmmaker in spring 1950.[85] One of the principal themes of his career was the atomic bomb. Born and raised not far from Hiroshima, Shindō visited the destroyed city immediately after August 6. Shocked as he stood in front of a wiped-out train station, Shindō "felt that he himself was struck by the bomb."[86] Later, he would go on to produce films such as *Child of the Atomic Bomb* (*Genbaku no ko*, 1952) and *The Lucky Dragon* (*Daigo fukuryūmaru*, 1959) in which he pleaded for world peace and "no more Hiroshimas."

The Bells of Nagasaki was a film project that Shindō took on while still at Shōchiku. The objective was not to indict the United States but to tell a story about the "progress of science" and "the beauty of human love" through a dramatized story of a real scientist.[87] The first synopsis, completed April 1, 1949, takes the story back to 1932, when Nagai was still an assistant in the physical treatment section of the Nagasaki Medical College.[88] There, Nagai specializes in radiology, which was a marginalized field in the profession. Nagai is portrayed as a diligent and inquisitive scientist, studying day and night until he falls asleep at his desk. Despite financial hardships, the doctor enjoys the faithful companionship of his wife Kiyono and their two children. Every Sunday, the Nagai family attends mass; they are Catholics in a city known for its long tradition of Christian worship.

As the crisis of war looms in the backdrop, Nagai abruptly feels a sharp pain in his left arm. He soon finds out that he is ill with leukemia, a life-threatening "atomic disease." Yet the doctor refuses to give up his work at the college. Backed by his loyal wife, he continues to pursue the "inquiry of truth." On August 8, 1945, Nagai leaves his home, seen off by Kiyono, and stays the night at the college. The next day, the atomic bomb is dropped on the city. The college catches fire, but Nagai survives the blast, and so do his children, who had been sent to the countryside. Kiyono, however, does not survive. When he returns home, Nagai discovers a pile of ashes and a rosary owned by his now deceased wife. The final lines of the screenplay present a determined Nagai continuing to explore atomic medical science in the face of ill health and family tragedy.

SCAP had no problem with the script except for one thing: the Nagasaki bombing. After reading a story that dramatized the Nagai family's suffering, the CIE pressured Shōchiku to eliminate references to the nuclear explosion. Shōchiku responded by adding an intertitle before the scene of ground zero. The text, which was added in the revised synopsis, described the atomic bomb as a vehicle for punishing the Japanese military while "sav[ing] the innocent nation who were [sic] longing for peace in their hearts."[89] Yet to SCAP, this disclaimer was not enough. While acknowledging that the story about the "life of [the] scientist is OK," the CIE insisted that scenes involving the bomb "will serve no constructive purpose."[90] This forced a crucial change in the second revision. Shōchiku's re-revised synopsis, submitted to the CIE on June 4, 1949, dropped all references to the bomb. After Nagai leaves for his office on August 8, 1945, the script jumps to him lying on his sickbed, his wife having died mysteriously. The text ends with the two children vowing to "live courageously" in spite of their father's fading health.[91]

SCAP's intervention stymied Shindō's project and led to an impasse. Shōchiku would not pick up the project until the following summer—after the screenwriter had already left the company to shoot films on his own. The final synopsis lists two additional cowriters, Mitsuhata Sekirō and Hashida

Sugako, while Ōba remained as director.[92] The team did not compromise. Even though the occupiers remained wary of the project, Shōchiku submitted the final prints with the scene of the atomic bomb. The film made it to the commercial screens on September 22, 1950.[93] In the film, the bomb strikes in a sequence that begins when Nagai's two children, playing in a river stream, observe a giant plume of smoke covering the skies beyond the mountains. After showing the mushroom cloud from three different angles, the narrative cuts to Nagai, standing in the rubble of his home, picking up the rosary of his dead wife. The doctor soon falls seriously ill, but decides to continue the study of radiology. He is sad that he will soon no longer be able to look after his two children. The film ends in 1949, when the Pope visits the city of Nagasaki. He praises Nagai in front of a large audience.

The final product was a result in no small measure of Shōchiku's insistence and determination. But it also materialized because of SCAP's policy relaxation. The film version of *The Bells of Nagasaki* was completed at a time when the occupation government was gradually—and cautiously—allowing the disclosure of information about the atomic bomb. As Japanese citizens began to learn about Hiroshima and Nagasaki, it became more difficult to suppress media coverage. The Soviets' successful test of their first bomb on August 29, 1949, rendered the censorship of nuclear news obsolete. The dissolution of the CCD in November also removed a powerful—and military—controlling agent. Once released, *The Bells of Nagasaki* collected decent earnings in the box office.[94] Critics' reactions were favorable. *Kinema junpō* ranked the film sixteenth among the best films of 1949. One reviewer praised the movie for its "serious[ness]." "One can say that it was among the best of recent films by Shōchiku," he noted.[95]

Daibosatsu Pass

While talk about the atomic bomb gradually entered the popular media, the period film (*jidaigeki*) began to make a quiet comeback. In the early postwar era, Japanese companies were eager to revive this once-popular genre that depicted historical pre-Meiji era stories. However, the occupiers found this problematic because of the "feudalistic" emphasis on swordfights, violence, and a "code of revenge and loyalty." To SCAP's chagrin, the period film too often introduced themes of personal retaliation, murder, treason, and fraud without regard for the law.[96] A similar anxiety surrounded the *kabuki* theater, which was nearly banned by MacArthur for its apparent display of "feudalism."[97] The period-film genre, which often drew inspiration from *kabuki* stories, faced pressure. SCAP's control was especially thorough when David Conde ran the Motion Picture and Theatrical Branch of the CIE. "American censorship was tough," recalled period-film director Itō Daisuke in reference to the Conde years. "[We] could not slash people [with swords] at all."[98]

Daibosatsu Pass (*Daibosatsu tōge*) was a project that gained life after Conde's departure. Based on Nakazato Kaizan's period novel (*jidai shōsetsu*) set in the late Tokugawa era, the story chronicles the travails of Tsukue Ryūnosuke, a blind samurai known for his soundless (*otonashi*) style of swordsmanship. Originally a newspaper serial that eventually turned into a twenty-volume epic, Kaizan's novel inspired Nikkatsu to make a film version in 1935. Sustained by a 17,000-yen budget, the Nikkatsu production, noted *Kokusai eiga shinbun,* dramatized the story on a "grand scale" and enjoyed a rare seventeen-day "long run" in major cities.[99] Immediately after the war, SCAP banned this film along with 235 others that appeared "harmful." [100] In spring 1948, Shōchiku decided to produce a remake of this story. The CIE rejected the synopsis "on the ground that this story is a revival of a banned film."[101]

Kaizan's story, however, was too popular for Japanese filmmakers to abandon or ignore. A year after Shōchiku's project reached a dead end, the Tōyoko Motion Picture Company decided to film the story. This young production firm struggled with financial difficulties in early 1949 and was desperate to overcome its plight.[102] The company soon formed a partnership with two other small producers and give birth to the so-called fourth exhibition circuit—an alternative to the Shōchiku, Tōhō, and Daiei chains.[103] Tōyoko believed that Nakazato's story was very exploitable: its scale was "comparable to *Les Miserables,*" noted one of its liaisons.[104] The popular period story presented an opportunity to salvage the company from its financial woes and bring success to its business.[105]

Yet to persuade the occupiers required careful thinking. The banned 1935 production, which was largely based on the novel's first episode, "The Episode of the Kōgen Ittō School [of sword fighting]," was peppered with scenes that SCAP was likely to oppose.[106] The story, for example, opened with Tsukue's brutal murder of an innocent old man for no apparent reason. Shortly before a ceremonial sword match, Tsukue rapes Ohama, the wife of his opponent. At the match, the protagonist inflicts a fatal wound on his enemy. After her husband's death, Ohama marries Tsukue and has a child by him. Meanwhile, the dead opponent's younger brother pledges revenge and begins a search for the protagonist. The episode concludes with a bloody swordfight between a master swordsman and the Tokugawa shogunate's watchdog organization to which Tsukue now belongs.[107]

Tōyoko made a conscious effort to differentiate its project from the 1935 version. The first script, which the CIE received on August 20, 1949, fused plots and characters of multiple episodes. It made for a compressed narrative with abrupt plot developments.[108] The first half begins some five years after the episode of the Kōgen Ittō School takes place. Tsukue becomes acquainted with Otoyo, a young woman who works at an inn where he stays for several nights. A set of flashbacks reveals that her face and figure are identical to those of Ohama, to whom Tsukue was once married. In the novel, the couple have a tragic relationship beginning with her rape and his slaying of her first husband. In the script, Tsukue and Ohama constantly quarrel until he kills her. The Tōyoko script avoids the subplot of rape and offers no concrete explanation for her death. Tsukue once remarks that Ohama died "because of my selfishness," but he leaves the actual cause a mystery.[109]

Tsukue and Otoyo are drawn to one another through their personal tragedies. The stoic swordsman first learns of Otoyo when he overhears her conversation with her lover. The two are runaways from their hometown, where their kin had arranged marriage partners against their will. The couple decides to commit suicide, but she survives. Tsukue is drawn to her because of her resemblance to Ohama as well as her tragic past. Their relationship is threatened by the appearance of Kinzō, the groom in Otoyo's arranged marriage. Desperate to bring her back to him, Kinzō threatens to kill Otoyo and burn down their village if she does not return to him. In a surprising twist, Otoyo chooses to marry the profligate son out of fear of his reckless behavior.

The second half of the script follows a group of soldiers who are fleeing from the Tokugawa army. Tsukue has capriciously joined the ten rebellious men, who are now surrounded in a hut and attacked with explosives. He survives but loses his eyesight. Still in love with the stoic protagonist, Otoyo escapes from Kinzō's hands and takes care of the blind swordsman. In the original story, Otoyo soon becomes ill but agrees to spend a night in bed with a feudal lord (tonosama) for money to heal Tsukue's vision. The Tōyoko script portrays her as simply fallen ill. Otoyo then sends a letter (and money) to Tsukue, who learns of Otoyo's loyalty to him as well as her decision to commit suicide. Perhaps in order to conceal his pain, Tsukue reacts to the news with his signature line: "Those who wish to die will die on their own." The script ends thus.[110]

Tōyoko's aim was not to subvert the occupation forces. The overall purpose of the film, the company insisted, was to apply a "new interpretation" to an old story and "affirm life through [the story of a] samurai living in a romance."[111] But to the occupiers, the script appeared far from cheerful or uplifting.

The CIE, for instance, disliked the film's presentation of suicide—which happens twice, both involving Otoyo. Equally problematic was the portrayal of the stoic protagonist. Even though Tōyoko toned down the violence and cruelty, Tsukue, according to the CIE, appeared little more than a "pessimist" and "egoist." The overall tone of the film was "extremely dismal," ending abruptly "with hopeless [and] unbearable emotions." The "negative" and "unconstructive" tone of the story made it unacceptable.[112]

Tōyoko claimed that their first script was a "constructive" period film, but nonetheless agreed to make some revisions.[113] Three weeks later, the company submitted a revised script that offered changes in a handful of scenes. It replaced Tsukue's signature line that feigned indifference to suicide with a moment of silence. Admitting that the script contained some "nihilistic" elements, the company toned down Tsukue's seemingly detached attitude toward government and political leadership. The new script also softened the rebel group's anger at Tsukue for appearing to lack honor and loyalty; Tōyoko decided to modify this scene because it could show that the picture "affirmed *bushido*." Finally, the script altered Kinzō's dialogue, for it promoted arson, murder, and disruption of public tranquility.[114]

The changes did not impress the CIE, which continued to question some of the script's "feudalistic" scenes. One concerned the dialogue during the ceremonial match.[115] Another troubling scene came with Tsukue's remark: "Sword is heart and character."[116] The CIE also deplored dialogue that championed the samurai code of honor and loyalty.[117] Women's subservience was another problem. The CIE crossed out dialogue that portrayed Otoyo's tendency to submit to Kinzō.[118] In addition, the presence of suicide itself—in dialogue and practice—continued to bother the occupiers.[119] All in all, the CIE reached a clear verdict: the new script "did not depart to a great extent from the original story."[120] Tōyoko was unable to make the film during the occupation.[121]

SCAP took a tough line against the period film. During the first three years of the occupation, the output of *jidaigeki* features was limited to single digits.[122] While Tōyoko was working on the script of *Daibosatsu Pass,* the CIE received requests for permission to film popular period stories involving Tange Sazen, Miyamoto Musashi, and Nakamura Yukinojō.[123] The CIE denounced the trend, arguing that filmmakers were "not showing good faith" in seeking to revive stories that showcased "blind allegiance."[124] Roughly a year before the occupation ended, the Motion Picture Association of Japan requested SCAP to allow the screening of the banned period films.[125] In the final days of his service, the CIE's Donald Nugent finally expressed willingness to open the market for these movies.[126]

The departure of occupation officials led to a large-scale revival of period films. Between 1954 and 1961, Japanese studios churned out well over one hundred period films per year.[127] Tōyoko's *Daibosatsu Pass* finally entered the production phase and was released in 1953. It had grown into an ambitious trilogy with Kataoka Chiezō playing the leading role. Five years later, Tōei released yet another trilogy of the same historical epic. Uchida Tomu's version of *Daibosatsu Pass,* starring Kataoka once again, appeared in wide-screen color and enjoyed wide viewership. The heyday of the period film arrived after MacArthur's departure.

Filmmaking in defeated Japan was a challenging exercise. While liberated from the ideological strains of the Home Ministry, Japanese companies struggled to resurrect their businesses in the aftermath of a devastating war. These filmmakers also had to deal with the U.S. occupiers, who imposed their own political agenda on the content of the movies. Although MacArthur granted a greater level of freedom to filmmakers than they had during war, he also imposed new constraints that hampered their creative activities. Japanese cinema in occupied Japan developed in this controlled political climate. It was a process that involved compliance, ambivalence, and resistance. Autonomous productions could not occur during the occupation. The Japanese film industry did not fully recover from the war until the mid-1950s.

The struggles of Japanese film companies raised Hollywood's hopes of expanding into the transpacific market. Thanks to their large stockpile of new films, U.S. studios gained the ability to compete against the Japanese film industry with quantity. American companies also renewed their confidence in the quality of the filmic products. Like most trade observers in Japan, they believed that Japanese companies were able to manufacture "very few superior pictures" that would emulate Hollywood's finest narratives.[128] In addition, SCAP's presence generated assurance and motivation. In addition to granting Hollywood a place in the Japanese market, the occupiers seemed determined to expand the transpacific film trade. Things were looking good for American movies.

Hollywood executives, however, soon realized that serious challenges lay ahead. To their surprise, the difficulties did not involve Japanese film companies but rather their own allies in the U.S. military and government. The transition from war to peace altered the political attitude of American officials and administrators. Once the occupation began, the corporatist harmony of the war years was replaced by an unexpectedly tense institutional relationship—one that would strain Hollywood's ties with U.S. authorities.

Chapter 4

Corporatist Tensions

Hollywood versus the Occupation

It was an odd decision. On a routine summer day in August 1946, a censor from SCAP's Civil Censorship Detachment came across *Mr. Smith Goes to Washington* (1939). This award-winning Frank Capra film told the uplifting story of Jefferson Smith, a junior senator who launches a vigorous crusade to restore justice on Capitol Hill. Relentless, passionate, and unbending, Smith—a "young Abraham Lincoln," the director later stated in his autobiography—stands up to corrupt state politics to defend the integrity of American freedom and democracy. His moral drive peaks in a twenty-four-hour filibustering act, which coaxes the guilty senators to confess their wrongdoings. The film ends with rounds of cheers and applause awarded to the fatigued hero. By commending Smith for his bravery, tenacity, and noble ideals, Capra aimed to champion his country and deliver a "ringing statement of America's democratic ideals."[1]

The CCD censor did not see things in Capra's way. Hardly impressed with the director's intended message, he dismissed the film for "ridiculing the dignity and the efficiency" of Washington politics. In the story, senior politicians who interact with Smith flourish through graft, media manipulation, and racketeering. Although the corrupt characters serve to accentuate Smith's enduring righteousness, the censor concluded that the film painted a "misleading and unfavorable picture of the American democracy they are copying—particularly in view of the fact that Mr. Smith's campaign for honesty finally triumphs despite the entire U.S. Senate." Although the film had been shown in Japan prior to the war, the wary SCAP official now requested the film's withdrawal. To the dismay of the famed director, *Mr. Smith Goes to Washington* was kept away from the Japanese until 1954, two years after the end of the occupation.[2]

Mr. Smith Goes to Washington was not the only film that suffered an unexpected fate. A number of other American productions fell prey to the scrupulous process of the occupation's film censorship. While directly interfering in the production of Japanese cinema, SCAP also developed an entangled network with the U.S. State Department and the U.S. Army to regulate the content of American movies. This censorship apparatus welcomed films that meshed with SCAP's political agenda, at time commissioning "reorientation" narratives for nationwide release. When confronting films that appeared to undermine the occupiers' mission, they demanded cuts and deletions in the editing room. During the occupation, U.S. officials offered privileged treatment to Hollywood studios, but they also went on to corral and control their cultural manifestations. America's "chosen instrument" was subjected to MacArthur's "democracy by intervention."

The censorship of Hollywood cinema reveals that the new corporatist climate of the postwar era often involved unease and frustration. The occupiers' desire to remold culture did not always synchronize with Hollywood's yearning for institutional autonomy. As the occupation progressed, the friction between the politics of cultural expression and the business of film presentation gradually widened the rift between U.S. authorities and Hollywood's top representatives. At one point, the Motion Picture Export Association threatened a complete withdrawal from the island nation, and the corporatist alliance faced a collapse. Even though the working relationship managed to last until the end of the occupation, Hollywood's bond with the U.S. government and military was fragile. In a climate of conflicting ambitions, occupation corporatism was a tense and even unhappy exercise in collaboration.

A New Corporatism

The American movie campaign in postwar Japan began on a strong note. After the successful opening of *His Butler's Sister* and *Madame Curie,* the Central Motion Picture Exchange went on to release roughly two to three new feature films every other week. The CMPE landed hit after hit in the opening months, from a heart-warming story about a Catholic priest (*Going My Way,* 1944) to an action-packed western (*Tall in the Saddle,* 1944) to the romantic war film (*Casablanca,* 1943). In Tokyo, the May 1946 *Kōgyō herarudo* reported that Hollywood was garnering "extremely superior" commercial results. Even in "regional areas" where "a considerable number of years and months were expectedly required for foreign films to become common," Hollywood, the trade magazine continued, was "defying this conventional wisdom." The supply of prints was simply "not enough" to meet the "soaring demand" for American movies.[3]

Hollywood's campaign during the first few months was loyal to the plans devised during the war. The choice of films was based on the Office of War Information's list of forty-five movies. Michael M. Bergher, the film officer who temporarily managed the CMPE, remarked that the new releases offered a glimpse of "the way American and the peoples of other democracies think and live."[4] Financial arrangements were inflexible. SCAP required the CMPE to arrange film exhibitions in a "normal commercial manner" and to draw the operating costs from its earned income. The films' returns were to be deposited in Japanese bank accounts.[5] Since its operation was approved "only because it is in furtherance of the Army education program," the CMPE was not allowed to transfer their yen earnings back to the United States. "No remittances of film rentals can be expected for a long time," the U.S. military authorities noted.[6]

The apparent popularity of U.S. movies delighted Hollywood, but SCAP was not entirely pleased. MacArthur's office was troubled because a number of American releases appeared to lack pedagogical value. One occupation official cautioned that Hollywood could deliver "an incorrect meaning of democracy to the Japanese."[7] SCAP grew frustrated also because it had little control over the first round of films that entered the Japanese market. Owing to the OWI's "equal participation" arrangement, the early lineup, noted another U.S. official, included "inferior films from at least two companies" while missing "several superior films of at least one company," since each U.S. studio was allowed to export no more than five feature productions.[8]

Problems with film content soon prompted the occupiers to develop a new procedure to seek greater control. The new process began with the Motion Picture Export Association. This trade apparatus collected lists of films from member studios and chose the exports for each market.[9] After 1934, U.S. feature films were internally censored by the Production Code Administration, which suppressed politically and morally offensive representations. The MPEA became a second filtering mechanism, aimed specifically to prevent state interference and popular criticism in off-shore markets. One film scholar thus referred to the MPEA as a "foreign distribution sister" of the PCA.[10] The MPEA's guidelines were simple: "Represent the very best in American Cinematic Art,... carry a true projection of U.S. domestic life, and... [accord] with objectives of the occupation."[11]

The State Department would examine the industry's selection. Immediately after the war, the newly created International Motion Picture Division (IMPD) co-opted the functions of the OWI and the Office of Inter-American Affairs. One of its main missions was to distribute 16 mm documentaries and newsreels—what government officials proudly called "factual films"—through noncommercial channels overseas. While doing so, the IMPD also served as an "informal liaison" to Hollywood and worked to "eliminate objectionable matter or treatment from export films."[12] The office examined the list of MPEA films and returned feedback before they were recommended for foreign markets.[13] John Begg, chief of the division, once noted that this was not outright censorship but an act of consultation "upon the request from the industry... [in order to] further international understanding."[14]

The U.S. Army also monitored Hollywood entertainment. The Civil Affairs Division (CAD), founded March 1, 1943, actively participated in the cultural reconstruction of the occupied territories. Determined to "expose the essential falsity" of "police state ideology," the Motion Picture Section of the Reorientation Branch at the New York field office of the CAD assembled documentary and newsreel programs for overseas publics.[15] The CAD's authority also extended to Hollywood's commercial productions.[16] Its criteria for judgment was based on technical superiority as well as the manifestation of "political, social and cultural themes deemed proper and not reflecting discredit on the U.S. or the Allies."[17] The CAD's interaction with Hollywood was at times forceful and demanding. In contrast to the State Department, U.S. Army officials often presented their decisions as "orders" with which Hollywood was expected to comply.[18]

In Japan, SCAP examined U.S. film products. The Civil Information and Education Section remained close to the U.S. film industry, as it housed the CMPE until it was privatized in May 1947. Meanwhile, it took part in the censorship of American cinema—a practice that continued until the end of the occupation. In examining Hollywood's lineup, this civilian agency chose to accept a mixture of politically "innocuous" amusement with message-heavy "reorientation" productions. The goal was to maximize turnout with a "balanced program," a portion of which was reserved for films that would "further... the objectives of the Occupation."[19] The Civil Censorship Detachment, the other arm of SCAP's cultural apparatus, influenced Hollywood's transpacific programming through its own acts of censorship. As was the case with Japanese cinema, military censors prioritized the establishment of order and security to protect SCAP's political and security agendas.[20]

The most significant SCAP policy was contained in Circular Twelve. Plans for this directive originated in the summer of 1946, when the two censorship offices worked out a blanket rule for foreign-film imports. On December 5, the CIE issued its criteria in "Admission of Foreign Magazines, Books, Motion Pictures, News and Photograph Services, et Cetera, and Their Dissemination in Japan." This key policy, commonly known as Circular Twelve, outlined the basic principles for a diverse range of international media products. The occupiers opened the market for foreign-film companies under the following four conditions: (1) Only one distributor per nation could engage in business; (2) each company could distribute as many as the maximum number of films its host country brought to Japan in any given year prior to the war; (3) SCAP would reserve the right to monitor film content to judge its "suitability in furthering the information and education objective of the Occupation"; and (4) screenings of these products were acceptable only within "normal commercial channels."[21]

On the surface, Circular Twelve was an open invitation for foreign-film distributors. It quickly triggered an "application rush" from as many as fourteen countries in a three-month period.[22] The eager parties included Great Britain, which inaugurated its postwar campaign with *The Seventh Veil* on December 3, 1947. The French followed suit the following year with the release of *La Belle et la Bête* on January 24. The Italians desired to engage in the film business as well. They began with *Paisà,* a neorealistic production by Roberto Rossellini, on September 6, 1949. The Russians had already broken into Japan in 1946, with two films *Music Girl in Moscow* and *Stone Flower,* but they benefited from the circular as well. Less-known movie-making countries such as Mexico and Argentina lacked a track record of business with the Japanese, but their products entered the market by way of complex business arrangements with other international distributors with commercial licenses.[23]

Yet in practice, this SCAP policy was discriminatory. As a "control procedure" that used prewar statistics to set a quota for celluloid imports, the directive privileged American movies—the most dominant cinematic imports in Japan before Pearl Harbor—over other foreign cinemas (see table 4.1).[24] The one-distributor-per-nation rule curbed the business prospects of small independent companies and assured the dominance of the MPEA, which obtained a commercial license from SCAP in May 1947 to operate on its own.[25] Yet Circular Twelve also reinforced the occupiers' authority over Hollywood. By assuring SCAP's right to examine and censor the narrative products for "information and education" purposes, the new rule preserved the U.S. government's power over America's "chosen instrument." In this way, Hollywood was subject to MacArthur's political orientation, even while enjoying a privileged position above other international cinemas.

Table 4.1. Statistics of Foreign Films in Japan, 1946–1951

	1946	1947	1948	1949	1950	1951	Total
United States	39	90	75	91	137	187	619
France	0	0	17	30	16	13	76
United Kingdom	0	2	14	18	17	19	70
Soviet Union	0	2	9	3	3	2	19
Italy	0	0	0	2	4	6	12
Mexico	0	0	0	1	1	1	3
Argentina	0	0	0	0	2	0	2
Sweden	0	0	0	0	0	2	2
Austria	0	0	0	0	0	1	1
Foreign Film Total	39	94	115	145	180	231	804

Source: Data on U.S. films are drawn from Hata Akio, ed. *Nijusseiki Amerika eiga jiten, 1914–2000*
(Tokyo: Katarogu hausu, 2002), 825–99; data on other foreign imports are from Allcinema movie database
(http://www.allcinema.net/prog/index2.php).

Censoring Hollywood

The process of censoring Hollywood differed from that of censoring Japanese
cinema. Whereas Japanese films were monitored from inception to exhibition, Hollywood only went through postproduction censorship. This meant
that the occupiers did not interfere in the filmmaking process itself, but determined the suitability of each celluloid narrative based on its synopsis, press
book, published reviews, and finished print. However, the experience of U.S.
film censorship was rigorous and demanding. This stemmed from SCAP's cau-
tious handling of the media in general and the active involvement of the U.S.
Army and State Department—two institutions that had little to do with the
censorship of Japanese cinema. The occupiers' concern with film content
spanned a myriad of genres and representations. Evidence suggests that the
occupation apparatus, as a whole, was most concerned and interested in four
major themes.

War

The war theme was not a problem exclusive to Japanese cinema. Occupation censors were alarmed with Hollywood's war-related films as well. U.S.
productions of this kind were undesirable because they could both anger and
demoralize the traumatized population. Equally troubling was the possibility that war-related productions might portray the United States as a violent

Table 4.2. The Breakdown of American Films by Genre

Genre	1946	1947	1948	1949	1950	1951	Total
Adventure/Action							
War	2	2	0	2	5	15	26
Swashbuckler	0	3	4	1	6	2	16
Western	3	5	2	10	19	41	80
Crime/Mystery	3	8	3	11	10	15	50
Imperial/Colonial	2	1	4	3	1	4	15
Other Adventure	1	0	4	4	6	14	29
Drama							
Biopic	3	5	3	3	3	5	22
Romance/Melodrama	5	14	13	12	9	9	62
Comedy/Comedy Drama	7	18	18	16	33	16	108
Historical Drama	2	6	2	5	2	7	24
Musical/Music Film	2	9	8	9	3	15	46
Other Drama	9	19	14	15	40	44	141
Total	39	90	75	91	137	187	619

Note: In determining the genre categories for each film, I have largely relied on the American Film Institute, ed., *The American Film Institute Catalog of Motion Pictures Produced in the United States.* 6 vols. (Berkeley: University of California Press, 1989). An online version is available at http://afi.chadwyck.com/home.

and belligerent nation. A CCD censor once warned that "American pictures...may be construed by the Japanese as glorifying war heroes."[26] Such anxiety led occupation censors to approach Hollywood with caution.

The occupiers' anxiety about the war-film genre was evident in such films' conspicuous absence in the approved list for Japan. In the early months of the occupation, the war pictures that did make it to the theaters were anti-Nazi pictures such as *Casablanca* (1943) and *Watch on the Rhine* (1943), most likely because they were far removed from the Pacific Theater. But even these films were deemed "questionable" because of their wartime backdrop.[27] Other Nazi-related pictures were not as lucky. One example was Alfred Hitchcock's *Lifeboat* (1944), which takes place in the aftermath of a German U-boat's sinking of a European passenger liner. The narrative unfolds almost entirely on an uncomfortable escape raft, on which the ten survivors, each representing a different social archetype, struggle to survive through the cruel weather, the shortage of food and water, and emotional angst. The problem with the film was not the war context per se but the presence of a Nazi captain, who confidently mans the drifting lifeboat on behalf of the hopeless and despairing passengers. Even though the cunning German perishes in the end, the CIE could not tolerate the film's "alleged depiction of Nazis as superior to

Figure 4.1. Still shot from Alfred Hitchcock's *Lifeboat* (1944). The film was banned because of the position of authority of the German U-boat captain (Walter Slezak, far left). Courtesy of the Wisconsin Center for Film and Theater Research, Madison, Wisconsin.

non-Nazis." This underrated Hitchcock classic never appeared on the screens of occupied Japan.[28]

The CCD found nothing but trouble in the Warner Bros. film *Counter-Attack* (1945). In this film about a Russian counteroffensive against the Nazi invasion on the Eastern front, a pair of Russian soldiers (Paul Muni and Marguerite Chapman) are trapped together with a handful of German military men beneath a half-destroyed building. Written by soon-to-be-blacklisted screenwriter John Howard Lawson, the story presented the Russians as courageous and relentless fighters against the sly Nazis, who attempt to seize the Russians' weapons and inflict serious injury on the heroine. The story ends with a train of Soviet tanks steadily advancing against German fire attacks, with the trapped Russians rescued shortly thereafter. The film bothered the CCD, which decided to suppress it in July 1946. The reason was not the sympathetic portrayal of the communists but the film's tendency to "glorif[y] war, individual heroism, self-sacrifice, and blind obedience."[29]

Representations of the Pacific War received even greater scrutiny than the battles that had raged in Europe. The timing appeared premature for release of feature films depicting military clashes in the Pacific. For this reason, certain war films that were chosen for Germany—such as *Across the Pacific* (1942), *So Proudly We Hail* (1943), and *Thirty Seconds over Tokyo* (1944)—were not shown in early postwar Japan.[30] Another film that did not make it to Japan was *Objective, Burma!* (1945), a story about an American-led parachute mission in Burma. Starring Errol Flynn as an army captain, the narrative highlighted the courage and determination of U.S. paratroopers who successfully destroy an enemy radio station and persevere in the jungles. To the occupiers, the biggest problem concerned the British. Before being considered for Japan, the film had already provoked a firestorm of protest in England, for it appeared to overlook British contributions to Allied campaigns in Southeast Asia.[31] In an August 6, 1946, memorandum sent to the State Department, the army placed this war movie on the list of recommended films for Japan, Germany, and Austria. The war picture, however, was scratched off the list. Two words were scribbled in the margins: "British objected."[32]

War films of this kind were problematic also because of their blatant racial caricatures and offensive attitudes toward the Japanese. Such characterizations surfaced in home-front films as well as combat pictures of the World War II era. Not surprisingly, the occupiers took pains to eliminate scenes that appeared to portray the Japanese in a negative light. The CIE, for example, requested the removal of phrases such as "Japs," "hara kiri," and "savages on the island" from *The Lady Is Willing* (1942), an otherwise innocuous comedy about a Broadway actress's romance with a pediatrician in New York City.[33] *A Medal for Benny* (1945) caused trouble for similar reasons. This home-front picture revolved around a romantic relationship in a Mexican-American community in a small California town. The heroine (Dorothy Lamour) loves a young serviceman who dies shortly after killing one hundred Japanese soldiers in the Philippines. The CIE's George Gercke reacted to this Paramount film because it referred to the soldier's actions in the Pacific "several times." He thus requested the deletion of "all references to the killing of the Japs." After viewing the edited film, the CCD intervened because it spotted a poster in one scene that read "Wipe the Japs off the Map." This scene was removed from the final product.[34]

The occupiers were particularly wary of dealing with the atomic bomb. This was evident in the skepticism expressed about Japanese films like *The Bells of Nagasaki*. Hollywood also faced considerable scrutiny. In *Tarzan and the Green Goddess* (1938), British and American expedition teams compete for a Mayan idol in the Guatemalan jungle. Even though the film had no direct connection with nuclear fission, the censors spotted an "unusual coinciden[ce]": the treasured object contained a secret formula for an explosive that could destroy the entire world. Both the CIE and the CCD suspended the film's release for a few months before finally agreeing to release it.[35] *Cinderella Jones* (1946), a Busby Berkeley musical, showcased a small-town woman's (Joan Leslie) attempt to land an intelligent marriage partner, whom she pursues by enrolling in an all-male technology institute. This light romantic comedy bothered the CIE because of a short scene in which the matrimonial candidate (a young professor at the institute) nearly touches an explosive chemical fluid. An older professor, beaker in hand, cautions that a single ounce of that liquid could "send the Rising Sun into the happy camping grounds." The CIE requested that Hollywood delete that line.[36]

Greater tension surrounded *The Beginning or the End* (1947). This mock documentary explored the creation of the atomic bomb during the Second World War. Much of the narrative follows the key leaders of the Manhattan Project, including Leslie R. Groves, Robert J. Oppenheimer, Vannevar Bush, and Enrico Fermi (whose roles were performed by professional actors), who labor day and night to produce the winning weapon before the Nazis. The film climaxes with two explosions. One is at the Trinity test in Alamogordo, New Mexico, which leads Harry S. Truman (who appears in a silhouette) to authorize the use of the bomb against Japan. The other is the unloading of Little Boy over Hiroshima, a city that burns to ashes under a giant mushroom cloud. The film defends Truman's decision as an attempt to "shorten the war by at least a year," but treats the policymakers and scientists as compassionate men who grapple with their conscience while supporting the president. Instead of making a one-dimensional propaganda piece, director Norman Taurog aimed to "make people think and talk ... [and] draw their own conclusions."[37]

Occupation authorities were ambivalent about this narrative. The documentary quality of the film actually impressed the CIE, which argued in February 1947 that *The Beginning or the End* would be "worth consideration" if it could educate "average people of the world with the atomic question."[38] The army disagreed, claiming that the film offered a "weak treatment of the subject." The CAD had no qualms about Taurog's interpretation of the Manhattan Project or Truman's decision making, but it objected to its storytelling through an "inappropriate interpolation of two romances."[39] In the film, the Manhattan Project is introduced through the presence of two fictitious characters. One of them is Matt Cochrane, a newly married scientist who dies shortly after an accidental exposure to radiation. The other is Col. Jeff Nixon, a military adviser who befriends Matt while overseeing the bomb making. After the *Enola Gay* returns from its Hiroshima mission, Jeff, who is engaged to the secretary of Leslie Groves, sadly informs Matt's now-pregnant wife of her husband's death. It was perhaps her tearful, melodramatic reaction that did not sit well with the army, which desired a more straightforward fact-based narrative.

In the end, this provocative MGM picture was left in limbo for three years, until SCAP's policy relaxed. The CIE finally approved the film for release in August 1950, shortly before Ōba Hideo's *The Bells of Nagasaki* made it to theater screens.[40]

Violence and Social Disorder

From the occupiers' vantage point, war was not the only theme that could undermine the "reorientation" of Japan. Depictions of social disorder, which arrived in a cargo of genres, were equally troubling. The cultural authorities believed that the display of disruptive behavior, underground activities, and corruption could set a bad example for the Japanese. On December 23, 1947, one SCAP official reported that between 30 to 40 percent of American films released in Japan depicted social disorder. He complained that these narratives undermined the overarching efforts to "eliminate the admiration for violence and disorder which has characterized so much of Japanese history and literature."[41] While supporting "social problem" films with constructive values—as with their interpretation of Akira Kurosawa's *Drunken Angel*—censors took issue with U.S. productions that appeared to inspire unrest and disharmonious acts.

On the most basic level, the occupiers deplored excessive displays of violence. Scenes of blood, murder, and torture cut across fixed genres. Censors tried their best to remove such representations. *The Wake of the Red Witch* (1948), for instance, introduced a gritty captain (John Wayne) manning a vessel peopled with rugged crew members who drink, brawl, and whip disloyal men. The CAD denounced this "second-rate" RKO production peppered with "hate, violence, and scenes of brutality."[42] The army also deplored *Arabian Nights* (1942), a Technicolor adaptation of the classic tales. The problem lay in two scenes. One was an early scene that displayed a half-naked man hanged in a public square with starving vultures looking down on him. The other scene showed a man tortured on a wooden wheel and stabbed to death. While ultimately approving this Middle Eastern fantasy, the army disputed such displays of physical cruelty and raw violence.[43]

Likewise, depictions of crime suffered the occupiers' opposition. In *Double Indemnity* (1944), an insurance agent in Los Angeles flirts with a femme fatale who conspires with him to murder her wealthy husband and claim the insurance money. The partners-in-crime kill the husband, but the blond seductress's desire to control the money results in their fatally shooting each other. Even though the woman's greed leads to the punishment of the criminals in the end, the State Department objected to this Billy Wilder classic for Japan, citing "policy reasons."[44] *Enter Arsène Lupin* (1944) was a tale about the popular French thief's stealing of jewelry and artwork, including Rembrandt's coveted oil paintings. Although Lupin's antics did not involve physical violence, the CCD deemed the film "questionable" for its dramatization of crime.[45] Before finally approving the film for distribution, the CCD specifically requested the elimination of the final scene, in which the captured criminal intimates his ability to escape from the police at will.[46]

The occupiers reacted to other apparent enticements to engage in disorderly behavior. One such theme, bootlegging, bothered censors because it seemed to mirror the seamy atmosphere of the Japanese black market.[47] In *Old Acquaintance* (1943), a Bette Davis melodrama partly set during Prohibition, an American moonshiner sells gin to one of the film's main characters in a hotel lobby. The CIE requested that Hollywood delete this scene, which ended with the following remark: "You don't have to worry about that stuff; I made it myself."[48] Another film that troubled the occupiers was *The Great Gatsby* (1948). Based on F. Scott Fitzgerald's classic novel, it offered a montage of wild party scenes at the protagonist Jay Gatsby's mansion on Long Island. The CIE claimed that those scenes lacked "constructive purpose.... The shots that exhibited speak-easies, rum runners, joy-riding, and bootlegging, were unnecessary."[49]

The occupation deplored gambling scenes for similar reasons. An example was *The Lady Eve* (1941), an Ernst Lubitsch comedy partly staged on a luxurious cruise liner. The CIE criticized the antics of "shipboard gamblers," who casually draw out their pocketbooks over poker and other card games.[50] *My Brother Talks to Horses* (1947) was a turn-of-the-twentieth-century drama about an eccentric boy who possesses a unique ability to communicate with horses. This unusual talent lands the boy in the hands of desperate bettors, who demand accurate predictions to win at the racetrack. The CIE criticized the film for presenting these "horse-racing and gambling aspects."[51]

The occupiers also targeted swashbucklers. For this popular genre, violence was not the sole reason that caused alarm. Fencing scenes and saber sequences, whether in European or Caribbean settings, appeared to resemble the bloody swordfights of Japan's period-film genre (*jidaigeki*). This, the occupiers feared, could rekindle the Japanese "feudalistic" mind-set.[52] The army once reminded

Figure 4.2. *The Mark of Zorro* (1940). SCAP criticized swashbucklers like this Rouben Mamoulian production because the sword-fighting scenes might rekindle the Japanese "feudalistic" mind-set. Courtesy of the Wisconsin Center for Film and Theater Research, Madison, Wisconsin.

SCAP: "It is suggested that your Headquarters, if screening... [American swash-bucklers], take note of instances of excessive swordplay, inasmuch as the special conditions in Japan relating to this type of action require special care."[53]

The opening scene in *The Mark of Zorro* (1940) was a case in point. Set at a military academy in Madrid, the scene introduced a group of Spanish men rhythmically clattering their swords and, from horseback, flinging their blades at human-shaped targets. The CIE required Hollywood to "alter" this portion of the narrative that treated swordplay as a "fine and fashionable art of killing" (as boasted in the opening caption).[54]

A similar scene appeared in *Adventures of Don Juan* (1949). In this Technicolor swashbuckler set in seventeenth-century Europe, the playboy protagonist, portrayed by Errol Flynn, coaches Spanish swordsmen at the royal academy. In addition to displaying young trainees rattling their sabers in front of the royal family, the film showed swordfights in several other parts, including a dramatic showdown between Don Juan and the evil duke who has sought to seize dictatorial power in Spain. The CIE acknowledged that the film dealt with a "semi-classical" character immortalized by Byron and Molière. But the amount of violence and swordplay, which occupied "approximately 1 1/2 reels of the total film," was simply unacceptable. The CIE stipulated that the distributor reduce such footage to an unspecified "logical amount."[55]

The occupiers approached the Hollywood western with equal caution. This genre featured brawls, fistfights, gunplay, and violent showdowns, as in John Wayne's *The Spoilers* (1942), which contained "too much gunplay and unnecessary killing throughout the picture," according to the CCD.[56] Westerns also hammered on the theme of revenge—which SCAP viewed as a feudalistic trait. The CIE thus was reluctant to clear the Warner Bros. film *Dallas* (1950), which highlighted a sheriff's tenacious pursuit of a band of outlaws. The CIE warned that the presentation of vengeance and retaliation, which propelled the sheriff into action, would make it problematic for Japan.[57] The CCD also argued against *Trapped,* a 1937 B western about a cowboy's attempt to avenge the death of his brother. The film featured raucous gunfights, a "lack of respect for human life," and "revenge as an underlying motive."[58]

The occupiers found the western genre threatening also because it undermined the power of constitutional law. *The Spoilers* exemplified this problem quite clearly as it displayed a corrupt judge. The censor also pointed out that John Wayne's attempts to take possession of a gold mine with his posse "glorif[ied] the men who take the law into their own hands."[59] Trivializers of law and justice appeared in other westerns, such as *The Bad Bascomb* (1946), a film about the adventures of a notorious bank robber and his gang. In this film, the protagonist appears to be an amiable character who develops a fatherly bond with an orphan girl. What disturbed CIE was not just the film's display of "the usual fanfare of killings" but its portrayal of the outlaws as humane characters with whom the Japanese audiences might easily sympathize.[60]

Race and Colonialism

In principle, the representation of race relations had to honor the spirit of egalitarianism and democracy. For this reason, interactions among white and nonwhite peoples faced a degree of scrutiny; films that highlighted discriminatory attitudes came in for the occupiers' criticism. For example, the CIE denounced *Romance of Rosy Ridge* (1947), a film about the American South in the post–Civil War years, because of its presentation of the Ku Klux Klan.[61] *The Spoilers* included a Chinese man who was "made fun of." Despite his marginal role in the narrative, the CCD could not accept the imprisonment of this Asian character, particularly when "guards make uncomplimentary remarks about him."[62]

Questionable representations of race often surfaced in colonial contexts. One example was William Wyler's *The Letter* (1940). Set in British Malaya, the narrative follows the trial of Leslie Crosbie (Bette Davis), the wife of a rubber plantation owner who murders a male friend, Jeff Hammond. After her acquittal, Leslie admits to having a long-term affair with the man she killed. Toward the end of the film, she confesses that her jealousy peaked when she discovered that Jeff had married a "native woman" with "a cobra's eyes" (Leslie's words). In the end, Jeff's widow (Gale Sundergaard), wearing a fully embroidered one-piece dress and marble-sized jewelry, fulfills her revenge by stabbing Leslie to death. The CIE gave preliminary clearance to this film, but the army found *The Letter* "entirely unsuitable."[63] The main problem was the "inter-racial theme" that bred hatred, jealousy, and violence between the colonizer and the colonized.[64]

Another prewar film, *Storm over Bengal* (1938), proved controversial. The film featured an Indian insurrection against British rule. The captain of the British Army barely escapes several plots to capture him, before the Indian rebels are eventually contained by the British troops. SCAP was unhappy with the dramatized conflict between "inferior" peoples and Westerners. Worrying about the representation of the Allied forces, the CIE noted that the film appeared to "buttress the past Japanese propaganda line that the British and Americans are 'imperialistic' and racially intolerant."[65]

The Tarzan episodes commonly alarmed the occupiers. The CIE, for instance, voiced dismay over *Tarzan and the Green Goddess* (1938). The chest-thumping hero, who in this episode roams the Guatemalan jungle, interacts with two European expedition teams vying for a legendary Mayan idol. One censor complained that the film, which painted the natives as powerless, faceless, and submissive, showed "imperialism at its worst."[66] The occupiers found *Tarzan and the Amazons* (1945) undesirable for similar reasons. Because of a plot that dramatized European archaeologists' greedy attempts to steal the treasures of the Amazon women, the CIE criticized the tensions formed between "white" and "non-white."[67] After encountering similar themes in the Tarzan episodes time and again, a CAD official complained: "Our office fails to find sufficient value for a program of films selected for maximum educational content in the best ways of life in America in the Tarzan series."[68]

In contrast, the occupiers endorsed the interaction of Euro-American civilization with non-Western societies if the relationship was peaceful and harmonious.

A favored example was *Anna and the King of Siam* (1946). Set in the early 1860s, the John Cromwell film begins with a widowed British woman's arrival in Siam, where she undertakes a job as language tutor for the royal family. The film underscores her growing friendship with the Siamese king, who expresses a desire for "scientific" thinking, "modernization," "progress," and English-language education. To the king and his people, Anna preaches the ideals of law and democracy—praising Lincoln as a leader "chosen by the people." She also promotes Euro-American social customs (such as bowing and dinner table etiquette), knives and forks (as an alternative to chopsticks), ladies' ballroom dresses, and certain English vocabulary (such as "jurisdiction"). The CCD believed that the film would make a valuable contribution because it showed an "introduction of progressive Western thought into a Far Eastern nation."[69]

The Man-Eater of Kumaon (1948) passed the test also because of its allegedly sympathetic portrayal of East-West relations. The story was framed around an American hunter's duel with a giant tiger in the Kumaon jungle of northern India. The blood-thirsty beast takes down a number of local villagers, and at a pivotal moment, it harms a pregnant woman. Disturbed at the lack of constructive messages, the army expressed discontent with this suspenseful tale.[70] SCAP, however, approved it not just because it was "simple, relatively pleasant and harmless," but also because it portrayed the American hunter's association with Indian villagers as a harmonious one. The CIE advocated the film's release because it painted a "sympathetic relationship...between westerners and Asiatics."[71]

Americanism

Hollywood films that idealized American life earned the occupiers' greatest praise. These "model pictures" largely involved two types. One was the celebration of the individual. Occupation censors commonly praised biographical pictures and fictional accounts that personalized success through hard work, perseverance, and compassion toward others. These Horatio Algeresque stories portrayed the greatest achievements of "democratic" life. Not all admired figures, such as Anna Leonowens in *Anna and the King of Siam,* were American, but many of these celluloid narratives were based on the actual life stories of U.S. heroes. Overall, the occupiers believed that these stories of notable individuals could present the United States as a beneficent nation, genuinely committed to helping others around the world.[72]

One such example was *Abe Lincoln in Illinois* (1940). This acclaimed biopic dramatized the life and career of the iconic leader before his presidency. In the narrative, a young passionate Lincoln departs from his father's log cabin and settles in a nearby town to start a small business. His charisma and disposition earn him the respect of a Whig Party politician, who recruits him to run for an office in the state legislature. Despite fears of splitting the country apart, Lincoln later decides to run for the U.S. Senate on a platform supporting emancipation. The film ends shortly after he winds the famous debates with Stephen Douglas. Although historians have sometimes disputed Lincoln's achievements and contributions, occupation censors could find nothing but praise for the film's treatment of the famous American. The CCD trumpeted the film as a "suitable" product that "would have a beneficial effect in helping to 'democratize' the Japanese people."[73]

Pride of the Yankees (1942) was another highly favored product. The narrative focused on the career of Lou Gehrig, the renowned first baseman of the New York Yankees. The pure and kind-hearted Gehrig, as the film portrays him, grows up poor in a lower Manhattan neighborhood. Following a brief period of studies at Columbia University, Gehrig is recruited to play ball for the Yankees. As the team's first baseman playing alongside Babe Ruth, Gehrig becomes a World Series champion and a record-holder in consecutive games played. He has a happy marriage. The story turns grim when the hero is diagnosed with a life-threatening neurological disease, which forces his retirement. Like Lou Gehrig in real life, the on-screen incarnation appears in front of a packed stadium for a special ceremony honoring his achievements. The Hall of Famer delivers a "moving" speech, thanking his teammates and family for their faith in his abilities.

The occupiers regarded *Pride of the Yankees* as an ideal film for the Japanese public. A story that touted diligence, modesty, and enthusiasm—all while the hero maintains a happy marriage—seemed to make for a great life story that a democratic society could offer. The theme of baseball was also a positive asset. A sport that blends teamwork and individual performance, baseball—a popular sport in Japan during the 1920s and 1930s—was something that the CIE praised for carrying the "spirit of democracy."[74] Even though the film was produced by Samuel Goldwyn Productions, an independent studio that did not belong to the MPEA, the occupiers sought to include the film in its lineup. The CIE cabled the army, noting that *The Pride of the Yankees* was "wanted especially."[75] The CAD approached Goldwyn to request the biopic for Japan, and the producer complied. The MPEA made special arrangements for Goldwyn so that he could earn revenue from Japan, despite his company's status as a non-MPEA studio.[76]

Films that championed successful American women, real or fictional, received the utmost praise. This was perhaps not surprising since SCAP strove to promote women's political and social rights. *The Farmer's Daughter* (1947) is a story about a young European immigrant woman in Minnesota who aspires to become a nurse and ends up in national politics. Overcoming financial hardships and media defamation, she runs an election campaign against a dubious candidate and eventually wins a seat in Congress. This heartening story won the CCD's accolades for contributing "to the Occupation objectives of democratization."[77] *Woman of the Year* (1942) portrayed the life of the fictional Tess Harding (Katherine Hepburn), a journalist who juggles her professional career with a rocky love life with sports columnist Sam Craig (Spencer Tracy). Following their marriage, Tess remains professionally and politically active and wins an honor as "America's Outstanding Woman of the Year." Although at times frustrated with her absence from home, Sam ultimately embraces her as Tess Harding Craig rather than Mrs. Sam Craig. The CIE praised this Hepburn-Tracy film as an elite picture that performed an "information job" to educate Japanese on women's life in America.[78]

Films about community life, the other type of "model picture," complimented the story of the individual. The films that fell under this category usually depicted modest families living in small-town America. Occupation officials supported these community-oriented narratives for their presentation of respectable social mores and family values or, as the army once put it, "a positive healthful approach towards life in America."[79] These movies underscored cooperation, compassion, and peaceful resolution of conflicts. They presented life in America as an ideal type for the Japanese to look on and emulate.

One of the most celebrated pictures within this body of movies was *State Fair* (1946). The main characters of this colorful musical belonged to the Frake family, a farmer's household that decides to visit the State Fair in Iowa. At the annual festival, the daughter Margy (Jeanne Crain) meets a newspaper reporter—the man of her dreams—and the two commit to marriage. Her brother Wayne (Dick Haymes) fails to get engaged to a singer with whom he falls in love at the fair, but he, too, finds happiness once he rekindles a romantic bond with a childhood sweetheart. The father returns home a happy man after his prize boar wins a competition. The mother is equally content after her entry wins in the "pickle and mincemeat" contest. These were rather mundane achievements to dramatize in a Hollywood drama. But this celebration of a simple life delighted the occupiers. The CIE was eager to release the film in Japan, because it presented the "true" lifestyle of Americans.[80]

Figure 4.3. *State Fair* (1945), a Rodgers and Hammerstein musical, was personally endorsed by General MacArthur. This Midwestern story presented the best aspects of the "American way of life." The image comes from a "scenario book" that introduced the film's full dialogue with a Japanese translation. *Motion Picture Library* 18 (September 1948), front cover. Author's collection.

MacArthur himself, known as a fan of gritty Hollywood westerns, encouraged the Japanese public to watch this family movie to grasp a "wholesome picture of American home life."[81] Backed by the Supreme Commander's personal endorsement, Hollywood rushed to release the film on September 21, 1948, even though it was not yet able to punch Japanese subtitles on Technicolor prints.

Our Town was another model film. Based on a Thornton Wilder play, the 1940 United Artists production offers a nostalgic portrait of "ordinary life" in small-town America. Anchored in the relationship of two neighboring families, the film depicts the joys of life and the sorrows of death as the years pass by. The children of the two families happily marry and the wife delivers a child at the end of the story. Even though the delivery nearly kills her, she is encouraged to live by the spirit of her dead mother-in-law. The CIE found this an "exceptionally useful picture" that captured an idyllic life in small-town America. When the arrival of the film prints was delayed, a frustrated CIE official urged the army to "convince the producer that it is his patriotic duty to allow the use of his film in furthering the occupation objectives in Japan."[82]

The occupiers' attitude toward these idealized portraits of American life contrasted starkly with films that depicted or alluded to communism. In *No Leave, No Love* (1946), a romantic comedy that highlights a World War II veteran's marriage to a radio commentator, the CIE found a troublesome dialogue that referred to a Texan as originating from Russia. That line was eliminated before the film's release.[83] In *Miss Tatlock's Millions* (1948), a comedy in which an aging caretaker scrambles to remain employed at a large California estate, the CIE found some unsuitable references about a "fighting liberal" character accused of being a Communist.[84] Censors suggested deletion of a line in *The Affairs of Susan* (1945), a story about a USO actress (Joan Fontaine) and her affairs with three men (told in the form of a flashback), because it also made references to a Communist.[85]

Another problematic film was *The Grapes of Wrath* (1940). This adaptation of John Steinbeck's popular novel conveyed the bleakness of the Depression through the experiences of the Joad family, who migrate from the drought-ridden Oklahoma farmlands to California in search of a better life. Following a long and arduous truck ride on Route 66, the Joads reach the West Coast but struggle to secure steady work in the face of business exploitation, labor competition, and police violence. The army fought the overseas release of this Oscar-winning classic, claiming that this story of poverty and social inequality during the Dust Bowl era "no longer [held] true" by the end of World War II.[86] The army was overall unhappy with the lack of "progress" and "reform" over the course of the narrative, and specifically reacted to a scene in which state police beat up the migrant workers. This action, the CAD noted, replicated the "Nazi ideal."[87] The CIE was distressed as well. It maintained that the film's portrayal of social unrest would lend itself to "exploitation by Japanese Communists."[88] Hardly seen as a "model" portrait of the United States, the film was unable to enter postwar Japan until 1960.

Explicitly anti-Communist films, such as *The Iron Curtain* (1948), enjoyed the occupiers' accolades. Based on an actual spy case in Canada, this Twentieth Century–Fox film featured a Soviet agent in North America who supplies secret information to the Canadian Embassy in Ottawa during and after the Second World War. Despite the Soviets' relentless efforts to prevent his defection, the protagonist decides to cooperate with the Western Allies in order to have his wife and newborn child live in a free "democratic" country. The subject matter piqued considerable interest among occupation officials. When the film was first released in 1948, the CIE rejected it, presumably because of the its ideologically charged content. But a year later, it decided to approve its release.[89] The CCD took a close look at the film as well. It carefully compared the film's English dialogue to the Japanese subtitles and, in a rather unusual move concerning Hollywood productions, invited high-ranking intelligence officials for a special screening to evaluate the film's value in defeated Japan.[90] Despite vitriolic criticism by the Soviets, the film was passed and received heavy promotional treatment.[91] Three days before its commercial release, the CIE even hosted a special screening for a group of Japanese filmmakers to teach them how to "debunk communism."[92]

The MPEA versus the Occupation

The occupiers' political control over American movies evoked conflicting opinions in Hollywood. On one level, industry representatives were pleased with the U.S. government and military's assistance in setting up the Central Motion Picture Exchange. Yet their true desire was to resume individual studio business as soon as possible. Since the planning stages of the postwar campaign, Hollywood representatives had repeatedly lobbied for greater independence and autonomy, claiming that a "joint operation of any type [is] not deemed in [the] best interests of occupying authorities or industry itself."[93] But U.S. authorities flatly rejected the idea, noting that it was "impossible to consider admitting...nine separate companies to contribute to the objectives of the occupation."[94] As their movies began to fill the Japanese screens, U.S. companies increased their complaints about lack of fairness and reciprocity in the negotiation process. Conflicting desires exacerbated the tension between Eric Johnston's MPEA and U.S. government and military authorities, even threatening the collapse of their corporatist alliance.

The MPEA's qualms about the occupiers concerned three matters. First, the MPEA was unhappy with the process of film censorship. A lot of this was due to the involvement of multiple agencies, which rendered the procedure cumbersome and time consuming. Controversial and potentially harmful pictures could remain in the censors' hands for months. The MPEA charged that the procedure was simply "too slow" and that delayed clearances created a danger in "satisfy[ing] distribution schedules."[95] Hollywood was serious in making such complaints, because the paucity of fresh releases could strain the industry's relationship with exhibitors who had long-term contracts for an uninterrupted stream of American products. In spring 1947, the American film program fell into trouble because it was "unable to release a single new production" due to the absence of cleared films. This forced Hollywood to screen reruns of old titles as a stopgap measure. The MPEA thus called for greater efficiency to expedite the clearance of its films.[96]

Second, MPEA officials disputed the occupation's censorship criteria. Expecting preferential treatment at first, Johnston's office quickly came to realize that the occupiers were determined to cull as many "reorientation" productions as possible without much regard to profitability. Shortly after the new filtering system went in effect, the MPEA charged that "too many dramatic subjects and too few light subjects have been selected."[97] Hollywood representatives perceived the censors' selectivity as a violation of the "equal participation" approach. At Johnston's headquarters in New York, studio heads grumbled about the uneven representation of stars and company products—as SCAP even went out of its way to enlist films by Samuel Goldwyn, a non-MPEA company.[98] The trade association groused at the lack of "fair representation."[99]

Hollywood's trouble with the occupiers' standards also stemmed from inconsistency. The MPEA occasionally spotted discrepant judgments made by a single office. On one occasion, MPEA vice president Irving Maas questioned the CIE's decision to grant "reorientation" status to The Jolson Story (1946), a biopic of the famous minstrel singer, while not rewarding the same status to Jolson Sings Again (1949), its sequel.[100] A greater problem was the existence of separate standards per office. MPEA personnel were particularly discontent with the Civil Affairs Division of the U.S. Army, which made it clear that "industry preferences should have secondary consideration to objectives of the occupation."[101] During the early months of 1948, the CAD began to withhold clearance of entertainment-heavy narratives that SCAP had actually approved.

Even SCAP complained that the army appeared to "take an attitude that only films of reorientation content should be shown."[102] This uncompromising attitude outraged MPEA leaders. In a letter to Maas, a local Hollywood representative in Tokyo furiously charged that the CAD was "dumber than we could ever imagine."[103]

The third and final problem concerned finances. Although initially agreeing to operate according to the terms set by the occupation establishment, the MPEA quickly grew frustrated with the occupiers' decision to block the transfer of yen earnings from Japan (see table 4.3). The desire to convert the holdings grew as the industry's commercial returns began to accumulate. But more important, Hollywood noticed that its overall holdings were shrinking due to the rampant inflation in the Japanese market. As the value of the yen dropped precipitously from 15 to 360 yen to the dollar during the first three years, the MPEA ratcheted up its demand to be able to extract its companies' earnings. Maas found it only fair to make such a demand, especially since "everyone familiar with our operation in Japan... [knows] that MPEA has rendered an indispensable service in reeducating and reorienting the Japanese."[104]

The time was ripe for a showdown. The moment arrived in spring 1949, when the MPEA's license in Japan was about to expire. On March 28, 1949, Paramount executive (and MPEA board member) George Weltner landed in Tokyo and held meetings with a handful of occupation officials.[105] Back in the United States, Johnston's office pressed its case against the CAD in New York. The negotiations disappointed Hollywood. In a letter to the MPEA, Carter B. Magruder of the CAD claimed that the "continued shortage of dollar

Table 4.3. The CMPE's Yen Earnings and Converted Earnings

	Yen receipts in yen (after deduction of operating expenses)	Yen receipts in dollars (then current rate)	Yen used for conversion	Converted yen in dollars	Exchange rate (yen per dollar)
1946	99,750,151.82	6,650,010.12	0	0	15
1947	398,666,475.09	9,775,135.91	0	0	15–50
1948	757,407,224.10	8,711,269.07	0	0	50–270
1949	1,052,323,959.01	2,802,734.37	151,155,062.10	454,400.67	270–360
1950	1,862,376,583.57	2,731,972.64	878,866,433.40	2,438,887.94	360
Total	4,170,524,393.59	30,671,122.11	1,030,021,495.50	2,893,288.61	

Source: Charles Mayer to G. P. Waller, May 23, 1951, Box 7494, Folder 22, Records of the Supreme Commander for the Allied Powers, Record Group 331, National Archives II, College Park, Maryland.

exchange...makes it impossible to permit the conversion of yen into dollars from export funds."[106] When the MPEA compromised by requesting partial remittance, the Department of Army, according to the minutes of an MPEA board meeting, "flatly rejected it."[107] This pushed the MPEA to the breaking point. After repeatedly warning army officials that "further film deliveries to Japan would be discontinued," the MPEA decided to halt the shipment of new prints on June 30, the end of the U.S. fiscal year.[108]

Hollywood's decision caused an uproar in Japan. Newspapers and magazines covered the news extensively, pleading for the continuation of the American screen program; an editorial in *Tokyo shinbun,* for example, demanded that the occupiers bring "more American movies" to Japan so as not to "inflict great disappointment" on the Japanese public.[109] Exhibitors were equally vocal. In a petition submitted to SCAP, a group of American-movie exhibitors in Chiba Prefecture urged MacArthur to keep Hollywood on the screens to "propagate [the] American way of democracy."[110] The suspension also moved fan organizations such as the American Movie Culture Association, a nationwide institution run by the culture elites (see chapter 7). In a letter submitted on June 1, Hori Makoto, chairman of the organization, urged MacArthur to "reopen the way for the continuous importation of American pictures," as they have given the Japanese "hope to live and [a] new view of life, in other words, [the] way of American democracy."[111]

Hollywood's pressure prompted the occupiers to consider a compromise. During the following two months, Johnston visited Washington to participate in a series of discussions with army officials, congressmen, and senators.[112] In early August, the Department of Army agreed to convert up to $1.6 million during the fiscal year.[113] SCAP approved the deal. In a move to transfer the governing authority to the Japanese, it arranged for the MPEA to sign a new contract with the Japanese Ministry of International Trade and Industry.[114] The *Motion Picture Herald* called the resolution a "smashing victory" for the MPEA.[115] This decision produced "great satisfaction" among MPEA studios, which agreed to extend their collective operation in Japan for another year.[116] Although the problem of frozen funds would outlast the occupation, Hollywood authorities, for the time being, were content with the partial transfer of their earnings to their U.S. bank accounts.

Following the new arrangement with the army, U.S. studios found a censorship apparatus in the process of relaxing its practices. In November 1949, the CCD ceased its operation (as planned). Following its run-in with Hollywood, the army dropped out of sight. During the final two years of the occupation, the CIE virtually stood as the sole censor of incoming U.S. pictures. The criterion for censorship no longer centered on "reorientation" quality; during the final two years, the occupiers sought what they broadly called "superior" or "meritorious" productions that touted high aesthetic and production values.[117] One film that met this qualification was Billy Wilder's *Sunset Boulevard* (1950). This dark story about an obscure writer's fatal affair with an aging film star might have been axed by U.S. censors had it been examined a few years earlier. Yet when the Oscar-winning film reached SCAP in October 1951, the CIE issued praise "not because of what it says but because of its artistry and maturity."[118] The final two years of the occupation saw a stark increase in Hollywood's releases in Japan. By this time, many films that formerly would have been banned made it to the screens.

Film censorship was a means to an end. It belonged to a larger political mission designed to "re-educate" and "reorient" the Japanese. The newly augmented transpacific apparatus—consisting of the State Department, U.S. Army, and SCAP—approached Hollywood with motivation and rigor, and shaped the lineup of U.S. releases. The content of the films was also affected. Occupation censors pressed for cuts and edits, and often got their way. The heads of U.S. studios were not pleased. Unhappy and outraged with the occupiers' policies, the MPEA criticized the censorship establishment, even threatening a complete withdrawal from the Japanese market. Occupation corporatism was at times an uneasy experience. It was a tense negotiation of power among American institutions.

The fragile bond between occupation officials and the MPEA placed the U.S. film industry's local employees in a difficult bind. Practicing business on the ground demanded an intense effort to maximize profits in the Japanese market, but it also required the assistance of U.S. authorities. Working in occupied Japan called for a balancing act. This difficult task fell on the Central Motion Picture Exchange—the MPEA's subsidiary office in Tokyo. This East Asian outpost of U.S. studios would have to figure out ways of boosting the industry's market share while maintaining favorable working relations with the U.S. occupation.

Chapter 5

Fountains of Culture

Hollywood's Marketing in Defeated Japan

On the back cover of its February 1947 issue, *Eiga no tomo* (Friends of the movies), a popular monthly magazine that showcased American movies, ran a full-page advertisement that portrayed Hollywood in a distinct fashion. The "protagonist" of the colorful text was not a specific film or a top star but a page-high Oscar statue glittering with an aura of prestige. Next to it was the circular logo of the Motion Picture Export Association, the global distribution office for major U.S. studios. Above the MPEA seal, a nine-line blurb boasted that "the best guide to understanding American culture is American cinema!" Hollywood films, the ad continued, offered "the world's best sellers" and "well-acclaimed stage plays," as well as "music, sports, dance, science, [and] American history." The prose concluded with the following line: "American movies are ... fountains of culture [*bunka no izumi*] and knowledge, as we desire it!"[1]

This Oscar ad was one of the thousands of publicity texts that circulated across defeated Japan. Once the occupation opened the floodgates of U.S. cinema, fans around the nation were swamped with glitzy Hollywood publicity. Much of the hype originated from the Central Motion Picture Exchange, the U.S. film industry's distribution outpost in Japan. After occupation censors evaluated the films, the CMPE determined the selling points, marketing strategies, and publicity methods to generate attraction. Over a six-year period, the distributor sent over six hundred feature films across Japan. Many of them became instant classics that would entertain and inspire fans for generations.

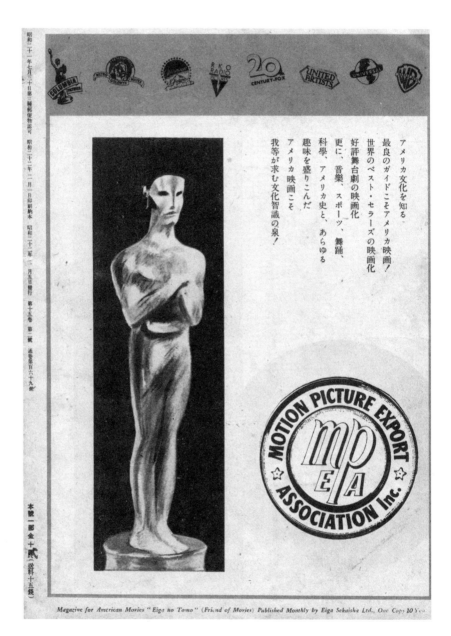

Figure 5.1. The Oscar advertisement in *Eiga no tomo*, February 1947, back cover. Author's collection.

Hollywood's marketing campaign entailed an aggressive effort to hype action, spectacle, and glamour. In so doing, the CMPE used the U.S. movie industry's standard methods of star and genre marketing. But the distributor also did something unique: it actively promoted Hollywood as *bunka* ("culture"). Since the interwar period, the term had held a dual meaning. First, it enjoyed wide usage as a signifier of intellectual and artistic activity. As an equivalent of the German word *Kultur,* it strongly connoted an aura of "high culture" stemming from Europe. Second, it indicated the "way of life" of nations and communities. Borrowing from the American (anthropological) definition of the term *culture,* the term *bunka* signified what one U.S. cultural historian described as "the structures of meaning associated with every part and every product of human life."[2]

The CMPE made active use of the term *bunka*. Not unlike the Japanese government and film industry during the war, the CMPE enlisted the term to showcase a "national" identity. By drawing together the variety of films made by member studios, the distributor celebrated Hollywood as a kaleidoscopic manifestation of an "American" way of life. The CMPE also used the term to associate Hollywood with cultural superiority. By presenting its films as *bunka,* the U.S. distributor dignified its commercial products as well as the values represented in them. These filmic products by and large privileged the power of men over women, Anglo-Saxons over other European ethnicities, whites over peoples of color, and "civilization" over "savagery." In catapulting its collective imagination onto the Japanese, the CMPE reified and amplified dominant social norms of American public life.[3]

Hollywood's *"bunka* strategy" partially stemmed from political considerations. In promoting cinema as a "fountain of culture," the CMPE sought to showcase the political utility of the films to the Supreme Commander for the Allied Powers. The CMPE employed this marketing strategy to justify the release of its narrative products and to reassure skeptical U.S. officials. The goal was to maintain corporatist relations with SCAP by demonstrating Hollywood's effectiveness as a "chosen instrument."

Yet the presentation of Hollywood as *bunka* was also an economic maneuver. It was a means of maximizing patronage by gearing its appeal to the outlying consumer. In the months following a crushing loss in war, the Japanese developed a new fascination with American ideas and culture. Tens of thousands of people sought to learn the values and lifestyles of a "superior" nation that defeated their own.[4] The CMPE catered to this budding zeal by presenting Hollywood products as an expansive tapestry of American life. In doing so, the CMPE also reinforced the effort to distinguish the Hollywood brand from rival commodities in the marketplace—particularly Japanese cinema, which Hollywood representatives repeatedly denounced as "vulgar" (*geretsu*) and "lowbrow" (*teizoku*).[5] Selling *bunka,* then, was a strategy with layered implications. It was an attempt to advance Hollywood's political and economic interests by elevating the cultural status of American movies.

Operation Hollywood

The Central Motion Picture Exchange was a changing institution. The distribution outpost of the Motion Picture Export Association was founded as an institutional arm of SCAP's Civil Information and Education Section. During its first three and a half months, when it was headed by Michael M. Bergher, the office operated under the close oversight of MacArthur's headquarters. But the U.S. film program was never designed to permanently remain under such conditions. On March 6, 1947, the CMPE submitted a letter requesting permission to operate independently of SCAP.[6] MacArthur granted the wish shortly thereafter. On May 26, occupation authorities, in an unusual move, issued the CMPE a commercial license to "import and distribute American motion pictures throughout Japan." While still constrained by SCAP's commercial regulations, the permit enabled the film distribution office to operate as full-fledged business institution in a controlled marketplace.[7]

The anchor of the business institution was Charles Mayer. A Far Eastern manager for Twentieth Century–Fox prior to the war, Mayer served the U.S. Army's Far Eastern Command before landing in occupied Japan under Hollywood's payroll.[8] On June 16, 1946, Mayer took over the operation from Bergher and assumed the title of managing director. He quickly secured residence at the Shinbashi Dai-ichi Hotel—one of the few high-rises near occupation headquarters—and commuted to work in a chauffeured Cadillac. Unlike Bergher, who was fluent in Japanese and socialized with his Japanese colleagues on a daily basis, Mayer rarely interacted with the rank and file and fired employees at will.[9] While respected by his superiors in New York, Mayer earned a reputation among the Japanese as a pontificating boss. Local employees grudgingly nicknamed him "Emperor Mayer" or the "MacArthur of CMPE."[10]

Mayer approached his job with two goals in mind. First, to assist the occupation forces in Japan. In an outline of company policy, the managing director vowed to be "helpful to the Occupation Forces in their endeavor to bring to the Japanese people a means of seeing democracy at work."[11] Mayer's desire to collaborate with SCAP was evident in the efforts to assist the CIE's visual

Figure 5.2. Portrait of Charles Mayer, managing director of the Central Motion Picture Exchange. Courtesy of Hidano Atsushi.

education program. The CMPE not only continued to preface commercial screenings with United Newsreel narratives, but it also integrated the CIE's own newsreels into its commercial screenings.[12] This service, with "no compensation," exposed the CIE films to an "aggregate attendance of well over

100,000,000 Japanese," noted Mayer in 1951.[13] The CMPE also reconciled the differences between the MPEA and occupation authorities. In the fall of 1948, amid the tense negotiations between MPEA and the Civil Affairs Division of the Department of Army, Mayer attended a board meeting at the MPEA headquarters in New York and called for a continuation of business in Japan. In a room full of skeptical studio executives, Mayer advocated the idea of "establishing good will," particularly as "occupation forces [on the ground] were cognizant of the value of American pictures in Japan."[14]

Second, while assisting the occupation government, Mayer extended Hollywood's commercial practices. "The primary function of the screen is to amuse and entertain," he once proclaimed.[15] In developing his business across the four main islands, Mayer expanded Bergher's apparatus into a bureaucratically managed institution that resembled the studio offices in the United States. Mayer did this by transferring CMPE's one-room office to the Kanesaka building, a six-story high-rise in the busy Shinbashi district of Tokyo, and by founding regional branches in Nagoya, Osaka, Fukuoka, and Sapporo.[16] The company parceled its labor into four departments: publicity, production (seisaku, which involved the subtitling of imported prints), accounting, and general affairs. Each of these departments was run by a manager (usually a foreign national) who assigned a specialized task—such as poster making, bookkeeping, or outdoor sales marketing—to each lower-level employee. The staff size quickly grew into the hundreds.[17]

Mayer's business offensive began with data management. His office adopted a zonal system to oversee the business by region and kept detailed records of population size as well as the number of theaters and their feature programs in each city. It also gathered data on movie attendance and fiscal earnings per theater.[18] Sales and publicity agents visited exhibitors around the country to collect fan surveys and exit polls.[19] Commercial data, film reviews, and other relevant information were regularly sent back to the MPEA headquarters in New York. In an effort to maximize productivity, Mayer periodically circulated performance data to regional branches and inspired competition among the local offices. Each year the company recognized one regional branch (usually Nagoya) for its strong efforts and results.[20]

The decisions regarding film distribution relied on accumulated data. Since the number of prints was limited (four to ten prints per film during the first year and a half), the CMPE was unable to blanket the country with nationwide releases "in theaters everywhere."[21] Mayer, thus, strategically positioned the films based on audience taste and profitability. In general, films with "high" cultural content—such as literary adaptations, biographical films, and Broadway plays—opened in first-run theaters in big cities where the CMPE could count on the turnout of educated and well-to-do audiences. Films with less high-cultural value—such as Tarzan episodes, westerns, and Abbott and Costello comedies—typically appeared in second-run venues in urban working-class neighborhoods (such as Asakusa) and regional cities. Films deemed to possess exceptional prestige and quality—such as *The Best Years of Our Lives* (1946), *Pride of the Yankees* (1942), and *Rhapsody in Blue* (1947)—debuted in coveted road shows, generally one per big city.

The promotion of these films abided by standardized routines. For each feature release, the CMPE prepared a package of materials dubbed "basic publicity" and circulated it across cities.[22] This included visual accessories, such as posters and billboards crafted by Japanese artists and designers, block advertisements for newspapers and magazines, and recorded announcements for the airwaves.[23] The distributor also distributed "press sheets" to exhibitors. Modeled after the industry's press books circulated in the United States, these promotional broadsides offered synopses, (laudatory) reviews, advertising strategies, logos, illustrations, and sample announcements for use in theaters.[24]

The CMPE also took advantage of existing publicity channels. For example, it supplied stills, news reports, and exclusive information to a select group of newspapers and film magazines. Mayer also worked with a local publisher to churn out dialogue books coupled with Japanese-language translations. Enthusiasts could use these publications to better understand the on-screen stories and also to learn English—a popular activity during the early postwar era. The distributor also relied on journalists, critics, and culture elites (see chapter 7) to enhance publicity. Intent on drawing favorable reviews from these professional writers, the CMPE offered "suggestions" on the tone and content of movie reviews, urging the critics to treat Hollywood as a respectable source of "worldly knowledge."[25] Those who failed to satisfy the CMPE's standards were banned from the company's screening room.[26] In one instance, Mayer refused to lend Hollywood's still photos to *Kinema junpō* because it lauded European films over Hollywood films in its annual critics' poll. Japanese journalists complained about this "nonsense" for a full year until the managing director finally lifted the ban.[27]

In addition, Mayer hired professional lecturers to directly engage with moviegoers.[28] The oral publicists visited a wide array of public spaces, including theaters, schools, universities, auditoriums, factories, gymnasiums, hospitals, municipal halls, community centers, and even private homes.[29] Their talks covered many different topics, including "Trends in American Movies," "On American Movies," "American Women and Home Life," and "School Life in America."[30] Mayer took particular pride in this publicity strategy. Several months before ending his tenure with the CMPE, Mayer noted that his lecturers had traveled "all over Japan, to give talks . . . in every remotest [sic] town and hamlet." By this time, the CMPE had orchestrated over nine thousand lectures for a total audience of approximately three million people.[31]

These regular lectures were augmented with larger public events. Mayer, for example, helped organize a large number of ad hoc exhibits of still photos, posters, and other visual materials. Taking advantage of display spaces in department stores, restaurants, train stations, office buildings, gymnasiums, and small shops, the CMPE showcased Hollywood culture and influenced popular taste.[32] During the spring and fall seasons—between the most lucrative summer and winter (New Year's) seasons—the CMPE launched citywide film festivals across the nation. These celebratory events involved parades, floats, window displays, trivia contests, and other eye-candy ballyhoo. Lucky fans would witness the company's publicity bus, the "Blondie," which made pit stops in a number of cities on special occasions.[33] Many of these events were enhanced by tie-ins with local businesses and media agencies.[34]

Selling *Bunka*

Mayer's operation hurled a wide array of ideas and representations at the Japanese. The content of Hollywood publicity consisted of three main types. One, of course, was the movie star. Picking up on the industry's activities during the interwar decades, the CMPE bombarded consumers with images of its top personalities on posters, billboards, magazines, exhibits, festivals, and other spaces. The weight given to the Hollywood star was evident in a number of ads that placed the top-caliber actors on center stage. In a full-page ad for *Johnny Belinda* (1948), for example, the CMPE disclosed nothing about the story but enlisted a full-size portrait of Jane Wyman. The advertising copy touted her "great performance . . . [that rewarded her with an] Academy Award this year!!"[35] Likewise, a full-page ad for *Pride of the Yankees* made no mention of Lou Gehrig, whose life story the film was about, but championed the film with the following line: "Gary Cooper wears a Yankees uniform and blasts a home run!" The image of Cooper's face filled the ad.[36]

The second type of information was the film genre. The classification of films by "story type" also remained key to Hollywood's business during the occupation era as a means of cultivating attention, attraction, and a sense of familiarity for the consumer. In a 1947 ad in *Kinema junpō,* for example, the

CMPE coupled still photos of a handful of female stars with a list of genres. The categories included "romantic drama," "filmic adaptation of best sellers and plays," "action-adventure spectacles," "music films," "thriller films," "cartoon films in bright color," and "news short films." No reference was made to individual films.[37] Subsequent campaigns often revolved around these and other genre traits. A full-page ad introduced *Sorry, Wrong Number* (1948) and *Notorious* (1946) together under the following copy: "Look! Two Great Masterpieces of Thriller Films."[38] Westerns were often paired for publicity as well. An ad that coupled *San Antonio* (1945) with *Fury at Furnace Creek* (1948), for example, appeared in the May 1950 issue of *Eiga no tomo*.[39]

While relying on such standardized practices, Hollywood actively promoted Hollywood as a manifestation of "culture," or *bunka*. Mayer and his team repeatedly insisted that U.S. cinema embodied "culturalism" (*bunkasei*) or "cultural significance" (*bunkateki igi*).[40] In 1948 the CMPE lecturer Tsuchiya Tarō remarked that his mission was to use the movies to implant a "correct awareness" of *bunka,* which encompassed the "humanity [*ninjō*], manners [*fūzoku*], customs, temperament, national character, daily practice [of the] American people" as well as the "politics, thought, society, ideals, [and] history" of the United States.[41] Likewise, an employee in Nagoya argued that the understanding of Hollywood's "culturalism" was vital for the "construction of a democratic nation, Japan."[42]

The CMPE made *bunka* a cornerstone of its campaign. On the back cover of the June 1, 1946, edition of *Kinema junpō,* the distributor listed a group of new feature films—including a crime film, a biopic, and a western—with the following headline: "The Window of Culture has Opened!" (*Hirakareta bunka no mado*).[43] Soon, posters, billboards, magazine ads—just like the "Oscar ad"—came out with the following slogan: "American movies are fountains of culture!" American movie festivals hosted "exhibits [of] American culture."[44] Lecturers waxed eloquent about *bunka,* in such talks as "Educational Qualities of American Films," "American Cinema and Culture," "Democracy and American Cinema," "Cultural Life in America," and "Democratic Spirit as Seen in American Movies."[45] In June 1950, the CMPE announced the founding of its Culture Department (*bunkabu*). Its mission, noted *MPEA News,* was to "promote [and] enlighten [the public with] American culture through American movies."[46]

The word *bunka* connotes ambiguity and abstraction. The CMPE, however, enlisted the term in a concrete manner to enhance the attraction value of the diverse studio products. Doing so required adjustment, manipulation, and reinvention of meaning. We now turn to four films to better understand how the

CMPE tried to sell its films as *bunka*. We will investigate how the distributor marketed individual products in a larger effort to promote Hollywood as a "window to American culture."

Rhapsody in Blue

Rhapsody in Blue (1945) was a combination of two filmic genres, the first of which was known in Japan as the "music film" (*ongaku eiga*). This story about George Gershwin stood alongside other successful music-heavy films like *Music for Millions* (1944) and *Song of Love* (1947), which interlaced songs, dance, and concert performances into the narrative. The second genre was the "biographical picture" (*denki eiga*), or biopic. This group of pictures narrated the life stories of notable women and men, including Marie Curie (*Madame Curie*, 1943), Emile Zola (*The Life of Emile Zola*, 1937), and Alexander Graham Bell (*The Story of Alexander Graham Bell*, 1939). An Oscar-nominated musical biopic, *Rhapsody in Blue* offered Gershwin's compositions through the presentation of his life story. In this sense, the Irving Rapper film was similar to other musical biographies like *Swanee River* (1939) and *The Jolson Story* (1946), which brought an assortment of songs and dance numbers to audiences.

Rhapsody in Blue, however, was unique because of the distributor's privileged handling of it. Instead of subjecting it to the normal cycle of one- or two-week turnarounds, the CMPE designated the Gershwin story as the first bona fide road-show film in postwar Japan.[47] This meant that the eighteen-reel film would remain in theaters as long as attendance was strong. In order to make the most of this presentation format, the CMPE generated extra hype with advance publicity on radio and in print. A week before its opening, the distributor created a spectacle by arranging a gala premiere packed with what the trade saw as an "unusual lineup of [distinguished] people," including university presidents, politicians, SCAP personnel, and members of the imperial family.[48] The film went on to enjoy an impressive ten-week run at the Marunouchi Subaru-za in Tokyo, and reached thousands of fans through prestige theaters throughout the country.[49] The success of this film set the tone for other road shows in ensuing months.[50]

The bulk of the film's narrative centers on George Gershwin's rise to fame in the music profession. Growing up on the Lower East Side of New York City, Gershwin teaches himself how to play the piano at a penny arcade. Gershwin's raw skills impress his parents. As soon as the family purchases a second-hand piano, Gershwin begins professional training and, after several years, takes on his first job as a relief pianist at a nearby vaudeville theater. Gershwin, then, briefly works for a music publisher. A breakthrough comes when Gershwin meets a sympathetic music mogul who hires the aspiring talent on a two-year contract. The New York native soon becomes a hit creator of popular songs.

According to the narrative, Gershwin's success as a musician stems from his unbending will to express his creativity. Although his teachers and employers try to impose conformity, Gershwin insists on the use of idiosyncratic chords (the diminished ninth) and rhythms (syncopation) in pursuit of originality. Harsh criticism of his stage compositions fails to stop him. Confident but never fully satisfied, Gershwin churns out new musical pieces for the stage and orchestra. Determined to hone his composition skills, Gershwin even sojourns in Paris. The film introduces an impressive array of selections from compositions, including "Blue Monday Blues," "An American in Paris," "Cuban Overture," and "Porgy and Bess."

As a typical narrative of classical Hollywood, romance intertwines with the other main line of action and bears an impact on the final resolution.[51] In *Rhapsody in Blue,* the amorous possibilities threaten Gershwin's success in the music world. The composer develops a rapport with two women. One is Julie Adams, an aspiring singer for whom Gershwin writes shows and songs. The other is Christine Gilbert, a divorced painter who falls in love with Gershwin in Paris. The composer has romantic feelings particularly for the latter, but Christine ultimately chooses to keep a distance from him out of respect for his creative activities. Julie does the same when Gershwin approaches her after Christine drops out of sight. An internationally acclaimed musician, Gershwin painfully realizes that his fame has isolated him from others. "Maybe way down deep I'm just a family man," he laments late in the film, but one "without a family."

Gershwin remains determined to create music in the absence of a romantic partner, but his body begins to deteriorate at the height of his career. During a live performance on stage, Gershwin begins to lose control of his fingers. A mysterious headache soon leads to his physical collapse. When his brother Ira pleads with him to take a rest, the ailing composer, breaking out in tears, replies: "I must write!" A few moments later, during a live radio concert of "Concerto in F" in New York, the conductor interrupts the program to announce Gershwin's death. The ending credits appear over a concert of "Rhapsody in Blue" attended by Julie and the remaining Gershwin family. As Julie's tearful eyes observe the stage, a shot of Oscar Levant (played by himself) overlaps with a confident Gershwin gracing the keyboard. The camera zooms out and captures the concert from the sky. In the final shot, rays of sunlight peek through the heavenly clouds, as if to honor Gershwin's creative work as a divine accomplishment.

The marketing of *Rhapsody in Blue* in Japan was anchored in its musical value. In the company newsletter, the CMPE promised that the Warner Bros. film would offer a "flood of American music."[52] The Gershwin film lacked top-value Hollywood stars, but it boasted an array of renowned artists in the music profession. Highlights included the vaudeville act of Al Jolson, the orchestral command of Paul Whiteman, the bouncing fingers of Levant, in addition to the performances of other real-life musicians. Instead of selling the film as a typical star-centered narrative, the CMPE's full-page magazine ads aligned the names of these "famous artists" together with Robert Alda and Joan Leslie, the lead actors in the film.[53]

Musical content was an equally significant aspect of film marketing. The CMPE trumpeted *Rhapsody in Blue* as a chronicle of U.S. music history, specifically championing the "true essence of jazz" in it.[54] This musical genre already enjoyed widespread popularity in Japanese cities during the 1920s, alongside social dance, radio, and record players. During the occupation, jazz revived as a common staple at cabarets, dance halls, and nightclubs. Many of these facilities were SCAP's "off-limits" venues for exclusive use by the occupation forces, but the Japanese public readily encountered this musical genre at concert halls, on the radio, in magazines, and at the movies.[55] This revival of jazz made it all the more important for the CMPE to sell *Rhapsody in Blue* as a film concerning "genuine jazz music."[56] At the very least, the assortment of big-name artists and their music, the distributor noted, would deliver "great stimulation and excitement to the music world in Japan."[57]

The CMPE's promotion of *Rhapsody in Blue* as a "jazz film" was more than an innocent act. It reflected an effort to showcase a superior "national culture" by touting the musical genre as a white man's art. The distributor did so by underscoring the genre's ties to classical music, which CMPE regarded as a "high class" creation worthy of distinction.[58] The early scenes of the film highlight Gershwin's training in the European tradition. His mentor, Professor Franck, treats Schubert, Wagner, and Beethoven as role models who pursued musical artistry over fame and material wealth. In Paris, Gershwin meets Maurice Ravel, and the two enjoy an evening sharing their music. At key intervals, the film takes pains to dramatize the orchestra performances of "Rhapsody in Blue" and "Concerto in F" with contrast lighting, close-ups, and long shots.

The CMPE underscored this transatlantic influence. It rendered the title of the film in Japanese as *American Symphony* (*Amerika kōkyōgaku*), which intimated that the artist's musical inspirations largely stemmed from Europe. Movie ads developed a sense of formality by interjecting a photograph of conductor Paul Whiteman smiling on stage with a baton.[59] The CMPE reminded

Figure 5.3. Magazine advertisement for *Rhapsody in Blue. Eiga no tomo,* April 1947, back cover. Author's collection.

consumers that Gershwin's brilliance was most evident in his talent for "modern musical composition."[60] Interestingly, in celebrating Gershwin's ties to classical music, the CMPE did not underscore the African-American influence on his creative works. Although the film introduced black performers like Anne Brown and Hazel Scott and suggested the influence of Negro spirituals and the blues on Gershwin's compositions, the CMPE chose not to promote the biracial connection. The distributor essentially sold jazz as a white man's music and chose to overlook its multicultural roots.

The association of jazz with whiteness also involved an effort to mask ethnic difference. The CMPE lauded Gershwin's accomplishments in *Rhapsody in Blue* as a "pride of America," but the biographical tale was virtually about a generic white man.[61] The film itself largely removed the composer's Russian Jewish origins and portrayed the protagonist as an "ordinary" working-class boy who earned fame and glory through hard work and perseverance—just like the hero of a Horatio Alger novel. Making no mention of his ethnic and religious background, the distributor praised Gershwin's work ethic and humility, while underscoring the fact that the film could demonstrate "the energetic fighting spirit of Americans" to the Japanese people.[62] Little was said about religious and ethnic diversity, as well as the composer's encounters with anti-Semitism. Through the publicity of *Rhapsody in Blue,* the CMPE presented America as a "melting pot" devoid of internal complexities. Dealing with a text that painted jazz as white, the CMPE sold the Gershwin biopic as a rags-to-riches story of an ethnically uprooted white American..

Little Women

Little Women (1949) belonged to a genre that the U.S. trade labeled the "woman's film," a female-starring narrative that studios marketed primarily to women.[63] In Japan, it was treated as a "literary and artistic" film (*bungei eiga*). Based on the famous children's novel by Louisa May Alcott, the MGM film portrayed the daily life of a struggling New England family during the Civil War. By the time of its release in 1949, the story was already familiar to the Japanese. In addition to the translated edition of the novel available before the war, an earlier RKO adaptation starring Katherine Hepburn had hit the theaters in the fall of 1934.[64] Produced fifteen years later, the new film—a rare Technicolor product—enjoyed top billing. In Tokyo, *Little Women* inaugurated the road-show opening of the Kōtō gekijō during the busy New Year's season. Commercial results were not as outstanding as with *Rhapsody in Blue,* but the woman's film stayed in the theater for a full month.[65] The distributor aggressively marketed the film in other cities outside the metropolis. On the press sheet, the CMPE boasted that the promotion of *Little Women* was widespread.[66]

The story begins in a family gathering. On a bright, snowy afternoon, the girls of the March family gather at home to prepare for a Christmas celebration. The four sisters—Meg, Jo, Beth, and Amy—have starkly different personalities, but their relationship is close. In preparing for the holiday, they rehearse a play that Jo wrote and visit a nearby store to buy Christmas presents. The anchor of the family is the mother, Marmee, whose caring words and moral support glue the family together. The bond of the Marches is evident in the sisters' decision to buy Christmas presents for their mother—even by sacrificing their meager belongings. Laurie, their next-door neighbor, envies the family because they always seem to enjoy "such a good time."

Two problems jeopardize the family's well being. First, the March household is struggling financially after a failed investment made a few years earlier. On Christmas morning, the sisters rejoice when they see sausage, pancakes, and coffee on the breakfast table, but the maid reminds them that such food was served everyday when the sisters were little. As a result of their plight, the family is forced to beg for money from a wealthy aunt, while bearing her biting sarcasm. Second, the father is absent from home, serving in the Union Army. The sisters console and cheer one another—singing, dancing, and practicing their play—but they miss their father. In one of the "moving" moments, the sisters cuddle around Marmee to read the father's letter from the battlefield.

The threat to family unity increases as the narrative moves forward. Social pressure isolates the March sisters from the wider community. Amy faces mockery from her peers at school, while she and Meg overhear a rich mother and daughter badmouthing the Marches at an evening ball. Changing emotions also threaten a familial breakup. Meg develops a romantic relationship with a young Union soldier, and Jo sees this as a threat to the sisters' togetherness. Jo chooses not to marry Laurie in order to maintain the family close, but leaves for New York City to pursue a career as a fiction writer. In the middle of the film, a telegram abruptly announces that the father has been wounded in the war. The sisters anxiously see off their mother, who rushes to a hospital in Washington, DC, to help her ailing husband. Worst of all, Beth suffers from scarlet fever and dies toward the end amid the sorrowing of her sisters and friendly neighbors.

Notwithstanding these hardships, the protagonists stick together by exchanging their love and compassion. Marmee shares her Christmas breakfast with a starving family, and endlessly pours out her affection to her children. Jo sells her hair to help finance her mother's trip to Washington. Beth befriends an elderly gentleman, and makes a pair of slippers for him. Shortly before her unwelcome death, Beth courageously tells Jo: "We will always be a family, even if one of us is gone." After her quiet passing, Jo writes *My Beth,* a book written in honor of her deceased sister. As if to reward their unselfish actions, the film concludes with the family's triumph against the odds. Amy and Meg, both happily married, return home to mother and friendly neighbors. Jo accepts a marriage proposal from Professor Bhaer, whom she met in New York, but she does so on the condition that the family will stay close. The final shot tilts up to a colorful rainbow peeking through the clouds, symbolizing the brightened emotions of a united family.

The marketing of *Little Women* was anchored on family warmth and unity. The CMPE's press sheet maintained that the film introduced the life of a "happy family" that overcomes three adversities: "Dad's injury, Jo's heartbreak, and saddest of all, Beth's death."[67] The joy, compassion, and endurance of the March household made the film "a most splendid, a most family-oriented, healthy product."[68] The distributor expected broad audience appeal also because of Margaret O'Brien. During the early postwar years, this child actress became a popular icon in Japan through other family-oriented pictures like *Journey for Margaret* (1942), *Our Vines Have Tender Grapes* (1945), and *Meet Me in St. Louis* (1945). According to the press sheet, O'Brien's role as Beth in *Little Women* was crucial in inspiring others around her to "share the sorrows, and pursue love and happiness."[69] In stressing her character's significance to her sisters and parents, the CMPE reinforced the notion that the movie was a family story that would appeal to all generations.[70]

The distributor also portrayed the film as a woman's story. The reason was clear: the CMPE found it effective in attracting young female audiences.[71] In its publicity blurbs, the CMPE characterized *Little Women* as "a story of love involving the four sisters" and "a story of poor but beautiful girls"; other taglines urged audiences to "weep at the rose-colored chronicle of the sisters" and root for the "young girls, healthily growing up under the wings of love [to] be beautiful!"[72] The efforts to play up sisterhood resulted in a "four-sister craze" in the big cities. In Tokyo, Nagoya, and Osaka, the CMPE arranged "four-sisters" contests and invited girls with four siblings to free screenings.[73] Furthermore, in an effort to expand the attendance of women, the CMPE hyped the romantic angle.[74] In the narrative, heterosexual relations inspired the actions of three out of the four siblings (Jo, Amy, and Meg); Jo's emotional oscillation between family and Professor Bhaer is a central focus of the film's second half. The CMPE stressed that "no other film is as fantastic, moving, and romantic" as *Little Women.*[75]

Moreover, the CMPE cloaked the LeRoy film with an aura of respectability. During the marketing of *Rhapsody in Blue,* the distributor emphasized high class with musical artistry. With *Little Women,* the CMPE underscored the literary original. Alcott's novel, as the CMPE described it, was worthy of serious attention because it reflected the "sincerity" and the "ambience of a devout Christian." The Japanese could identify with the story because it portrayed "a quaint love of family that would transcend the ages . . . and national boundaries."[76] The quality of the original rendered the film version a "literary masterpiece."[77] In Tokyo, the CMPE collaborated with the translator of the novel and advertised the book on posters and billboards.[78] In Nagoya, the CMPE erected a human-sized book of *Little Women* in front of the city's largest bookstore. Decorated with brightly colored ribbons, it advertised the film adaptation to book lovers in town.[79]

Star promotion was another way of cultivating respectability. Seeking to lure the female population, the CMPE displayed the film's four young actresses—June Allyson, Elizabeth Taylor, Margaret O'Brien, and Janet Leigh—who had "absolute" marketing value. The aim, however, was not to sell their pretty faces. The CMPE made sure to stress their "elegant performances" as members of the March family.[80] In addition, the distributor devoted ample attention to director Mervyn LeRoy, who was known in Japan for such delicate melodramas as *Random Harvest* (1942) and *Waterloo Bridge* (1940). On the press sheet, the CMPE extolled LeRoy as a "great director" who refined the film with "sensitive coaching."[81]

Furthermore, the CMPE underscored the Victorian backdrop.[82] The film took pains to represent the fashion, architecture, and mannerisms of this genteel lifestyle in Technicolor—a format that added strength to the visual presentation.[83] With this in mind, the CMPE publicized *Little Women* as a story about "noble sentimentality" (*kōga na kanshō*).[84] The film's representation of Victorian life was particularly apparent in the gendered behavior of the protagonists. For the March girls, the priorities in life lay in the home and marriage. Even Jo, who leaves for New York to pursue a professional career, returns to her home in Concord, Massachusetts, uniting with her romantic partner at the very end. Her pursuit of personal freedom only leads her back to the Victorian "cult of domesticity," which others in the family actively embrace.[85]

This portrayal of restrained female behavior did not owe solely to the Victorian elites of the mid-nineteenth century. As literary scholars have noted, Alcott's original story actually contained an element of rebellion against the constrained gender norms of the era. Using the character of Jo March, Alcott expressed her vigorous desire for independence and self-expression, even while the novel ultimately privileges women's self-restraint and service to the codes of domestic behavior.[86] The 1949 film version was more conservative. As Robyn McCallum has noted, Mervyn LeRoy's remake suppressed much of these transgressive desires and reified the "post–World War II antifeminist ideology that sought to remove women from the workforce and reinstate them in the home."[87] The CMPE's promotion of "noble ambience" (*kōga na funiki*), then, was a marriage of nineteenth-century genteel culture and the social clout of early cold war America. Hollywood wedded the gender norms of American Victorianism with the growing conservative turn toward "domestic containment."[88]

Union Pacific

The Hollywood western was a success story in Japan. During the pre–Second World War decades, the action-packed hits of William S. Hart and Tom Mix had won a passionate following by catering to fans across the nation. This trend revived shortly after the war with John Wayne's breakthrough hit *Tall in the Saddle* (1944). To the CMPE, however, the popularity of the genre was a curse as well as a blessing. While delighted with high turnouts, Charles Mayer worried that the oversell of a single genre could precipitate audience disinterest in other filmic products.[89] The greater problem was SCAP's ambivalence. As discussed in the previous chapter, occupation censors took the western with a grain of salt, complaining of its glorification of violence, revenge, and racist acts against nonwhites. Mayer was serious when he publicly confessed that the success of the western was "not something to boast about."[90] He was well aware that the popular genre was creating political and institutional problems.

Union Pacific (1939) entered postwar Japan in this context. Like most other westerns released during the occupation, the Cecil B. DeMille epic was not a privileged product like *Rhapsody in Blue* or *Little Women,* nor was it a fresh commodity.[91] The film actually debuted in Japan several months before Pearl Harbor; after the war, the CMPE re-released the film twice, in 1947 and 1949.[92] In Tokyo, the Nikkatsu chain became its primary exhibitor. Many nonmetropolitan theaters also screened this product. Commercial results were strong during both releases, but the film stayed in theaters for only one or two weeks.[93] The film, in essence, was a "second-tier" product that CMPE promoted to the "mass" (*taishū*) audiences.[94]

The main plot concerns the construction of the transcontinental railroad. Toward the end of the Civil War, Washington politicians, in an effort to reunite the torn nation, discuss a plan to build a transportation line across the American West. Endorsed by Abraham Lincoln and his supporters, the mission to lay the tracks from Ohama, Nebraska, to California commences under the hands of the Union Pacific railroad. The idea, however, invites political resistance in Capitol Hill, as opposing senators scoff at the ambitious project as a "crazy dream" and a "monumental folly." While paying lip service to Lincoln's plan, a rich Chicago banker decides to support the Central Pacific, a rival company based in California. Henceforth, the two companies race to build tracks to Ogden, Utah. The first to reach Ogden would gain control over the operation.

The narrative personalizes this corporate struggle in the relationship of two men. On one side is Captain Jeff Butler—the hero of the story—who oversees work for the Union Pacific. On the opposite side is Dick Allen, the corrupt banker's henchman hired to thwart the westward construction. The two men had bonded during their service in the Union Army in the Civil War, but now they work for archrivals. The duo also vie for the love of Molly Monahan, an Irish-American tomboy type who works for the postal service. Dick passionately pursues Molly with a wedding ring in hand, but the heroine is in love with the more stoic Jeff. The ramifications of her actions are bigger than her personal relationships. Without her knowing it, Molly's romantic decisions greatly affect the course of the railroad competition.

Several troubling actions place the Union Pacific in jeopardy. Dick tries to sabotage the operation by enticing its workers into gambling and alcohol. A short-tempered worker kills his foreman and pressures others to boycott their manual labor jobs. A band of Sioux ominously observe the passing steam train. Later, they stage an all-out assault against the railroad workers. Jeff is haunted by other crises. He nearly loses his life when a corrupt card player, a henchman of Dick's boss, tries to shoot him in the back. When Dick and his men steal a bag full of loan money for the Union Pacific, Jeff fails to recover it. Not realizing that Dick is behind the heist, Molly, in an effort to prevent Dick's men from killing Jeff, agrees to marry the thief. At the lowest point of the film, Jeff apparently has lost the money and the girl.

Yet thanks to Jeff's dogged efforts and the help of others, the tide turns in favor of the Union Pacific. For instance, Jeff's men launch a counterattack on those who run the saloon. After realizing that Dick stole the loan money, Molly persuades her husband to return the sack of cash to the Union Pacific. The battle against the Sioux nearly ends with a total wipeout of the construction workers, but Jeff and Molly cable for help. The U.S. Army storms to the rescue and chases away the indigenous foes at the last minute. When the railroad workers face their final obstacle to success—a storm-ridden, rock-solid mountain standing in the way—Jeff recommends that the tracks be laid around the mountain instead of through it. Thanks to the hero's wit, the Union Pacific beats the Central Pacific to Ogden.

The triumph of the Union Pacific inspires other resolutions. At Promontory Point, where the two lines meet, the dignitaries pound in the golden spike. A distinguished California speaker touts the new creation as the "greatest railroad enterprise of the world." Personal skirmishes also reach a resolution. The final showdown takes place between Jeff and the banker's right-hand man. Dick loses his life in an attempt to save Jeff, but the villain perishes at the hands of the hero's friends. Dick's death draws Molly closer to Jeff, while the crowd celebrates the technological marvel of the railroad. The final shot displays a diesel train zooming past the camera, decades later. The transcontinental railroad, the ending suggests, has inspired the modern age.

In general, the CMPE's promotion of *Union Pacific* was similar to the marketing of westerns since the prewar years. The distributor, first and foremost, promoted the film as a story about the conquest of the natural landscape. Echoing Frederick Jackson Turner, who famously argued that the area west of the Mississippi was shaped by a moving "frontier" that divided "civilization" from "savagery," the CMPE treated the film's action ground as a process (not place) that unfolded in the "arid landscape of the vast west."[95] In this drama that takes place far from the urban experience, audiences, the CMPE noted, should expect to enjoy the protagonists' efforts to overcome the "challenge against the grand wilderness." The scale and grandeur of the landscape was the central emphasis in the film's Japanese-language title: *The Great Plains* (*Daiheigen*). Many Japanese learned to see the American West as a symbol of freedom and openness.

The publicity for *Union Pacific,* handled similarly to that of other westerns, also showcased star power. The CMPE hyped the film's charismatic icons. A focal point of this marketing involved Barbara Stanwyck, already a well-known actress in Japan. But the CMPE cast even greater attention on Cecil B. DeMille, the producer and director of the Paramount product. Since the 1910s and 1920s, the director had achieved fame and respect in Japan for his historical epics such as *Intolerance* (1916) and *The Ten Commandments* (1923). The distributor thus did not hesitate to tout him as an "artistic mind" and "extraordinary director." By praising *Union Pacific* as a "large picture scroll" of the American West, the CMPE strove to wed the visual grandeur of the Hollywood western with the "spectacular" scope and scale of a DeMille film.[96]

The selling of *Union Pacific* also relied on thrill and suspense. Not unlike the marketing of westerns prior to the war, the CMPE peppered its ads with such lines as "breathtaking tension," "heroic and fierce struggles," and "[the efforts to] eliminat[e] the evil plots and actions of the greedy businessmen." Yet the distributor deviated from convention in the handling of violence specifically between whites and Native Americans. Like many other westerns, *Union Pacific* climaxes with a large-scale Indian raid that nearly kills the white protagonists. Although tempted to sensationalize this spectacular moment, the distributor ultimately sought "not to emphasize the ethnic struggle between Indians and whites too strongly in print [advertising]." The CMPE feared that cinematic scenes of cross-racial tension in the American West could foster unfavorable emotions toward the (white) American occupiers in defeated Japan. It thus urged publicists to concentrate on star marketing in an effort to move forward in "an era of peace after war."[97]

While toning down the elements of racial conflict, the CMPE asserted that *Union Pacific* was filled with pedagogical value "necessary for the study of the youth." According to the distributor, the Paramount picture illustrated a noteworthy "history on the construction of the Union Pacific Railroad." The CMPE crafted block ads that showcased a steam locomotive blazing forward at full speed. Its press sheet devoted a full-length article to the political and business motivations that created the railroad company, as well as the process through which the iron highway was built across the American West. The article concluded with information about the present state of the Union Pacific line, which apparently enabled travel from Chicago to San Francisco in a matter of thirty-nine hours. Its train cars, CMPE noted, were "famous for their magnificent modern facilities."[98]

In showcasing the triumph of the railroad line, the CMPE was attempting something bigger: the celebration of America's "progressive" achievements. *Union Pacific* belonged to a larger group of contemporary films that cultural historian Richard Slotkin referred to as the "progressive epic" western, which tended to glorify "all persons, tendencies, and crises that yield higher rates of production, faster transportation, more advanced technology, and more civilized forms of society."[99] In marketing the film in Japan, the CMPE amplified the film's triumphant interpretation of U.S. history by emphasizing the "pioneer spirit" of white Americans as well as their "conquest" of the rugged natural landscape.[100] This effort was more than a means of boosting the film's entertainment value. It revealed the distributor's attempts to paint the Hollywood western as a pedagogically useful and respectable genre. The marketing of *Union Pacific* did not simply reflect the contemporary U.S. climate in which the DeMille epic was made. It also revealed the CMPE's active response to the political sensitivities of the occupation program.

Cry of the City

Cry of the City (1950) was a low-budget production of mediocre quality. Similar to *Union Pacific,* it told a Manichaean story of good versus evil, but it involved men in trench coats, a prison break, and criminal antics under neon lights. This Twentieth Century–Fox film was an urban crime story, which film scholars have identified as a film noir.[101] In defeated Japan, *Cry of the City* walked the borders of a "crime film" (*hanzai eiga*), a "crime melodrama" (*hanzai merodorama*), and a "gangster film" (*gyangu eiga*). The film debuted in Tokyo on February 28, 1950, only a few months after it opened in the United States. Records suggest that the film was not a commercial hit. It stayed in most Japanese theaters for no longer than a full week. The CMPE did not give privileged treatment to this production.[102]

The narrative concerns the entangled lives of two Italian American men. One is Vittorio Candella (Victor Mature), a stoic police lieutenant who devotes his life to justice and law enforcement. An honest, respected man in his precinct, Candella tirelessly works to maintain peace and order on a modest salary. The other protagonist is Martin Rome (Richard Conte). A petty criminal who grew up in the same Italian American neighborhood as Candella, Rome routinely gambles and steals to make a quick buck. The film begins shortly after Rome holds up a restaurant and kills a policeman. The opening scene depicts him lying unconscious on a hospital bed, apparently injured during his criminal act. Surrounding Rome are his mother, father, and siblings, who feel for their ailing son, soon to be sent to the electric chair.

Rome's one hope in life is his girlfriend, Teena Riconti. Worried about her injured boyfriend's health and future, Teena quietly slips into the hospital to see him. The two reaffirm their affection for one another. However, a nurse discovers her presence, and the police soon search for her. The news about the girlfriend immediately reaches Niles, a crooked lawyer who, in an attempt to defend one of his clients, seeks Rome's confession for a jewel robbery—one that the ailing protagonist did not commit. Shortly after Rome regains full consciousness, the corrupt attorney proposes a deal that involves his confession in exchange for a reduced criminal sentence (for the murder of the policeman). When Rome refuses, Niles hints that his gang will find Teena and "work...on her for a few days" to force her into a false confession of the jewel robbery. Desperate to protect his girlfriend, Rome gains help from a janitor and escapes from prison.

Rome's first destination is Niles's office. There, he discovers that the attorney had been part of the jewel robbery. Rome not only seizes the stolen treasures from Niles but also forces him to reveal the name of a conspirator: Rose Given. The two men soon clash violently. Niles shoots and misses, and Rome stabs him to death. The fugitive then returns home, where he reunites with his brother Tony, an admirer of his rebellious antics. Rome's mother and father, however, are not as pleased and express shock in his second act of killing. Fighting her strong affection for her oldest son, the mother tells Rome to leave the house. Then, by pure chance, Candella visits the Rome household to talk to Rome's mother. Rome threatens the lieutenant at gunpoint and quietly slips into the night.

Rome's escape soon takes a physical toll. He begins to suffer from a high fever. But he is determined to find Given. With the help of Brenda, a former girlfriend, he secures first-aid treatment from an unlicensed doctor. Brenda also gives him a car ride to Given's apartment. There, Rome bargains for a car, five thousand dollars, and a way out of the United States. Given offers cash and an escape route to South America. Rome tells her to meet in front of a locker at a subway station, where the jewelry is hidden, but he double-crosses her by tipping off Candella. At the locker, the police arrest her, but Candella is shot by Given and badly injured. Rome escapes amid the chaos.

The gunshot wound does not stop Candella from pursuing Rome. He leaves his hospital bed to visit an apartment where Teena is said to be hiding. He does not find her but learns that Rome is meeting her at a nearby cathedral. In the pews, Rome tries to persuade Teena to flee the country with him. Teena declines, noting that he had "changed" after killing the two men. Candella additionally reveals that the people who helped Rome's escape—the janitor, the doctor, and the blonde girlfriend—will be serving jail time because of him. Teena, with tears in her eyes, quietly leaves the building. Noticing that Candella is injured, Rome then attempts one last escape. The barely conscious law officer shouts: "In the name of the law, Rome, stop!" The fugitive refuses, and dies after Candella shoots him in the back. Tony, who now appears, confesses that his brother had asked him to steal money from their mother, but that he could not. As the narrative closes, Tony's morals are preserved.

Cry of the City was armed with two known actors from previously released films, Victor Mature (*My Darling Clementine,* 1946) and Richard Conte (*Calling Northside 777,* 1948). Thanks to these personalities, the CMPE decided to play up the film's "male beauty" (*danseibi*). While presuming that the film's primary audience was men, the lineup would "enchant women," the press sheet boasted.[103] Another emphasis was on the urban setting. In the press sheet, the CMPE compared *Cry of the City* to *The Naked City* (1948).[104] Although lacking the prestige of the Jules Dassin film, *Cry of the City,* the distributor argued, also offered a "realistic" filming of the "actual landscape."[105] It was an "epic tale" that "exceeded *The Naked City* in thrill!!"[106]

But at the heart of the marketing campaign was genre, specifically the film's gangster angle. Like the Hollywood western, the gangster narrative was a filmic product that the occupiers resisted, as it depicted violence, crime, social disturbance, and glorified villains. The CMPE attempted to avoid political condemnation by calling *Cry of the City* a "new gangster movie." By labeling the film as such, the CMPE did not shy away from building excitement with words such as "sirens," "sound of gunshots," and "people's screams."[107] Yet the distributor also assured that this new genre did not overglorify crime or violent action. Even while featuring multiple murders and shootings, the narrative did not have excessive shoot-'em-up violence, and the final showdown between hero and villain ends with the single shot Candella fires at Rome's back. The CMPE went on to claim that *Cry of the City* was "not a third-rate gangster film that aimed [to yield] excitement through the shoot-out of police and gangster in a big city."[108]

The "new" gangster film was also devoid of moral ambiguity. The CMPE made this clear by noting that *Cry of the City* was centrally concerned with the demise of the villain. The actual film, like other crime-world narratives made under the 1934 production code, depicted the criminals as morally flawed characters who gradually lose their place in society. At the beginning of the narrative, Teena and the Rome family are all highly sympathetic to the lawbreaking protagonist and worry about his health and future. But as a result of his escape, his murder of the attorney, and his evident greed for money, his father, mother, Teena, and Tony lose respect for him. The process through which the villain loses the support of his friends and family considerably differs from Japanese equivalents like *Drunken Angel,* which maintained sympathy for the gangster (Mifune Toshirō) even after his death. The CMPE made a conscious effort to distinguish its product from morally ambiguous crime narratives. It stressed that the film "depicted the miserable travails of a gangster in a thorough manner."[109]

In a similar vein, the promotion of *Cry of the City* underscored the "humanistic theme." While taking pains not to glorify the gangster, the distributor portrayed the film as a story about a policeman who "tried to believe in human goodness." In the film, this theme is evident in Candella's efforts to console Rome's parents, who are shocked and demoralized by their son's turn to crime. The lieutenant also tries to prevent Tony from following in his brother's footsteps—and eventually succeeds. The CMPE stressed that *Cry of the City* "was a moving masterpiece that denied the gangster and celebrated humanism." In the spirit of underscoring law enforcement as a compassionate and righteous activity, the distributor encouraged tie-ins with local police forces. This enabled the distributor to boost the film through crime prevention activities.[110]

The CMPE's intention was to treat this "humanistic" drama as an American story. Despite the film's Italian American backdrop (Rome's family occasionally speak in Italian), the distributor chose to de-emphasize the ethnic angle of this urban crime film. Instead, the publicists noted that *Cry of the City* was ultimately a story about two "life-long friends in New York, one who became a police man and the other a gangster."[111] As with the marketing campaign of *Rhapsody in Blue,* the CMPE chose to portray the central characters as generalized white Americans, and the film as one where law and morals triumph over crime and evil intentions. The promotion of the "new gangster film," in this regard, reinforced the occupiers' efforts to present white mainstream norms as the "American" model of justice and peacekeeping. The CMPE, in this manner, sold *Cry of the City* as a proestablishment film.

Hollywood's marketing in defeated Japan was a unique exercise. Working under the rules set by the U.S. occupiers, it temporarily overrode its studio-based mind-set and engaged in a collective operation. This institutional structure enabled American companies to aggregate their resources and generate far-reaching promotional campaigns. Another unique characteristic was the *bunka* campaign. Determined to maximize its commercial opportunity in defeated Japan, the CMPE, in addition to hyping stars and genres, sold its movies as culturally "superior" products that represented the "American way of life."

As can be seen, the idea of "America," as presented by Hollywood, was hardly uniform. It consisted of a hodge-podge of representations that cut across studio products and genres, and included themes and stories that might cast the United States in a negative light. Yet through content adjustment, emphasis, and manipulation, the CMPE made a conscious effort to present its "imagined community" as a respectable model for Japanese life and behavior. This resulted in the celebration of "high art" (*Rhapsody in Blue*), the underscoring of social harmony (*Little Women*), the championing of technological triumph (*Union Pacific*), and the condemnation of criminal violence (*Cry of the City*). This *bunka* strategy reflected dual intentions: it aimed to diffuse the occupiers' ill feelings and to expand the industry's market share. The CMPE's promotional campaign reached moviegoers around Japan and inspired their thinking. Its influence was particularly strong at a crucial juncture of cultural encounter: the movie theater.

Chapter 6

Presenting Culture

The Exhibition of American Movies

On July 1950, Irving A. Maas landed in Japan with a sigh of relief. After a brief visit to Korea, where a bloody war had just broken out between North and South, the vice president of the Motion Picture Export Association whisked himself away on "the last plane in the evacuation airlift" and arrived safely in Tokyo. In contrast to the war-torn Korean market, business in Japan was encouraging. The country was "largely in the hands of responsible nationals who have taken the initiative in setting up film deals," he thought.[1] While pleased with a number of developments in Japan, Maas took particular notice of exhibitors' enthusiasm. Three years earlier, when he first visited the island nation, Maas was impressed with the exhibitors' "fast recovery," but he expressed concern about some of their "imprudent" (hiryōshinteki) practices, such as the tendency to overpack small theater spaces.[2] Although such practices did not disappear, his second trip gave him a different outlook.[3] On his return to the United States, the MPEA representative told *The Film Daily* that American-film exhibition was "well run" in the Japanese market. Hollywood, he concluded, "has found fertile ground for enlightenment."[4]

Maas spoke of a business arena that witnessed a rapid influx of Hollywood culture. While advertising its movies via newspapers, lectures, radio, and city-wide festivals, the Central Motion Picture Exchange interacted with exhibitors to control and manage the sites of film presentation. The CMPE did this by suspending ties with reluctant nationwide chains and turning instead to small circuits and independents that were mushrooming in cities across the nation. The distributor not only sought to maximize the exposure of its narrative

PRESENTING CULTURE   113

products, but it also employed a rigorous reform campaign to cultivate an air of refinement at the movies. In an effort to transform dingy theater spaces into what Charles Mayer called "shrines of culture" (*bunka no dendō*), the CMPE instructed its affiliates in the "proper" modes of doing business and promoted competition via a "good movies to good theaters" policy.

Hollywood's growing presence drew the attention of hundreds of exhibitors. A multitude of small outlets chose to work with the CMPE in hopes of gaining institutional legitimacy, prestige, and a steady stream of popular American movies. Theaters equipped with capital, facilities, and personal connections usually "won" privileged distribution contracts. They became first-run houses and, in special cases, road-show theaters emblazoned with the familiar marquee: "Home of American Movies." Exhibitors that lacked such resources operated as second- or lesser-run theaters, and at worst they lost the rights to handle American features. The competition among exhibitors gave rise to a mix of "privileged" and "unprivileged" American-movie exhibitors in a growing marketplace.

The exhibition of U.S. films was an uneven collaboration. It was an interplay and alignment of power shaped among the involved business parties. Much of this owed to Hollywood, which wielded considerable influence on the terms of film distribution and, at times, the methods of theater management. Yet the vigor of film exhibition was also shaped by the theaters themselves. Eager to carve their niche in a competitive business, theater owners and managers actively invested their finances, devised creative advertising, and set out to lure consumers to the movies. They adapted, mediated, and reinvented Hollywood culture in search of survival and success in the trade. The enlightenment campaign spread across cities in this fluctuating business environment. Movie theaters were vital intermediaries that disseminated Hollywood culture on the ground.

Japan, Year Zero

The Second World War was a miserable time for film exhibitors. The years of military action overseas increasingly strained their business at home. While filmmakers coped with diminishing artistic opportunities under the watchful eyes of the Home Ministry, theater owners suffered from product shortages and controlled management. The screen programs lost flexibility and variety. As the warring empire grew desperate, exhibitors were forced to reduce their screen hours or, worse, to close down. The final year of the war was literally disastrous for exhibitors. The B-29 air raids demolished hundreds of theaters and left deep scars on surviving ones. By the time Japan finally conceded to the Allies, some 530 theaters had been burnt to ashes. The number of movie houses stood at 845—about a third of the prewar total.[5]

In a climate of scarce resources, Hollywood decided to play it safe by turning to established networks. Shortly after his arrival in Japan, Michael M. Bergher rekindled distribution deals with the nationwide chains of Tōhō and Shōchiku. There were two advantages to this strategy. First, the CMPE could showcase its films in the nation's prestige theaters, such as the Shinjuku Musashino-kan (owned by Tōhō) and the Hōgaku-za (Shōchiku) in Tokyo, where foreign cinemas had traditionally enjoyed lucrative returns. Second, U.S. films could gain exposure outside metropolitan centers. Even after a devastating war, the two circuits still maintained a wide network that could broaden the circulation of American movies. During the first seven-and-a-half months after opening with *His Butler's Sister* and *Madame Curie,* American movies flourished through these established theater channels.

Change came with the arrival of a new director. Shortly after taking over the distribution business, Charles Mayer decided to increase the exposure of Hollywood products. On August 27, 1946, the distributor held a meeting with Tōhō. In an unprecedented move, the CMPE demanded that the exhibitor allocate a "minimum playing time [*sic*] of 50% for American pictures" in all existing venues (some seventy of them).[6] Similar demands were made to Shōchiku.[7] Concerned that the screen time for their own companies' film products would greatly diminish, Tōhō and Shōchiku refused to accept the distributor's terms. Tōhō's Sashō Shōzaburō, for instance, complained that the new proposition would bring "financial difficulty" to the company.[8] In mid-October, the CMPE decided to part ways with the two nationwide exhibitors. Conflicting interests brought an end to the relationship.[9]

Following its brief stint with Tōhō and Shōchiku, the CMPE turned to alternative venues. One was Nikkatsu, a former film producer that had operated exclusively as an exhibitor during the war.[10] Starting on May 1, 1947, the exhibitor agreed to commit twenty-nine theaters exclusively to showing American films (ten displayed Japanese films; three were split half-and-half).[11] Meanwhile, the CMPE approached a growing body of small-time exhibitors and independents. During the early postwar era, the exhibition field witnessed an unprecedented growth of small-size venues in cities across the nation. Only a year after the war, as many as five hundred new theaters had blossomed. *Kinema junpō* remarked that movie theaters were sprouting as fast as "bamboo shoots right after a shower."[12] The CMPE aggressively courted these up-and-coming exhibitors. Three months after the breakup with Tōhō and Shōchiku, the CMPE was able to lock up 275 venues with long-term contracts.[13] By May 1947, 728 movie houses were exhibiting Hollywood features.[14] *Eiga geinō nenkan* observed that the breakup with Tōhō and Shōchiku encouraged the small-time theaters to "actively acquire American movies." Motivated exhibitors, the almanac noted, were achieving "success" as American-movie exhibitors.[15]

Reforming Exhibition

The CMPE's attitude toward independent exhibitors was rigorous. Relying on its bargaining power as the sole handler of American products, it imposed higher rental costs on Japanese exhibitors. Traditionally, the rental fee of a Hollywood movie was 15 to 25 percent of its box office return.[16] Following a precedent used against Tōhō and Shōchiku, the CMPE demanded a blanket 50 percent rental fee of all exhibitors—a rate that, even in the United States, was set only for special road-show screenings for prestige films such as *Gone With the Wind* (1939).[17] The distributor, in addition, instituted the system of block booking and blind buying. This arrangement enabled the CMPE to sell packages of twenty-six or fifty-two films without granting exhibitors the right to choose the specific titles. In many cases, the distributor required the "bicycling" of prints from one theater to another. This was a means of making up for the shortage of film supplies.[18]

Furthermore, the CMPE moved to reform exhibition practices. Although happy with its leverage over the small-time exhibitor, the CMPE quickly noted that its affiliates often lacked the resources or discipline to succeed. Most of these independent businesses, *Asahi shinbun* complained in November 1946, were saddled with "poor theater facilities" and were "hardly comparable to the theaters of Tōhō and Shōchiku."[19] The CMPE lamented that these Japanese movie houses lacked the ability to "draw the upper classes."[20] Intent on distancing the community of American-movie exhibitors from the trade's unflattering reputation as "lowbrow" and "illegitimate," Mayer preached the "responsibility of the exhibitor" to its affiliates.[21] On September 26, 1948, at a board meeting at the MPEA headquarters in New York, Mayer reported to his superiors that the CMPE was doing its best to "educate the Japanese people in methods of theatre operation."[22]

Mayer's office reached out to exhibitors in multiple ways. It published *MPEA News,* a monthly newsletter, which offered advice on theater management.

Regional branches occasionally issued handouts for exhibitors in their area. The CMPE also organized a series of forums and informal gatherings with theater managers across regions. These sessions offered a rare chance for exhibitors, scattered across cities, to bond in a community as Hollywood exhibitors. "For the first time in [the] history of film business in that country," boasted the MPEA's newsletter published in the United States, the "nation's exhibitors from every province [were] invited to sit down with distributors, air grievances and offer suggestions for improvement in service and operations."[23]

One of the main emphases of this reform campaign was to assure the sanctity of the contract. To the distributor's dismay, many Japanese exhibitors violated their deals by diverting Hollywood's prints to theaters without contracts and by presenting non-Hollywood features in spite of exclusive screening arrangements. The CMPE repeatedly condemned such practices and punished exhibitors with fines and contract suspensions.[24] The company also curtailed illegal activities conducted by its own employees. Noticing that its sales agents sometimes demanded bribes, gifts, and meals, the distributor encouraged exhibitors to report "inappropriate" behavior by its own employees. The managing director fired those who appeared to profit under the table.[25]

Mayer's office, then, called for qualitative improvements to the theaters. While aware of the general shortage of equipment and resources, the CMPE was greatly dismayed at the poor hygiene of theaters. Observers during the occupation era commonly pointed out that theaters suffered from poor ventilation, high humidity (during summers), and uncomfortable temperatures (hot in the summer, cold in the winter).[26] It was not rare to encounter rats, mice, fleas, and ticks; poor physical conditions even forced SCAP to sterilize the theaters in Tokyo to prevent the spread of typhus and other contagious diseases.[27] The CMPE repeatedly advised theaters to sweep the floors, clean the toilets, and wash the entrances. If theaters could not afford to buy soap, they could at least refresh the air a few times a day, particularly during the hottest summer afternoons.[28] The distributor also stressed the importance of equipment maintenance—specifically projectors and screens. Sanitation was a relatively easy task, the distributor stressed, because it simply "did not cost money."[29]

The CMPE also promoted effective advertising. The reason was simple: publicity, noted Charles Mayer, was "the most important [aspect of] the movie business."[30] As a way of generating public attention, the distributor, in *MPEA News,* urged exhibitors to bolster their structures with large marquees, colorful neon lighting, and flamboyant decorations.[31] The company also suggested the use of daily publications (mostly newspapers) as well as tie-ins to create an extra buzz in the community.[32] Poster and still-photo exhibits were particularly

Figure 6.1. The Central Motion Picture Exchange cautioning against "excessive erotic advertising." *MPEA News* 21, n.d., 4. Courtesy of Yamada Noboru.

effective in drawing attention, noted the CMPE.[33] In addition, exhibitors were encouraged to publish their own movie programs—"cultural guides" according to the distributor. The CMPE recommended that theaters distribute these to consumers free of charge.[34]

The CMPE's concern with publicity involved content as well as form. Eager to perpetuate the demand for movies, Mayer's office instructed exhibitors to announce upcoming films on their programs and screen trailers.[35] The distributor also called for clarity in publicity. One of the problems was the exhibitors' tendency to publicize both the ongoing and forthcoming releases on the same marquee. In an attempt to eliminate confusion, the distributor instructed its affiliates to publicize the featured film on the marquee, while advertising upcoming pictures indoors.[36]

The CMPE, in addition, advocated respectable content in advertising. The distributor noticed that exhibitors at times violated its standards of decency. On one occasion, the CMPE spotted a troubling ad for *Anna and the King of Siam*. Created by an exhibitor in Wakayama Prefecture, this visual display featured a scantily clad Asian (presumably Thai) woman posing in the style of Edouard Manet's infamous painting *Olympia*. The ad identified the Twenti-eth Century–Fox film as a "Picture scroll of lust and eroticism hidden deep in the palace" and warned that "Children should refrain from watching this movie." Outraged at this distorted portrayal of an Oscar-winning production, the CMPE suspended film distribution to this theater for a full month.[37]

The CMPE further instructed exhibitors to create a respectable atmosphere in the theater. This, for example, required theaters to select appropriate music for intermissions and to avoid the use of regional dialects in their introductory announcements.[38] The CMPE was also concerned with social order. Since the prewar decades, Japanese exhibitors commonly employed a "packing-in" (*tsumekomi*) or "flowing-in" (*nagashikomi*) system, in which exhibitors allowed audiences to fill the theater space without any regard for seating capacity. The CMPE criticized exhibitors who dangerously crammed their venues, arguing that the practice overlooked hygiene, safety, and moviegoers' enjoyment.[39] As an alternative to the packing-in format, the CMPE urged exhibitors to limit admission to seating capacity. Regulated seating was better than otherwise, CMPE argued, because "audiences purchase tickets to enjoy the movie, not to learn how to survive in packed trains."[40]

Good Movies to Good Theaters

The CMPE's campaign did not end with recommendations. It urged business reform by relying on competition for products. William Schwartz, publicity manager of the CMPE, once noted that improvements in theater operation would depend on the "competitive spirit" of the venues.[41] The distributor in-creasingly put forth this agenda after its first year. During his first visit to Japan in October 1947, MPEA vice president Maas called for a "superior theater policy" that rewarded favorable distribution arrangements for better-equipped movie houses.[42] Maas's policy was soon implemented in Tokyo. A year after the break with Tōhō and Shōchiku, the CMPE assigned its affiliates into three groups: "A," "B," and "C" (the latter was the Nikkatsu chain). In November, the distributor decided to break up the "A" and "B" categories to privilege theaters that had "better" services and facilities.[43] This practice soon became known as the "good movies to good theaters" policy.[44]

The CMPE pursued quality improvement by making extensive use of the run system. It provided best-conditioned theaters with new releases. These venues typically enjoyed their status as first-run theaters, usually operating in conspicuous locations in large metropolitan centers. Following the screenings in these coveted outlets, prints were passed on to second-, third-, and lesser-run theaters. These lower-ranked theaters were typically second-class venues in metropolitan areas or local cities with modest population size. More likely than not, these theaters were forced to screen damaged prints. To a select group of theaters, CMPE granted a special road-show status. Usually given to only one theater per large city, the road-show format guaranteed exclusive screening of prestige films before they reached the first-run houses.[45] These "rankings" of theaters were never permanent. If the quality of lesser-run venues improved considerably, CMPE "upgraded" them with favorable runs. Theaters with diminishing services could easily lose their status as well.[46]

Moreover, the CMPE gave awards and prizes to theaters with impressive services. In 1947 the distributor inaugurated an annual award of "superiority" for a select number of theaters from across the country. The criterion for judgment involved the overall quality of presentation. This included the cleanliness, service, comfort, and quality of equipment.[47] The CMPE also hosted contests designed to improve the theaters' mode of presentation. In these events, the distributor doled out prizes to theaters with "superior" management, promotional efforts, and sales strategies.[48] At one contest, the CMPE announced that it would release *Gulliver's Travels* (1939), a rare Technicolor animation, to theaters that carried out superlative efforts in promotion, service, and sales. If the winners were able to maintain their high standards, the CMPE might supply other prestige features, such as *State Fair* (1945).[49]

Moreover, the CMPE granted what it considered a "symbolic privilege." To qualified exhibitors, the distributor gave permission to embellish the front walls and marquees with the familiar logos of American studios and their umbrella organization, the Motion Picture Export Association. American-movie exhibitors could also display a large emblem that read: "Home of American Movies."[50] The CMPE treated the slogan as a status symbol for the Japanese to seek and earn. In July 1947, *Motion Picture Herald* noted that "dozens" of first-run houses had been "sold on the prestige value of setting up permanent display fronts with identification proclaiming that theirs is 'The Home of American Movies'."[51]

Cultures of Exhibition

The exhibitors' response to Hollywood was not monolithic or uniform. Some were unhappy with the CMPE's hard-nosed business attitude and complained that the 50 percent rental fee was simply too expensive. For example, Kawakita Nagamasa, a well-known handler of European films, groused that the high rental costs of American films were "doing permanent harm" to the Japanese movie business "by causing bad exhibition conditions."[52] These exhibitors could turn to Japanese companies, which were struggling throughout the occupation era but were gradually restoring their output.[53] Another option was European cinema. Although their presence in defeated Japan was limited, imports from Britain, France, Italy gradually increased. In 1946 foreign films released through official channels were all American; three years later, over 150 foreign productions circulated in the market, 61 of which were not from the United States (see table 4.1).

To many others, however, Hollywood was a source of opportunity. Hundreds of aspiring theaters—varying in location, size, services, and reputation—worked with Hollywood to make a name for themselves in a competitive marketplace. In a time when Japanese filmmaking was struggling, Hollywood seemed to promise a rich lineup. Becoming an American-movie exhibitor appeared to bring other advantages, such as public attention, cultural respectability, and institutional legitimacy. Although the reasons and motives varied by the exhibitor, the CMPE's imposing business agenda did not stop them from working with Hollywood. American-movie exhibitors interacted with Hollywood to fulfill their own objectives. In so doing, they invested their energy and services to expand the draw of the American brand.

We now turn to three exhibitors that exemplified the entrepreneurial spirit of the exhibition community. Two of them, the Marunouchi Subaru-za in Tokyo and the State-za in Nagoya, were "privileged" theaters that thrived on long-term contracts with the CMPE. The third, the Nagasaki daiichi kokusai gekijō, was a small "unprivileged" venue that screened CMPE's products for less than two months. How did each exhibitor work with the CMPE? What were their business strategies? How successful was each theater as an American-movie exhibitor? In what ways did they adapt and reinvent Hollywood entertainment? The answer to such questions requires a close look at their individual operations.

Marunouchi Subaru-za

The Marunouchi Subaru-za was a special theater. Located in the busy Marunouchi district in the heart of Tokyo, this mortar-covered wooden structure specialized in Hollywood's new releases during the early postwar years. Movie fans adored this prestige theater decorated with the epitaph "Home of American Movies" on the front wall; the trade championed this midsized venue as a an "ideal [site of] exhibition."[54] Fans flocked from various areas of the metropolis, as well as from its "satellite cities"—including Chiba, Urawa, Omiya, Hachioji, Yokosuka, and Kamakura—to savor the experience at this coveted theater.[55] The aura that boosted the theater's reputation in the wake of the war endured throughout Japan's recent past. Forty years later, a famous film critic recalled the occupation era and emphatically wrote: "One cannot discount the Subaru-za from any social history of postwar Japan. . . . [The theater was] beyond first-rate."[56]

The Subaru-za came to life in the largest urban market in Japan. By the summer of 1947, Tokyo, with an estimated population of 4.7 million, was home to as many as 155 movie theaters. In order to oversee the 44 theaters under contract, the CMPE divided the metropolis into three geographic zones.[57] Marunouchi was a district of particular interest to the CMPE. Traditionally, it thrived as a financial center. It was also adjacent to the Ginza, a lively commercial area that flourished as a hub of "modern" life during the interwar years. Despite the destruction wrought by the war, the district was a convenient access point for train and bus systems, and it continued to maintain a reputation as a place where the political, business, and culture elites congregated.[58] The climate stood in stark contrast to the "low city" neighborhoods such as Asakusa, a working-class district known to draw a much higher proportion of "ordinary" citizens—including factory workers, engineers, small shopkeepers, and farmers—to popular entertainment.[59]

This distinguished theater originated from a meeting on February 9, 1946, when a group of nine young and middle-aged men gathered in Tokyo to inaugurate an exhibition company, the Subaru Enterprises, Co. Ltd. Most of the founders were outsiders to the movie business with more work experience with the Mitsubishi conglomerate, but all were determined to break new ground in the exhibition field.[60] In the company prospectus, the founders expressed dismay at the "unhealthy" state of the existing theater business and the "vulgarity" of the movies. Through the management of their own venues, they vowed to replace "lowbrow" movies with "superior" products, while transforming "outdated" theaters into "cultural institution[s]."[61] As a way of displaying their commitment and cooperative spirit, they named the company after a famous constellation of stars: the Pleiades, which in Japanese is called Subaru.[62] Armed with a modest capital of 180,000 yen and a novice's zeal, Subaru Enterprises set out to make a name for itself in the postwar movie market.

In starting their business, the Subaru-za decided to court the support of the occupation forces. Tōyama Fukio, the company's inaugural president, utilized

Figure 6.2. Principal officers of Subaru Enterprises and the Central Motion Picture Exchange posing in front of the Subaru-za in Tokyo. Charles Mayer is in the front row, sixth from the right. Courtesy of Asaoka Hiroshi.

his acquaintanceship with Michael Bergher.[63] The distributor's response was favorable. In a memo dated April 17, 1946, the inaugural head of the CMPE "welcomed" the company's desire to build an "upscale" theater and promised to support the plan. Bergher's colleagues at the Civil Information and Education Section were also pleased with the idea. Major H. L. Roberts assured "full support" for the construction and maintenance of such a theater, and requested that Japanese authorities allow Subaru Enterprises to construct new venues.[64] Thanks to the occupiers' backing, Subaru Enterprises was able to open three movie houses by the end of the year: the Meiga-za, the Orion-za, and the Subaru-za.

The three theaters were each widely known as a "shrine" of Hollywood's new releases. The Subaru-za, however, earned the highest accolades because of its presentation format. On March 25, 1947, the Subaru-za became the first "permanent" road-show theater in the nation.[65] Employed by New York's Astor Theater to showcase such prestige productions as *Gone with the Wind,* the road-show system not only granted exclusive screenings of a given film before other theaters, but it also allowed for extending the dates of the screenings, based on popularity of the feature presentations. The lineup was largely devoid of B westerns and *Tarzan* movies that circulated in less-coveted venues. Instead, the Subaru-za received what one manager labeled "artistically high" films that included literary epics (*Jane Eyre,* 1944), Broadway adaptations (*The Philadelphia Story,* 1940), acclaimed melodramas (*Random Harvest,* 1942), biographical films (*Rhapsody in Blue,* 1945), Technicolor productions (*The Yearling,* 1946), and prestigious "male melodramas" (*The Best Years of Our Lives,* 1946).[66] A third of the theater's releases were Oscar winners.

The road-show system enabled the Subaru-za to market its products broadly. Since the distribution format guaranteed the possibility of longer runs, the Subaru-za was able to allocate greater funds for advertising than the average movie house. The exhibitor, thus, was able to cast its net widely, relying on posters, billboards, still photos, magazines, radio, and electric news boards.[67] Over half of the promotional budget went to newspaper ads. Subaru Enterprises particularly valued the major newspapers—the *Asahi, Yomiuri,* and *Mainichi*—because of their large circulation. Major newspapers were "effective a few times [more]" than other publications, a company publicist claimed, because they reached out to the hard-working *salari man* and "penetrated deeply into households."[68]

The Subaru-za also devoted considerable effort to publishing programs for sale in the theater. Even though program publications were commonplace among elite exhibitors since the prewar years, the Subaru-za's were lavish in design and meaty in content—sometimes running up to forty pages.[69] A company publicist boasted that theirs was "close to being a magazine."[70] Each program amplified the feature presentation with articles and essays written by film critics, industry professionals, and the culture elites who joined the American Movie Culture Association (see chapter 7). The programs included synopses, profiles of stars and production crew, commentaries, still photos, and illustrations of the films' memorable scenes. While differing in content from issue to issue, these Subaru programs overall presented the films as artistic works, celebrating Hollywood's on-screen world as a representation of "high culture" and "sophisticated" lifestyle typical of the United States. They became known as "Subaru souvenirs" (*Subaru miyage*) and have become collectors' items.[71]

While cultivating attention and respect through various print materials, the Subaru-za also took pains to dignify its social atmosphere. The key strategy was reserved seating. Instead of allowing moviegoers to crowd in, the theater limited admission to seating capacity. This policy, rarely seen before the war, guaranteed unusual comfort to patrons. It helped restore spatial order by guaranteeing that viewers, as an ad on *Yomiuri shinbun* boasted, could simply "sit and relax in their seats."[72] Reserved seating also developed a respectable atmosphere by treating patrons, as the exhibitor boasted, as "ladies and gentlemen."[73] Differing from its rivals, the Subaru-za specifically asked (male) audience members to place their hats beside their laps during the screenings. It also prohibited smoking in the auditorium.[74] Furthermore, in order to cultivate a refined milieu, the theater employed young usherettes to escort patrons to their designated seats.[75] Managers closely monitored their uniforms, hairstyle, makeup, bowing manners, and language.[76]

An additional attraction inside the theater was the love seats installed in the back rows. These "romance seats," as they were dubbed, were an instant hit. Although only twelve such seats were installed, this amenity drew a flurry of media attention. Romance seats also had social ramifications. They colored movie going with an aura of romance, as did a number of its feature productions. They enticed fans to date at the movies. Romance seats, furthermore, encouraged moviegoers to view heterosexual dating as a wholesome experience. By wooing couples to a respectable atmosphere that the exhibitor strove to maintain, the Subaru-za helped disassociate heterosexual dating from the "lowly" *kasutori* culture—a budding subculture shaped by sleazy pulp magazines and sexually driven amusements.[77] Romance seats assisted the promotion of public romance as an acceptable and even respectable experience.[78]

The Subaru-za's mode of business also achieved temporal order. In most other theaters, patrons could wander in and out at will; under the Subaru-za's policy, ticket-holders could only attend one screening, at a specific time and date inscribed on the bill. This arrangement encouraged punctuality. The Subaru-za's obsession with time management became apparent in the auditorium as well, where screen curtains were used as punctuation after each show, as well as between shorts (newsreels, trailers, etc.) and feature presentations.[79] In addition, the company carefully controlled the screen time of each presentation. The theater's vice manager saw to it that each screening would run exactly on schedule, in particular by preventing technicians from skipping reels or accelerating the speed of the projection.[80] In one of its programs, a Subaru-za manager admitted that his seating system created confusion at first. Yet once audiences had sampled the less-congested space, they appeared to enjoy it. The manager took pride in the fact that many of his patrons "scheduled a few hours [of movie viewing] in their monthly plans."[81]

To cap off its efforts to elevate its prestige value, the Subaru-za hosted premieres and special screenings with Japan's top elites. The exhibitor regularly invited the most visible and prominent figures, such as politicians, professors, public officials, business executives, and various culture elites—writers, journalists, artists, intellectuals, musicians, doctors, and film critics. On special occasions, SCAP officers and the imperial family were also present. Perhaps the most noteworthy screening took place on March 26, 1948, the day the Subaru-za hosted the gala premiere of *Gulliver's Travels*. The premiere of the 1939 Technicolor animation, which was cohosted by the American Movie Culture Association, welcomed a diverse array of dignitaries led by Crown Prince Akihito—who was turning into a popular celebrity. The public appearance of the young prince attracted a large crowd of onlookers and journalists at the front entrance. A company executive who presided at the event confessed: "I couldn't stop my tears from flowing out of my eyes. I stood there glancing at His Highness ascending the stairs, amid the flare of strobe lights and spotlights."[82]

Their various efforts to scale up entertainment earned the Subaru-za profits, prestige, and nationwide attention. But these rewards were not permanent. As Subaru-za basked in the limelight, the number of American-movie exhibitors—first- and second-run venues in particular—multiplied in the metropolis. By 1949 the Subaru-za's business had become "more challenging" because of the appearance of theaters with better facilities.[83] Subaru Enterprises also suffered from unwise business decisions. Beyond running the three theaters in Marunouchi, the company acquired two other movie houses—one in Kyoto and the other in Osaka—and invested in a seaside bathing resort, a tennis club, and an amusement park project. These hasty investments drove the company into debt; Subaru Enterprises temporarily lost ownership of the Subaru-za and had no choice but to fire a quarter of its employees.[84] In December, the company lost its screening rights for American movies and turned to European distributors to stay in the business.[85] Ironically, the Subaru-za fell victim to its remarkable success.

Nagoya State-za

While the Marunouchi Subaru-za was enthralling thousands of Tokyoites with its popular road-show screenings, Hollywood was discovering a passionate following in Nagoya. Once damaged by intense Allied bombings, the nation's third-largest city, with an estimated population of eight hundred thousand, underwent rapid recovery. By spring 1948, an impressed journalist noted—perhaps with some exaggeration—that the "downtown area" was "showing a level of prosperity far beyond the prewar years."[86] Movie going became a lively pastime in this climate of recovery. According to an official history of the city, as many as eleven theaters had resumed their business only two weeks after the war.[87] The first CMPE film was *His Butler's Sister* (1943), which debuted in Nagoya a week after it did in Tokyo. At the Yaegaki gekijō, a war-surviving theater that exhibited the Deanna Durbin movie, the two-story space was jam-packed with zealous movie fans. Those who visited the venue recalled that the second floor of the building was about to "collapse onto the ground."[88]

The volume of movie going in Nagoya was far more modest than in Tokyo. By 1948 there were thirty-seven theaters in the city, nine of which exclusively featured Hollywood films.[89] The CMPE, however, found the city promising for three reasons. First, the CMPE's Nagoya office was thorough and active. Each year, Mayer commended the Nagoya branch for its commitment to improving the business.[90] Second, the exhibition business seemed to match the needs of the public. *Zenkoku eigakan shinbun,* a trade paper for film exhibitors, lauded the number of theaters in Nagoya as "ideal" relative to its population size.[91] Finally, the quality of the theaters appeared high. In a memo to SCAP's CIE, penned in November 1947, Mayer noted that American-movie exhibitors in Nagoya were "being patronized not only for the enjoyment received from the picture, but also due to the fact that some sensible treatment is received from the management."[92]

The Nagoya State-za appeared in this thriving theater scene, having been completed on October 30, 1946. Like the Subaru-za, the Nagoya theater was located in a lively downtown district: it was built on the Hirokoji, a traffic-heavy commercial avenue within walking distance from the principal train station. For its first three years, the structure was a Shōchiku exhibitor (then named the Shōchiku eiga gekijō, or Shōei for short). Managed by Nishioka Matsuo, a former school teacher who took great pride in pursuing an "ideal exhibition format," the theater captured the attention of the trade as a "modern movie theater" in the Chubu region.[93] The theater's business undoubtedly impressed the CMPE during this time. On July 1, 1949, it became a road-show theater for new Hollywood releases.[94] Now renamed the State-za, it opened with a ten-day screening of *Song of Love* (1947), a high-end biopic about Robert and Clara Schumann.[95] Equipped with five hundred seats, State-za prospered as "a queen of exhibitors," as the theater itself regularly boasted.[96]

The CMPE provided the State-za with a privileged lineup of Hollywood features. Like the Subaru-za, the Nagoya theater was able to offer multiweek screenings of prestige features, usually a few weeks after they debuted in Tokyo. Oscar-winning features such as *The Treasure of the Sierra Madre* (1948, a grim treasure-hunting tale by John Huston), *Johnny Belinda* (1948, a turbulent life story of a deaf and mute woman), and *Joan of Arc* (1948, a biopic of the French saint during the Hundred Years War) broke at this theater, weeks before appearing in the city's first-run houses. Others, such as *The Yearling* (1946, a tear-jerker about a young boy and a fawn), *San Antonio* (1945, a western set in late-nineteenth-century Texas), *Little Women* (1949, adapted from the Louisa May Alcott novel), and *The Adventures of Don Juan* (1948, the Errol Flynn swashbuckler), were Technicolor features, which were difficult to come by. The length of the screenings was overall shorter than at Subaru-za. Road-show films in Nagoya usually lasted two to four weeks.

The State-za complemented its screenings with intense marketing. Just like the road-show venue in Tokyo, the State-za made extensive use of the local press—including the *Chubu nihon shinbun, Tokai mainichi shinbun,* and *Chukyo shinbun*—to advertise its feature presentations across the greater Nagoya region. Taking advantage of its conspicuous location, the exhibitor also erected a ninety-five–foot "windmill ad tower" to publicize its upcoming pictures.[97] Inside the theater, the State-za offered movie programs for each feature presentation. In contrast to the Subaru-za's hefty publications, the Nagoya theater's programs were four-page broadsides that briefly introduced the feature presentation, its cast of characters, and upcoming films.[98] Events and activities were abundant. In conjunction with the feature screenings, the exhibitor, for example, hosted concerts (to tie in with music-heavy films like *Song of Love* and *Paleface,* for example) and glass-case exhibits.[99] Premieres of road-show films were commonplace. One such occasion, the advance screening of *Arabian Nights* (1942) was so popular that the theater later "apologized" to those who were unable to enter the theater.[100]

The State-za also featured several "high-tech" amenities, which earned the CMPE's accolades. Unlike most of its rivals in the area, the State-za, for example, had an electric generator that enabled the theater to continue screenings during power blackouts—a common problem during this era. Equally impressive was its projection and sound equipment—which the CMPE praised as "superior" to that at other venues.[101] The theater also was proud of its newly added automatic doors. Its sixteen entry points could be opened and shut with the click of a button.[102] The State-za, furthermore, installed full-scale heating and cooling systems. This was a luxury that most exhibitors, even the Subaru-za, did not possess. During the hot summer season, the State-za advertised comfort in the form of "high-speed cooling."[103] Its ads commonly boasted that the indoor temperature was "ten degrees [Celsius] cooler than outdoors."[104]

While bragging about their cutting-edge machinery, the State-za strove to create a hospitable atmosphere. Learning from its rivals and predecessors including the Subaru-za, the Nagoya theater decided to open with full-time reserved seating. Patrons were encouraged to purchase tickets in advance, after verifying the screening times listed in the newspaper ads. To make things convenient, the theater made available a phone line, so that moviegoers could inquire about the films and screen times, and in addition, purchase advance tickets without visiting the ticket booths.[105] Later, by the following fall, the State-za switched its seating system to a "free capacity" format, which allowed its seats to be filled on a first-come, first-served basis. Even then, the theater continued to pursue audience comfort by restricting admission to seating capacity.[106]

The theater provided other comforts for its patrons. For example, they installed what one journalist marveled as "luxurious" chairs and an oval ceiling—which also improved the theater's sound quality.[107] The exhibitor added additional chairs in its lobby, veranda, and lounge and offered free tea.[108] An artificial pond provided aesthetic pleasure at the theater's "front garden," located on the right side of the entrance.[109] There, fans could sit and enjoy a water fountain, a miniature water mill, and koi in the pond, and forget that they were in the "heart of the city."[110] Overall, contemporaries were impressed with the theater's welcoming atmosphere. *Zenkoiku eigakan shinbun* wrote that the State-za offered services that were "impossible to imagine prior to the war." Theater owners from out of town visited State-za to study the business.[111]

The State-za flourished during the first two years of business. As the U.S. film industry's flagship theater in the Chubu region, its road-show screenings, according to *MPEA News,* broke box office records.[112] It earned the CMPE's honors as one of the twelve best theaters in 1950.[113] However, the novelty value of the theater gradually wore off. In July 1951, the State-za lost its road-show status and was "downgraded" to a first-run theater. Until the CMPE ceased to operate at the end of the year, the exhibitor joined one of the two first-run circuits in the city, releasing Hollywood films with a one-week turnaround. In April 1952, the State-za underwent a large-scale renovation and became a steel-structured, concrete-clad theater with 1,100 seats. Six months later, it resumed exhibition with *Gone with the Wind,* this time as an MGM affiliate. But the new State-za's relationship with Hollywood was rather brief. A year and a half later, the State-za returned to screening Japanese cinema as a Shōchiku affiliate.[114] By this time, other theaters in the vicinity took over the State-za's former role as a leading Hollywood exhibitor in the greater Chubu region.

Daiichi kokusai gekijō

On August 9, 1945, the United States dropped Fat Man, a deadly plutonium bomb on the historic port city of Nagasaki, three days after bombing Hiroshima. The surprise attack was a catastrophe for the city, instantly killing eighty thousand people. As in Hiroshima, the bomb left permanent scars in the minds and bodies of survivors—especially the aftereffects of radiation. Yet, unlike Hiroshima, the downtown district of Nagasaki was not totally destroyed, due to the city's hilly geography.[115] Social and commercial activities in Nagasaki revived weeks after the devastating bombing. It was in this climate that movie going also rose from the ashes. The earliest screenings began as early as several weeks after the war ended, when a handful of theaters began to show worn-out productions of Shōchiku, Tōhō, and Daiei.[116]

The size and scale of this urban market was modest. According to a 1947 survey, this city of 174,000 only had five exhibitors; in fact, only twenty-seven venues existed in the entire Nagasaki Prefecture.[117] Japanese cinema appeared far more dominant than foreign imports, and partly for this reason, the trade often criticized the city's moviegoers for their "lowliness." In the *Yūkan taimuzu* on New Year's Day 1950, for example, one journalist lamented that "conscientious" productions "did poorly at the box office" and that "types [of films] that did not require deep thinking" thrived in the mainstream.[118] Yet the transition from war to peace sparked a growing interest in things American.[119] After suspending its business with the Tōhō and Shōchiku chains, the CMPE released its films through the Nagasaki Central Theater, the first permanent American-movie exhibitor in town.[120] By spring 1950, three theaters were showcasing Hollywood films exclusively in the war-damaged city.

The Daiichi kokusai gekijō (DKG) was born during this time of recovery. This movie house was the brainchild of a group of returnees from Manchuria who founded an exhibition company in Fukuoka City.[121] The company's activities revolved around the Kokusai eiga gekijō, a 1,200-seat theater located in downtown Fukuoka.[122] The company soon decided to expand across the greater Kyushu region. Aijima Masato, a publicist for this company, was assigned the task of developing a theater chain. His first job was to build a movie house in Kagoshima, a large theater that seated 866.[123] Following his venture in southern Kyushu, Aijima arrived in Nagasaki and purchased the Wakakusa eiga gekijō, a theater exhibiting Japanese and European films.[124] They renamed it the Daiichi kokusai gekijō, or the "first international theater." Its business began on March 10, 1948.[125] The theater in Nagasaki was by far the company's smallest structure, with an official seating capacity of 282.[126]

The Kokusai eiga gekijō in Fukuoka was a prestige house that reigned as a leading Hollywood exhibitor in Kyushu. Like the Subaru-za in Tokyo, it broke box office records and won a CMPE award as one of the ten best theaters.[127] Although owned by the same company, the DKG lacked the status and amenities that the Fukuoka theater enjoyed. Unable to operate as an American-movie exhibitor, the DKG began as an affiliate of Daiei—a company, according to one film historian, that was "least interested [among the Japanese majors] in producing artistic films."[128] During the first year and a half, the DKG showed a hodge-podge of the company's period films, comedies, and gangster films. In selling these films, the DKG often turned to sensationalism. For example, the company advertised *Goblin Courier* (*Tengu hikyaku*, 1949), a suspenseful period film, as a duel between an "evil long-nosed goblin" (*tengu*) and a "thief [who appears like a] whirlwind. . . . blood [and] smoke will rise from the Tokaido [road]!"[129] The promotion of *Handsome Boss* (*Bibō no kaoyaku*, 1949), a gangster film, highlighted the story of an "evil protagonist" who "roamed around with a pistol, murdering and philandering."[130]

Although business with Daiei was profitable, the exhibitor desired to diversify its screen program. This led to breaking with the Japanese company in fall 1949 and working with European distributors—British, French, and Italian companies—to showcase their novelty products. The DKG then turned to Hollywood. The reason why U.S. cinema appealed was not its arsenal of prestige films that the Marunouchi Subaru-za or the Nagoya State-za enjoyed. To the Nagasaki exhibitor, the biggest allure of American products were the action-packed westerns and adventure films. The DKG particularly desired to exhibit the "*Tarzan* episode" type—which was in high demand according to contemporary citywide surveys.[131] In order to bring these lucrative products to his theater, Aijima visited the CMPE's Tokyo headquarters (rather than the Fukuoka branch), gifts in hand, to negotiate directly with Charles Mayer. After a few rebuffs, the distributor chose to reward the exhibitor's enthusiasm.[132] On February 21, 1950, the DKG became one of three American-movie exhibitors in Nagasaki.[133] Nonetheless, the DKG began to boast of its "exclusive" screenings of the CMPE's new releases.[134]

The films that the DKG received were eclectic. In contrast to the lineups of the Marunouchi Subaru-za or the Nagoya State-za, which consisted of a steady stream of prestige films, the Nagasaki theater screened films that cut across genre and cultural status. The DKG, thus, strove to accomplish two things. First, it sought to widen its fan base. When it advertised John Wayne's *Wake of the Red Witch* (1948), an ocean adventure led by a rugged sea captain, it hyped the "epic" of "adventure and romance" that would be of interest for "all fans."[135] The blurb for *The Adventures of Huckleberry Finn* (1947) stressed that the film was based on Mark Twain's "[literary] masterpiece," which "families could absolutely enjoy."[136] Second, the exhibitor sought to attract culture elites and educated audiences. This, for example, showed in the ad for *Welcome Stranger* (1947), a "witty" film on a par with *Going My Way* (1944).[137]

Ninotchka (1939), a popular comedy that dramatized the visit of Soviet officials to Paris, became a film that "intellectuals absolutely cannot miss."[138]

The DKG aggressively promoted these films via extended publicity. In addition to relying on local newspapers such as *Minyū* and *Nagasaki nichinichi shinbun,* it plastered the city with posters and handbills just as its rivals did. Some of the ads, Aijima later recalled, were intentionally pasted upside down to draw the attention of passersby.[139] In order to identify the target audience for each product, the DKG did something creative: it asked its employees to follow the patrons after the day's final screening. Although far more impressionistic than a thorough statistical survey, this method enabled the exhibitor to approximate the residential areas of interested consumers. After its employees conducted their research on foot, the DKG tailored poster and flyer advertisement to specific neighborhoods to achieve greater turnout. The theater, in addition, arranged special events, such as premieres, roundtables, and contests—often together with newspaper companies.[140] It also reached out to schools, film circles, and businesses.[141] It especially targeted the Nagasaki Mitsubishi shipyard (Mitsubishi Nagasaki zōsenjo)—the biggest company in the area. The exhibitor in particular adjusted advertising according to the company's monthly pay cycle to lure shipyard workers.[142]

While generating extensive ad campaigns and outreach, the DKG strove to reap profits by admitting ticket-holders regardless of seating capacity. Unlike road-show theaters in big cities, the DKG—one of the smallest movie houses in the city—had no interest in employing limited seating. Not only that, the Nagasaki exhibitor decided to rip off the back-row seats to accommodate standees.[143] While bringing chaos and discomfort to the viewing experience, this practice multiplied regular attendance far beyond the number of available seats. One survey taken during the busy Obon festival season in the summer of 1950, for example, revealed that the DKG was operating at an astonishing 747 percent beyond capacity.[144] Aijima recalled that because of the intense overcrowding, children who were unable to slip out to the restroom urinated during the screenings.[145]

Such mode of conducting business evidently did not please the distributor. Seven weeks after switching to American movies, DKG abruptly lost distribution rights of the CMPE's movies for good. In the following months, the DKG handled Tōei's new releases, at times resorting to "vulgar" hyperbole. For example, during the week of November 8, the DKG hosted a double feature of *Tokyo jūya* (Ten nights in Tokyo, 1950) and *Sutorippu Tokyo* (Strip Tokyo, 1950), the latter of which featured two female nude dancers, Hirose Motomi and Pearl Hamada. The ad for the screenings during this "seduction week" (*nayamashi shūkan*) displayed a photograph of a naked woman wearing high heels and promised to "draw you into a vortex of love and lust."[146]

For the DKG, however, the appeal of U.S. cinema remained strong. The brief business partnership with the CMPE confirmed that Hollywood could draw large crowds on a regular basis. It also enabled the theater to enhance its screen programming and widen its customer base. After spring 1950, the DKG continued to seek opportunities to exhibit American movies. It soon acquired the independent productions of Samuel Goldwyn and Walt Disney, which won the right to enter the Japanese market during the final two years of the occupation.[147] During the mid-1950s, the DKG prospered as an American-movie exhibitor. The brief stint with the CMPE was merely a preview of the exhibitor's later involvement with Hollywood.[148]

The exhibition of Hollywood films grew throughout the occupation. U.S. films found increased screen time in metropolitan centers as well as local cities where Hollywood culture had previously received minimal exposure. On October 1948, *Ningen keisei* reported that American movies were now screened in cities of five or six thousand, reaching "ten times the moviegoers of the prewar [years]."[149] By the time of MacArthur's departure, U.S. films were shown in some 1,100 theaters.[150] At many of these venues, the quality of film presentation seemed to improve as well. In a letter to an occupation official dated May 21, 1951, Charles Mayer expressed satisfaction with the expanding number of affiliates as well as their efforts to elevate the cultural standards of film exhibition. Mayer wrote: "We have...constantly campaigned for better, cleaner, safer, less-crowded theatres, and refused to show our pictures where excessive over-crowding was the regular practice, or where certain minimum standards of hygiene were not observed." He concluded, "We succeeded in this campaign to a considerable extent."[151]

The Marunouchi Subaru-za, the Nagoya State-za, and the Nagasaki daiichi kokusai gekijō were three movie houses that epitomized the energy and vivacity of the exhibition field. Although they ran the theater business in different places and in overlapping moments, they all enjoyed wide patronage in their communities. The Subaru-za led the way as the flagship theater in Tokyo. A road-show venue that showcased Hollywood's prestigious selections, it earned a national reputation as a "shrine of culture" in the movie business. The State-za basked in the limelight on a smaller scale. "Privileged" and equipped with "modern" facilities, this Nagoya theater spearheaded Hollywood's activities in the greater Chubu region. The DKG lacked the cultural status that the leading Hollywood exhibitors enjoyed, nor did it gain the Central Motion Picture

Exchange's full respect. It represented the business of a second-tier exhibitor in a modest-sized (and bomb-struck) city, with limited opportunities to screen American movies. Yet these lesser known theaters were no less vital in presenting Hollywood culture to local communities.

The exhibition of Hollywood cinema was a fluid exercise in collaboration. It operated in a larger interactive climate of business competition. The CMPE was an engine of this development. Determined to restore and expand its constituents, it wielded institutional power to secure the best available theaters and elevate the cultural standards of their business practices. Yet the exhibitors themselves were equally crucial. Intent on profiting from Hollywood, they actively engaged with the CMPE, presented U.S. film culture in the communities, and amplified the appeal of "America" in the Japanese market. Even though their relationship to the distributor involved tense moments, these exhibitors complemented CMPE's efforts to boost the attraction of American movies. Hollywood's "enlightenment campaign" expanded through the uneven workings of film exhibition. This business collaboration brought together a multitude of moviegoers—a subject to which we now turn.

Chapter 7

Seeking Enlightenment

The Culture Elites and American Movies

In 1949 Hori Makoto, an eminent professor and a member of the House of Councillors, penned a letter to General MacArthur. In the letter Hori expressed his deep appreciation for Hollywood motion pictures, not solely for providing pleasure and amusement in the cities and towns across the country, but, more important, for offering knowledge and information about the victor's moral values and cultural lifestyles. "American motion pictures," he stated in a tone of thankfulness, were "an important social force in edifying the Japanese nation. By presenting aspects of American democracy in a way we can all understand, these films are giving our people a better understanding of America and an insight into the better way of life in a democratic society."[1]

Hori's remarks captured the sentiments of a large number of learned and well-to-do patrons of Hollywood culture. During times of great change and shifting allegiances in Japan, American cinema drew together an impressive group of prominent individuals from a range of professional fields. This included politicians, journalists, writers, artists, musicians, film critics, and others—a group I will broadly call the "culture elites."[2] Like Hori, these prominent individuals approached Hollywood movies in part for plain amusement, but also to make better sense of American values as represented on the screen. The culture elites' fascination with Hollywood soon led to the founding of a nationwide organization, the American Movie Culture Association (Amerika eiga bunka kyōkai), which promoted the cultural significance of Hollywood entertainment in over sixty cities across the nation.[3]

The AMCA appeared in a social climate that General MacArthur took pains to control as head of the Allied Powers. Founded as a semiofficial publicity arm of the Central Motion Picture Exchange, it took on the mission of boosting interest in the narrative products. Charles Mayer was particularly eager to make use of the culture elites, believing that their reputation and wisdom would inspire moviegoers to see American motion pictures. He not only initiated the plan to bring these distinguished individuals together but also regularly provided "guidance" to maximize their function as agents of his "enlightenment campaign."

But the AMCA is also a story about the Japanese culture elites. While the seeds of the movement were sown by the CMPE, the culture elites actively participated in this interactive climate to better understand the "American way of life." Their other goal was to educate the greater population. Dismayed that the greater masses appeared incapable of comprehending Hollywood narratives in a satisfying manner, the culture elites joined forces to deliver new ideas and ways of thinking to the outlying population. Through these pedagogical practices, the culture elites not only conveyed knowledge and information to the public, but also reinforced their social status in an era of change and uncertainty. The AMCA reveals how an expanding group of prominent individuals re-established themselves by adopting an "organic" function in early postwar Japan. It shows how they did this by confirming their allegiance to the U.S. occupiers in times of dynamic transition.[4]

Film Criticism from War to Defeat

The world of motion picture entertainment was also a world of print. Writing and critiquing the movies became an institutionalized practice as cinema became a national pastime during the 1910s and 1920s. Early on, film-specific magazines such as *Katsudō shashinkai* and *Kinema record* carved a space for filmmakers, critics, and others to share their knowledge, research, and reactions to the screen medium.[5] The interwar era extended this practice. A host of new periodicals, led by *Kinema junpō* (1918), *Eiga geijutsu* (1925), and *Eiga hyōron* (1925), expanded the infrastructure for critical expression. In time, this climate bred a lively group of professional film critics—such as Iijima Tadashi, Hazumi Tsuneo, and Imamura Taihei—who also became leading public intellectuals of their day. Film criticism also spilled into mainstream newspapers and magazines such as *Kaizō, Sekai,* and *Bungei shunjū.* The range of this critical enterprise soon came to include journalists, musicians, literary scholars, and other noted professionals.

The critical community talked freely and passionately about a variety of matters. Its members not only analyzed, dissected, and evaluated the movies in their own terms, but they passionately disputed one another over the quality of a given narrative product.[6] Their interests commonly lay in the aesthetic and technological dimensions of the movies, such as cinematography, audiences, projection, lighting, music, sound technology, and subtitling. Efforts to compare the cinema to the other arts (such as literature, music, and theater) abounded.[7] Critics of this era looked to the West for inspiration. This was evident in their common excitement about U.S. and European films, as well as their translation of essays by German expressionists, French impressionists, and Hollywood moguls.[8] While gaining inspiration from these foreign imports, critics generally looked down on Japanese cinema. Disdain, distrust, and disappointment often permeated their discourse.[9]

The Pacific War altered the tone of expression. As in other intellectual fields, the climate of war inspired a "political turn" in the critical profession. Thanks in part to the Home Ministry's continuing pressure, Japanese movie critics increasingly turned to support the expansionist mission of the imperial government. Many left-wing writers "converted" (tenkō) to supporting the state establishment, while their uncompromising cohorts suffered mockery and imprisonment by the Special Higher Police. Instead of outright denouncing Japanese cinema for its "lowbrow" and "immature" disposition, critics, in this tightening political climate, delivered advice on how to utilize the movies for popular "training" (kunren) and "instruction" (shidō).[10] Film aficionados increasingly identified respectable quality in Japanese cinema. In 1939 Iijima Tadashi observed that the reduction of foreign imports led to an increasing number of "artistic products" from Japanese filmmakers. The prolific writer expressed "a great deal of respect... [and] joy" about this.[11]

At the same time, critics' views of international cinemas altered. While celebrating Nazi cinema as a model of art and mass mobilization, they gradually took a hostile attitude toward Hollywood. Even though the late prewar imports from the United States continued to fascinate many viewers, critics began to refer to American movies as "commerce-centered," "mechanical," and "opiumesque" entertainment.[12] The rhetoric turned militant as war with the United States became a reality. For example, in *Eiga to minzoku*, Hazumi Tsuneo urged readers to mount "criticism against American cinema," which has "continued to defend the fortress of American democracy."[13] Tsumura Hideo pushed things even further. Referring to the "Greater East Asian War" as a "thought war" (*shisōsen*), the staunch nationalist critic, in *Eiga seisakuron,* declared his will to "resolutely break from American cinema" and "declare war to destroy it."[14]

The outcome of the war devastated this critical community. Defeat shattered the morale and confidence of the once vocal jingoists. Those who willingly joined the imperial cause stood in a state of shame and bewilderment, only to regret the decisions they made earlier. Others expressed "repentance" (*hansei*) for lacking the courage to preserve their political and intellectual integrity against the pressures of the imperial war machine. Those suppressed during the war came out with a vengeance. Iwasaki Akira, a left-wing critic who was imprisoned because of his dissent, deplored the former jingoistic activities of his peers as "nothing less than [that of] war criminals."[15]

The occupation era marked a reversal from the years immediately prior to it. One after another, critics gave up their loyalty to Japanese cinema and vented harsh words against it. Criticisms commonly addressed technical shortcomings stemming from resource shortages, such as the darkness of screens or poor sound quality.[16] But the more damning words addressed deeper problems. For example, Tsumura, after doing his best to support Japanese filmmaking over the course of a losing war, remarked in 1950 that Japanese cinema had fallen "twenty years behind" the world's "top-level movie culture," particularly because of its "handicraft-like [mode of] production" and "elementary technique" of local filmmaking.[17] In *Eiga kanshō dokuhon,* a 1948 publication on the methods of film viewing, Iijima charged that Japanese cinema was short on "intelligence." While acknowledging that many wartime filmmakers suffered from the Home Ministry's "regulatory policy for [film] production," Iijima observed that postwar movie making largely lacked the "awareness of the greater society . . . [as well as] a sense of . . . collective responsibility in community life."[18]

Once again, critics began to display their allegiance to Hollywood. To Futaba Jūzaburo, the attraction lay in the crisp and coherent narrative style. In a 1950 tome titled *Amerika eiga (American Cinema),* Futaba outlined three admirable traits: rational (and efficient) craftwork, fast tempo, and cross-cutting techniques. In contrast to the "incoherence" and "contradictions" that seemed to pervade Japanese cinema, the narrative structure of American movies, the critic mused, was "well-calculated," "coherent," and "clearly structured." Hollywood, the critic marveled, had achieved "scientific perfection."[19] Others welcomed the values that were congruent with the occupiers' mission. Murakami Tadahisa, for instance, praised Hollywood for more than just offering a "free and delightful" experience as an entertainment medium. While acknowledging that the Japanese used to condemn American movies during the war for their "shallowness," Murakami now believed that Hollywood's commitment to wide-reaching recreation stemmed from its "democratic" aspirations. He urged readers to "grasp the energy" from the films to further their "recovery for tomorrow."[20]

The Culture Elites Organize

The Supreme Commander for the Allied Powers approached the critical universe with a skeptical eye. Aware of the critics' political function during the war, the Civil Censorship Detachment closely monitored the critics' expressive activities, as it did other literary and journalistic writings. But the occupation apparatus did more. On July 9, 1948, Harry Slott of the Civil Information and Education Section summoned a group of newspaper and magazine critics to directly "instruct" them on the practice of film criticism. Confident that critics "can greatly help" in rendering the movies "both entertaining and educational," the CIE informed the participants: "The job of the critic is to awaken the public to take an interest in improving the quality of films."[21] Like the imperial Japanese government that preceded it, MacArthur's SCAP headquarters treated critics as influential agents. "Instructing" and "educating" them became an important task for the "democratic" reconstruction of Japan.

Hollywood approached the field of film criticism with a different intention. It aimed to use the authority of the critical community to boost its commerce in the Japanese market. Beginning on August 28, 1946, Charles Mayer of the Central Motion Picture Exchange began inviting prominent and well-to-do individuals to special screenings, intent on using their "big-name endorsements" to develop advance publicity. The participants' mission was more than to simply discuss the films in the media. They were expected to render the films' "high level of culturalism" accessible to the lay public.[22] Mayer believed that the culture elites could expand the ranks of Hollywood's consumers by "systematizing the instruction of [filmic] appreciation."[23] This strategy soon became known as an "enlightenment campaign."[24]

Mayer's plan drew enthusiastic responses from academics, literary critics, poets, novelists, playwrights, dancers, musicians, artists, critics, and many other professionals. These culture elites immediately formed the Committee for the Instruction and Appreciation of American Cinema (Amerika eiga kanshō shidō iinkai) in Tokyo and erected regional offices in Osaka, Kyoto, and Kobe.[25] Its core members soon decided to expand the size and scope of the organization. This enlarged organization was renamed the American Movie Culture Association. On July 8, 1947, this new organization held a "flamboyant" inauguration ceremony in Tokyo. After a sequence of speeches by noted dignitaries, participants enjoyed a special screening of a literary adaptation: *Jane Eyre* (1944).[26]

The AMCA outlined its objectives in a mission statement. The articles of the new organization declared the intent of "appreciating American movies broadly and culturally" and of organizing activities so as to "contribute to the reconstruction of a democratic [and] cultural nation."[27] The new organization did not reject the study of Hollywood's "artistic nature," which prewar critics passionately explored. But it devoted greater effort to understand "America's lifestyle, philosophy, science, education, politics, religion...language, customs, and the subtleties of human nature."[28] In order to run the organization smoothly, the AMCA delegated logistical labor to its secretariat, while enlisting the culture elites for its American Movie Appreciation Committee. The main headquarters was located inside the CMPE's Tokyo office. This assured close access to Hollywood representatives in planning various activities.[29]

The AMCA attracted a larger number of culture elites from a variety of professions. Its founders consisted of literary scholars (Tatsuno Takashi, Hosoiri Tōtarō, and Honda Akira), journalists (Eito Toshio and Nakano Gorō), psychologists (Hatano Kanji and Shikiba Ryūzaburō), film/cultural critics (Iijima Tadashi and Haruyama Yukio), an artist (Fujita Tsuguharu), a playwright (Kikuta Kazuo), and a composer (Horiuchi Keizō). In addition, three prolific female writers—Hayashi Fumiko, Masugi Shizue, and Sakanishi Shiho—joined the group. These respected professionals were admirers of Hollywood. Most of them also looked down on Japanese cinema, because of its supposed poor craftsmanship and inferior cultural content. Few treated local cinema with the same respect that American films enjoyed.

Soon after its founding, the AMCA began to reach out to the greater public. It recruited fellow culture elites in and outside Tokyo and welcomed others to join with a fifteen-yen membership fee. In an era when day-to-day survival was a challenge for many, this financial requirement could have hindered community building. Yet within a matter of months, the new recruits hatched regional branches in Yokohama, Kyoto, Osaka, Nagoya, Wakayama, Matsue, Toyama, Shimabara, and Gifu. Before long, the AMCA was boasting over seventy branches and a total membership of over ten thousand from across Japan.[30]

The AMCA's members performed countless activities to sustain this expansion. They began by organizing premieres and exclusive screenings of select

American films.[31] Although the size of these events varied by location, they commonly attracted occupation personnel, public officials, celebrities, and distinguished figures in their respective locales.[32] In Tokyo, the AMCA invited prime ministers (such as Katayama Tetsu), cabinet members, and the imperial family. In other cities, mayors, governors, and municipal officers were regular participants. Unlike regular commercial screenings, the AMCA's events typically began with formal introductions by the culture elites and, at times, by SCAP officials and CMPE representatives. A unique air of formality enveloped these screenings.[33]

Outside the theaters, the AMCA shared its views of Hollywood culture in print. Determined to educate the lay public, members of the organization wrote about the political, social, cultural, and historical contexts of the movies. In order to spread the word widely, the AMCA founded its own newsletter, *Amerika eiga bunka* (American movie culture), which one member praised as a "cultural resource... [that] developed a new trend in film journalism." Local branches also developed their own publications. Their quality varied from professionally printed periodicals, such as the Nagoya branch's magazine *Hollywood,* to coarsely handwritten mimeographs like *Kudamatsu A.M.C.A. News* of the Kudamatsu branch in Yamaguchi Prefecture.[34]

The AMCA, in addition, organized a myriad of public lectures. As Hori once underscored, the AMCA aimed to "enlighten" mass audiences by way of a "classroom system."[35] In these events, each speaker waxed eloquent about the movies from their own professional perspective. For instance, journalists would offer first-hand reports on U.S. cities in response to the urban setting of a film; novelists would compare a literary adaptation to the original novel; doctors would decipher the psychology of sociopathic protagonists in thrillers and murder mysteries; female essayists would discuss the role of women in cinema and society.[36] These "movie classrooms" were held in movie theaters, city halls, high schools, college campuses, and even private homes.[37] The words of the experts also circulated through "information records," or recorded lectures that introduced the background and cultural values of films.[38]

The AMCA's lectureships took place alongside the CMPE's own speaker events, which relied on salaried employees who spread the word about Hollywood cinema across Japan. The AMCA's lectures differed in the lineup of noted professionals and were equally widespread. The activities of Haruyama Yukio provide an example. A famous commentator on a radio show called *Fountain of Words* (*Hanashi no izumi*), this noted poet and cultural critic made countless public appearances on behalf of the AMCA.[39] He held public lectures around the country during the occupation era. His twelve-day trip to

western Japan in the fall of 1950, for example, involved the following whirlwind schedule:

November 16: lecture at Kita-za (theater), Izumo Kon City; roundtable in
                 the evening
November 17: lecture at Kon Municipal High School
November 18: roundtables at Women's College and Sumiyoshi-za (theater)
November 19: lecture at Masuda-kan (theater); roundtable at Maruya Inn
                 (hotel), Ishimi Masuda City
November 20: interview with newspaper reporters; roundtable at Matsue
                 kaikan (theater), Matsue City
November 21: lecture at Yonago City Hall; lecture at Kokuyū tetsudō
                 kōkibu club
November 22: lectures at Yonago West High School and Yonago sentoraru
                 gekijō (theater)
November 23: roundtable at Ayabe shōkō kaikan (hall)
November 24: lecture at Maizuru High School; roundtable at local film
                 circle
November 25: roundtable at Junmei Elementary School, Fukuchiyama City
November 26: lecture at Osaka sennichimae sentoraru (theater)
November 27: lecture at Miyatsu High School; roundtable at local
                 public hall[40]

During his visits to the different venues in distant cities, Haruyama mingled
with a wide range of interested listeners. In a 1948 article that discussed his
visits to a handful of cities along the Sea of Japan, Haruyama recalled meeting
high school principals, newspaper editors, college professors, working women,
students, and employees of a railway company. The interest in the movies, Haruyama concluded, was "far more nationwide" than other literary and cultural
activities.[41]

Furthermore, the AMCA selected "superior" Hollywood movies. From its
first year, the association conducted a survey of American films to determine
the "superior" narratives that made notable "contributions to society."[42] Relying on the mobilizing power of its regional branches, the AMCA solicited
input from across the nation, inviting the participation of the Ministry of
Education, major newspaper companies, magazine publishers, film critics, and
relevant political, artistic, religious, and educational institutions.[43] The top selections were usually prestige films that gained critical acclaim in the United
States. For example, the top five films from the 1948 survey, which involved

some 2,500 culture elites, were the following (in order of rank): *The Best Years of Our Lives* (1946), *The Life of Emile Zola* (1937), *Arsenic and Old Lace* (1944), *The Farmer's Daughter* (1947), and *The Bells of St. Mary's* (1945). At the third American Movie Anniversary organized by the CMPE, Takase Sōtarō, the Minister of Education, thanked Samuel Goldwyn, the producer of *The Best Years of Our Lives*, and Hollywood for restoring "power and joy in our lives."[44]

Interpreting Hollywood, Imagining America

The AMCA made its name felt around the country at a remarkable speed, and this happened for good reason. The organization had earned SCAP's moral and institutional backing. Charles Mayer and the CMPE actively assisted the AMCA and coordinated screenings, roundtables, and other activities. Most significant, the culture elites were motivated. While engaging with their own professional activities, these learned men and women invested great energy in running the organization's day-to-day activities. Many of them became voluntary contributors as lecturers, writers, panelists, and radio personalities. What drove these individuals to take part in the organization? Why were they attracted to Hollywood? What were their thoughts and objectives?

To answer these questions requires a close look at some of the key individuals who actively participated in running the AMCA. We now turn to look at three important figures whose personal aspirations dovetailed with the AMCA's widespread action. Their stories do not represent the thoughts and careers of all members, but they offer us a window on the personal motives and actions that energized the AMCA community. The initiatives of these individuals were essential for the AMCA to flourish. Their thoughts and actions greatly contributed to the prosperity of the organization.

Nakano Gorō

Nakano Gorō was an outspoken man. Born in 1909, this graduate of Tokyo (Imperial) University spent the first half of his career as a journalist for *Asahi shinbun*. On the eve of Pearl Harbor, Nakano was a foreign correspondent in New York and Washington, DC. He cabled firsthand news about the United States. Deported from the United States seven months after the war began, he toured a number of cities across Japan to promote anti-American views to the population.[45] His writings, such as the 1943 book *Keishō* (Alarm bell), was imbued with outright fury: "Heat up the hostility to destroy America!/Hate

enemy America!/Hate enemy American public!/Hate enemy American civilization!/Hate enemy Americanism!" he exclaimed.[46] Nakano's opinions on
Hollywood were equally negative. In *Tekikoku Amerika no eiga senden* (*Movie
publicity by enemy America*), a book published three months before Japan's surrender, the raging journalist condemned U.S. cinema as a "morale-boosting
stimulant and…anesthetic drug" peppered with "erotic" and "hedonistic"
stories.[47]

Japan's defeat forced Nakano to reassemble his thinking. To a man once
so passionate for the imperial cause, defeat instantly transformed his wartime
jingoism to outright shame. Soon after the war, Nakano broke his silence by
saying that Japan's involvement in the Pacific War was a "rotten mistake."[48] In
the early occupation days, he began to repent his thoughts and actions that supported Japan's imperial expansion, while furiously blaming the bureaucrats and
militarists for misleading the greater population. Nakano also turned to the
United States for inspiration. He no longer deplored America as a materialist
and decadent society but expressed awe at the former enemy as a "superior civilization" that overwhelmed the Axis states in almost every conceivable aspect.
The United States was now his model for Japan's postwar reconstruction. It
was a ruler as well as an ally that could transform Japan into a "peace-minded
nation" (*heiwa kokka*).[49]

Nakano's professional activities in the wake of war reflected his intellectual
conversion. During the occupation, Nakano quit his job at *Asahi shinbun* and
became an independent critic. On newspapers, magazines, and radio shows, he
frequently voiced his thoughts about American culture and society, as well as
Japan's best course of action. Many of his essays were compiled in books such
as *Amerika zakkichō* (Notebook on America), *Amerikachō* (American style),
Amerika ni manabu (Learning from America), and *Amerika josei tenbō* (Outlook
on American women). In this context, Nakano joined the AMCA and became
a leading spokesperson. As a trustee, he regularly commented on Hollywood
movies and related them to broader issues of the politics, culture, and society
of the two countries.

Nakano's participation in the AMCA stemmed from a presumption that
American cinema was a superior vehicle for mass entertainment. From the
days of the Bluebird and Red Feather films of the 1910s, he wrote in 1947,
Hollywood represented "a sense of progress" that reflected the high cultural
status of the United States.[50] From an aesthetic standpoint, Hollywood's on-
screen images shined with "an astonishing degree of variation, color, and contrast [of light and dark]."[51] What also stood out in Nakano's mind were the
stars—such as Charles Chaplin, Bing Crosby, Ingrid Bergman, and Charles

Boyer—who appeared to have mastered the ways of drawing diverse emotions from the audiences. Because of such attributes, Hollywood cinema was, in Nakano's mind, a pastime that the "masses of all countries" could enjoy.[52] This stood in stark contrast to Japanese cinema, which satisfied the interests of only "a fraction of movie fans... and a small body of filmmakers in the business."[53] To the journalist-turned-critic, the difference between local (Japanese) and global (American) entertainment was stark.

Nakano was struck even more powerfully by what he took as Hollywood's lessons on American life. While aware that movies did not always capture reality, he contended that a number of U.S. films displayed the "bright and healthy family life" as well as the "relentless work ethic" of the American people.[54] Above all, Nakano believed that Hollywood showcased "democracy in action."[55] In a series of radio lectures addressed to teenage students in 1946, Nakano defined the elusive term "democracy" as a universal principle of individual freedom and the freedom of others. It was also an ideal that respected disagreement and minority opinion. Those who run a country need to take differing opinions seriously to best serve the public good, or otherwise, that society will fall under fascist or dictatorial rule. Democracy, furthermore, nourishes progress, happiness, and peace through hard work and action.[56] In Nakano's view, Hollywood was a medium that dramatized these important qualities. To him, American cinema was a "gospel of democracy" with a plethora of pedagogical messages.[57]

Nakano praised several specific films for offering meaningful lessons to the Japanese. *Boom Town* (1940) was one such example. The story introduced the off-and-on friendship of two business partners, Big John McMasters (Clark Gable) and Square John Sand (Spencer Tracy), who gambled on the oil bonanza in Texas and the Southwest at the turn of the twentieth century. A romance between Big John and Betsy Bartlett (Claudette Colbert) disrupts the partnership of the two wildcatters, and this leads them to part ways. As both men emerge as successful oil entrepreneurs, Big John begins to flirt with a blonde business associate. In an attempt to help Betsy, Square John arranges an antitrust lawsuit against Big John's oil firm. In court, Square John then testifies in support of his former partner, and this awakens Big John. In the end, the two men restore their friendship and resume their business partnership. The original romance revives and brightens the film's closure.

Nakano's fascination with this film had little to do with the central elements of the narrative, friendship or romance. He, instead, praised the film as a "100 percent American story." What fascinated him was the scale and dynamism of the petroleum industry in the oil states. More significantly, Nakano was excited to witness a high level of social fluidity. As friends and occasional rivals, Big John and Square John made their way up the socioeconomic ladder through hard work, bold financial investment, and good fortune. In the journalist's view, they were "American pioneers" who took advantage of economic opportunity. Prosperity in the United States stemmed from this "free and uninhibited life" that both women and men in America seemed to enjoy. *Boom Town,* then, showcased America's "youthful progress" as a nation. The film, Nakano believed, captured the "air of freedom of the New World."[58]

An even more impressive film from Nakano's perspective was *The Best Years of Our Lives.* The William Wyler picture portrayed the return of three Second World War veterans to Boone City, a fictional community in the American Midwest. The tone of the story was actually grim at times, as these men—particularly the working-class welder and the middle-class soldier who lost both arms in battle—struggled with psychological trauma and class prejudice. Yet to Nakano, the film deserved applause because it directly confronted the problems surrounding the repatriation of war veterans, with which the Japanese were all too familiar. *The Best Years of Our Lives* impressed the journalist also for conveying "passion and hope." The perseverance of the struggling protagonists, the compassion of the supporting cast, and the eventual triumph of the war veterans made for a "powerful" story that touted "a great culture of democracy" in the United States. For this reason he thought, *The Best Years of Our Lives* was "one of the very best movies" of recent times.[59]

These "democratic" messages embedded in Hollywood films were noble and valuable, but Nakano was concerned that the Japanese public lacked an attitude to appreciate them. While living in the United States as a foreign correspondent, Nakano discovered that American theaters welcomed citizens from all walks of life, be they "diligent workers or men and women with education and high social standing." In Japan, the movie-going climate did not welcome all classes. Japanese venues, he wrote in 1947, were "dominated by…adolescents covered with pimples or women of the night."[60] Nakano had little sympathy for these perceived audience groups, because they appeared to "cut school or escape from their workplaces while relying on their parents' financial support." Worse, Nakano continued, these moviegoers were likely to mimic gang activities after watching a gangster film, or indulge in "lewd behavior" after viewing a romance film—contrary to the occupiers' intentions. The movies were not to blame for such attitudes. These, Nakano charged, were the "sins" of Japan's movie fans.[61]

Nakano's goal as an educator was to promote what he, like many others, called a "correct" viewership. In order to promote "lessons of democracy" via the screen, Nakano urged moviegoers to take Hollywood seriously. He encouraged audiences to appreciate the richness and diversity of Hollywood's genres, tropes, and tastes. The AMCA trustee also advised fans to identify the films that they wanted to see, instead of visiting the theaters for an arbitrary escape. Nakano passionately preached the importance of studying the context and background of the movies. Instead of craving for Tinseltown gossip, Nakano argued that fans should read books on American society and life to decode the nuanced meanings embedded in the filmic narratives. Then the movies would nourish moral values and work ethic, thereby enriching a person's knowledge and everyday life. Ultimately, "correct" movie-going practices could elevate Japan's movie-going culture as a whole and approach that of the "superior" United States.[62]

Curiously, Hollywood, to Nakano, did more than offer a boatload of ideals that could guide Japan in a new direction. It also expanded his understanding of the immediate past—the Second World War—by providing useful lessons and perspectives. Defeat in war prompted Nakano to divorce himself from his wartime mind-set, but it did not drive him to forget or deny the horrors of that catastrophic experience. On the contrary, the journalist, now freed from an imperialist ideology that had once dictated his consciousness, developed a fascination with Americans' thoughts, experiences, and perspectives on the war. Nakano avidly consumed memoirs, reportages, and historical accounts of the Second World War, written by American veterans, journalists, and scholars. These accounts, he contended, could help explain Japan's involvement in the Pacific War.[63] Likewise, Hollywood, Nakano believed, projected American attitudes and ideals—keys to explaining the Allied victory. American movies, thus, were invaluable texts in accounting for the wartime past. They allowed him to develop what he later called an "objective" perspective on the Second World War.[64]

To Nakano, the making of a peace-minded Japan necessitated a comprehensive understanding of its destructive past. This was precisely what he pursued in his later years. After the occupation, Nakano remained a serious student of World War II. Labeling himself a "researcher of war history," Nakano, as an independent critic, wrote books and articles on this important subject and translated American war reportage into Japanese. The journalist-turned-critic also became nationally known as a collector of war-related books, letters, and memorabilia. He also served as a consultant for two World War II documentaries: *Arishi hino kamikaze tokubetsu kōgekitai* (The days of the Kamikaze Special Forces, 1953), which dealt with the Kamikaze pilots, and *Taiheiyō sensō no kiroku: Nihon kaku tatakaeri* (Record of the Pacific War: How Japan fought,

1956), an analysis of Japan's involvement in the Pacific War.[65] Nakano's quest for an "objective" understanding of war turned into an obsession that endured until his death in 1972.

Honda Akira

Honda Akira had much in common with Nakano. A professor of British literature at Hōsei University, he obtained an undergraduate degree from Tokyo (Imperial) University just like the *Asahi* journalist. Honda was also a public figure. Despite problems with physical health since his childhood, he was thriving as a prominent scholar and cultural critic by the late 1930s.[66] After Japan's defeat, Honda was a vocal supporter of the United States. While continuing his activities as a literary and cultural critic, the Aichi native sought inspiration from the outside world, particularly MacArthur's country of origin.[67] As part of this endeavor, Honda agreed to serve as an AMCA trustee, actively participating in the new organization. A passionate movie fan since his youth, Honda waxed eloquent about Hollywood in the early postwar years.[68]

Honda, however, differed from Nakano in one crucial respect. Unlike Nakano or most others in the association, he had been an opponent of Japanese militarism during the Second World War. An avid reader of liberal and left-wing works, including Karl Marx's *Das Capital* and Kawakami Hajime's *Shakai mondai kenkyū* (A study of social problems), Honda gained notoriety as a "progressive" thinker during the war and was blacklisted by government authorities.[69] In the months when Nakano was pumping anti-American fury to the masses, Honda, forced to abandon his profession, quietly retreated to the countryside and survived the hard times as an amateur farmer.[70] His distrust of Japanese cinema was clear throughout. In 1940, when thought control in Japan was intensifying, Honda crafted a short article for *Eiga no tomo* that criticized the government for forcing its politics on film producers. The obsession with "instruction," he argued, deprived the movies of artistic quality and mass appeal. It denigrated cinema to the realm of "preaching."[71]

In contrast to Japanese cinema, Hollywood seemed to lack that one-dimensional quality. Once the war came to a close, Honda, liberated from the Japanese war machine, joined the AMCA and fervently wrote about American movies.[72] Honda patronized Hollywood movies in part to find pleasure. In the months after the traumatic war experience, Honda continued to find hardship. Living at a time when the nation's future still remained in the dark, Honda approached American movies for emotional fulfillment. In an article published in *Eiga no tomo* Honda insisted that he "watches the movies to laugh."[73] Where

Hollywood succeeded as a source of pleasure and delight, Japanese cinema failed. In the same article, Honda criticized *Sensō to heiwa* (War and peace, 1947), which depicted a Japanese housewife's decision to remarry after hearing that her husband had died in China during combat. It turns out that her husband actually survived as a POW; his return to Japan yields suffering and agony to all three people. To Honda, this controversial film by director Kamei Fumio exposed the Japanese "lack [of] comfort [in their] minds." Kamei's film failed to deliver "any sense of hope" to the viewers.[74]

Whenever he was able to move beyond escapism, Honda engaged with American movies in search of aesthetic value. Unlike some intellectuals who despised the movies, Honda looked up to film as a "synthetic art" akin to literature and theater.[75] As a scholar of the written word, Honda paid special attention to screenplays and original stories. Films based on "superior" novels, such as William Shakespeare's *Romeo and Juliet* and Oliver Goldsmith's *Vicar of Wakefield,* could effectively engage and move the audiences, he claimed, even if the studios drastically modified the original texts. In Honda's mind, "high art" and "mass culture" were not mutually exclusive. Sophisticated artwork, he believed, could mesmerize the everyday consumer. What drew him to Hollywood was its ability to fuse "high" and "low" culture in a tight-knit narrative. According to Honda, Hollywood was proof that the artistic and the popular could go hand in hand.[76]

Furthermore, Honda valued Hollywood because of its pedagogical quality.[77] Despite his differing political orientation from Nakano, Honda shared with him the belief that American "culture" and "civilization" were superior to those of Japan.[78] U.S. movies, therefore, had much to offer—from social customs and material life to political values.[79] Most significant, Hollywood shined because it taught him about "humanism" (*hyūmanizumu*), a "mind-set to respect human beings."[80] During the war years, the term was curiously applied to describe a group of war films, such as Tasaka Tomotaka's *Gonin no sekkōhei* (Five scouts, 1938), that celebrated human bonding and emotional affection in relation to Japan's imperial polity.[81] Honda agreed that "humanism" implied a candid exposure of one's inner emotional qualities, but he also interpreted the term as a universal drive for compassion. Little of this appeared to exist in wartime Japan, but Americans, Honda believed, had exhibited this quality from the time of the Pilgrims on the *Mayflower* to the abolitionists like Harriet Beecher Stowe and beyond. Not surprisingly, Honda strongly advocated Hollywood for its championing of personal kindness and compassion.[82]

Honda's reading of American films often revolved around this humanistic theme. His commentary on *Sister Kenny* was typical. This 1946 RKO film was based on a famous written biography of Elizabeth Kenny, an Australian nurse, who developed an original treatment for children infected with infantile paralysis. Rejected by the stubborn medical establishment in Australia and England, Kenny used her self-taught methods to help sick boys and girls. Honda lauded the film's celebration of Kenny's "ultimate victory," but his appreciation was not limited to the uplifting finale. He also found virtue in the nurse's devotion to aid the "life and spirit" of all people as well as her will to confront the "big-name scientists" for the sake of "humanism." Moreover, he extolled the United States, where Kenny's unorthodox treatment received serious professional attention. "America," he wrote in awe, "is liberated from troublesome traditions," and its people "are not blinded by flamboyance, authority, or social status." For this reason, Americans were capable of "viewing the true disposition of humankind."[83]

Honda praised *Anna and the King of Siam* (1946) on similar grounds. As described earlier, the film narrated the story of a nineteenth-century British widow who went to Siam to serve as private tutor for the royal family. Like the occupation censors who lauded this film, Honda was moved by Anna Leonowens's tireless efforts to convey Western values to the king, his family, and his subordinates, while urging them all to respect one another as human beings. Interestingly, the Siamese palace did not appear to him as a distant space. Instead, its "stubborn feudalism" turned out to "completely [mirror] our Japan." While unconvinced that a woman could single-handedly "destroy" long-standing traditional behavior, Honda admired the effort Anna invested to "liberate" the Siamese women and other subjects of the king. Even though the story largely concerned the British, Honda argued that the John Cromwell film ultimately symbolized the "prayers of the humanistic Americans."[84]

Honda's applause for Hollywood humanism reflected his urge for vindication. His embrace of humanistic attitudes arose from his anger toward the Japanese military and those who voluntarily supported it with a "narrow-minded patriotism."[85] The scholar was convinced that the U.S. films he encountered after the war were aimed at the "reeducation" of those in Japan who had committed "inhuman crimes" during the war.[86] But Honda's goal was not to restore his dignity at the expense of the wartime jingoists. Despite his consistent antiwar views, this literary scholar held himself guilty for allowing the war to happen. His remorse was particularly directed toward the young people who were indoctrinated to fight.[87] Unable to prevent many of his own students from dying in battle, Honda candidly confessed his sense of culpability: "It was we adults who ruined Japan and put it into such a miserable state."[88] Honda's search for humanism was for others as well as for himself. The compassion he witnessed in the likes of Elizabeth Kenny and Anna Loenowens encouraged him to seek a new, pacifist Japan where the innocent and the vulnerable would be safe from harm.[89]

Honda's critical activities continued after the occupation, but his attitude toward young people changed over the course of time. In the spirit of a true educator, he advised students and adolescents through his books and other writings.[90] Yet his tone turned increasingly critical of youth in the late 1950s and early 1960s, as they engaged in political protests and student movements against the establishment.[91] Likewise, his respect for Hollywood diminished. By 1958 Honda complained that the Japanese market was saturated with "foolish" foreign films that "showcased" murder, violence, and eroticism.[92] What remained constant with him was his commitment to humanism and pacifism, which he passionately defended throughout his life. Honda was a maverick intellectual who remained true to his ideals. In the early postwar years, Hollywood was an opportunity for him to grapple with his own deep-seeded concerns.

Sakanishi Shiho

Sakanishi Shiho was an extraordinary woman. Born in Hokkaido in 1896, she came of age in Tokyo before deciding to gain an education in the United States. In 1922, Sakanishi enrolled in Wheaton College in Norton, Massachusetts, and earned her undergraduate degree four years later. Then, she attended graduate school at the University of Michigan in Ann Arbor. After obtaining a PhD in philosophy, Sakanishi began working at the Library of Congress as its first area specialist on Japan.[93] Her main job was to catalogue and collect Japanese-language books and resources. In her spare time, Sakanishi translated poems and *kyōgen* plays into English.[94] Her life in Washington DC was a fulfilling one, but the war forced her to abandon her career as an archivist.[95] Suspecting her to be a threat to national security, the Federal Bureau of Investigation detained her immediately after Pearl Harbor. She was forced to leave the United States in June 1942. On the ship bound to Japan, Sakanishi encountered Nakano Gorō. Little did she know that their paths would cross a few years later at the AMCA.[96]

Yet unlike the jingoistic Nakano, Sakanishi never hated the United States, even during the height of the war. To her, Pearl Harbor was a source of shock, not outrage.[97] Her analysis of Japan's prospects in the war was far from cheery. A keen observer of American power, Sakanishi was convinced that Japan could never win against the Allies.[98] When the Japanese government and military summoned her to gather information about the enemy nation,

Sakanishi delivered sobering assessments and annoyed the authorities.[99] The end of the war brightened her feelings. Shortly after MacArthur's arrival, Sakanishi temporarily worked for SCAP's Civil Intelligence Section.[100] She also started writing extensively in Japanese, and quickly became a prominent essayist, translator, and literary critic. In this context, she joined the AMCA with the other culture elites. As a trustee, Sakanishi—together with Nakano, Honda, and others—played an active role in expanding the organization.

As a spokesperson for the AMCA, Sakanishi advocated Hollywood films as a source of entertainment. In Japan, she complained, the public traditionally embraced a kind of "fastidiousness" (*keppekisa*) and was reluctant to consider "the act of having fun" as something "necessary for human beings."[101] The movies, as a result, became commonly associated with youthful delinquency and vice.[102] Sakanishi was more broad-minded. She fought against the stigma attached to the movies and encouraged public viewership.[103] Especially, in light of the fear and shock of defeat, people, she believed, needed release and encouragement.[104] Sakanishi specifically advocated Hollywood films because their signature optimism seemed to have therapeutic value. She thus argued that Hollywood cinema did more than invoke "mindless sentiments." It healed the "wounds of our minds, so that we could gain confidence and hope once again."[105]

Sakanishi also promoted American cinema to encourage popular self-education. To her eyes, Japanese moviegoers lacked the skills to improve their knowledge and understanding of the world. According to her, fans were good at memorizing the names of the actors, the films in which they appeared, the profiles of directors, and so on. But their efforts largely ended with fact and trivia gathering, far short of a "true [filmic] appreciation."[106] As an AMCA spokesperson, Sakanishi sought to alter this tendency. She actively promoted the study of the movies through books and family discussions.[107] Additionally, she encouraged critical thinking. Sakanishi's goal was not to impose her knowledge on the lay population. In promoting the movies as educational texts, she urged everyday consumers to ask questions and think critically about pertinent issues, just as she thought it was being done in the United States.[108]

Hollywood was a perfect medium for self-education. Sakanishi asserted this because U.S. cinema seemed to offer "culture [and] intellectual content" (*bunka kyōyō*).[109] She resisted the tendency to regard the movies as pure escapism, claiming that "American life as it appears on screens is, on the whole, a faithful depiction of real life."[110] Her statement may appear naïve, but it reflected her admiration for U.S. films that addressed serious social issues. These included alcoholism (*The Lost Weekend,* 1945), anti-Semitism (*Crossfire,* 1947), and family matters (*The Human Comedy,* 1943). Sakanishi favored these and other movies because of their accessibility, clarity, and "warm understanding and sympathy" toward people.[111]

Furthermore, Sakanishi lauded Hollywood because it taught people about "social responsibility" (shakaiteki sekinin).[112] Since SCAP's arrival, the Japanese had a welcome opportunity to "pursue [their] happiness freely," but Sakanishi worried that people were beginning to act too selfishly.[113] She thus preached the significance of self-reliance and respect for others as members of a new democratic society. Sakanishi especially called on women and families to adopt an attitude of social responsibility. As romantic partners, mothers, or caretakers of elders and siblings, women had to carry the burden of responsibility to protect the ideals of "freedom, equality, independence, autonomy, and human rights."[114] Social responsibility was not solely for the captains of society. Men, women, the young, and the old all needed to work with one another other to build a truly democratic community.

Many American movies seemed to preach the values of social responsibility. Sakanishi cited *Penny Serenade* (1941) as an example. In this episodic narrative peppered with popular songs, a young couple (Cary Grant and Irene Dunne) gets married and expect the birth of a child, until a large earthquake induces a miscarriage. They decide to adopt a five-month-old baby girl from an orphanage. To Sakanishi, this process of adoption was moving. The people at the orphanage, she noted, were patient and sympathetic to both the children and parents. The generosity of the institution enabled the young couple to adopt an "unfortunate child" and nourish a "warm family."[115] The young couple also impressed Sakanishi. By pouring love and affection to their child, the parents in *Penny Serenade* were also "being rewarded many, many times." This sentimental film taught a simple lesson of life: "For one to be happy, other people must be happy too."[116] Sakanishi lauded the Columbia Pictures movie for injecting "social significance" into on-screen amusement.[117]

The theme of family responsibility seized center stage in *The Yearling* (1946). In the early months after the Civil War, the Baxter family toils every day to survive in the forests of Florida. Survival to them is a difficult and cruel task: the father, for example, nearly loses his life after being bitten by a snake; the son (played by Claude Jarman Jr.) is forced to kill his pet deer to protect the crops in the yard; an unending storm levels their farm field. This Technicolor story, imbued with a "pioneer spirit," moved Sakanishi tremendously. She appreciated the boy's affection for the deer, as well as the "warm connection between human beings." What stood out the most was the father-son relationship. In this film, the bond between men enabled the family to overcome their difficulties. Sakanishi wrote that this relationship was a "noble" one.[118]

I Remember Mama (1948) was another film that impressed Sakanishi. This RKO film followed the daily life of a Norwegian-American family in early twentieth-century San Francisco. Throughout the narrative, the Hansons struggle to keep their family together through hard times. In spite of their financial plight, the illness of their youngest daughter, and the death of a gruff uncle, the family stays close to the mother (Irene Dunne), who shares compassion and kindness with everyone. The narrative celebrates the bond between kin and the maturation of children in a caring family. Sakanishi felt that *I Remember Mama* was powerful because it "effectively depicted the American family, and successfully represented the close relationship of husband and wife, parent and child."[119] Sakanishi also appreciated the treatment of women in the film. In contrast to the rather self-centered men—the father, uncle, and son— the female protagonists, especially Mrs. Hanson, "supported the men" through adversity. Sakanishi was delighted to see women's active efforts to support the family.[120]

Sakanishi's sympathetic reading of Hollywood movies was part of her urge to transform the Japanese into what she later called "desirable citizens."[121] Unlike Nakano, her goal in life was not to excavate the truth of the past. Her aim was to urge the Japanese to become "good citizens" in the present and the future. This was not an easy task, as it required responsible action everywhere—in schools, neighborhoods, offices, governments, and, most important to her, the household.[122] In the years after SCAP's departure, Sakanishi continued her education activities. She published books and essays on democracy, culture, and society, and advised various organizations, from the International House of Japan, the Nihon hōsō kyōkai (Japan Broadcasting Corporation), and the United Nations Education, Scientific and Cultural Organization (UNESCO). While doing so, Sakanishi continued to praise Hollywood for "reflect[ing] American attitudes, principles, and the American way of life... [and] leav[ing] the audience with something to think about." Until her death in 1976, Sakanishi tirelessly strove to building a democratic society from Japan's ashes. To a considerable degree, Hollywood, to her, was a tool with which to erect a socially responsible community.[123]

Nakano, Honda, and Sakanishi were bright minds in different professions. During the interwar era, they developed respectable careers through hard work and dedication. They held distinct ideological positions during the global conflict. But their paths unexpectedly converged in the wake of the Second World War. During the occupation, these talented individuals, together with hundreds of others, joined the AMCA and took part in its outreach activities.

Their activities were extensive. In countless occasions, they watched, wrote, lectured, debated, and meditated on American movies. The CMPE was impressed with the solidarity of the culture elites. In 1950 Charles Mayer noted that the "AMCA was not an appreciation circle for the masses, typified by an ordinary movie fan group, but an instructional nourishment institution for [serious] movie appreciationists."[124] Hollywood's top business organizations also took notice of the culture elites. In 1949 the Motion Picture Export Association praised AMCA as a "highly influential" organization that had "no counterpart in any other country in the world."[125] Four years later, Eric Johnston commended the AMCA for turning Japan into "an immense classroom in which millions of its people learned about us and our way of life through our motion pictures."[126]

Hollywood's satisfaction with the AMCA stemmed from its efforts to promote the movies as respectable, dignified, and educational amusement. The AMCA functioned to further the U.S. film industry's "enlightenment campaign." But the culture elites had much to gain as well. To these prominent admirers of Hollywood, the AMCA was a meeting ground where they could enrich their knowledge and intellect through dialogue and discussion. It also offered a space for community building. By taking part in this organization, members could cultivate a larger social identity apart from the lay movie-going public, which seemed in dire need of instruction for cultural elevation. The members of the AMCA appreciated the camaraderie beyond Hollywood's expectation. In 1954, three years after MacArthur left Japan, the AMCA renamed itself the Organization to Appreciate Superior Films (Yūshū eiga kanshōkai) and continued to engage with the movies. Even though the organization also turned attention to European, Japanese, and other national cinemas, Hollywood remained a central object of its exploration. Many of its participants became lifelong colleagues. Their critical activities continued throughout the twentieth century.

The culture elites were prominent actors in defeated Japan. The movie-going climate, however, involved more than these distinguished individuals. While the AMCA set out to convey their beliefs and passion to the larger public, tens of thousands of "ordinary" fans consumed Hollywood cinema with an equal degree of excitement. Many of them took part in forming larger communities of moviegoers. One of the most lively fan groups convened around a popular movie magazine that circulated widely in defeated Japan. Hollywood culture also grew from the youth—the core constituent of this publication.

Chapter 8

Choosing America

Eiga no tomo and the Making of a New Fan Culture

Nakano Yutaka was excited. A resident of Matsumoto, a city in the heart of mountainous Nagano Prefecture, he did not lose hope when many of his peers seemed to sink in despair in the drab aftermath of the catastrophic world war. What kept his spirits high, Nakano explained in 1948, was the cultural fertility of his hometown. This modest city of eighty thousand was home to thirty bookstores, fifteen schools, several dance halls and an "excellent" music school. Even more important to him was its lively movie culture. Junior high and high school students gathered in film clubs; school teachers took students to the movies; and galleries assembled photo exhibits of movie posters and stills. Of the city's six movie theaters, Nakano particularly cherished the two "modern" venues that specialized in American cinema: the Sentoraru-za and the Denki-kan. In a time when people suffered from "bleak conditions" following the war, films like *Boys Town* (1938), *The Human Comedy* (1943), and *Rhapsody in Blue* (1945), Nakano exclaimed, became "our beacon of hope." "We trek to the Sentoraru-za and the Denki-kan," the only two American-movie exhibitors in the wider Shinshu region, "as if we were going to church."[1]

Nakano was far from unique in the passion and excitement he expressed for American movies. He shared a common view with a larger circle of young consumers who read *Eiga no tomo* (Friends of the movies), a popular magazine that specialized in Hollywood cinema during the early postwar era. Immediately after Japanese theaters began to screen American films, this colorful publication became a widespread resource on Hollywood culture. Led by Yodogawa Nagaharu, its editor in chief, it also invited reader participation in various forms. In particular, *Eiga no tomo* distinguished itself as the host of Tomo no kai (Meeting of friends)—a fan club that attracted some ten thousand moviegoers in over sixty cities. This popular publication inspired young people to form a larger community of Hollywood fandom in defeated Japan.

Eiga no tomo's success did not emerge from a void. Larger forces assisted its creation and popularity. A crucial player that influenced the magazine was the Supreme Commander for the Allied Powers, which endorsed its publication in an era of paper and resource shortages.[2] Yodogawa's publication also depended on the Central Motion Picture Exchange, which permitted direct access to stills, portraits, and fresh news straight from the United States. To the CMPE, *Eiga no tomo* was a useful marketing tool, because it reached out to youth. By relying on the magazine as yet another instrument for Hollywood publicity, the distributor could cultivate new patrons beyond the American Movie Culture Association and the culture elites.

Yet, while benefiting the U.S. film industry, *Eiga no tomo* also empowered the "ordinary" moviegoer. The popular magazine brought together a new generation of fans, who crowded the theaters, gossiped with friends, wrote lots of fan mail, and organized group activities in their hometowns and surrounding areas. Although moviegoing continued as a casual pastime, the magazine's followers often visited the theaters for cultural and intellectual nourishment. Inspired by the magazine's call for action, many of them eagerly built a respectable community of Hollywood patrons. These young moviegoers were hardly "reckless" or "idle" consumers, as the culture elites often perceived them to be. Nakano Yutaka and his peers were determined participants who proudly built a new social space to gain knowledge, pleasure, and self-esteem.

Additionally, *Eiga no tomo* inspired the Japanese by presenting a pro-American worldview. Through its celebration of Hollywood culture, Yodogawa's magazine fostered a community of movie enthusiasts who gravitated toward the ideals and lifestyles of the United States. Seeking to enrich their everyday lives, these cultural consumers passionately engaged with "things American" and reinvented their thinking. Emerging in an era after the nation's collective agenda was demolished by the war, this monthly magazine brought Hollywood fare to its readers and inspired community organizing under a U.S.-led government. *Eiga no tomo* and its readers, in this sense, were political actors who supported the occupation. In developing their fan community, the young moviegoers actively chose to live under an American umbrella and to search for a better future.

The Rebirth of *Eiga no tomo*

The buzz about Hollywood films was a product of many hands. It involved filmmaking in the United States, the marketing efforts of the Central Motion Picture Exchange, the business aspirations of American-movie exhibitors, and the organizational activities of the culture elites. Hollywood culture also sprang from the expanding field of print. Immediately after Japan's defeat, the publishing business underwent a quick recovery. Movie magazines and newspapers began to circulate in cities across the nation.[3] According to one report from January 1947, as many as twenty-three movie and trade magazines were published in Tokyo alone.[4] The list of publications included standard trade magazines such as *Kinema junpō* (Cinema report), popular fan magazines such as *Screen* and *Kindai eiga* (Modern cinema), children's magazines such as *Eiga shōnen* (Boys' cinema), and "highbrow" texts such as *Eiga geijutsu* (Film art) and *Eiga hyōron* (Film critique). The industry's reports appeared in *Rengō tsūshin* (Allied news), *Nihon bunka tsūshin* (Japan cultural news), and *Jiji tsūshin* (Current news). Local cities published their own movie newspapers and magazines, with such titles as *Eiga to supōtsu* (Movies and sports), *Kinema nyusu* (Cinema news), and *Sukurīn nyusu* (Screen news).

The history of *Eiga no tomo* preceded this postwar publication boom. The magazine was founded in January 1931, nine months before the Manchurian Incident. Published by Tachibana Kōichirō's Eiga sekaisha (Movie World Company), it began with a broad coverage of Japanese, European, and Hollywood cinemas. The early issues sprinkled "serious" trade talk with popular gossip about sex, as it actively participated in the larger literary milieu of "erotic, grotesque, nonsense" (*ero guro nansensu*).[5] Soon, the war forced *Eiga no tomo* to adopt a strong political tone.[6] Even though actresses such as Greta Garbo and Myrna Loy continued to grace the pages, the magazine's objective shifted from pure recreation to "accurate instruction."[7] As the Japanese military extended into the heart of China, the magazine's contributors frequently debated the Home Ministry's film policies and the Japanese film industry's ideological responsibilities. This "political turn" lasted until 1943, when government restrictions and material difficulties forced the publication to discontinue.[8]

Immediately after the war, Tachibana and his staff at Eiga sekaisha decided to revive the defunct magazine. The editorial team made two major changes. First, it chose to focus exclusively on American movies. By concentrating on Hollywood, the editors reasoned, the magazine would not only appeal to U.S. movie fans, but also assure the magazine a precious allotment of printing paper from SCAP's Civil Information and Education Section.[9] Second, the editors decided to present "uplifting" content. Unlike some of their earlier issues, which were peppered with risqué material, the postwar issues vowed to deliver "serious" information that could enrich the intellect. Echoing the CMPE's desire to portray Hollywood as an enlightening force, an editor once stated that "from American movies we must first learn. [We need to] read and acquire their rich culturalism [*bunkasei*] with our good conscience!"[10]

The decision paid off. On April 1946, the first postwar issue of *Eiga no tomo* came to life. Its cover did not feature a Japanese actress, as was commonplace before the war. Instead, readers encountered a smiling portrait of Deanna Durbin, the star of *His Butler's Sister* (1943). Above her cheery face, in roman script (instead of Japanese characters), was the ornately inscribed magazine title: EIGA NO TOMO. Due to the shortage of resources, the magazine only had thirty-four pages—less than half the length of the meatiest prewar issues. However, the editors were proud of their revived periodical. In an editorial column, those who brought back the magazine explicitly articulated a new mission: "The spring of reconstructing Japan should start with American movies! Bright and joyful and filled with democratic culture, American movies will surely provide insight for Japan's democratization." Acknowledging the "defeat of the old Japan," the editors promised to lead the way to a "new beginning."[11]

Eiga no tomo was a "privileged" monthly that relied on the support of the Central Motion Picture Exchange. This relationship enabled the editors to maintain an exclusive focus on Hollywood. The coverage began with the U.S. film industry's latest releases. In each issue, the editorial staff contributed synopses, previews, and analyses of the new feature productions from *Going My Way* (1944) to *The Ghost and Mrs. Muir* (1947) and *Miracle on 34th Street* (1947). The emphasis on timeliness was clear, as yet-to-be-released films often enjoyed extended attention. Readers, for example, encountered production updates on *The Beginning or the End* (1947), a quasi documentary about the Manhattan Project, twice before it reached Japanese screens—once when the MGM film was still in the production phase (June 1946), and the second time immediately after the product was completed (May 1947).[12] Topical essays introduced films that were new or unseen by the Japanese. In an article titled "American Films during the War," the writer remembered a string of pictures—including *Bataan* (1943), *Thirty Seconds over Tokyo* (1944), and *Yankee Doodle Dandy* (1942)—he encountered during a six-month period in early postwar Shanghai. A piece on the "Latest Tendency of American Films" bracketed new films by theme and genre, such as literary adaptations, boxing pictures, social problem films, and politically controversial productions.[13]

映画之友

ァメリカ映画専門紹介誌

EIGA NO TOMO

Greer Garson

8

Magazine for American Movies

Figure 8.1. Front cover of the August 1946 issue of *Eiga no tomo*. Greer Garson, a popular star in early postwar Japan, was famous for her roles in *Madame Curie* and *Random Harvest*. Author's collection.

Hollywood stars also enjoyed the spotlight. *Eiga no tomo* stimulated reader interest with wide coverage of actors, directors, and other filmic personalities. Stills and portraits of screen actors, "directly shipped from America," filled the pages from cover to cover.[14] Articles on famous individuals were equally abundant, ranging from one-paragraph snippets on budding actors to multipage biographies of big-name idols. A collection of these articles appeared as a 1951 hardcover book titled *Sutā dokuhon* (Book of stars).[15] In contrast to newspapers and magazines peppered with sensationalized gossip, *Eiga no tomo* treated American celebrities with dignity and respect. The two-page "Life Story of Maureen O'Hara," for example, portrayed the acting career and family life of the Irish-born star as one sustained by her modest and caring disposition.[16] In "Glamour, Ingrid Bergman," an article tracing the actress's professional career that was translated from *Stars and Stripes,* the Swedish actress's "natural beauty" and "passion for work" were lauded.[17] Bob Hope, who visited Japan in October 1950, created a splash in the magazine. In a pair of articles, *Eiga no tomo* documented his Japan tour, marveling at his friendliness and approachable character.[18]

While hyping the stars, *Eiga no tomo* also presented itself as a resource on American values and life. The magazine vowed to enrich the "study of American culture" for a population that possessed few firsthand opportunities to observe the outside world.[19] This began with the teaching of language. In the early postwar era, studying English became a popular activity among the Japanese. Radio shows such as *Kamu kamu eigo* (Come, come English) and instruction books such as *Nichibei kaiwa techō* (Japanese-English conversation manual) became instant hits.[20] *Eiga no tomo* fostered this learning atmosphere by drawing from Hollywood. In its first issue of the postwar era, the magazine presented an excerpt of dialogue from *Abe Lincoln in Illinois* (1940) and coupled it with a line-by-line translation into Japanese. "Nothing beats American movies as a way of studying vivid English," the magazine boasted.[21] Dialogue translations remained a popular column in later issues.[22]

Eiga no tomo also commented on customs and social aspects of American life. Intent on bringing background knowledge to Japanese moviegoers, the magazine offered background articles on a plethora of topics—from styles of jazz music to trends in women's swimwear to different forms of social dance to the gold rush in California to trends in contemporary American literature.[23] The magazine also relied on the expertise of the culture elites. Honda Akira, for instance, praised comedies like *Adam's Rib* for successfully portraying both the sad and funny sides of life. To capture the two polar emotions, wrote the literary scholar from Hōsei University, was a sign of a "true artist."[24]

Nakano Gorō's writings were equally laudatory. In an article titled "Thoughts on American Movies," the trustee of the American Movie Culture Association praised U.S. cinema as a "universal language" that "diffused and expressed ideas freely across the world." He urged the Japanese to digest every bit of the "breathing, lively democracy" that surfaced on the screens.[25] Ishida Aya, dean of Bunka gakuin, a private school for women, hailed the U.S. film industry's projection of "American idealism, humanistic sentiment, and lyricism." In contrast to the propagandistic films of Japan during the war, American cinema, she maintained, did a "far better job" in encouraging its citizens' "voluntary" service to their country. Impressed with a society in which "bankers and janitors each developed their own philosophy of life and creative ideas, and were allowed to express them freely," she touted the American people as "artists of everyday life."[26]

A People's Magazine

Eiga no tomo benefited from the culture elites. Their contributions brought knowledge, dignity, and respectability to the magazine. But its goal was not to preach down to the lay reader. The editorial team's intention was the opposite: to broaden its constituent base by cultivating an interactive climate with readers. In so doing, the monthly rendered Hollywood's "high" cultural content accessible to the "ordinary" reader, particularly young audiences in their teens and twenties. Its targeting of the coming-of-age readership was evident in the editorials that routinely addressed the student population.[27] *Eiga no tomo* once claimed to make itself a "fun textbook" for young readers. It desired to plant "*Eiga no tomo* in school libraries across Japan."[28]

The efforts to court young readers stemmed from the new editor in chief, Yodogawa Nagaharu. Born in 1909, Yodogawa, the son of a geisha-house owner, grew up an avid fan of the movies. After graduating from a five-year middle school, he moved to Tokyo to study at the Nihon University. There, he did not attend a single class but "roamed around [town] enjoying watching new foreign movies," he later confessed.[29] After dropping out of college, he briefly worked for Eiga sekaisha as a writer and assistant. With a passion for the movies that kept growing, Yodogawa soon joined the Osaka office of United Artists in the 1930s and Tōhō studio during the war, while maintaining ties with Eiga sekaisha as a critic and writer.[30] His extensive writings on such films as *Pinocchio* (1940), *Gulliver's Travels* (1939), and *Our Town* (1940) were *Eiga no tomo*'s highlights on the eve of war.[31]

Figure 8.2. Yodogawa Nagaharu (far left) lecturing at a gathering of the Tomo no kai (Meeting of friends) in Yokohama, July 31, 1949. Courtesy of the Kawakita Memorial Film Institute.

After the war, Yodogawa joined the Central Motion Picture Exchange.[32] As a lecturer for the Hollywood distributor, he immediately earned a reputation as a popular and charismatic speaker—a "god of movie promotion," an inspired fan recalled decades later.[33] Although he was excited about the opportunity to deal with fresh U.S. releases, the strict and compartmentalized work climate of the company dismayed him. "[We] were salary men, employees, nothing more," Yodogawa groused.[34] Things turned sour when the company accused him of pocketing outside pay as a contributor to a movie magazine. Yodogawa immediately resigned from the CMPE, labeling its crusty managing director Charles Mayer a "MacArthur wannabe."[35] This run-in was welcome news to Tachibana, who quickly hired him as *Eiga no tomo*'s editor in chief. Enthralled by its new acquisition, Eiga sekaisha immediately announced that Yodogawa's talent "would add substantial weight" to the once-defunct magazine.[36]

Yodogawa's job involved two main objectives. The first goal was to maintain favorable ties with the CMPE. Despite bitter feelings toward Mayer, the

editor chose to work with the Hollywood distributor in a civil manner. This
assured the magazine's exclusive focus on American movies. The CMPE returned the favor by praising Yodogawa's work. In the April 1949 issue, which
marked the magazine's third anniversary after the war, Mayer penned a letter to
"thank" Eiga sekaisha for "familiarizing readers with American movies" and
"endeavoring to introduce upcoming releases" to the lay public.[37] In a one-on-
one interview with Yodogawa, the CMPE representative fondly stated that he
was "always thinking of [Yodogawa] when looking at *Eiga no tomo.*"[38]

While maintaining amicable working relations with the Hollywood distributor, Yodogawa also strove to render the content of the magazine accessible
to the wider public.[39] At the heart of his mission was establishing what he
called an "egalitarianism of intellect" (*kyōyō no byōdō shugi*). Yodogawa observed in a 1950 book titled *Eiga sansaku* (Strolling in the movies), that since
the prewar years the Japanese public was split into two spheres: a minority
group of "people with a very high intellect"—the culture elites—and the
great majority of "lowbrows" (*mīchan hāchan*). The widening gap of the two
groups accelerated the "deterioration...[of] morals" in early postwar Japan.
To Yodogawa, the problem lay not in the ordinary citizen but the "coldness
and lack of vigor" of the learned elites, who "despised" ordinary citizens and
ultimately "rejected" them. The chief editor was determined to close the culture gap by redistributing knowledge to the general public. A college dropout
without an elite background, he was sympathetic to the so-called lowbrows
with whom he identified more closely. In Yodogawa's view, the shared ownership of knowledge was more than a means of empowering the ordinary
citizen. It was a means of practicing the democratic mores of the United
States.[40]

In an effort to elevate the knowledge of his readers, the editor elicited popular involvement. He began by expanding the readers' pages. In the prewar
editions, *Eiga no tomo* included a two-page column titled "Club," which offered an assortment of movie-related essays penned by fans.[41] Yodogawa not
only revived this fan section, but founded new readers' pages such as the "Our
Town" column (an allusion to the 1940 film based on Thornton Wilder's play),
in which readers from across the country, both urban and rural, reported on
the popularity of American movies in their hometowns. A monthly Q&A
section entertained fans with answers to their questions of various sorts (e.g.:
In which films did Greta Garbo star? Which Japanese stars appeared in Hollywood movies? How are subtitles added to film prints?). Yodogawa's magazine
devoted unusual effort to interacting with readers. One staff member recalled
that his main obligation was to respond to readers' questions and queries.
"There was not a single day in which letters from our readers did not arrive to

the office. . . . To answer their questions was a particularly painstaking job," he reminisced in a memoir published in 2000.[42]

Eiga no tomo also conducted polls and surveys to gauge fan opinion. The magazine periodically compiled "random" interviews to capture the voices of different age groups and occupations. A one-page article in the July 1948 issue, titled "American Movies Discussed on the Street," for example, included brief commentaries by eight Tokyoites, including a male student, a female schoolteacher, a Buddhist monk, and a curator at the Ueno zoo.[43] Another article from June 1951 listed popular opinions culled from around the nation. The two-page piece introduced a total of nineteen individuals (school principals, baseball players, public officers, movie exhibitors, and others), both celebrities and lay people. The survey included their favorite films, frequency of visits to theaters, and degree of passion for the movies.[44]

Large-scale surveys took place once a year in the magazine's "public opinion poll." In these extended surveys, *Eiga no tomo* asked readers to respond to a string of questions on the movies. Typical questions involved the best and worst films of the year and favorite stars and directors. The results were published a few months after the readers submitted their responses. For example, the first postwar survey demonstrated that the most popular stars, new releases, and prewar productions were the following:

Most Popular Male Star
1. Gary Cooper   1,968 votes
2. John Payne   1,878 votes[45]
3. Gregory Peck   1,783 votes

Most Popular Female Star
1. Ingrid Bergman   3,598 votes
2. Greer Garson   2,889 votes
3. Claudette Colbert   1,677 votes

Best New Release
1. *Casablanca*   2,102 votes
2. *Going My Way*   1,644 votes
3. *Madam Curie*   1,133 votes

Best Prewar Production
1. *Gone with the Wind*   2,807 votes
2. *Rebecca*   441 votes
3. *Fantasia*   370 votes[46]

Later surveys entertained readers with additional questions, such as the frequency of visits to movie theaters, the films that provoked interest in the original novel or story, and the preference between black-and-white and Technicolor features or between the road-show and the packing-in type of theater.[47]

The social profile of Hollywood fandom is difficult to grasp, but the results of the annual surveys strongly suggest that the core body of readers were young people. Even though Yodogawa would sometimes boast that fan response to an annual survey encompassed people from little children to senior citizens, the largest constituent of respondents belonged to the age group fifteen to twenty-five.[48] The surveys did elicit the participation of consumers from a wide range of professions—including office workers, public officials, farmers, fishermen, and factory workers. Yet by far the most enthusiastic respondents were high school and college students (see table 8.1). The editorial staff also discovered the passions of young fans from the comments and writings submitted to the readers' columns. By December 1948, the editor was convinced that "80 percent of the readers of movie magazines today were postwar fans."[49]

The demographics of readership showed that there were fans throughout the country. Fan mail and survey responses indicated fan interest in every prefecture. The proportion of popular representation, however, was rather lopsided. Usually, at least a third of respondents were Tokyoites. Prefectures with major metropolitan centers (and CMPE branch offices), such as Osaka and Fukuoka, followed.[50] Responses were uneven between the sexes. In the annual surveys, there were two to three times more male respondents than women. Yet this did not mean that women were marginal readers of the magazines. A number of female fans wrote to fan columns. Each issue showcased ads for women—such as lipstick and perfume—and distinguished women contributed essays to the magazine. The editorial staff believed that the modest participation of women in the surveys reflected "traditional" social norms, which discouraged women from public participation, not their lack of passion for American movies.[51] Convinced that women constituted a core foundation of the magazine's readership, Yodogawa called for the "active [participation] of the modern woman."[52]

Writing about Hollywood

Eiga no tomo's call for popular participation inspired passionate reactions from readers. In their spare time between their studies, work, and social obligations, fans wrote to the magazine, itching to share their joy and excitement

Table 8.1. Statistical Data of *Eiga no tomo*'s Annual Surveys

	1947	1948	1949	1950	1951	1952	1953	1954
Occupation								
Student	No Data	858 (19.7%)	1,575 (63.3%)	No Data	1,391 (55.7%)	8,359 (68.3%)	4,127 (64.0%)	4,237 (60.1%)
Office Worker	No Data	683 (15.6%)	409 (16.5%)	No Data	455 (18.2%)	1,759 (14.4%)	631 (9.8%)	830 (11.8%)
Other	No Data	2,824 (64.7%)	503 (20.2%)	No Data	653 (26.1%)	2,118 (17.3%)	1,691 (26.2%)	1,982 (28.1%)
Sex								
Male	No Data	No Data	1,784 (71.7%)	2284 (68.5%)	1,869 (74.8%)	8,343 (68.2%)	4,331 (67.2%)	4,672 (66.3%)
Female	No Data	No Data	661 (26.6%)	1049 (31.5%)	630 (25.2%)	3,893 (31.8%)	2,092 (32.4%)	2,318 (32.9%)
No Answer	No Data	No Data	42 (1.7%)	0 (0.0%)	0 (0.0%)	0 (0.0%)	26 (0.4%)	59 (0.8%)
Region								
Tokyo	No Data	No Data	844 (33.9%)	1,164 (34.9%)	754 (30.2%)	4,102 (33.5%)	2,063 (32.0%)	2,327 (33.0%)
Major Prefectures	No Data	No Data	461 (18.6%)	659 (19.8%)	420 (16.8%)	2,054 (16.8%)	1,141 (17.7%)	1,229 (17.4%)
Other	No Data	No Data	1,182 (47.5%)	1,510 (45.3%)	1,325 (53.0%)	6,080 (49.7%)	3,245 (50.3%)	3,493 (49.6%)
Total	8,777 (100.0%)	4,365 (100.0%)	2,487 (100.0%)	3,333 (100.0%)	2,499 (100.0%)	12,236 (100.0%)	6,449 (100.0%)	7,049 (100.0%)

Source: Eiga no tomo. "Major Prefectures" consist of Hokkaido, Aichi, Osaka, and Fukuoka; they housed CMPE's regional offices.

with the larger community. Readers' comments typically began with pure ela-
tion. "How wonderful are American movies," noted a fan in September 1948.
"I love American movies from deep in my heart."[53] Another fan expressed
similar emotions. "What is my only source of entertainment?" she asked her-
self. "Of course that is American movies.... I am certain that I would lose half
of my life's joy without [them]."[54] Some of the most passionate fans lived in
the hinterlands, where U.S. cinema was not readily accessible. One moviegoer
in Miyagi Prefecture noted on February 1949, "As soon as I found out that
American movies were being released, I took a two-hour train ride to Sendai
[City] to see *Watch on the Rhine* (1943). I still cannot forget how much I was
moved by that movie."[55] Similarly gushing comments came from a resident
from remote Sado Island. After watching *Princess O'Rourke* (1943), his first ever
Hollywood experience, the writer was pleased to report, "I was able to enjoy
it from my heart."[56]

Despite its obvious entertainment value, Hollywood furnished its patrons
with more than mere escapism. Many moviegoers praised American movies
for their therapeutic quality, especially their characteristic happy ending that
restored joy and confidence to life. One fan, for example, wrote in October
1948 that Hollywood movies "eliminate our worries in life" and "give us
courage."[57] After watching *Miracle on 34th Street,* another enthusiast wrote that
this movie would "recover the dreams that are being lost and provide warmth
to this cold world" of today.[58] To Naka Akio, a Siberian expatriate who ab-
horred the occupation era as a "dark social climate [marred by] inflation," Hollywood shone as a "beacon of light." Watching the movies "gave [him] confidence" to live a "bright and fun" life. The film that impressed him the most,
he wrote in December 1948, was *The Best Years of Our Lives* (1946)—which
dramatized the perseverance of ailing war veterans and their families. This film
restored "his fighting spirit to combat the struggles in life" in future days.[59]

To many fans, the Hollywood star was the greatest allure. However, the
readers of *Eiga no tomo* often looked beyond the good looks and sex appeal of
celebrities. They carefully examined and evaluated the quality of acting and
performance. In an essay titled "[Joseph] Cotten and [Henry] Fonda," one
moviegoer examined the "contrasting acting style" of the two stars. Com-
paring their performance in several recent releases, the writer concluded that
both stars were superior in their "profound acting ability." The two, however, differed on one count: Cotten's expressions, thanks to his earlier training
in theater (with Orson Wells), offered "depth" and "contrast," while Fonda
was able to present "wit" and "humor" in his internal expressions.[60] Another
moviegoer championed *The Life of Emile Zola* (1937), the biopic of the French

realist writer, for the "moving" acting of Paul Muni (Emile Zola) and Joseph Schildkraut (Albert Dreyfus). In particular, the latter's performance as Albert Dreyfus was the "highlight" of the film, thanks to his "complex psychological" expressions.[61]

In addition to evaluating the performance of the stars, Hollywood admirers critiqued directorial talent. One reader, for instance, attributed the success of *Arsenic and Old Lace* (1944), a movie adapted from a popular Broadway play, to its director, the "great" Frank Capra. This film risked becoming a mediocre "slapstick comedy," but Capra, the writer remarked in 1949, was able avoid "boredom" with "brilliant" music, cinematography, and acting. "Only Capra could have pulled this off," the writer concluded.[62] Another fan penned an essay on Irving Rapper, his favorite director. Judging from the notes he scribbled after each screening, the writer approved of the director because his films (such as *Rhapsody in Blue*) offered a "dissection of human [life]" without being "preachy" about it. The fan predicted that the director would continue to remain popular in years to come.[63]

A great number of *Eiga no tomo*'s readers yearned to better understand the United States—the society that gave rise to Hollywood. In an age when overseas travel was rarely a reality, American movies served as educational texts about the wider world, particularly U.S. values. Many fans, thus, paid close attention to the practice of life at the movies. These moviegoers learned many things. For example, after viewing *It Happened on 5th Avenue* (1947), a film about a struggling drifter in New York City, one reader was surprised to learn that housing problems actually existed in American society.[64] *The Bells of St. Mary's* (1945) moved another fan because it revealed the prevalence of Christianity in America. Impressed with the story about a young Catholic priest's tireless efforts to help the Church and its children, the fan noted that one could "truly understand" the film only by coming to terms with the priest's religion. "Why does one offer the other cheek after being struck on one cheek? Why did the nun, right before joining the Church, pray in a posture that resembled that of Jesus the night before his crucifixion? Only by understanding these things," the fan concluded, could one make sense of the "beauty, purity, and cheerfulness" of the Bing Crosby film.[65]

The culture elites often praised the "humanistic" traits that surfaced in Hollywood. Many readers of *Eiga no tomo* offered similar remarks. In an essay titled "The Humanity of American Movies," one reader opined on the subject of *Going My Way,* a film in which a compassionate Catholic priest mentors a group of delinquents and devotes himself to building a church for them. Wrote the fan, "Haven't we forgotten the most important thing: respecting humanity?... Wasn't it because of this that we were drawn into a shameful war?"[66] *The Best Years of Our Lives* evoked equally celebratory comments. One viewer expressed "gratitude" to the William Wyler movie for delivering a "heartwarming" story about the three American GIs and their difficulties in adapting to civilian life. Witnessing the help and support offered by the protagonists' friends and neighbors, another reader noted, "Love for society—what the Japanese today need is this."[67] Perhaps reacting to these and other films, Takahashi Katsuichi, a fan in Tokyo, noted that the greatest attraction of American movies was its treatment of people with a "warm heart" and its strong faith in "human goodwill." This trait, he argued, constituted a "scent of human[ism]."[68]

Fans who wrote to *Eiga no tomo* commonly associated this "humanistic" trait with "democracy." This was clear in the words of one Tokyoite, who argued that films produced by the "democratic nation" on the other side of the Pacific were shaped by a "faith in human goodwill" that existed even inside a "bloody movie."[69] Others identified traits of democracy more broadly in a wide variety of genres that appeared on the theater screens. To one fan, "democratic values" appeared in almost every Hollywood story, from the log cabin president's early life (*Abe Lincoln in Illinois*) to a set of entangled personal dramas in New York City (*Tales of Manhattan,* 1942) to a farmer's life on the frontier (*The Southerner,* 1945).[70] Another fan argued that American movies taught viewers "respect for humanity, a glorious frontier spirit, a wholesome entertainment quality." On the whole, Hollywood, he argued, presented to viewers a "democratic way of thinking."[71]

Meeting of Friends

Fan contributors were excited to share their thoughts in the readers' columns, but some among them were determined to do more. Realizing that not everyone was viewing the movies with an eye for aesthetic, cultural, or intellectual content, eager fans urged others to develop an inquisitive mind like their own. To the chagrin of these enthusiasts, their fellow citizens in their hometowns and surrounding communities often appeared to lack a genuine appreciation for American movies. A high school student in Onomichi, for example, complained that most of his peers treated American movies only as "entertainment." Even though local theaters provided discount tickets for students, his peers often chose not to go and watch such films as *Madame Curie* (1943) and *Sister Kenny* (1946). Those who went, furthermore, would complain about the "loud music" and "drowsy" content.[72] A fan from Saga also noticed low turnout for Hollywood productions in his community. "Movie houses are not filled every day of the week," he observed. "Isn't this a proof that citizens in Saga Prefecture have a low ability to appreciate American movies?"[73] A resident in Tokushima attributed the short screen time of Hollywood movies to the audiences' failure to grasp their deeper value. "There is a lot of room in which to improve the quality of American movie spectatorship" in his city, he complained.[74]

Disappointed but hardly discouraged, readers of *Eiga no tomo* decided to take action. In the readers' columns, many of them provided suggestions for improving one's movie viewing. One fan in the March 1948 issue encouraged readers to look more closely at the plot, the actors' performance, the sets, and the cinematography—all of which produced "hidden effects" that a casual viewer could easily overlook. "We might simply say that the movie [we] just saw was fun," the writer informed his peers, "but [we also need to] think what was good about it."[75]

Others suggested new methods of spectatorship. One moviegoer, for instance, recommended note-taking on the performance of actors, the quality of the films, as well as their ideological viewpoints. "Gaining something [meaningful]" from the movies, he stressed, would enrich the "life of fans."[76] Another reader was more specific. In the June 1948 issue, Yoshisuji Manji introduced an eight-step viewing method that he promoted to his peers:

1. Memorize the plot of the film by reading *Eiga no tomo*.
2. Envision the star's performance before attending the theater.
3. Envision the scenes before attending the theater.
4. During the screening, compare the actual performance with what you had previously envisioned.
5. Examine the director's cinematography, techniques, etc.
6. Observe how viewers around you are reacting to the movie.
7. After the screening, compare the film with Japanese movies.
8. Critique the movie with your friends.[77]

Following these steps made it possible for him to "enjoy American movies even better [than before]."[78] Others claimed that the best way to elevate one's viewing was to adopt an independent mind. One fan specifically urged others to view the writings of professional film critics with a grain of salt, because they tend to "constrain our ways of viewing."[79]

Many motivated readers, in addition, took part in Tomo no kai (Meeting of friends), the fan club hosted by *Eiga no tomo*. The idea of Tomo no kai originated with a young high school student who visited the editor's office to request a guest lecturer for his film club at Ueno High School. Yodogawa was reluctant, but he agreed to come. In April 1948, he visited the campus and talked to a group of fourteen high school students. The topic of discussion was the career of Charlie Chaplin, the filmmaker whom he most admired, and one of his silent features, *The Kid* (1921).[80] Pleasantly surprised with the experience, Yodogawa came to think the magazine could run such social events on a larger scale. That fall, *Eiga no tomo* began holding regular meetings at the Ueno High School.[81] Soon named Tomo no kai, this assembly in Tokyo drew a large following. Less than a year later, the size of the audience reached nearly five hundred.[82]

Eiga no tomo aimed to promote similar experiences outside of Tokyo. It encouraged readers, movie fans, and exhibitors to run Tomo no kai's regional branches, embracing new members in the spirit of the cowboy hero who welcomed a visitor from out of town with a hearty, "Welcome, stranger."[83] To expand its membership, the magazine listed meeting times and reports for each branch. It accommodated new club members with a "Tomo no kai badge" and the publication of a newsletter, *Green Years,* a compilation of fan letters from around the country. As the meetings in Tokyo increased in size and number, Tomo no kai branches took root in Kyoto, Nigata, Okayama, Nagoya, Itami, Taira, Kawaguchi, Hamamtsu, Hakodate, Himeji, Matsuyama, Oita, and Osaka.[84] The activities in these branches attracted local and out-of-town fans. Tomo no kai meetings in Kyoto, for example, accepted visitors from Osaka, Okayama, Kobe, Himeji, and Wakayama, while at Nigata, participants came from Nagaoka, Shinhatsuda, and Kashiwazaki.[85] In the February 1951 issue, *Eiga no tomo* reported the existence of some ten thousand members in at least sixty-one regional branches.[86]

The editor took particular pride in running the club. Now the principal organizer of Tomo no kai's Tokyo meetings, Yodogawa visited cities and towns—near and far. Between deadlines and desk work, he routinely spoke in front of crowds of all sizes.[87] In late 1951, Yodogawa went on a lecture tour to western Japan. On this whirlwind trip, spanning eight cities in eighteen days, he mingled with enthusiastic members at schools, movie theaters, and other public spaces. In his limited spare time, he took part in media interviews and roundtables.[88] This successful excursion led to a trip to northern Japan a few months later. Greeted warmly by Tomo no kai members at every stop he made, Yodogawa described the trip as "an unforgettable experience."[89] Throughout the 1950s, the charismatic editor spent countless hours speaking in front of interested fans. He was a major influence on audiences in developing a larger community of Hollywood film lovers.

The fans who took part in the meetings were as enthusiastic as the magazine's editor. They took charge in organizing a wide array of activities at their local gatherings. One of the most common events was guest lectures. In Tokyo and Yokohama, audiences eagerly listened to Yodogawa's eloquent speeches on the films, stars, and directors. In other branches, organizers invited film critics, journalists, magazine editors, artists, cartoonists, writers, poets, SCAP officials, CMPE's publicists, and even Japanese movie stars.[90] The subject matter of these talks varied widely. Speakers like Yodogawa typically delivered in-depth discussions of Hollywood's stars and new releases. Those familiar with movie making uncovered the "behind-the-scenes" secrets of filmmaking, sharing detailed knowledge of the processes of subtitling, script writing, and directing. Many others introduced audiences to Hollywood history in such lectures as "American Movies during the Silent Era," "On Technicolor Movies," and "American Movies during World War II."[91]

To these fans, merely listening did not satisfy their appetite for the movies. Itching to share their excitement with others, they organized group discussions. Fans would energetically, sometimes endlessly, debate the pros and cons of the new releases, the "best" and "worst" films of the year, as well as favorite stars and directors.[92] Participants also taught each other how to write fan letters to Hollywood stars (in English).[93] At times, group interaction adopted a more serious tone. In one meeting, for example, participants debated whether or not it was better to watch a movie without prior knowledge of its content.[94] In another gathering, the central topic was the relationship between cinema, realism, and humanism. According to a report of this session, discussions proceeded "with a degree of seriousness."[95] Sometimes, Tomo no kai members mused on ways to improve *Eiga no tomo,* as if they were members of the editorial staff.[96] Most of these events, as was the case at a meeting in Kanazawa City, yielded "lively agreements and disagreements," thereby representing the "youthfulness" of the "upbeat" members.[97]

The desire to participate also led to games and quizzes. Participants at a club meeting in Kyoto, for example, tried to name "three-time Oscar winners," "five postwar films by Clarence Brown," and "father-and-son filmmakers."[98] In Tokyo, Yodogawa asked participants to guess the names of specific movies from still photos and images. He also challenged participants to figure out the original, English-language title of the films from their Japanese counterparts.[99] Other activities included the "Who am I?" quiz, in which participants guessed the name of the star from hints and clues offered by the host.[100] Another was Twenty Doors, in which contestants had to guess the star that the host had imagined by asking up to twenty questions.[101] Successful contestants won modest prizes, such as free movie tickets, programs, and still photos.[102] Fans truly enjoyed these activities. A report from Osaka, for example, noted that "whirlwinds of laughter exploded here and there"![103]

Tomo no kai members also attended monthly meetings to share their appreciation of amateur and professional art. Fans exhibited still photos, posters, sketches, and portraits of the movies and stars, and turned the meeting into miniexhibits of Hollywood iconography.[104] Oftentimes, *Eiga no tomo*'s representatives, the CMPE's publicity agents, and theater managers were invited to share their publicity material of the newest releases. Some enthusiasts brought handmade posters, sketches, drawings, and calendars of the popular stars.[105] At a meeting at Kawaguchi, one young member painted famous Hollywood personalities in watercolors and presented them free to their peers.[106] At Nigata, a club member displayed a pamphlet about Margaret O'Brien and ten autographed still photos of movie stars. "We surrounded them, mesmerized," reported a local representative.[107]

Recorded music became another source of attraction. Tomo no kai often hosted a popular event, dubbed "record concerts."[108] On these occasions, members brought phonographs and records and shared their collections with the group.[109] This attracted crowds because recorded music was not affordable to many. The lineup of music included memorable tunes by George Gershwin (*Rhapsody in Blue*), Al Jolson (*The Jolson Story*, 1946), Frederick Chopin (*A Song to Remember,* 1945), and Jascha Heifetz (*They Shall Have Music,* 1939).[110] Record concerts sometimes turned into sing-alongs. At the tenth Tomo no kai assembly in Tokyo, Yodogawa played a recording of the music of Chopin and then the main theme song ("Always") from *The Pride of the Yankees* (1942). Afterward, one member sang standards from *The Blue Angel* (1930) and *Rose-Marie* (1936). Audiences "applauded loudly" and "demanded an encore," reported the pleased editor.[111]

Each year, Tomo no kai branches across Japan capped the year's meetings with a Christmas celebration. Even through Christianity was a minority religion in Japan, Christmas began to become popular after the Meiji Restoration, largely as a secular and commercialized holiday that couples and families enjoyed.[112] Fans of *Eiga no tomo* celebrated the occasion primarily in a secular fashion, but they did so with sincerity and respect. In various regional meetings, members called for donations and purchased Christmas trees to decorate together.[113] They listened to music and sang Christmas songs such as "Silent Night," "White Christmas," and "Jingle Bells," with piano accompaniment.[114] Exchanging presents became a common practice.[115] In the winter of 1949, over four hundred and fifty Tokyoites assembled to appreciate Christmas together.

Fans decorated their Christmas trees, sang carols, exchanged presents, and were entertained by a choral group.[116] The celebration at Okayama, while smaller in scale, was no less fun. There, a group of about twenty-five members met for cocoa and cake, and listened to recorded Christmas songs.[117] In Nagoya, some eighty fans assembled to talk about the movies and exchange presents with one another.[118] To these energetic fans, Christmas brought optimism and warmth, while strengthening the bond with their peers through a new, "American" custom. Tomo no kai's practice empowered their own community.

Cinema, Culture, and America

Eiga no tomo was not the only place where movie fans congregated in defeated Japan. As commercial screenings revived in cities, filmgoers increasingly took part in group activities to share their excitement and passion in larger communal settings. Workers and union members, for example, formed "movie circles" (*eiga sākuru*). These left-leaning moviegoers organized to seek discounted admission rates and, more importantly, to pressure Japanese filmmakers to pursue "high art" in their filmmaking. This, according to one observer, was a way to get "democratic good movies" from (profit-oriented) Japanese companies.[119] At schools and campuses across Japan, young audiences formed movie study groups and clubs (*eiga kenkyūkai* and *eiga kenkyūbu*). Although such organizations had existed before the war, SCAP's new educational curriculum expanded these movie-related activities, thanks to the creation of new junior high schools, high schools, and universities around the nation. In 1948 a local trade paper made note of the "nationwide eruption" of these student-run organizations.[120]

Eiga no tomo was a centerpiece of this diverse moviegoing community. It grew into a prominent site of fan congregation within months after its first postwar publication. Whereas most of the film clubs at schools and workplaces were small gatherings in a single town or city, Yodogawa's periodical absorbed moviegoers from around the nation. Owing to its wide circulation, the monthly publication was able to bring together movie fans from distant cities and regions in ways that most other organizations could not. Moreover, this community thrived because of its accessibility. In contrast to the American Movie Culture Association, which endeavored to distinguish itself from the mass population, *Eiga no tomo* had a welcoming atmosphere that elicited the participation of the "lay" moviegoer. The individuals who took part in its shared climate constructed Hollywood fandom from the ground up.

This fan-driven magazine also bolstered a larger climate of cultural activities (*bunka katsudō*) that blossomed after the war. In this era of transition, men and women eagerly took part in a wide range of youth organizations (*seinendan*), "cultural circles" (*bunka sākuru*), and study groups (*gakushū sākuru*) in their search for fulfillment and meaning. These local organizations promoted various artistic, literary, and cultural activities, including oil painting, calligraphy, photography, folk songs (*minyō*), haiku, novel reading, and creative writing. To be sure, such grassroots activities were not unique to the occupation; during the Fifteen Years' War from 1931 to 1945, for example, student groups, youth centers, and women's organizations mobilized the public to support the war effort through collection drives, self-education meetings, and morale-boosting campaigns.[121] Yet the "MacArthur era" instilled a greater level of openness for public dialogue, debate, and activism. According to one historian, these diverse "cultural movements" after the war were both "conscious [and] subconscious" attempts by the Japanese public to "resurrect their selfhoods and search for direction" in times of large-scale change.[122]

Eiga no tomo played an important role in shaping this expanding climate of popular activity. Instead of painting Hollywood culture as salacious, risqué, and morally offensive, the magazine celebrated it as dignified, refined, and respectable entertainment from which the youth could gain both fun *and* useful meaning. This editorial agenda brought together a new generation of young people who were itching to reconnect with society, rebuild their rhythms of life, and enrich their minds by engaging with the movies. While enjoying fun and games, fans also strove to expand their intellectual and cultural horizons together with their peers. Just like many other "cultural organizations" that mushroomed in the war-scarred landscape, *Eiga no tomo* nourished a space for young women and men to heal their psychological damage from the war era and build a new collective identity. The readers of Yodogawa's magazine were far from passive recipients of meaning. Determined to find new directions in their individual and collective lives, they actively took part in the magazine's social and cultural activities.

Eiga no tomo, furthermore, was a site of Americanization. It accelerated the permeation of American values in the fabric of everyday life. Throughout the occupation era, *Eiga no tomo* maintained a near-exclusive focus on Hollywood and, by extension, things American. Its colorful pages full of stills and articles, the eloquent lectures by Yodogawa and others, and the myriad activities at the Tomo no kai meetings all brought about a renewed fascination with a range of American products and ideas—from music, fashion, politics, to ideas and daily life.

The imagination, negotiation, and dissemination of American culture was a complex process. While operating within a larger political structure established by U.S.-led occupation forces, the spread of American values was never a one-way street. The monthly magazine and its expanding body of readers imagined and reinvented "America" in their own terms, through their negotiations and interactions with Hollywood culture. The acts of cultural negotiation fostered a climate of admiration and respect, thereby reinforcing the perception of the United States as a superior society for the Japanese to emulate. In the end, *Eiga no tomo* was a centripetal force that directed the popular fans to look on the United States in a favorable light. In so doing, it accelerated the weaving of pro-American sentiment into the fabric of Japan's everyday life.

The life of *Eiga no tomo* outlasted the occupation. In the issues published after MacArthur's departure, the magazine continued to introduce the latest Hollywood pictures and stars, the cultural value of the films, and firsthand reports of U.S. show business. The readers' columns were expanded. Each month, *Tomo no kai*'s branch reports captured the fun and fulfillment of the avid moviegoers across Japan. In the post-occupation era, *Eiga no tomo* gradually opened its pages to cover other foreign cinemas that began to enter the market. Hollywood, however, continued to shape the heart and soul of the magazine. Despite trials and travails, the magazine served as a haven for Hollywood fans until its publication discontinued in 1968.

Yodogawa continued to edit the magazine throughout this time. In addition to enriching *Eiga no tomo,* the editor endlessly wrote essays, articles, and film reviews for books and magazines.[123] In 1961 this energetic film critic appeared on television to introduce *Laramie* (1959), a TV western show.[124] His success with the show led to a regular appearance on the small screen as a host of weekly movie airings. His lectures at Tomo no kai continued throughout the postwar era—long beyond the final issue of *Eiga no tomo*—until his death in 1998. Today, movie fans continue to hold Tomo no kai meetings in Tokyo once a month. In these events that draw passionate moviegoers, we may see glimpses of the collective spirit that first took root shortly after the Second World War.[125]

Conclusion

December 31, 1951: Tokyo. It was a cold winter day, but the streets were bustling with energy. As the final hours of the year slipped away, swarms of people—women, men, and children—crowded the stores and shopping streets as they prepared for another New Year's celebration. It was hard to imagine that six years had already passed since the end of the war: although the miseries of defeat remained etched in people's minds, many of them were starting to look toward the future, hoping to build a better life. The times were still tough for most, but the lives of citizens were slowly starting to look up.

For Hollywood, New Year's Eve marked the end of an era. It was the last day of the Central Motion Picture Exchange's operation. After nearly six years of extended work throughout Japan, the transpacific outpost of the U.S. studios had proudly fulfilled its mission. Charles Mayer, who completed his duties a month earlier, had already left the country.[1] He was replaced by a handful of U.S. studio representatives who arrived in Tokyo, one after another, to set up their own branch offices and start afresh.[2] A new era of business dawned the following day. The "enlightenment campaign" came to an end with this transition.

Hollywood's transpacific operation produced notable results. The alliance formed with the U.S. government and military rewarded American film studios with a greater presence in the Japanese market. Journalists, film critics, and market observers commonly remarked on a "Hollywood craze" in big and small cities; trade papers reported that U.S. cinema was able to claim some 40 percent of the market share—doubling the figures of the prewar decades.[3]

Studios were pleased with the outcome. A report submitted by Irving Maas of the Motion Picture Export Association indicated that Japan, by fall 1951, had become "the unit's best market."⁴ *Kinema junpō* praised the Central Motion Picture Exchange for its "epoch-making achievement."⁵

The enlightenment campaign also pleased the U.S. occupiers. Despite tense moments with the MPEA, occupation authorities were overall happy with Hollywood's efforts to promote American culture and values. In October 1951, Gen. M. B. Ridgeway of the U.S. Army lauded the CMPE's assistance in distributing SCAP's newsreels, its contribution to the "formation and stimulation of groups of study of the United States through motion pictures," and its presentation of "superior American Motion [*sic*] pictures" that "helped to implant something of the significance of American democracy." Ridgeway personally commended Charles Mayer as a "sympathetic and energetic participant," who assisted the occupation "far beyond the [expected] requirements."⁶

Moreover, Hollywood's campaign greatly influenced the Japanese. It stimulated the business of hundreds of small-time film exhibitors, who vied to showcase U.S. movies in their theaters. Although the CMPE's demands were rigorous and the competition among exhibitors was intense, many of them successfully carved a niche, and some won instant fame as a "Home of American Movies." In addition, Hollywood empowered its consumers. They flocked to American movies en masse, in search of excitement, amusement, and enlightenment. Many of them sought collective appreciation of Hollywood cinema. Their organized activities helped resurrect the social life, self-esteem, and group identity of moviegoers. Hollywood deeply affected the hearts and minds of the Japanese.

The end of the enlightenment campaign came with bigger changes. During the final year of the CMPE's operation, President Truman dismissed General MacArthur from his command of United Nations troops in Korea. This striking decision also relieved him from his command in occupied Japan. The aging general departed Japan on April 16, 1951, seen off by thousands of onlookers on the streets. Seven months later, the United States, Japan, and nearly fifty other countries signed the Treaty of Peace in San Francisco. When this went into effect the following April, the occupied island nation regained its sovereignty. Economic recovery began to accelerate during the transition of political leadership. During and after the Korean War, Japanese light and heavy industries expanded quickly. Fast-speed growth in output and productivity ushered in a major economic boom—the "Jinmu boom"—during the mid-1950s.

The social fabric of Japan changed as well. The revival of the Japanese economy sped up the expansion of big cities, further widening the gap that separated urban and rural communities. Expansion of transportation lines enabled commuters to reach commercial and business districts in city centers from multistory apartments that were starting to sprout in the outlying "bed towns." The white-collar *salari man*—the "new [postwar] middle class," to borrow the phrase of a classic sociological study—increasingly became central to this urban experience.[7] The savings and spending power of Japanese consumers increased. Armed with greater disposable income, citizens were beginning to enjoy leisure time. Things were turning optimistic for many Japanese.

Yet during the years after MacArthur, Japan remained under America's firm grip. On the security front, Japan was heavily dependent on U.S. hard power. The United States–Japan Security Treaty, signed together with the San Francisco Peace Treaty, authorized U.S. troops to operate in military bases across Japan. Even though the Japanese government founded its Self-Defense Forces in 1954 to boost its own defense capabilities, the primary instrument of national security was the U.S. military.[8] The economy, too, relied on U.S. support. During the early 1950s, Japan's industrial and financial sectors relied on America's "economic cooperation" policy, which increased military procurement for the war in Korea and enhanced Japan's market penetration in Southeast Asia.[9] The Japanese also sought technical assistance. Throughout the 1950s and 1960s, Americans offered unprecedented levels of training and advice on industrial production and business management. The famous "lean production" system of Japanese auto companies owed in no small measure to U.S. "tutelage" during this era.[10]

This era of "high speed growth" yielded diverse beliefs and ideas in the minds of the Japanese. Yet many continued to find inspiration in the ideals of American democracy and freedom. Intellectuals and culture elites often took part in new American Studies seminars and Fulbright programs for study abroad.[11] The craving for America continued to grow in the wider public arena. Scores of citizens listened to radio programs such as "Tales from America" (*Amerika dayori*), read magazines like *Reader's Digest,* and listened to popular music including jazz, country western, and rock and roll. The fashion culture of New York and Los Angeles—dresses, nylons, hairstyles—became the buzz of town, and many adapted those styles as they strolled along the streets. The "new [postwar] middle class" aped American-style consumerism in seeking to own the so-called three sacred treasures (*sanshu no jingi*)—refrigerator, washing machine, and television. For many Japanese during this era "the middle-class 'American way of life' became the utopian goal and the dream."[12]

Hollywood continued to wield influence in this cultural climate, but under different institutional conditions. By the time the CMPE dissolved, film policy was in the hands of the Japanese government. SCAP's Circular Eight, which replaced the earlier Circular Twelve in the spring of 1950, broke up the one-distributor-per-nation rule and installed a new quota system. The Ministry of Finance gained the authority to manage film imports. Within a few years after the occupation, the doors were opened to as many as forty-five foreign distributors and scores of licensed intermediaries.[13] At the same time, Japanese bureaucrats also controlled fiscal transfers. Under the new system, foreign distributors were able to increase their currency exchanges, but withdrawals from Japan were capped at $6 million per year. This regulation troubled many distributors.[14]

In this new system, Japanese cinema regained its momentum. After surviving the hard times right after the war, filmmaking in Japan made a big comeback in the mid-1950s. By this time, six major studios—Tōhō, Shōchiku, Daiei, Tōei, Nikkatsu, and Shin Tōhō—commanded a firm lead in filmmaking. A handful of new pictures—Kurosawa Akira's *Rashomon* (1951), Mizoguchi Kenji's *The Life of Oharu* (*Saikaku ichidai onna,* 1952) and *Ugetsu* (*Ugetsu monogatari,* 1953), and Kinugasa Teinsuke's *The Gates of Hell* (*Jigokumon,* 1953)— won international awards and brought confidence to citizens. In the absence of occupation and government censorship, the content of cinema diversified. Japanese companies manufactured a plethora of genre films—including period films, modern dramas, war pictures, and science fiction—to cater to diverse local constituencies. The annual output of domestic films rose throughout the 1950s and peaked in 1960 at 547. This was more than double the total count of foreign imports during that year.[15]

Similar to the 1920s, the postwar boom of Japanese cinema threatened Hollywood's business. But this time, U.S. companies were determined to protect their power in the market. While Japanese studios were increasing their output, U.S. companies geared up their sales and marketing campaigns for big-time productions. Popular hits included action-packed spectacles (*Ben Hur,* 1959) to romantic dramas (*Roman Holiday,* 1953), nail-biting thrillers (*Psycho,* 1960), social-problem films (*Blackboard Jungle,* 1955), and westerns (*Shane,* 1953).[16] The screenings were often coupled with actual visits by top-billed stars, which rarely happened prior to the war. The arrival of William Holden, Elizabeth Taylor, Marilyn Monroe, and Alfred Hitchcock—among many others—generated much media buzz and fan frenzy.

U.S. studios also defended their operations through team work. Facing the familiar binary obstacle of the Japanese government and film industry, American companies, unlike during much of the prewar era, quickly coordinated their actions on the ground. They also worked closely with the MPEA,

Figure 9.1. Advertisement at the Kitano theater in Osaka for Alfred Hitchcock's *Psycho* (1960). Courtesy of Komaki Toshiharu.

which dispatched its own representatives to lobby on the members' behalf. The industry's united front became evident on February 25, 1956, when Eric Johnston visited Japan. During his historic one-week trip to a country in which his predecessor Will H. Hays never set afoot, the MPEA head met with Japanese cabinet members, film moguls, bureaucrats, and scores of other local representatives. At the negotiation tables, Johnston offered an extension of "technical assistance to Japan's movie firms," while calling for expanded quota allotments and the full remittance of the accumulated yen (now amounting to 16.7 billion yen, or some $4.6 million).[17] In a meeting with Finance Minister Ichimada, Johnston argued his case in light of Japan's improved economy and accumulation of dollar reserves.[18]

Japan's ties to the Hollywood product was strong. Throughout the 1950s, U.S. cinema maintained a loyal following among most of the culture elites. Members of the Organization to Appreciate Superior Films (Yūshū eiga kanshōkai), which grew out of the American Movie Culture Association, continued to look to Hollywood for inspiration, even while extending respectful

attention to other imported cinemas. Many of these learned moviegoers up-
held a familiar double standard: valuing Japanese cinema less than U.S. (and
European) imports.[19] Young fans and other "ordinary" consumers passionately
consumed American movies. *Eiga no tomo, Screen,* and other Hollywood-heavy
magazines enjoyed a large following throughout the decade. Magazine fan
clubs, study groups, and film circles continued to engage with Hollywood.
When Samuel Goldwyn visited Japan in 1956, he was impressed with the
lively fan activities, and much more: "They [the Japanese] are actually carrying on the spread of our theories of life, which had previously been so widely
disseminated through our military leaders." "Japan," the producer continued,
"is immensely interested in our country, our views and beliefs. They are more
anxious to carry on trade with us than any other nation."[20]

Hollywood's postoccupation campaign did not lead to its instant domination. The Japanese government and film industry pushed back the surge of
American movies. According to one source, U.S. shares in the Japanese box
office declined from 40 percent in 1955 to 30 percent in 1957 and 21 percent in 1959.[21] However, this downturn was temporary. Hollywood's returns
picked up in the following decade, while Japanese companies struggled to
cope with the rise of television, the migration of youth to the big cities, the
aftereffects of poor investment decisions, and the continuing influx of U.S.
movies.[22] Japanese studios were forced to downsize their operations, and those
hit the hardest, Shin Tōhō (1961) and Daiei (1971), went bankrupt. In 1973
a veteran film critic, albeit prematurely, declared that Japanese cinema had
"found [its] closure . . . and collapsed."[23] Subsequent years did not look good
for Japanese companies; some turned to pornography for survival (Nikkatsu)
and others disintegrated after accumulating massive debts (Shōchiku). Much
of Japanese filmmaking during the 1980s and 1990s was small-scale independent productions.[24]

The situation of Hollywood was more favorable. While the popularity of
Japanese cinema dwindled, U.S. studios achieved record highs at the box office. Movie fans flocked to such hit products as *West Side Story* (1961), *The
Sound of Music* (1965), *The Exorcist* (1974), *Star Wars* (1977), *E.T.* (1982), *Back to
the Future* (1985), and *Top Gun* (1986).[25] In 1988 the *New York Times* reported
that Japan was the largest foreign consumer of Hollywood films, contributing at least $140 million in the previous year. "American movies are every-
where," the writer noted.[26] That figure multiplied to $317.8 million six years
later, when Japan accounted for "almost 16 percent of [Hollywood's] entire
international total."[27] The twentieth century ended on a high note. The once
hostile East Asian nation became the biggest patron of American movies.

Japan today hardly resembles the scorched landscape of the early postwar era. It now flourishes on an impressive industrial and post-industrial economy—the second largest in the world. Its culture and values have greatly diversified, thanks to the influx of goods, people, ideas, and institutions from around the globe. Yet despite these drastic changes, Japan's ties with "America" have remained strong. Politically and militarily, the island nation shares a firm bond with the U.S. government.[28] Trade and commerce have continued in high levels. Citizens crave U.S. culture and lifestyles, as they flock to Disneyland, McDonald's, Starbucks Coffee, hip-hop music, and of course, Hollywood movies. This bicultural intimacy over the decades demonstrates the enduring influence of U.S. power, as well as Japan's lasting affinity for things American. Understanding the history of the two societies require a close look at this transpacific dialectic. Border-crossing interactions of this kind have greatly influenced their respective experiences in the postwar world.

Appendix

First Forty-Five Films Selected for Distribution in Japan after the War

Columbia
Here Comes Mr. Jordan
The Men in Her Life
Once upon a Time
Counter-Attack
Ladies in Retirement

Paramount
Going My Way
No Time for Love
Our Hearts Were Young and Gay
The Uninvited
Two Years before the Mast

Twentieth Century-Fox
Tales of Manhattan
Captain Eddie
The Keys of the Kingdom
Remember the Day
Sun Valley Serenade

Republic
Lake Placid Serenade
Yellow Rose of Texas
Song of Nevada
In Old Oklahoma
San Fernando Valley

MGM
Lost Angel
Madame Curie
Babes on Broadway
Our Vines Have Tender Grapes
Men of Boys Town

RKO
All That Money Can Buy
Snow White and the Seven Dwarfs
Kitty Foyle
Abe Lincoln in Illinois
Tall in the Saddle

United Artists
The Gold Rush
I'll Be Seeing You
The Southerner
Our Town
Dangerous Journey

Universal
Shadow of a Doubt
The Spoilers

Flesh and Fantasy
Enter Arsène Lupin
His Butler's Sister

Warner Bros.
Watch on the Rhine
The Corn Is Green
Now, Voyager
Casablanca
Always in My Heart

Source: *Kinema herarudo* 1:3 (February 1946): 2–3.

Notes

Preface

1. *Eiga hyōron,* October/November 1945, 1–3.
2. Hazumi Tsuneo, *Amerika eiga dokuhon* (Tokyo: Tōzai shuppansha, 1947), 15, 18, 3.
3. Hazumi, *Amerika eiga dokuhon,* 195, 197.
4. *Sentoraru nyūsu,* 1, n.d., 1.
5. See, for example, Kazuo Kawai, *Japan's American Interlude* (Chicago: University of Chicago Press, 1960); Michael Schaller, *The American Occupation of Japan: The Origins of the Cold War in Asia* (New York: Oxford University Press, 1985); Howard B. Schonberger, *Aftermath of War: Americans and the Remaking of Japan, 1945–1952* (Kent, OH: Kent State University Press, 1989); Yoneyuki Sugita, *Pitfall or Panacea: The Irony of U.S. Power in Occupied Japan, 1945–1952* (New York: Routledge, 2003); Eiji Takemae, *Inside GHQ: The Allied Occupation of Japan and Its Legacy* (New York: Continuum, 2002).
6. Mire Koikari, *Pedagogy of Democracy: Feminism and the Cold War in the U.S. Occupation of Japan* (Philadelphia: Temple University Press, 2008); Yukiko Koshiro, *Trans-Pacific Racisms and the U.S. Occupation of Japan* (New York: Columbia University Press, 1999); Takeshi Matsuda, *Soft Power and Its Perils: U.S. Cultural Policy in Early Postwar Japan and Permanent Diplomacy* (Stanford and Washington, DC: Stanford University Press and Woodrow Wilson Center Press, 2007); Naoko Shibusawa, *America's Geisha Ally: Reimagining the Japanese Enemy* (Cambridge: Harvard University Press, 2006).
7. John W. Dower, *Embracing Defeat: Japan in the Wake of World War II* (New York: W. W. Norton and the New Press, 1999), 558, 24–25, emphasis in original.
8. Hollywood has received marginal attention in the scholarship on the occupation. For example, see Dower, *Embracing Defeat,* 150, 195, 252. One exception is a Japanese-language book by Tanikawa Takeshi, which explores U.S. cinema in relation to the U.S. State Department's film policies formulated during the Second World War and their implementation by SCAP during the occupation era. A pioneering and useful account, Tanikawa's book is largely a study of official policymaking by U.S. government and military authorities and less so on Hollywood itself. We are also left to wonder about the impact of Hollywood's penetration on the "ground level" and the response of the Japanese population to the policies and programs

implemented from above. See Tanikawa Takeshi, *Amerika eiga to senryō seisaku* (Kyoto: Kyoto University Press, 2002).

9. On "chosen instrument," see Emily Rosenberg, *Spreading the American Dream: American Economic and Cultural Expansion, 1890–1945* (New York: Hill and Wang, 1982), 59–62.

10. Standard works on Hollywood's overseas trade include Heide Fehrenbach, *Cinema in Democratizing Germany: Reconstructing National Identity after Hitler* (Chapel Hill: University of North Carolina Press, 1995), 51–91; H. Mark Glancy, *When Hollywood Loved Britain: The Hollywood "British" Film* (New York: Manchester University Press, 1999); Thomas Guback, *The International Film Industry: Western Europe and America since 1945* (Bloomington: Indiana University Press, 1969); Andrew Higson and Richard Maltby, eds., *"Film Europe" and "Film America": Cinema, Commerce, and Cultural Exchange, 1920–1939* (Exeter, UK: University of Exeter Press, 1999); Ian Jarvie, *Hollywood's Overseas Campaign: The North Atlantic Film Trade, 1920–1950* (New York: Cambridge University Press, 1992); Paul Swann, *The Hollywood Feature Film in Postwar Britain* (London: Croom Helm, 1987); John Trumpbour, *Selling Hollywood to the World: U.S. and European Struggles for Mastery of the Global Film Industry, 1920–1950* (New York: Cambridge University Press, 2002); Jens Ulff-Moller, *Hollywood's Film Wars with France: Film-Trade Diplomacy and the Emergency of the French Film Quota Policy* (Rochester, NY: University of Rochester Press, 2001). Key overviews include Toby Miller, Nitin Govil, John McMurria, Richard Maxwell, and Ting Wang, *Global Hollywood 2* (London: British Film Institute Publishing, 2005); Kerry Segrave, *American Films Abroad: Hollywood's Domination of the World's Movie Screens* (Jefferson, NC: McFarland, 1997); Kristin Thompson, *Exporting Entertainment: America in the World Film Market, 1907–1934* (London: British Film Institute Publishing, 1985).

11. Robert C. Allen, "From Exhibition to Reception: Reflections on the Audience in Film History," in *Screen Histories: A Screen Reader*, ed. Annette Kuhn and Jackie Stacey (Oxford: Oxford University Press, 1998), 15. An exception in the literature is Richard Maltby and Melvyn Stokes, eds., *Hollywood Abroad: Audiences and Cultural Exchange* (London: British Film Institute, 2004).

12. In 2004, *Variety* reported that Japan was the industry's "biggest theatrical market outside the U.S." *Variety*, October 19, 2004, 5. On Japan's primacy to Hollywood, see Toby Miller, "Hollywood and the World," in *American Cinema and Hollywood: Critical Approaches*, eds. John Hill and Pamela Church Gibson (Oxford: Oxford University Press, 2000), 147; Kerry Segrave, *American Films Abroad*, 290.

13. For recent works on "Americanization," see Fehrenbach and Uta G. Poiger, eds., *Transactions, Transgressions, Transformations: American Culture in Western Europe and Japan* (New York: Berghahn Books, 2000); Richard Kuisel, *Seducing the French: The Dilemmas of Americanization* (Berkeley: University of California Press, 1993); Robert W. Rydell and Rob Kroes, *Buffalo Bill in Bologna: The Americanization of the World, 1869–1922* (Chicago: University of Chicago Press, 2005); Uta G. Poiger, *Jazz, Rock, and Rebels: Cold War Politics and American Culture in a Divided Germany* (Berkeley: University of California Press, 2000); Kristin Ross, *Fast Cars, Clean Bodies: Decolonization and the Reordering of French Culture* (Cambridge: MIT Press, 1995). For a useful overview, see Jessica C. E. Gienow-Hecht, "Cultural Transfer," in *Explaining the History of American Foreign Relations*, 2nd ed., ed. Michael Hogan and Thomas Paterson (New York: Cambridge University Press, 2004), 257–78. One should also note that the scholarship on anti-Americanism has grown over the past several years, particularly after the terrorist attacks on September 11, 2001. See, for example, Jessica C. E. Gienow-Hecht, "Always Blame the Americans: Anti-Americanism in Europe in the Twentieth Century," *American Historical Review* 111:4 (October 2006): 1067–91; Michel Gobat, *Confronting the American Dream: Nicaragua under U.S. Imperial Rule* (Chapel Hill: University of North Carolina Press, 2005); Greg Grandin, "Americanism and Anti-Americanism in the Americas," *American Historical Review*, 111:4 (October 2006): 1042–1066; Peter J. Katzenstein and Robert O. Keohane, eds., *Anti-Americanism*

in *World Politics* (Ithaca: Cornell University Press, 2007); Alan McPherson, *Yankee No!: Anti-Americanism in U.S.-Latin American Relations* (Cambridge: Harvard University Press, 2003).

14. See, for example, William Marotti, "Japan 1968: The Performance of Violence and the Theater of Protest," *American Historical Review,* 114:1 (February 2009): 97–135; Barbara Sato, *The New Japanese Woman: Modernity, Media, and Women in Interwar Japan* (Durham: Duke University Press, 2003), 35; Miriam Silverberg, *Erotic Grotesque Nonsense: The Mass Culture of Japanese Modern Times* (Berkeley: University of California Press, 2006), 9; Sugita, *Pitfall and Panacea.* One exception is sociologist Yoshimi Shunya, who argues that "from the late 1940s on, the process of widespread, overwhelming Americanization began." Yoshimi's research largely focuses on the postoccupation decades. Yoshimi Shunya, "Consuming 'America': From Symbol to System," in *Consumption in Asia: Lifestyles and Identities,* ed. Chua Beng-Huat (New York: Routledge, 2000), 206. Also see Yoshimi, *Shinbei to hanbei: Sengo nihon no seijiteki muishiki* (Tokyo: Iwanami shoten, 2007).

15. I owe this reading to Henry Jenkins's notion of "convergence culture." See Henry Jenkins, *Convergence Culture: Where the Old and New Media Collide* (New York: New York University Press, 2006), 1–24.

16. My use of the term "hegemony" involves political, military, economic, and cultural control. I have received inspiration from the following books: Quintin Hoare and Geoffrey Nowell Smith, eds., *Selections from the Prison Notebooks of Antonio Gramsci* (New York: International Publishers, 1971), esp. 5–23, 279–318; T. J. Jackson Lears, "The Concept of Cultural Hegemony: Problems and Possibilities," *American Historical Review* 90:3 (1985): 567–93; Thomas J. McCormick, *America's Half-Century: United States Foreign Policy in the Cold War and After,* 2nd ed. (Baltimore: Johns Hopkins Press, 1995), esp. 5–6; John Storey, *Inventing Popular Culture* (Malden, MA: Blackwell Publishing, 2003), esp. 48–62.

17. For recent works that address the growing intimacy of America and Asia after World War II, see, for example, Gregg Brazinsky, *Nation Building in South Korea: Koreans, Americans and the Making of a Democracy* (Chapel Hill: University of North Carolina Press, 2007); Warren I. Cohen and Nancy Bernkopf Tucker, "America in Asian Eyes," *American Historical Review* 111:4 (November 2006): 1092–1119; Seth Jacobs, *America's Miracle Man in Vietnam: Ngo Dinh Diem, Religion, Race, and U.S. Intervention in Southeast Asia* (Durham: Duke University Press, 2004); Christina Klein, *Cold War Orientalism: Asia in the Middlebrow Imagination, 1945–1961* (Berkeley: University of California Press, 2003); Gavan McCormack, *Client State: Japan in the American Embrace* (New York: Verso, 2007); Bradley R. Simpson, *Economists with Guns: Authoritarian Development and U.S.-Indonesian Relations, 1960–1968* (Stanford: Stanford University Press, 2008); James L. Watson, ed., *Golden Arches East: McDonald's in East Asia* (Stanford: Stanford University Press, 1997).

1. Thwarted Ambitions

1. *Kokusai eiga shinbun,* 89, 2–3.

2. On America's rise to power after the Civil War, see, for example, Paul Kramer, *The Blood of Government: Race, Empire, the United States, and the Philippines* (Chapel Hill: University of North Carolina Press, 2006); Walter LaFeber, *The New Empire: An Interpretation of American Expansion, 1860–1898,* 35th anniversary ed. (Ithaca: Cornell University Press, 1998); Erez Manela, *The Wilsonian Moment: Self-Determination and the International Origins of Anticolonial Nationalism* (New York: Cambridge University Press, 2007).

3. Richard Abel, *The Red Rooster Scare: Making Cinema American, 1900–1910* (Berkeley: University of California Press, 1999); Kristin Thompson, *Exporting Entertainment: America in the World Film Market 1907–1934* (London: British Film Institute, 1985), 5.

4. Robert Anderson, "The Motion Picture Patents Company: A Reevaluation," in *The American Film Industry*, rev. ed., ed. Tino Balio (Madison: University of Wisconsin Press, 1986), 133–52.

5. David Bordwell, Janet Staiger, and Kristin Thompson, *The Classical Hollywood Cinema: Film Style and Mode of Production to 1960* (New York: Routledge and Kegan Paul, 1985).

6. Thompson, *Exporting Entertainment*, 1–99, 199–211.

7. Bordwell, Staiger, and Thompson, *Classical Hollywood Cinema*.

8. Carl Laemmle, "The Business of Motion Pictures," *Saturday Evening Post* 200 (August 27, 1927): 10–11, repr. in *The American Film Industry*, ed., Tino Balio (Madison: University of Wisconsin Press, 1976), 157.

9. Douglas Gomery, *Shared Pleasures: A History of Movie Presentation in the United States* (Madison: University of Wisconsin Press, 1992), 3–82.

10. Tino Balio, ed., *The American Film Industry*, rev. ed. (Madison: University of Wisconsin Press, 1986), 125–26; Ian Jarvie, *Hollywood's Overseas Campaign: The North Atlantic Movie Trade* (New York: Cambridge University Press, 1992), 284–301; Richard Koszarski, *An Evening's Entertainment: The Age of the Silent Feature Pictures, 1915–1928* (Berkeley: University of California Press, 1990), 203–10; Stephen Vaughn, "Morality and Entertainment: The Origins of the Motion Picture Production Code," *Journal of American History* 79:1 (June 1990): 42–44.

11. Leigh Ann Wheeler, *Against Obscenity: Reform and the Politics of Womanhood in America, 1873–1935* (Baltimore: Johns Hopkins University Press, 2004), esp. 46–95, 133–80; Vaughn, "The Devil's Advocate: Will H. Hays and the Campaign to Make Movies Respectable," *Indiana Magazine of History*, 101:2 (June 2005): 125–52.

12. Gregory D. Black, *Hollywood Censored: Morality Codes, Catholics, and the Movies* (New York: Cambridge University Press, 1994); Lea Jacobs, *The Wages of Sin: Censorship and the Fallen Woman Film, 1928–1942* (Madison: University of Wisconsin Press, 1991).

13. Balio, *The American Film Industry*, 253. For more details, see Tino Balio, *Grand Design: Hollywood as a Modern Business Enterprise, 1930–1939* (Berkeley: University of California Press, 1993).

14. On the "open door" approach, see William Appleman Williams, *The Tragedy of American Diplomacy* (New York: W. W. Norton, 1972).

15. Ruth Vasey, *The World According to Hollywood, 1918–1939* (Madison: University of Wisconsin Press, 1997), 8, 38.

16. Vasey, *World According to Hollywood;* John Trumpbour, *Selling Hollywood to the World: U.S. and European Struggles for the Mastery of the Global Film Industry, 1920–1950* (New York: Cambridge University Press, 2002), 30–32.

17. Jarvie, *Hollywood's Overseas Trade*, 305.

18. Vasey, *World According to Hollywood*, 42, 50, 121, 156; Trumpbour, *Selling Hollywood to the World*, 65–66.

19. Quoted in Jarvie, *Hollywood's Overseas Trade*, 309. Vasey, *World According to Hollywood*, 42–43.

20. *The Film Daily Yearbook, 1932* (New York: Film Daily, 1932), 964.

21. Vasey, *World According to Hollywood*, 39–43.

22. See, for example, H. Mark Glancy, "MGM Film Grosses, 1924–1948: The Eddie Mannix Ledger," *Historical Journal of Film, Radio and Television* 12:2 (1992): 128–29; Will H. Hays, "Government Co-Operation in Maintaining Foreign Markets for American Motion Pictures," October 23, 1943, 800.4061 Motion Pictures/332, Records of the U.S. Department of State, Record Group 59, National Archives II, College Park, Maryland (hereafter cited as State Department Records, NA).

23. Thompson, *Exporting Entertainment*, esp. 100–37; Trumpbour, *Selling Hollywood to the World*, esp. 63–116; On Europe's resistance to Hollywood, see Andrew Higson and Richard

Maltby, eds. *"Film Europe" and "Film America": Cinema, Commerce and Cultural Exchange 1920–1939* (Exeter, UK: University of Exeter Press, 1999).

24. *The Film Daily Yearbook, 1928* (New York: Film Daily, 1928), 941.

25. Thompson, *Exporting Entertainment,* 139–40; Glancy, *When Hollywood Loved Britain: The Hollywood "British" Film* (New York: Manchester University Press, 1999), 17–20.

26. Thompson, *Exporting Entertainment,* 137.

27. The *Film Daily Yearbook, 1930 (New York: Film Daily, 1930),* 999.

28. Sherman Cochran, *Inventing Chinese Networks: Western, Japanese, and Chinese Corporations in China, 1880–1937* (Berkeley: University of California Press, 2000); Thomas J. McCormick, *The China Market: America's Quest for Informal Empire, 1893–1901* (Chicago: Ivan R. Dee, 1967).

29. *Los Angeles Times,* November 12, 1916, III20.

30. The *Film Daily Yearbook, 1928,* 943.

31. W. G. Beasley, *Japanese Imperialism, 1894–1945* (New York: Oxford University Press, 1987), 1–155; Charles E. Neu, *The Troubled Encounter: The United States and Japan* (Malabar, FL: Robert Krieger, 1987).

32. Thomas C. Smith, *Political Change and Industrial Development in Japan: Government Enterprise, 1868–1880* (Stanford: Stanford University Press, 1955); Kozo Yamamura, ed., *The Economic Emergence of Modern Japan* (New York: Cambridge University Press, 1997), esp. 50–158, 203–38.

33. The population of Japan grew from thirty-five million in 1873 to fifty-six million in 1920. Marius B. Jansen, *The Making of Modern Japan* (Cambridge: Harvard University Press, 2000), 447, 556.

34. Andrew Gordon, *Labor and Imperial Democracy in Prewar Japan* (Berkeley: University of California Press, 1991); Jansen, *Making of Modern Japan,* 555–64; Carol Gluck, *Japan's Modern Myths: Ideology in the Late Meiji Period* (Princeton: Princeton University Press, 1985), 159–60.

35. Jansen, *Making of Modern Japan,* 568. Silverberg, *Erotic Grotesque Nonsense,* 22.

36. See, for example, Silverberg, *Erotic Grotesque Nonsense;* Takemura Tamio, *Taishō bunka: Teikoku no yūtopia* (Tokyo: Sangensha, 2004); Louise Young, "Marketing the Modern: Department Stores, Consumer Culture, and the New Middle Class in Interwar Japan," *International Labor and Working-Class History* 55 (Spring 1999): 52–70.

37. Yoshimi Shunya, "Amerikanaizēshon to bunka no seijigaku," Inoue Shun, Ueno Chizuko, Ōsawa Makichi, Mita Munesuke, and Yoshimi Shunya, eds., *Gendai shakaigaku,* vol. 1, *Gendai shakai no shakaigaku* (Tokyo: Iwanami shoten, 1997), 172.

38. Silverberg, *Erotic Grotesque Nonsense,* 51–72.

39. Tanaka, *Nihon eiga hattatsushi,* vol. 1 (Tokyo: Chūō kōronsha, 1963), 237.

40. Tanaka, *Nihon eiga hattatsushi,* vol. 1, 237.

41. Aaron Gerow, "Jigoma to eiga no 'hakken': Nihon eiga gensetsushi josetsu," *Eizōgaku* 58 (1997): 34–50.

42. Tanaka, *Nihon eiga hattatsushi,* vol. 1, 94–129.

43. Jeffrey A. Dym, *Benshi, Japanese Silent Film Narrators, and their Forgotten Narrative Art of Setsumei* (Lewiston, NY: Edwin Mellen Press, 2003), esp. 1–117; Hidaki Fujiki, "Benshi as Stars: The Irony of the Popularity and Respectability of Voice Performers in Japanese Cinema," *Cinema Journal* 45:2 (Winter 2006): 68–84.

44. It is worth noting that cinema in Japan, as Joseph Anderson and Donald Richie have stated, was "essentially an urban affair." Anderson and Richie, *The Japanese Film: Art and Industry,* expanded ed. (Princeton: Princeton University Press, 1982), 412.

45. Kokusai eiga tsūshinsha, ed., *Nihon eiga jigyō sōran: Shōwa 5 nendoban* (Tokyo: Kokusai eiga tsūshinsha, 1930), 159–61; Kokusai eiga tsūshinsha, ed., *Eiga nenakn: Shōwa 16 nendoban* (Tokyo: Kokusai eiga tsūshinsha, 1941), 50–51.

46. *Kokusai eiga shinbun* 47 (December 1930): 21–22.

47. Kokusai eiga tsūshinsha, ed., *Nihon eiga jigyō sōran: Shōwa 3–4 nendoban,* (Tokyo: Kokusai eiga tsūshinsha, 1928), 322–23.

48. Kokusai eiga tsūshinsha, *Nihon eiga jigyō sōran: Shōwa 3–4 nendoban,* 59; Kokusai eiga tsūshinsha, ed., *Nihon eiga jigyō sōran: Taishō 15 nendoban* (Tokyo: Kokusai eiga tsūshinsha, 1925), 54; *Kokusai eiga shinbun* 142 (January 15, 1935): 2.

49. Kokusai eiga tsūshinsha, *Nihon eiga jigyō sōran, Shōwa 3–4 nendoban,* 321.

50. Kokusai eiga tsūshinsha, *Nihon eiga jigyō sōran, Taishō 15 nendoban,* 53–54.

51. Fujiki Hideaki, *Zōshoku suru perusona: Eiga sutādamu no seiritsu to nihon kindai* (Nagoya: Nagoya University Press, 2007), 112.

52. Tanaka, *Nihon eiga hattatsushi,* vol. 1, 242–46.

53. On the Bluebird films, see Yamamoto Kikuo, *Nihon eiga ni okeru gaikoku eiga no eikyō* (Tokyo: Waseda University Press, 1982), 48–66; Jeannette Delamoir, "Louise Lovely, Bluebird Photoplays, and the Star System," *Moving Image* 4:2 (Fall 2004): 64–85. On the Red Feather and Butterfly films, see Tsukada Yoshinobu and Yamanaka Toshio, "Burūbādo eiga no kiroku, tsuiho" (unpublished manuscript, 1984), esp. 9–12, National Film Center, National Museum of Modern Art, Tokyo, Japan. On Universal, see *Kokusai eiga shinbun* 61 (September 1, 1931): 14.

54. Yamamoto, *Nihon eiga ni okeru gaikoku eiga no eikyō,* 67–100.

55. Kokusai eiga tsūshinsha, *Nihon eiga jigyō sōran, Shōwa 3–4 nendoban,* 185.

56. Kokusai eiga tsūshinsha, *Nihon eiga jigyō sōran, Shōwa 2 nendoban* (Tokyo: Kokusai eiga tsūshinsha, 1927), 472–73.

57. *Kokusai eiga shinbun* 27 (May 1, 1929): 5.

58. United Artists, for example, compiled "black books" that listed quota laws, holidays, monetary regulations, taxes, duties, censorship rules, trade papers, competitors, insurance plans, etc. of each foreign market. For Japan, see "Far East: India-straits Settlements," Box 5, Folder 4, Series 1F, United Artists Collection, Wisconsin Center for Film and Theater Research, Madison, Wisconsin (hereafter cited as UA Collection, WCFTR).

59. *Kokusai eiga shinbun* 69 (January 1, 1932): 24. Also see *Kinema junpō,* January 1, 1932, 68; *Kinema junpō,* December 1, 1927, 11; *Kokusai eiga shinbun* 161 (November 5, 1935): 8–9. *Kokusai eiga shinbun* 53 (May 1, 1931): 8; *Kinema junpō,* August 11, 1928, 41.

60. Kokusai eiga tsūshinsha, *Nihon eiga jigyō sōran, Shōwa 2 nendoban,* 504–11.

61. *Kinema junpō,* October 1, 1930, 18.

62. *Kokusai eiga shinbun* 172 (April 20, 1936): 19.

63. *Kokusai eiga shinbun* 178 (July 20, 1936): 45.

64. Yodogawa Nagaharu, *Yodogawa Nagaharu jiden, jō* (Tokyo: Chūō Kōronsha, 1988), 347–53.

65. See, for example, *Kinema junpo,* November 11, 1927, 65; *Kokusai eiga shinbun,* 2 (August 1927), 6; *Kinema junpo,* June 21, 1920, 12; *Kinema junpo,* December 1, 1922, 2.

66. Richard Maltby, *Hollywood Cinema,* 2nd. ed. (Malden, MA: Blackwell, 2003), 142.

67. On genre, see Steve Neale, *Genre and Hollywood* (New York: Routledge, 2000), esp. 9–29.

68. *Kokusai eiga shinbun* 86 (September 1932): n.p.

69. *Kokusai eiga shinbun* 35 (January 1930): n.p.

70. *Kokusai eiga shinbun* 40 (June 1930): n.p.

71. Eileen Bowser, *The Transformation of Cinema, 1907–1915* (Berkley: University of California Press, 1990), 103.

72. *Kinema junpō,* November 11, 1927, 65; *Kokusai eiga shinbun* 2 (August 1927): 6; *Kinema junpō,* June 21, 1920, 12; *Kinema junpō,* December 1, 1922, 2.

73. Nanbu Keinosuke, *Eiga sendensen* (Tokyo: Dōbunkan, 1956), 37.

74. Kokusai eiga tsūshinsha, *Nihon eiga jigyō sōran, Taishō 15 nendoban,* 11. Kokusai eiga tsūshinsha, *Nihon eiga jigyō sōran, shōwa 3–4 nendoban,* 314.

75. *Nihon eiga,* June 1937, 63. Joseph Anderson and Donald Richie claim that the standard rate during the interwar era was 35 percent. See Anderson and Richie, *The Japanese Film: Art and Industry,* 173.

76. Kokusai eiga tsūshinsha, *Nihon eiga jigyō sōran: Shōwa 2 nendoban,* 472–73.

77. Kokusai eiga tsūshinsha, *Nihon eiga jigyō sōran: Shōwa 2 nendoban,* 473.

78. Kokusai eiga tsūshinsha, ed., *Kokusai eiga nenkan: Shōwa 9 nendoban* (Tokyo: Kokusai eiga tsūshinsha, 1934), 40.

79. Yamamoto, *Nihon eiga ni okeru gaikoku eiga no eikyō,* 68–69, 210–11.

80. Fujiki, *Zōshoku suru perusona,* 292–362. On *Kingu,* see Satō Takumi, *"Kingu" no jidai: Kokumin taishū zasshi no kōkyōsei* (Tokyo: Iwanami shoten, 2002).

81. See, for example, Gonda Yasunosuke, quoted in Fujiki, *Zōshoku suru perusona,* 71; *Kinema junpō,* June 11, 1930, 46; *Nihon eiga,* October 1936, 22; *Nihon eiga,* November 1936, 28.

82. Barbara Sato, *The New Japanese Woman: Modernity, Media, and Women in Interwar Japan* (Durham: Duke University Press, 2003), 31.

83. *Kokusai eiga shinbun,* 4 (September 1927), 101.

84. The *Film Daily Yearbook, 1925* (New York: Film Daily, 1925), 659.

85. Peter B. High, "The Dawn of Cinema in Japan," *Journal of Contemporary History,* 19:1 (January 1984): 23–57; Hiroshi Komatsu, "Some Characteristics of Japanese Cinema before World War I," in *Reframing Japanese Cinema: Authorship, Genre, History,* ed. Arthur Nolletti Jr. and David Desser (Bloomington: Indiana University Press, 1992), 229–58.

86. Tanaka, *Nihon eiga hattatsushi,* vol. 1, 194–218.

87. Komatsu, "Some Characteristics of Japanese Cinema," 229–58.

88. Joanne Bernardi, *Writing in Light: The Silent Scenario and the Japanese Pure Film Movement* (Detroit: Wayne State University Press, 2001), esp. 67–96.

89. Satō Tadao, *Nihon eigashi,* vol. 1 (Tokyo: Iwanami shoten, 1995), 187–202, 253–54.

90. Satō, *Nihon eigashi,* vol. 1, 36–44.

91. David Bordwell, *Ozu and the Poetics of Cinema* (Princeton: Princeton University Press, 1988); David Bordwell, *Figures Traced in Light: On Cinematic Staging* (Berkeley: University of California Press, 2005), 83–139; Mark Le Fanu, *Mizoguchi and Japan* (London: BFI Publishing, 2005).

92. Satō, *Nihon eigashi,* vol. 1, 170–74.

93. Fujiki, *Zōshoku suru perusona,* esp. 188–290, 331–62; Deguchi Fumihito, "Nani ga hakujin konpurekkusu o umidashitaka," *Nihon eiga to modanizumu, 1920–1930,* ed. Iwamoto Kenji (Tokyo: Riburo pōto, 1991), 104–23.

94. Bordwell, *Ozu and the Poetics of Cinema,* 18.

95. Komatsu, "The Foundation of Modernism: Japanese Cinema in the Year 1927," *Film History* 17 (2005): 365.

96. Kokusai eiga tsūshinsha, *Nihon eiga jigyō sōran: Taishō 15 nendoban,* 44–45.

97. Iwamoto Kenji, "Jidaigeki densetsu," in *Jidaigeki densetsu: chanbara eiga no kagayaki,* ed. Iwamoto Kenji (Tokyo: Shinwasha, 2005), 8–32.

98. Yamamoto, *Nihon eiga ni okeru gaikoku eiga no eikyō,* 258–78, 343–61; Mitsuyo Wada-Marciano, *Nippon modan: Nihon eiga no 1920, 30 nendai* (Nagoya: Nagoya University Press, 2008). 69–114.

99. Mitsuhiro Yoshimoto, *Kurosawa: Film Studies and Japanese Cinema* (Durham: Duke University Press, 2000), 207.

100. Fujiki, *Zōshoku suru perusona,* 213.

101. *Kokusai eiga shinbun* 9 (November 1927): 245; *Kokusai eiga shinbun* 48 (January 1931): 25.

102. *Kokusai eiga shinbun* 161 (November 5, 1935): 9.

103. *Kokusai eiga shinbun* 161 (November 5, 1935): 10.

104. *Kokusai eiga shinbun* 165 (January 5, 1936): 62–67.

105.   Japanese studios secured screen time in three ways: by directly owning theaters (these theaters were called *tokuyaku kan*), by renting prints on a percentage basis (*buai kan*), and by renting prints on a flat fee (*keiyaku kan*). The figures for each studio are sums of the three types of theaters. Katō Atsuko, *Sōdōin taisei to eiga* (Tokyo: Shinyōsha, 2003), 32, 275.

106.   *Kokusai eiga shinbun* 148 (April 20, 1935): 2.

107.   Inoue Masao, *Bunka to tōsō: Tōhō sōgi, 1946–1948* (Tokyo: Shinyōsha, 2007).

108.   Kokusai jiji tsūshinsha, ed., *Nihon eiga jigyō sōran: Shōwa 5 nendoban,* 154–56.

109.   *Kokusai eiga shinbun* 161 (November 5, 1935): 31.

110.   Kokusai eiga tsūshinsha, ed., *Kokusai eiga tsushin: 1934 nendoban,* 122–24. On Fukuoka, see *Kokusai eiga shinbun* 42 (August 10, 1930): 39; *Kokusai eiga shinbun* 27 (May 10, 1929): 27. On Nagoya, *Kokusai eiga shinbun* 44 (October 10, 1930): 14–16. On the Chukyo region, see *Kokusai eiga shinbun* 51 (April 5, 1931): 35–36.

111.   Thompson, *Exporting Entertainment,* 147.

112.   Fukuda Kizō, "Taishōki ni okeru eiga tōsei jōkyō, sono ichi," *Seikei daigaku bungakubu kiyō* 10 (February 1975): 51–65. Hase Masato, "Kenetsu no tanjō: Taishōki no keisatsu to katsudō shashin," *Eizōgaku* 53 (1994): 124–38; Makino Mamoru, *Nihon eiga kenetsushi* (Tokyo: Pandorasha, 2003), 78–164.

113.   Fukuda Kizō, "Eiga tōitsu kenetsu no naiyō to mondai: Eiga tōsei ni kansuru kenkyū 2," *Seikei daigaku bungaku kiyō* 11 (February 1976): 46–55; Gregory J. Kasza, *The State and the Mass Media in Japan, 1918–1945* (Berkeley: University of California Press, 1988), 54–71.

114.   Makino, *Nihon eiga kenetsushi,* 228–61.

115.   Peter B. High, *The Imperial Screen: Japanese Film Culture in the Fifteen Years' War, 1931–1945* (Madison: University of Wisconsin Press, 2003), 82–85; Kasza, *State and the Mass Media in Japan,* 168–93.

116.   High, *Imperial Screen,* 70–82; Katō, *Sōdōin taisei to eiga,* 50–71.

117.   See chapter 5 for a discussion *bunka.* For more on bunka, see Nishikawa Nagao, *Kokkyō no koekata: Kokumin kokkaron josetsu, zōho* (Tokyo: Heibonsha, 2001), esp. 222–70; Nishikawa, *Chikyū jidai no minzoku = bunka riron: Datsu "kokumin bunka" no tameni* (Tokyo: Shinyōsha, 1995), esp. 46–107; Tessa Morris-Suzuki, *Re-Inventing Japan: Time, Space, Nation* (New York: M. E. Sharpe, 1998), 60–78.

118.   Katō Atsuko, "Taishū goraku kara eiga kokusaku e," in *Mediashi o manabu hito no tameni,* ed. Ariyama Teruo and Takeyama Akiko (Tokyo: Sekai shisōsha, 2004), 208–32.

119.   Katō, "Taishū goraku kara eiga kokusaku e," 215.

120.   Michael Baskett, *The Attractive Empire: Transnational Film Culture in Imperial Japan* (Honolulu: University of Hawaii Press, 2008), 72–105.

121.   Katō, *Sōdōin taisei to eiga,* 84–133.

122.   Peter B. High, *Teikoku no ginmaku: 15 nen sensō to nihon eiga* (Nagoya: Nagoya University Press, 1995), 94–112.

123.   Katō, *Sōdōin taisei to eiga,* 116–17.

124.   Kokusai eiga tsūshinsha, *Kokusai eiga nenkan: 1934 nendoban,* 39.

125.   *New York Times,* February 12, 1928, 111.

126.   Burman to Spring, December 20, 1937, 894.4061 Motion Pictures/14 F/A, State Department Records, NA.

127.   "Mutiny on the Bounty" folder, Production Code Administration Files, Special Collections, Margaret Herrick Library, Academy of Motion Picture Arts and Sciences, Los Angeles (hereafter cited as MHL). Makino, *Nihon eiga kenetsushi,* 410–12; Seno Tokuji, "Cinema Censorship in Japan," *Contemporary Japan,* June 1937, translated by Supreme Commander for the Allied Powers, May 7, 1957, Box 8654, Folder 19, Records of the Supreme Commander for the Allied Powers, RG331, National Archives II, College Park, Maryland (hereafter cited as SCAP Records, NA).

128. Quoted in Makino, *Nihon eiga kenetsushi,* 412.

129. American Ambassador to the Japanese Minister for Foreign Affairs, May 25, 1940, 894.4061 Motion Pictures/43, State Department Records, NA.

130. Makino, *Nihon eiga kenetsushi,* 410–11. American Ambassador to the Japanese Minister for Foreign Affairs, May 25, 1940, 894.4061 Motion Pictures/43, State Department Records, NA.

131. High, *Imperial Screen,* 70–82; Katō, *Sōdōin taisei to eiga,* 50–71.

132. American Consul General, "New Regulations for Motion Pictures in Japan," December 5, 1939, 894.4061 Motion Pictures/37, State Department Records, NA; "Japan," January 4, 1944, MPAA General Collections File Roll 9, Special Collections, MHL.

.   133. American Consul General, "New Regulations for Motion Pictures in Japan," December 5, 1939, 894.4061 Motion Pictures/37, State Department Records, NA.

134. R. D. Spierman to Joseph Grew, November 16, 1939, 894.4061 Motion Pictures/32, State Department Records, NA.

135. Division of Far Eastern Affairs, Department of State, memorandum, April 29, 1941, 894.4061 Motion Pictures/57, State Department Records, NA.

136. Nathan D. Golden, "Review of Foreign Markets during 1936" (Washington, DC: U.S. Department of Commerce), 99.

137. Yūji Tosaka, "Hollywood Goes to Tokyo: American Cultural Expansion and Imperial Japan, 1918–1941," (PhD diss., Ohio State University, 2003), 262.

138. AMPA to Joseph Grew, November 16, 1939, 894.4061 Motion Pictures/31, State Department Records, NA; Arthur Kelley to producers in United Artists, July 11, 1938, Box 5, Folder 4, Series 1F, UA Collection, WCFTR.

139. AMPA to Joseph Grew, November 16, 1939, 894.4061 Motion Pictures/31, State Department Records, NA.

140. AMPA to S. Ikeda, August 10, 1938, 894.4061 Motion Pictures/32, State Department Records, NA.

141. AMPA to S. Ikeda, October 1, 1938, 894.4061 Motion Pictures/32, State Department Records, NA.

142. AMPA to Joseph Grew, November 16, 1939, 894.4061 Motion Pictures/31, State Department Records, NA.

143. According to a conversation record between Joseph Grew and the representatives of the AMPA, the AMPA was preparing to contact the Hays Office in November 1939. Edward Crocker, "Conversation" Memo, November 13, 1939, 894.4061 Motion Pictures/31, State Department Records, NA.

144. January 10, 1940, 894.4061 Motion Pictures/39, State Department Records, NA.

145. Joseph C. Grew to U.S. Secretary of State, May 31, 1940, 894.4061 Motion Pictures/43, State Department Records, NA.

146. Joseph Grew to Japanese Minister of Foreign Affairs, May 31, 1940, 894.4061 Motion Pictures/43, State Department Records, NA.

147. *Kokusai eiga shinbun* 134 (September 20, 1934): 12.

148. Tosaka, "Hollywood Goes to Tokyo," 264–65.

149. Frederick Herron to Maxwell M. Hamilton, January 2, 1941, 894.4061 Motion Pictures/50, State Department Records, NA.

150. Herron to Maxwell M. Hamilton, February 14, 1941, 894.4061 Motion Pictures/54, State Department Records, NA; Milliken to Maxwell Hamilton, March 26, 1941, 894.4061 Motion Pictures/57, State Department Records, NA.

151. Division of Far Eastern Affairs memorandum, April 29, 1941, 894.4061 Motion Pictures/57, State Department Records, NA.

152. Frank S. Williams to Joseph Grew, August 28, 1941, 894.4061 Motion Pictures/72, State Department Records, NA.

153. "Japan," January 4, 1944, MPAA General Correspondence Files, Roll 9, Special Collections, MHL.

154. Manager, International Department of MPPDA, "Japan: Market for American Motion Pictures," undated memo, MPAA General Correspondence Files, Roll 11, Special Collections, MHL.

155. *Film Daily,* January 28, 1942, 1, 6.

156. In 1929, *The Film Daily Yearbook* reported that U.S. film share was 22 percent. *The Film Daily Yearbook, 1929* (New York: Film Daily, 1929), 1009. In June 1946, Eric Johnston noted that American representation on Japanese screens accounted for about 16 percent of the total film rentals. See *Motion Picture Letter,* 5:6, 3.

157. MPPDA Manager, "Japan: Market for American Motion Pictures, First Section" n.d. MPAA General Collections File Roll 10, Special Collections, MHL; MPPDA Manager, "Japan: Market for American Motion Pictures, Second Section," February 19, 1945, MPAA General Collections File Roll 10, Special Collections, MHL.

2. Renewed Intimacies

1. The two films were the first releases of the Central Motion Picture Exchange, but they were not the first U.S. films shown in postwar Japan. A handful of pre–World War II releases, kept in warehouses during the war years, were screened by Japanese distributors during the first months of the occupation.

2. CINCAFPAC to War Department, March 16, 1946, 894.4061 Motion Pictures/ 3–1646, RG 59, State Department Records, NA.

3. On corporatism, see Ellis W. Hawley, *The Great War and the Search for a Modern Order: A History of the American People and Their Institutions, 1917–1933* (New York: St. Martin's Press, 1979); Michael Hogan, "Corporatism," in *Explaining the History of American Foreign Relations,* ed. Michael Hogan and Thomas Paterson (New York: Cambridge University Press, 1991), 226–36; Thomas McCormick, "Drift or Mastery?: A Corporatist Synthesis for American Diplomatic History," *Reviews in American History* 10 (December 1982): 318–30.

4. On Hollywood's recovery from the Great Depression, see Tino Balio, *Grand Design: Hollywood as a Modern Business Enterprise, 1930–1939* (Berkeley: University of California Press, 1993), esp. 13–36.

5. Thomas Schatz, *Boom and Bust: American Cinema in the 1940s* (Berkeley: University of California Press, 1997), 14–21, 323–28.

6. Tino Balio, ed., *Hollywood in the Age of Television* (Boston: Unwin Hyman, 1990); Erik Barnouw, *Tube of Plenty: The Evolution of American Television,* 2nd rev. ed. (New York: Oxford University Press, 1990); Gary R. Edgerton, *The Columbia History of American Television* (New York: Columbia University Press, 2007), 3–59, 102–7.

7. Michael Denning, *The Cultural Front: The Laboring of American Culture in the Twentieth Century* (New York: Verso, 1997), esp. 362–422; Saverio Giovacchini, *Hollywood Modernism: Film and Politics in the Age of the New Deal* (Philadelphia: Temple University Press, 2001); K. R. M. Short, "Hollywood Fights Anti-Semitism, 1940–1945," in *Film and Radio Propaganda in World War II,* ed. K. R. M. Short (Knoxville: University of Tennessee Press, 1983), 146–72.

8. Patrick J. Hearden, *Roosevelt Confronts Hitler: America's Entry into World War II* (DeKalb: Northern Illinois University Press, 1997), esp. 53–87.

9. *New York Times,* December 9, 1941, 44.

10. Will H. Hays, "The Motion Picture in a World at War: Twentieth Anniversary Report to the Motion Picture Producers and Distributors of America, Inc.," MPPDA pamphlet (March 30, 1942).

11. Thomas Schatz, *Boom and Bust: Hollywood and the 1940s* (Berkeley: University of California Press, 2001), 155, 191; Susan Ohmer, "The Science of Pleasure: George Gallup

and Audience Research in Hollywood," in *Identifying Hollywood's Audiences: Cultural Identity and the Movies, ed.* Melvyn Stokes and Richard Maltby (London: British Film Institute, 1999), 61–80. "Problems Confronting the Motion Picture Industry," n.d., Reel 30, in *The Will Hays Papers,* ed. Douglas Gomery (Frederick, MD: University Press of America, 1986), hereafter cited as WHP.

12. Schatz, *Boom and Bust,* 180.

13. Thomas Doherty, *Projections of War: Hollywood, American Culture, and World War II* (New York: Columbia University Press, 1993), 60.

14. Hays, "The Motion Picture in a World at War," 1.

15. The *Film Daily Yearbook, 1943* (New York: Film Daily, 1943), 151.

16. Harmon to George Schaefer et al. May 1, 1942, Reel 30, WHP; The *Film Daily Yearbook, 1944* (New York: Film Daily, 1944), 146. Also see the documents in War Activities Committee Papers, Box 1, Series 3D, United Artists Collection, Wisconsin Center for Film and Theatre Research, Madison, Wisconsin (hereafter cited as UA Collection, WCFTR).

17. Schatz, *Boom and Bust,* 239. On the inclusiveness of the category, also see Dorothy Jones, "The Hollywood War Film: 1942–1944," *Film Quarterly* 1 (October 1945): 1–2.

18. David Culbert, ed., *Film Propaganda in America: A Documentary History,* vol. 2, *World War II: Part 1* (New York: Greenwood Press, 1990), 28–68; Clayton Koppes and Gregory Black, *Hollywood Goes to War: How Politics, Profits, and Propaganda Shaped World War II Movies* (Berkeley: University of California Press, 1986), 17–48.

19. Schatz, *Boom and Bust,* 221–32, 239–61; Michael S. Shull and David Edward Wilt, *Hollywood War Films, 1937–1945: An Exhaustive Filmography of American Feature-Length Motion Pictures Relating to World War II* (Jefferson, NC: McFarland, 1996).

20. *Variety,* March 14, 1944, 25.

21. Richard W. Steele, "Preparing the Public for War: Efforts to Establish a National Propaganda Agency, 1940–1941," *American Historical Review* 75:6 (October 1970): 1640–53.

22. John Morton Blum, *V was for Victory: Politics and American Culture during World War II* (New York: Harcourt Brace, 1976), 21–31.

23. Cordell Hull, "Departmental Order No. 768," August 11, 1938, 111.017/260, State Department Records, NA.

24. Michael McShane Burns, "The Origin and Development of the Division of Cultural Relations within the State Department: 1935–1944," MA thesis, University of North Carolina–Chapel Hill, 1968; Frank A. Ninkovich, *The Diplomacy of Ideas: U.S. Foreign Policy and Cultural Relations, 1938–1950* (New York: Cambridge University Press, 1981), esp. 8–60.

25. OWI Overseas Branch, "Manual of Information: News and Features Bureau," February 1, 1944, 2, National Archives Interlibrary Loans.

26. Koppes and Black, *Hollywood Goes to War;* James M. Myers, *The Bureau of Motion Pictures and Its Influence on Film Content during World War II: The Reasons for Its Failure* (Lewiston, NY: Edwin Mellen Press, 1998), esp. 61–204; Allan M. Winkler, *The Politics of Propaganda: The Office of War Information, 1942–1945* (New Haven: Yale University Press, 1978).

27. OWI, "Government Information Manual for the Motion Picture Industry," Records of the Historian, Box 3, Entry 6A, RG 208, Office of War Information Records, National Archives II, College Park, Maryland (hereafter cited as OWI Records, NA).

28. Will Hays to Clarence Cannon, June 18, 1943, "Motion Pictures, May–July 1943" Folder, Box 6, OF 73, Franklin D. Roosevelt Library, Hyde Park (hereafter cited as FDRL).

29. OWI Overseas Branch, "Manual of Information: News and Features Bureau" (February 1, 1944), 1–4. The information campaign in Latin America soon fell into the hands of Nelson Rockefeller's Office of the Coordinator for Inter-American Affairs. See Emily S. Rosenberg, *Spreading the American Dream: American Economic and Cultural Expansion, 1890–1945* (New York: Hill and Wang, 1982), 206–9; Coordinator for Inter-American Affairs, *History of the Office of the Coordinator of Inter-American Affairs: Historical Reports on War Administration* (Washington, DC: Government Printing Office, 1947), 67–82.

30. *Washington Post,* February 23, 1943, 1, 12; *New York Times,* 17 September 1944, X1; OWI, "OWI in the ETO: A Report on the Activities of the Office of War Information in the European Theatre of Operations," April 18, 1945, esp. 3–5.

31. Press Release, March 29, 1944, OF5015, Box 2, "Office of War Information 1944" folder, FDRL. Robert Sherwood to Elmer Davis, September 22, 1944, OF5015, Box 4, "Office of War Information 1942–1944" folder, FDRL.

32. On the OWI's Overseas Branch, see Theodore A. Wilson, "Selling America via the Silver Screen? Efforts to Manage the Projection of American Culture Abroad, 1942–1947," Reinhold Wagnleitner and Elaine Tyler May, eds., *"Here, There, and Everywhere": The Foreign Politics of American Popular Culture* (Hanover, NH: University Press of New England, 2000), 83–99.

33. *Variety,* November 3, 1943, 1, 41.

34. *Variety,* June 16, 1943, 20; *Motion Picture Herald,* July 22, 1944, 12; *Film Daily,* July 21, 1944, 1.

35. *Variety,* June 16, 1943, 1.

36. MPPDA, "Planning Report for 1945 of the International Subcommittee of the Public Information Committee of the Motion Picture Industry, Western Division," "MPAA International Committee 1948" folder, Special Collections, MHL.

37. Carl Milliken to James Ross, December 5, 1944, 611.0031/12–544 EG, State Department Records, NA.

38. Hays, "Government Co-Operation in Maintaining Foreign Markets for American Motion Pictures," October 23, 1943, 800.4061 Motion Pictures/332, State Department Records, NA.

39. Milliken to Francis Colt de Wolf, May 23, 1944, 800.4061 Motion Pictures/202, State Department Records, NA.

40. A. A. Berle to American Diplomatic officers, February 22, 1944, 800.4061 Motion Pictures/409A, State Department Records, NA.

41. See, for example, Francis Colt de Wolf, "Telecommunications in the New World," *Yale Law Journal* 55: 5 (August 1946): 1281–90.

42. Quoted in Kerry Segrave, *American Films Abroad: Hollywood's Domination of the World's Movie Screens* (Jefferson, NC: McFarland, 1997), 130.

43. Will Hays to Edward R. Stettinius, Jr., January 17, 1944, 111.673/15, State Department Records, NA.

44. Spyros Skouras to Francis Colt de Wolf, February 1, 1944, 800.4061 Motion Pictures/398, State Department Records, NA; *Film Daily,* October 17, 1944, 1, 4; *Film Daily,* October 18, 1944, 1, 8; *Film Daily,* May 18, 1945, 1, 3; Carl Milliken to W. H. H., "Re: Export Trade Association," March 9, 1945, Reel 10, MPAA General Correspondences, MHL; *Motion Picture Herald,* May 26, 1945, 26.

45. Hays, *The Memoirs of Will H. Hays* (New York: Doubleday, 1955), 505; *Variety,* December 15, 1948, 7, 56.

46. Carl Elias Millilen to Will H. Hays, March 9, 1945, MPAA General Correspondences, Roll 10, Special Collections, MHL.

47. "Amended Certificate of incorporation before payment of capital of Motion Picture Export Association inc. as of April 1 1950," Box 7, Folder 7, Gradwell Sears Papers, UA Collection, WCFTR.

48. *Variety,* November 13, 1946.

49. Irving Maas to Douglas MacArthur, March 9, 1951, "Motion Picture Export Association" folder, MacArthur Memorial Library, Norfolk, Virginia.

50. Thomas H. Guback, *The International Film Industry: Western Europe and America since 1945* (Bloomington: Indiana University Press, 1969), esp. 91–107; Paul Swann, "The Little State Department: Hollywood and the State Department in the Postwar World," *American Studies International* 29:1 (1991): 2–19.

51. *Variety,* September 26, 1945. On Johnston's background, see Douglas Gomery, *The Hollywood Studio System: A History* (London: British Film Institute, 2005), 178–83.

52. *Motion Picture Herald,* September 22, 1945, 13.

53. *Film Daily,* October 2, 1945, 1, 11.

54. Ralph A. Edgerton, "Hometown Boy Makes Good: The Eric Johnston Story," *Pacific Northwesterner* 33:4 (1989): 55–64. Also see Gomery, *Hollywood Studio System,* 175–84.

55. *Variety,* March 27, 1946, 21; Guback, *International Film Industry,* 90–107; Swann, "The Little State Department," 2–19.

56. Francis Harmon, *Hearings before the Special Committee on Postwar Economic Policy and Planning,* 79th Cong., 1st and 2nd sessions, H. Res. 60, Part 9, 2575 (Washington, 1946).

57. *Variety,* October 10, 1945, 16.

58. Ronald H. Spector, *Eagle against the Sun: The American War with Japan* (New York: Free Press, 1985).

59. Barak Kushner, *The Thought War: Japanese Imperial Propaganda* (Honolulu: University of Hawaii Press, 2006).

60. On "strategy of annihilation," see Russell F. Weigley, *The American Way of War: A History of United States Military Strategy and Policy* (Bloomington: Indiana University Press, 1973), esp. xvii–xxiii, 312–81. Also see Michael S. Sherry, *The Rise of American Air Power: The Creation of Armageddon* (New Haven: Yale University Press, 1987), esp. 219–356.

61. John W. Dower, *Embracing Defeat,* 87–120. On the final year of the Pacific War, see, for example, Richard B. Frank, *Downfall: The End of the Imperial Japanese Empire* (New York: Random House, 1999); Tsuyoshi Hasegawa, *Racing the Enemy: Stalin, Truman, and the Surrender of Japan* (Cambridge: Harvard University Press, 2005).

62. Marlene J. Mayo, "American Wartime Planning for Occupied Japan: The Role of the Experts," in *Americans as Proconsuls: United States Military Government in Germany and Japan, 1944–1952,"* ed. Robert Wolfe (Carbondale: Southern Illinois University Press, 1984), 3–51; Marlene J. Mayo, "Psychological Disarmament: American Wartime Planning for the Education and Re-education of Defeated Japan, 1943–1945," in *The Occupation of Japan: Educational and Social Reform,* ed. Thomas W. Burkman (Norfolk, VA: MacArthur Foundation, 1980), 21–140.

63. Eiji Takemae, *Inside GHQ: The Allied Occupation of Japan and Its Legacy* (New York: Continuum, 2002), 209–14, 225–29.

64. Takemae, *Inside GHQ,* 52–67.

65. See, for example, Gar Alperovitz, *Atomic Diplomacy: Hiroshima and Potsdam* rev. ed. (East Haven, CT: Pluto Press, 1994); Hasegawa, *Racing the Enemy.*

66. Dower, *Embracing Defeat,* esp. 69–73.

67. Michael Schaller, *Douglas MacArthur: The Far Eastern General* (New York: Oxford University Press, 1988), esp. 120–57.

68. See Naoko Shibusawa, *America's Geisha Ally: Reimagining the Japanese Enemy* (Cambridge: Harvard University Press, 2006), esp. 1–12, 54–95.

69. "A Fourth of July Message from General Douglas MacArthur," *Life,* July 7, 1947, 34.

70. U.S. Senate, 82nd Congress, 1st Session, Committees on Armed Services and Foreign Policy, *Military Situation in the Far East* (Washington, DC, 1951), 310–11.

71. Takemae, *Inside GHQ,* 106–13, 235–60.

72. On the New Deal mind-set in occupied Japan, see, for example, Theodore Cohen, *Remaking Japan: The American Occupation as New Deal* (New York: Free Press, 1987); Oliver Zunz, *Why the American Century?* (Chicago: University of Chicago Press, 1998). 159–82.

73. Takemae, *Inside GHQ,* 260–92.

74. Takemae, *Inside GHQ,* 339–46.

75. Toshio Nishi, *Unconditional Democracy: Education and Politics in Occupied Japan, 1945–1952* (Stanford: Hoover Institution Press, 1982), esp. 141–241.

76. Ariyama Teruo, *Senryōki mediashi kenkyū: Jiyū to tōsei, 1945 nen* (Tokyo; Kashiwa shobō, 1995); Yamamoto Taketoshi, *Senryōki media bunseki* (Tokyo: Hōsei daigaku shuppankai, 1996).

77. Douglas MacArthur, *Reminiscences* (New York: McGraw-Hill, 1964), 299.

78. Katō, *Sōdōin taisei to eiga,* 247–64.

79. General Headquarters, Supreme Commander for the Allied Powers (GHQ/SCAP), *Summation of Non-Military Activities in Japan and Korea, No. 1 (September–October 1945),* 159.

80. Eiga kōsha, "First *kondankai* meeting between MacArthur's Information Division and the Entrepreneurs of Japanese Movies business," September 21, 1945, National Film Center, ed., Senjika eiga shiryō, dai 1kan (Tokyo: Nihon tosho sentā, 2006), 324. This document cites the date of the meeting as September 21, but most other accounts state that the meeting took place on the 22nd.

81. GHQ/SCAP, *Summation of Non-Military Activities in Japan and Korea, No. 1 (September–October 1945),* 160.

82. Eiga kōsha, "First *kondankai* meeting," 328–29. Also see Shimizu Akira, "20.9.22 kara 23.8.19 made: Senryōka no eigakai no kiroku," *Firumu sentā* 7 (May 8, 1972): 9–11.

83. H. W. Allen, Memorandum concerning the "Elimination of Japanese Government Control of the Motion Picture Industry," October 16, 1945, Box 8565, Folder 31, SCAP Records, NA.

84. H. W. Allen, Memorandum concerning the "Elimination of Undemocratic Motion Pictures," November 16, 1945, Box 8550, SCAP Records, NA; *Kinema junpō,* August 15, 1954, 92.

85. Civil Information and Education Section, "Mission and Accomplishments of the Occupation in the Civil Information and Education Fields," "Civil Information and Education Fields" folder, Box 3, W. Kenneth Bunce Papers, Harry S. Truman Library.

86. Takemae, *Inside GHQ,* 184.

87. David Conde, "Nihon eiga no senryōshi," *Sekai* 237 (August 1965): 251.

88. ALD to Wadsworth, "Censorship of Films by CI&E," March 13, 1946, Box 8579, Folder 38, SCAP Records, NA; CIE, "Report of Conference on Coordination between CIE and CCD on Censorship and Production of Motion Pictures," May 1, 1946, Box 8541, Folder 1, SCAP Records, NA.

89. This list is derived from "Eiga seisaku ni kansuru kinshi jikō," November 1945, National Film Center, ed. Senjika eiga shiryō, 344–45; also see Kyoko Hirano, *Mr. Smith Goes to Tokyo: Japanese Cinema under the American Occupation, 1945–1952* (Washington, DC: Smithsonian Institute Press, 1992), 44–45.

90. Shadan hōjin eiga haikyūsha, "Eiga seisaku narabini kenetsu tou ni kansuru shiji," October 18, 1945, in National Film Center, ed. Senjika eiga shiryō, 342–43.

91. ALD (Chief, PPB) to CCD, May 13, 1946, Box 8579, Folder 38, SCAP Records, NA.

92. GHQ/AFPAC, "Basic Plan for Civil Censorship in Japan," July 10, 1945, Box 8565, Folder 26, SCAP Records, NA.

93. Takemae, *Inside GHQ,* esp. 382–95.

94. CCD Administrative Division, "Manual of Press, Pictorial, and Radio Broadcast Censorship in Japan," September 30, 1945, 7; Box 8565, Folder 26, SCAP Records, NA.

95. CIS, SCAPIN 658, January 28, 1946, Box 8550, SCAP Records, NA.

96. J. J. C. to PPB Sections, March 26, 1946, Box 8603, Folder 18, SCAP Records, NA.

97. CCD to CIE, May 10, 1946, Box 8603, Folder 7, SCAP Records, NA.

98. CCD, "A Manual for Censors of the Motion Picture Department," rev. version, September 12, 1946, Box 8603, Folder 7, SCAP Records, NA.

99. G-2 to G-1, December 20, 1948, Box 8579, Folder 3, SCAP Records, NA.

100. CIE Memorandum, October 16, 1945, "Consolidated Report of Civil Information and Education section Activities, 11 Oct 1945–1 Dec 1945," 26; National Diet Library, Tokyo, Japan (hereafter cited as NDL).

101. CIE Memorandum to Dyke, October 28, 1945, "Consolidated Report of Civil Information and Education section Activities, 11 Oct 1945–1 Dec 1945," 101–2, NDL.

102. Excerpts from Kodama Kazuo's diary, in Kodama Kazuo, *Yabunirami eigashi: Sengo no kiroku* (Tokyo: Yomiuri shinbunsha, 1974), 15.

103. *Variety,* January 9, 1946, 201.

104. H. W. Allen to Imperial Japanese Government, "Motion Picture Censorship," January 28, 1946, Box 8550, SCAP Records, NA. John B. Cooley to Imperial Japanese Government, "Census of Foreign Films in Japan," July 8, 1946, Box 8550, SCAP Records, NA. John B. Cooley to Imperial Japanese Government, "Illegally-Possessed Foreign Films in Japan," November 29, 1946, Box 8551, SCAP Records, NA.

105. *Asahi shinbun,* September 21, 1946, 3; John Albeck to Costello, June 25, 1946, Box 8520, Folder 3, SCAP Records, NA.

106. G-2 to CCPC, July 15, 1946, Box 8603, Folder 9, SCAP Records, NA; CIE to CPC, May 28, 1947, Box 5062, Folder 15, SCAP Records, NA; CPC to CIE, February 24, 1948, Box 8579, Folder 3, SCAP Records, NA.

107. CIE to ESS, February 19, 1951, Box 5231, Folder 3, SCAP Records, NA.

108. Marion Winer, "Statement of the Distribution of the '40-Program' Features and OWI Documentaries, a Joint Project between the OWI and the Motion Picture Industry Operating during the Approximate Period of 1943 to 1946," "MPA and MPEA" folder, Warner Bros. Collection, University of Southern California.

109. OWI, "OWI in the ETO," 11–13; *Film Daily,* December 15, 1944, 1, 11; *Film Daily,* January 9, 1945, 1, 13.

110. OWI Overseas Branch, "Guidance on Pictures and Features for the Far East," October 13, 1944, Box, Folder 3, Office of the Records of the Historian, RG 208, OWI Records, NA.

111. OWI "Operational Guidance for the Distribution of O.W.I. Documentaries and Industry Films in the Far East," December 22, 1944, Box 2, Folder 1, Office of the Records of the Historian, RG 208, OWI Records, NA.

112. Don Brown to Mildred E. Allyn, approved January 29, 1945, Box 2 Folder 1, Office of the Records of the Historian, OWI Records, NA. Civil Affairs Division Telecon, May 21, 1946, TT 5915, Box 741, Records of the Department of Army, Record Group 165, National Archives II, College Park, Maryland (hereafter cited as Army Records, NA).

113. Francis Harmon, "Harmon's Notes, No. 3," "Western Europe in the Wake of World War II: As Seen by a Group of American Motion Picture Industry Executives Visiting the European and Mediterranean Theatres of Operation as Guests of the Military Authorities," 1945, Paley Library, Temple University, Philadelphia.

114. Office of War Information, "OWI in the ETO," 11–13; *Film Daily,* December 15, 1944, 1, 11; *Film Daily,* January 9, 1945, 1, 13.

115. *Film Daily,* September 17, 1945, 1, 7.

116. *Nippon Times,* March 1, 1946, 3.

117. Interview with Oikawa Shirō, November 16, 1999, Tokyo, Japan; OWI, "Operational Guidance for the Distribution of O.W.I. Documentaries and Industry Films in the Far East," December 22, 1944, Box 2, Folder 1, Office of the Records of the Historian, OWI Records, NA.

118. Jiji tsūshinsha, ed., *Eiga geinō nenkan 1947 nenban* (Tokyo: Jiji tsūshinsha, 1947), 86; CIE to WARTAG, November 22, 1945, Box 7494, Folder 22, SCAP Records, NA; *Film Daily,* November 8, 1945, 2; *Film Daily,* December 10, 1945, 1, 6.

119. Notes on conference of Wadsworth, Putnam, Blake, Dibella, Kunzman, Costello, Conde, March 11, 1946, Box 8520, Folder 8, SCAP Records, NA.

120. CIE to G-1, June 23, 1947, Box 5062, Folder 15, SCAP Records, NA; CIE Memorandum, February 16, 1946, Box 1020, Folder 9, SCAP Records, NA.

121. Bergher to Chief of CIE, April 12, 1946, Box 489, Folder 12, SCAP Records, NA.

122. Nugent to Cullen, June 23, 1947, Box 5062, Folder 15, SCAP Records, NA; DRN to Office of C-in-C (Col Adams), October 12, 1951, Box 5088, Folder 15, SCAP Records, NA; *Film Daily,* May 6, 1946, 6; Bergher to CIE Chief, April 12, 1946, Box 5062, Folder 15, SCAP Records, NA; Bergher to CIE Chief, April 12, 1946, Box 489, Folder 12, SCAP Records, NA; *Variety,* May 8, 1946; *Progress* (Universal Studios), August 26, 1946, 10.

123. *Variety,* May 8, 1945.

3. Contested Terrains

1. Harry Slott, "Elimination of Objectionable Sequences from *Murderer* (Satsujinki)," July 27–28, 1949, Box 5305, Folder 3, SCAP Records, NA.

2. On the Soviet Union, see, for example, Peter Kenez, *The Birth of the Propaganda State: Soviet Methods of Mass Mobilization, 1917–1929* (New York: Cambridge University Press, 1985); Vance Kepley Jr., "The First 'Perestroika': Soviet Cinema under the First Five-Year Plan," *Cinema Journal,* 35:4 (Summer 1996): 31–53. On Nazi Germany, see David Welch, *The Third Reich: Politics and Propaganda* (London: Routledge, 1993). On wartime Japan, see Peter B. High, *The Imperial Screen: Japanese Film Culture in the Fifteen Years' War, 1931–1945* (Madison: University of Wisconsin Press, 2003).

3. Jessica C. E. Gienow-Hecht, *Transmission Impossible: American Journalism and Cultural Diplomacy in Postwar Germany, 1945–1955* (Baton Rouge: Louisiana State University Press, 1999), 5.

4. Hirano's otherwise excellent study of Japanese cinema during the occupation era oddly characterizes the mind-set of Japanese filmmakers as "receptiveness." See Kyoko Hirano, *Mr. Smith Goes to Tokyo: Japanese Cinema under the American Occupation 1945–1952* (Washington, DC: Smithsonian Institute Press, 1992), 95, 177.

5. On the notion of the "contact zone," see Mary Louise Pratt, *Imperial Eyes: Travel Writing and Transculturalism,* 2nd. ed. (New York: Routledge, 2008), 7.

6. Tanaka Junichirō, *Nihon eiga hattatsushi,* vol. 3, (Tokyo: Chūō kōronsha, 1986), 214–15

7. Jiji tsūshinsha, *Eiga nenkan 1950nen* (Tokyo: Jiji tsūshinsha, 1949), 6–7.

8. Kinema junpōsha, *Kinema junpō zōkan: Eiga 40nen zen kiroku* (Tokyo: Kinema junpōsha, 1986), 12.

9. Satō Tadao, *Nihon eigashi,* vol. 2 (Tokyo: Iwanami shoten, 1995), 160–61.

10. *Kōgyō herarudo,* December 1945, 1; *Kinema junpō,* April 1, 1946, 16–18.

11. Michael Lombardi, "The Tōhō Motion Picture Company's Future Plans and Policies," June 24, 1947, Box 8653, Folder 26, SCAP Records, NA; *Kōgyō herarudo,* October 15, 1946, 4; CCD to CIE, May 10. 1946, Box 8603, Folder 7, SCAP Records, NA.

12. Lombardi, "The Tōhō Motion Picture Company's Future Plans and Policies," June 24, 1947, Box 8653, Folder 26, SCAP Records, NA.

13. *Rengō tsūshin eiga geinō ban,* March 28, 1948, 2.

14. Jiji tsūshinsha, *Eiga nenkan 1950nen,* 29.

15. *Kinema junpō,* March 1, 1946, 4–5.

16. *Kinema junpō,* June 1, 1946, 8.

17. CCD Memorandum, March 17, 1947, Box 8578, Folder 29, SCAP Records, NA.

18. CCD Memorandum, December 8, 1947, Box 8618, Folder 10, SCAP Records, NA; CCD Memorandum, December 4, 1947, Box 8618, Folder 10, SCAP Records, NA. *Kinema junpō,* December 1, 1947, 23. Satō, *Nihon eigashi,* vol. 2, 187.

19. Inoue Masao, *Bunka to tōsō: Tōhō sogi 1946–1948* (Tokyo: Shinyōsha, 2007), 41–43.

20. *Kinema junpō,* July 1, 1946, 40–41; *Kinema junpō,* October 1, 1949, 38.

21.. *Rengō tsūshin eiga geinō ban,* January 18, 1948, 5.

22. Jiji tsūshinsha, *Eiga nenkan 1950nendo ban* (Tokyo: Jiji tsūshinsha, 1949), 66–69.

23. Gōdō tsushin, Publicity No. 53, October 4, 1948, Box 8603, Folder 9, SCAP Records, NA.

24. *Rengō tsūshin eiga geinō ban,* February 29, 1948, 5.

25. Nakayama Kikumatsu to Charles Mayer, February 28, 1950, Box 7475, Folder 1, SCAP Records, NA; Fair Trade Commission, "Main Text," February 27, 1950, Box 7475, Folder 1, SCAP Records, NA; *Kinema junpō,* April 1, 1950, 100.

26. Many contemporaries believed that Conde was forced to resign because of his sympathy toward liberal and left-wing politics. See Hirano, *Mr. Smith Goes to Washington,* 8. On Gercke, see *New York Times,* December 18, 1938, 156.

27. PPB DI Special Report, February 17, 1948, Box 8654, Folder 19, SCAP Records, NA.

28. CCD, "A Manual for Censors of the Motion Picture Department," Box 8603, Folder 7, SCAP Records, NA.

29. CCD Memorandum, June 27, 1947, Box 8579, Folder 25, SCAP Records, NA.

30. RHK Memorandum, August 23, 1946, Box 8663, Folder 25, SCAP Records, NA.

31. CIE Weekly Report, December 11, 1947, Box 5304, Folder 5, SCAP Records, NA; CIE Weekly Report, March 10, 1949, Box 5304, Folder 8, SCAP Records, NA.

32. Gishin Ikeda, "Report on the Motion Picture Association of Japan," May 27, 1947, Box 5278, Folder 5, SCAP Records, NA.

33. CCD's PPB, "Special Report: Japanese Motion Picture Code of Ethics," August 20, 1949, 15, Box 8578, Folder 14–15, SCAP Records, NA; Gishin Ikeda, "Agreement of the Motion Picture Producers Association," Box 8578, Folder 44, SCAP records, NA.

34. Gishin Ikeda, "Agreement of the Motion Picture Producers Association," Box 8578, Folder 44, SCAP Records, NA.

35. Hirata Tetsuo, *Reddo pāji no shiteki kenkyū* (Tokyo: Shin nihon shuppansha, 2002).

36. Hirata, *Reddo pāji no shiteki kenkyū,* 251–52.

37. Shindō Kaneto, *Tsuihōsha tachi: Eiga no reddo pāji* (Tokyo: Iwanami shoten, 1983), esp. 54–55; Hirata, *Reddo pāji no shiteki kenkyū,* 269.

38. CCD "Special Report: Japanese Motion Picture Code of Ethics," August 20, 1949, Box 8578, Folder 45, SCAP Records, NA.

39. CIE, "Report of Conference" (with Daiei), January 19, 1949, Box 5305, Folder 3, SCAP Records, NA.

40. CIE Weekly Report, June 16, 1949, Box 5304, Folder 8, SCAP Records, NA.

41. CCD, "Special Report: Japanese Motion Picture Code of Ethics," August 20, 1949, 15, Box 8578, Folder 38, SCAP Records, NA.

42. CCD, "Special Report: Japanese Motion Picture Code of Ethics," August 20, 1949, 15, Box 8578, Folder 17–21, SCAP Records, NA.

43. CIE Weekly Report, July 7, 1949, Box 5304, Folder 8, SCAP Records, NA.

44. Nugent to Chief of Social Education Bureau of Japan, April 8, 1952, Box 5093, Folder 14, SCAP Records, NA.

45. CCD, "Special Report: Japanese Motion Picture Code of Ethics," August 20, 1949, 15, Box 8578, Folder 24.

46. CCD, "Special Report: Japanese Motion Picture Code of Ethics," August 20, 1949, 49, Box 8578, Folder 24.

47. Kurosawa Akira, *Gama no abura: Jiden no yōna mono,* (rpr., Tokyo: Iwanami shoten, 2001); *Kinema junpō,* August 15, 1956, 93.

48. CIE Report, October 16, 1947, Box 5304, Folder 5, SCAP Records, NA.

49. CIE Report, "Meeting with Tōyoko Filmmakers," July 21, 1948, Box 5305, Folder 8, SCAP Records, NA.

50. CCD Weekly Report, February 17, 1948, Box 8654, Folder 19, SCAP Records, NA.

51. Tōhō studio, June 1, 1948, n.p.; Kurosawa, *Gama no abura,* 295.

52. Uekusa Keinosuke, *Waga seishun no Kurosawa Akira* (Tokyo: Bunshun bunko, 1985), 132.

53. Kurosawa, Uekusa, and Motoki, "Bachirusu no machi (kadai)," Box 5290, Folder 1, SCAP Records, NA; Uekusa, *Waga seishun no Kurosawa Akira,* 127.

54. An early synopsis names him Matsumoto, and the first script, dated October 30, 1947, names him Matsumura. The name is changed to Matsunaga in the revised script, dated November 13, 1947.

55. Tōhō Company, "Yoidore tenshi" screenplay, October 30, 1947, 5, Box 5290, Folder 1, SCAP Records, NA.

56. Tōhō Company, "Yoidore tenshi" screenplay, October 30, 1947, 93, Box 5290, Folder 1, SCAP Records, NA.

57. Tōhō Company, "Yoidore tenshi" screenplay, October 30, 1947, 101, Box 5290, Folder 1, SCAP Records, NA.

58. Tōhō Company, "Yoidore tenshi" screenplay, October 30, 1947, 90, Box 5290, Folder 1, SCAP Records, NA.

59. Tōhō Company, "Yoidore tenshi" screenplay, October 30, 1947, 122, Box 5290, Folder 1, SCAP Records, NA.

60. Tōhō Company, "Yoidore tenshi" synopsis, October 15, 1947, 2, Box 5290, Folder 1, SCAP Records, NA.

61. Tōhō Company, "Intention of Production for 'Yoidore Tenshi,'" October 15, 1947, Box 5290, Folder 1, SCAP Records, NA.

62. Tōhō Company, "Yoidore Tenshi" synopsis, October 15, 1947, 5, Box 5290, Folder 1, SCAP Records, NA.

63. Tōhō Company, "*Yoidore tenshi kaiteiban*" examined by CIE, November 13, 1947, Box 5290, Folder 1, SCAP Records, NA; Tōhō Company, "Yoidore tenshi" revised script, November 13, 1947, Box 5290, Folder 1, SCAP Records, NA.

64. Tōhō Company, "Yoidore tenshi" revised script, November 13, 1947, 108, Box 5290, Folder 1, SCAP Records, NA.

65. This scene already existed in the first script. Tōhō Company, "Yoidore tenshi" revised script, November 13, 1947, 89, Box 5290, Folder 1, SCAP Records, NA.

66. Tōhō Company, "Yoidore tenshi" revised script, November 13, 1947, 89, Box 5290, Folder 1, SCAP Records, NA.

67. John W. Dower, *Embracing Defeat: Japan in the Wake of World War II* (New York: W. W. Norton and the New Press, 1999), 121–67.

68. Tōhō Company, "Bachirusu no machi gaikan," Box 5290, Folder 1, SCAP Records, NA. Stephen Prince, *The Warrior's Camera: The Cinema of Akira Kurosawa,* rev. and expanded ed. (Princeton: Princeton University Press, 1999), 85.

69. Uekusa, *Waga seishun no Kurosawa Akira,* 147.

70. *Eiga nyūsu,* May 1948, 17.

71. Tōhō Company, "Yoidore Tenshi" revised script, November 13, 1947, cover page, Box 5290, Folder 1, SCAP Records, NA.

72. Nugent, "Japanese Feature Films for Okinawa," March 25, 1950, Box 5308, Folder 5, SCAP Records, NA.

73. Quoted in Stuart Galbraith IV, *The Emperor and the Wolf: The Lives and Films of Akira Kurosawa and Toshirō Mifune* (New York: Faber and Faber, 2001), 91.

74. Kurosawa, *Gama no abura,* 271–75.

75. Marlene J. Mayo, "Psychological Disarmament: American Wartime Planning for the Education and Re-education of Defeated Japan, 1943–1945," in *The Occupation of Japan: Educational and Social Reform,* ed. Thomas W. Burkman (Norfolk, VA: MacArthur Foundation, 1980), 21–140.

76. Hirano, *Mr. Smith Goes to Tokyo,* 49.

77. Monica Braw, *The Atomic Bomb Suppressed: American Censorship in Occupied Japan* (New York: M. E. Sharpe, 1991), 89–132; Robert Jay Lifton and Greg Mitchell, *Hiroshima in America: Fifty Years of Denial* (New York: G. P. Putnam's Sons, 1995), 40–64.

78. ESS to G-2, December 19, 1947, Box 8519, Folder 15, SCAP Records, NA.

79. Hirano, *Mr. Smith Goes to Tokyo,* 59–61.

80. Nagai Hiroshi, *Nagasaki no kane* (Tokyo: Hibiya shuppansha, 1949), 7.

81. Bratton to Charles Willoughby, January 6, 1948, Box 8519, Folder 16, SCAP Records, NA; Willoughby to Bratton, Norberg, and Duff and Bethune, March 31, 1948, Box 8519, Folder 16, SCAP Records, NA.

82. CCD to CIS, May 15, 1947, Box 8655, Folder 13, SCAP Records, NA.

83. CIS to G-2, March 28, 1948, Box 8519, Folder 16, SCAP Records, NA.

84. SCAP, "Manila no higeki," in Nagai, *Nagasaki no kane,* 195.

85. Shindō, *Shindō Kaneto no sokuseki,* vol. 4, 21.

86. Shindō, *Genbaku o toru* (Tokyo: Shin nihon shuppansha, 2005), 11.

87. Shōchiku, "Nagasaki no kane" script, April 1, 1949, Box 5267, Folder 8, SCAP Records, NA.

88. Shōchiku, "Nagasaki no kane" script, April 1, 1949, Box 5267, Folder 8, SCAP Records, NA.

89. Shōchiku, "Nagasaki no kane" second revised script, received by CIE April 26, 1949, 10, Box 5267, Folder 8, SCAP Records, NA.

90. Shōchiku, "Nagasaki no kane" revised synopsis, submitted to CIE April 26, 1949, cover, Box 5267, Folder 8, SCAP Records, NA; Harry Slott, "Conference on Revised Synopsis *The Bell of Nagasaki,*" May 2, 1949, Box 5305, Folder 3, SCAP Records, NA.

91. Shōchiku, "Nagasaki no kane" third revised synopsis, June 4, 1949, 11, Box 5267, Folder 8, SCAP Records, NA.

92. Hashida later recalled that she and Mitsuhata did much of the background research for the film. See Yamada Taichi, Saitō Masao, Tanaka Kōgi, Miyagawa Shōji, Yoshida Takeshi, and Watanabe Yutaka, eds., *Hito wa taisetsu na kotomo wasurete shimaukara: Shōchiku Ōfuna satsueijo monogatari* (Tokyo: Magazine House, 1995), 81–82.

93. CIE report, "Trailer for *Bells of Nagasaki,*" September 9–12, 1950, Box 5308, Folder 13, SCAP Records, NA.

94. *Kinema junpō,* November 1, 1950, 29.

95. *Kinema junpō,* November 1, 1950, 49.

96. Shimizu Akira, "20.9.22 kara 23.8.19 made: Senryōka no eigakai no kiroku," *Firumu sentā* 7 (1972): 9.

97. Shirō Okamoto, *The Man Who Saved Kabuki: Faubion Bowers and Theatre Censorship in Occupied Japan,* trans. Samuel Leiter (Honolulu: University of Hawaii Press, 2001).

98. *Kinema junpō,* August 15, 1956, in Kinema junpō sha, *Besuto obu Kinema junpō/jo: 1950–1966* (Tokyo: Kinema junpōsha, 1994), 529.

99. *Kokusai eiga shinbun,* 165 (January 1936), 62–67.

100. Takejiro Ōtani to Donald Nugent, July 3, 1951, Box 5233, Folder 2, SCAP Records, NA.

101. CIE Weekly Report, April 28, 1949, Box 5304, Folder 8, SCAP Records, NA.

102. CIE Memo, February 4, 1949, Box 5305, Folder 3, SCAP Records, NA.

103. *Kinema junpō,* October 1, 1949, 40; *Kinema junpō,* October 15, 1949, 40.

104. Slott, Hide, Yoshida, November 25, 1950, Box 5308, Folder 13, SCAP Records, NA.

105. CIE, "Story Conference *Daibosatsu Tōge,*" September 17, 1949, Box 5305, Folder 3, SCAP Records, NA.

106. Tōyoko, "Daibosatsu tōge (Dai ichi wa kanashiki ise) Shinario teisei ni tsuite," Box 5297, Folder 31, SCAP Records, NA.

107. Nakazato Kaizan, *Daibosatsu tōge 1* (Tokyo: Chikuma shobō, 1995), 11–136.

108. Tōyoko, "Daibosatsu tōge" script, submitted to CIE August 20, 1949, Box 5297, Folder 31, SCAP Records, NA.

109. Tōyoko, "Daibosatsu tōge" script, submitted to CIE August 20, 1949, 12, Box 5297, Folder 31, SCAP Records, NA.

110. Tōyoko, "Daibosatsu tōge" script, submitted to CIE August 20, 1949, 100, Box 5297, Folder 31, SCAP Records, NA.

111. Tōyoko, "Daibosatsu tōge (Dai ichiwa Kanashiki Ise): Shinario teisei ni tsuite," n.d., Box 5297, Folder 31, SCAP Records, NA.

112. Tōyoko, "Daibosatsu tōge" script, August 20, 1949, back cover, Box 5305, Folder 3, SCAP Records, NA.

113. Tōyoko, "On the Scenario Revision of *Daibosatsu Tōge* (Episode One: *Kanashiki Ise*)," received by CIE on September 12, 1949, Box 5305, Folder 3, SCAP Records, NA.

114. Tōyoko, "Daibosatsu tōge (Dai ichiwa: Kanashiki Ise): Shinario teisei ni tsuite," n.d., Box 5297, Folder 31, SCAP Records, NA.

115. Tōyoko, "Daibosatsu tōge (Dai ichiwa: Kanashiki Ise): Shinario teisei ni tsuite," n.d., Box 5297, Folder 31, SCAP Records, NA. The change concerned pages 10–15 of the revised script.

116. Tōyoko, "Daibosatsu tōge (Dai ichiwa: Kanashiki Ise): Shinario teisei ni tsuite," n.d., Box 5297, Folder 31, SCAP Records, NA. The change concerned page 17 of the revised script.

117. Tōyoko, "Daibosatsu tōge (Dai ichiwa: Kanashiki Ise): Shinario teisei ni tsuite," n.d., Box 5297, Folder 31, SCAP Records, NA. The change concerned pages 42–45 of the revised script.

118. Tōyoko, "Daibosatsu tōge (Dai ichiwa: Kanashiki Ise): Shinario teisei ni tsuite," n.d., Box 5297, Folder 31, SCAP Records, NA. The change concerned page 35 of the revised script.

119. Tōyoko, "Daibosatsu tōge (Dai ichiwa: Kanashiki Ise): Shinario teisei ni tsuite," n.d., Box 5297, Folder 31, SCAP Records, NA. The change concerned pages 18 and 46 of the revised script.

120. Harry Slott, Story Conference Report, September 17, 1949, Box 5305, Folder 3, SCAP Records, NA.

121. CIE Memo, November 25, 1950, Box 5308, Folder 13, SCAP Records, NA.

122. The yearly output, between 1945 and 1950, was 3, 7, 8, 15, and 29. See Kinema junpōsha, *Kinema junpō zōkan: Eiga 40nen zen kiroku,* 45.

123. CIE Synopsis Conference, June 20, 1949, Box 5305, Folder 3, SCAP Records, NA; CIE, April 15, 1948, Box 5305, Folder 11, SCAP Records, NA; Shōzaburo Sashō, "Motion Picture Biography of Miyamoto Musashi," November 4, 1950, Box 5308, Folder 5, SCAP Records, NA.

124. CIE, "Story Conference of *Daibosatsu Tōge,*" September 17, 1949, Box 5305, Folder 3, SCAP Records, NA.

125. Ōtani Takejirō to CIE, May 7, 1951, Box 5308, Folder 5, SCAP Records, NA.

126. Nugent to Motion Picture Association of Japan, November 13, 1951, Box 5308, Folder 5, SCAP Records, NA; Motion Picture Association of Japan to CIE, May 7, 1951, Box 5308, Folder 5, SCAP Records, NA.

127. Kinema junpōsha, *Kinema junpō zōkan: Eiga 40nen zen kiroku,* 44–46.

128. *MPEA News,* 10, n.d., 4.

4. Corporatist Tensions

1. Frank Capra, *The Name above the Title* (New York: MacMillan, 1971), 260.

2. Memorandum by R. H. K., August 16, 1946, Box 8578, Folder 33, SCAP Records, NA.

3. *Kōgyō herarudo,* May 1946, 3.

4. *Nippon Times,* March 1, 1946, 3.

5. B. M. Fitch, "WARTAG Routine," November 22, 1945, Box 1020, Folder 9, SCAP Records, NA.

6. WARTAG Routine, November 22, 1945, Box 7494, Folder 22, SCAP Records, NA.

7. CCD, "Summary of post-surrender American pictures," March 3, 1947, Box 8578, Folder 33, SCAP Records, NA.

8. Hersey to Chief of Civil Affairs Division, June 18, 1947, Box 5062, Folder 15, SCAP Records, NA.

9. Francis Harmon, *Hearings before the Special Committee on Postwar Economic Policy and Planning,* 79th Cong., 1st and 2nd sessions, H. Res. 60, Part 9, 2574 (Washington, 1946).

10. Jennifer Fay, "The Business of Cultural Diplomacy: American Film Policy in Occupied Germany, 1945–1949," PhD diss., University of Wisconsin–Madison, 2001, 139.

11. U.S. Army Teleconference, May 21, 1946, TT5915, Box 741, Records of the Civil Affairs Division, Record Group 165, National Archives II, College Park, Maryland (hereafter cited as CAD Records, NA).

12. Charles A. H. Thomson, *Overseas Information Service of the United States Government* (Washington, DC: Brookings Institution, 1948), 223.

13. CAD memorandum to State Department, August 8, 1946, 862.4061-MP/8–846, State Department Records, NA.

14. Harmon, *Hearings before the Special Committee on Postwar Economic Policy and Planning,* 79th Cong., 1st and 2nd sessions, H. Res. 60, Part 9, 2542 (Washington, 1946).

15. "A Statement of Policy," n.d., Reel 13, Motion Picture Association of America Papers, Special Collections, MHL. The same document is also available in Box 5066, Folder 2, SCAP Records, NA.

16. "Progress Report of Motion Picture Section for the FY 1948," June 30, 1948, Box 5066, Folder 2, SCAP Records, NA. On the CAD, see also H. Mark Woodward, "The Formulation and Implementation of U.S. Feature Film Policy in Occupied Germany, 1945–1948," PhD diss., University of Texas at Dallas, 1987, 91–111.

17. R. B. McRae memorandum to U.S. State Department, August 8, 1946, 862.4061-MP/8–846, State Department Records, NA.

18. Nugent to McClure, October 4, 1948, Box 5066, Folder 2, SCAP Records, NA.

19. CIE Teleconference, November 7, 1946, TT7300, Box 746, CAD Records, NA; CIE Teleconference, February 20, 1947, TT7748, Box 750, CAD Records, NA; CIE Teleconference, March 13, 1947, TT7869, Box 751, CAD Records, NA; CIE Teleconference, January 8, 1948, TT8942, Box 762, CAD Records, NA; CIE Teleconference, February 12, 1948, TT9087, Box 763, CAD Records, NA; Hersey to CAD, June 18, 1947, Box 489, Folder 12, SCAP Records, NA.

20. CCD, "A Manual for the Censors of the Motion Picture Department," August 15, 1946, Box 8603, Folder 7, SCAP Records, NA.

21. "Admission of Foreign Magazines, Books, Motion Pictures, News and Photograph Services, et Cetera, and Their Dissemination in Japan," attached to an unrestricted memorandum by the U.S. Political Adviser for Japan, December 12, 1946, 894.916/12–1246, State Department Records, NA.

22. John B. Cooley to K. Derevyanko, "Circular No. 12," Box 5062, Folder 15, SCAP Records, NA.

23. Donald Nugent to ESS, "British Movie License," June 17, 1947, Box 5062, Folder 15, SCAP Records, NA; RR to Diplomatic Section, June 2, 1947, Box 5062, Folder 15, SCAP Records, NA; Diplomatic Section memorandum, October 10, 1947, Box 5062, Folder 15, SCAP Records, NA; Jiji tsūshinsha, ed., *Eiga nenkan 1950nen,* 55–59.

24. Bratton to Willoughby, November 18, 1946, Box 8520, Folder 8, SCAP Records, NA.

25. SCAP to CMPE, "License to Engage in Business in Japan," May 26, 1947, Box 7494, Folder 22, SCAP Records, NA.

26. CCD, "Summary and Classification of 'Post-Surrender' imported American pictures, submitted for censorship up to 31 December 1946," March 3, 1947, Box 8578, Folder 33, SCAP Records, NA.

27. CCD, "Summary and Classification of 'Post-Surrender' imported American pictures, submitted for censorship up to 31 December 1946," March 3, 1947, Box 8578, Folder 33, SCAP Records, NA.

28. CIE Teleconference, August 29, 1946, TT6895, Box 743, CAD Records, NA.

29. PPB memorandum, June 16, 1949, Box 8603, Folder 22, SCAP Records, NA.

30. Fehrenbach, *Cinema in Democratizing Germany,* 261–62; Motion Picture Section, Civil Affairs Division to McClure, "Progress Report of Motion Picture Section for the FY 1948," June 30, 1948, Box 5066, Folder 2, SCAP Records, NA.

31. John Trumpbour, *Selling Hollywood to the World: U.S. and European Struggles for Mastery of the Global Film Industry, 1920–1950* (New York: Cambridge University Press, 2002), 183–85.

32. McRae to Acting Chief, ADO, Department of State, August 8, 1946, 862.4061 MP/8–846, State Department Records, NA.

33. Slott to Takada, January 29, 1948, Box 5304, Folder 12, SCAP Records, NA.

34. Memorandum by Walter Mihata, April 29, 1947, Box 8579, Folder 38, SCAP Records, NA.

35. Bernard D. Frew to Ken Dyke, October 31, 1945, in "Consolidated Report of Civil Information and Education Section Activities, 11 October 1945–1 December 1945" (unpublished manuscript), 117, NDL.

36. Slott to Takada, May 1, 1950, Box 5308, Folder 13, SCAP Records, NA.

37. *Los Angeles Times,* June 30, 1946, C2.

38. FEC Teleconference, February 27, 1947, TT 7784, Box 750, CAD Records, NA.

39. CAD Teleconference, April 17, 1947, TT8021, Box 853, CAD Records, NA.

40. "Pictures Cleared & on order for 1950," October 10, 1950, CIE (B)—08389, Records of the Supreme Commander for the Allied Powers, National Diet Library, Tokyo (hereafter cited as SCAP Records, NDL).

41. Wilder Johnson to CINCFE, December 23, 1947, Box 5062, Folder 15, SCAP Records, NA.

42. CAD to CIE, February 10, 1949, Box 595, SCAP Records, NA.

43. CAD checklist, "Feature films under consideration for overseas use," n.d., Box 5072, Folder 2, SCAP Records, NA.

44. State Department Teleconference, September 20 1946, TT 7053, Box 744, CAD Records, NA.

45. CCD, "Manual for Censors of Motion Picture Department," August 15, 1946, Box 8603, Folder 7, SCAP Records, NA.

46. CCD, "A Manual for Censors of the Motion Picture Department," August 15, 1946, Box 8603, Folder 7, SCAP Records, NA.

47. John Dower, *Embracing Defeat,* 139–48.

48. Slott to Tamura, July 2, 1948, Box 5305, Folder 8, SCAP Records, NA.

49. Slott to Mayer, April 26, 1950, Box 5308, Folder 13, SCAP Records, NA.

50. CIE Teleconference, July 18, 1946, TT6674, Box 741, CAD Records, NA.

51. CIE Teleconference, February 27, 1947, TT7784, Box 750, CAD Records, NA.

52. Kyoko Hirano, *Mr. Smith Goes to Tokyo: Japanese Cinema under the American Occupation, 1945–1952* (Washington, DC: Smithsonian Institute Press, 1992), 66–70.

53. CAD Checklist, Box 5072, Folder 2, SCAP Records, NA.

54. Slott to Tamura, February 12, 1948, Box 5304, Folder 12, SCAP Records, NA.

55. Slott to Mayer and William Schwartz, September 24, 1949, Box 5305, Folder 3, SCAP Records, NA.

56. Review Sheet by Sgt. Masuda, May 9, 1946, Box 8578, Folder 33, SCAP Records, NA.

57. Nugent to Mayer, August 28, 1951, Box 5088, Folder 15, SCAP Records, NA.

58. "Manual for Censors of Motion Picture Department," CCD, August 15, 1946, Box 8603, Folder 7, SCAP Records, NA. "CCD Master List," October 1945–September 1946, Box 8601, Folder 23, SCAP Records, NA.

59. Memorandum by Masuda, May 9, 1946, Box 8578, Folder 33, SCAP Records, NA.

60. Slott to Mayer, July 2, 1948, Box 5305, Folder 8, SCAP Records, NA.

61. CADNY to CINCFE, October 11, 1948, Box 543, Folder 11, SCAP Records, NA.

62. Walter Mihata and Hugh Walker to Motion Picture Department, n.d., Box 8578, Folder 33, SCAP Records, NA.

63. CIE Teleconference, April 16, 1948, TT9367, Box 765, CAD Records, NA.

64. Lt. Col. Rogers to Francis Harmon, October 6, 1948, MPAA General Correspondences, MHL.

65. Donald Nugent to CCD, May 31, 1946, Box 5060, Folder 18, SCAP Records, NA.

66. Notes on conference of Wadsworth, Putnam, Blake, Dibella, Kunzman, Costello, Conde, March 11, 1946, Box 8520, Folder 8, SCAP Records, NA.

67. K. C. Grew to Blakemore, November 25, 1950, Box 5081, CIE (B)-08388, SCAP Records, NDL.

68. Lt. Col. Rogers to Francis Harmon, October 6, 1948, MPAA General Correspondences, MHL.

69. CCD, "CCD Monthly Report," February 1–29, 1948, Box 8565, Folder 5, SCAP Records, NA.

70. Chief, New York Field Office to Civil Information and Education Section, December 25, 1948, "Misc. Incoming, Sept–Dec 48" folder, Box 48, RG-9, Records of the Supreme Commander for the Allied Powers, MacArthur Memorial Library, Norfolk, Virginia (hereafter cited as SCAP Records, MML).

71. SCAP to New York Field Office, January 13, 1949, "DACX Outgoing Misc, Jan–Jun 1949" Folder, Box 26, RG-9, SCAP Records, MML.

72. CCD, "Summary and Classification of 'Post-Surrender' imported American Pictures, submitted for censorship up to 31 December 1946," March 3, 1947, Box 8578, Folder 33, SCAP Records, NA.

73. CCD, "Summary and Classification of 'Post-Surrender' imported American Pictures, submitted for censorship up to 31 December 1946," March 3, 1947, Box 8578, Folder 33, SCAP Records, NA.

74. Quoted in Hirano, *Mr. Smith Goes to Tokyo,* 176.

75. CIE Telecon, August 29, 1946, TT 6895, Box 743, CAD Records, NA.

76. Ellis Arnall to Tracy S. Voorhees, November 3, 1949, Box 5074, Folder 10, SCAP Records, NA.

77. CCD Monthly Report, March 1948, Box 8565, Folder 6, SCAP Records, NA; Nugent to McClure, October 4, 1948, Box 5066, Folder 2, SCAP Records, NA.

78. Nugent to McClure, October 4, 1948, Box 5066, Folder 2, SCAP Records, NA.

79. McClure to Nugent, September 30, 1948, Box 5066, CIE(B)-00046, SCAP Records, NDL.

80. Harry Slott, "Request for showing of American film," August 26, 1948, Box 5035, Folder 9, SCAP Records, NA.

81. Lawrence E. Bunker to Charles Mayer, August 25, 1948, "MPEA" folder, OMS Correspondence, SCAP Papers, RG-5, SCAP Records, MML. Also see *Zenkoku eigakan shinbun,* September 25, 1948, 2.

82. CIE Teleconference, October 18, 1946, TT 7214, Box 745, CAD Records, NA.

83. Slott to Takada, January 29, 1948, Box 5304, Folder 12, SCAP Records, NA.

84. Hirano, *Mr. Smith Goes to Tokyo,* 246–47.

85. Slott to Tamura, March 26, 1949, Box 5305, Folder 3, SCAP Records, NA.

86. War Department Teleconference, September 6, 1946, TT6946, CAD Records, NA.

87. War Department Teleconference, September 20, 1946, TT7046, CAD Records, NA.

88. Nugent to Diplomatic Section, Box 5088, Folder 2, SCAP Records, NA.

89. G-2 Exec to CCD, June 30, 1949, Box 8603, Folder 24, SCAP Records, NA.

90. Sykes to CCD, July 1, 1949, Box 8603 AF or 8520, Folder 7; CCD to Sykes, July 1, 1949, Box 8520, Folder 7, SCAP Records, NA.

91. K. Derevyanko to Douglas MacArthur, August 15, 1949, Box 5072, Folder 2, SCAP Records, NA.

92. CIE Weekly Report, September 15, 1949, Box 5304, Folder 8, SCAP Records, NA.

93. Washington to CINCAFPAC, February 5, 1946, Box 419, Folder 28, SCAP Records, NA.

94. Schuler to Lefebre, January 29, 1946, Box 7494, Folder 22, SCAP Records, NA.

95. WAR to CINCFE, March 25, 1947, Box 489, Folder 12, SCAP Records, NA; CIE Teleconference, February 12, 1948, TT9087, Box763, CAD Records, NA.

96. CIE Teleconference, March 13, 1947, TT7869, Box 751, CAD Records, NA.

97. Hersey to Chief, Civil Affairs Division, June 18, 1947, Box 5062, Folder 15, SCAP Records, NA.

98. On April 21, 1949, R. W. Altschuler of Republic Pictures was "extremely disappointed" to find out that only one film from his company, *Angel and the Badman,* was selected during the previous six months. R. W. Altschuler (RKO) to John McCarthy, MPEA, April 26, 1949, Roll No. 14, Special Collections, MHL.

99. Hersey to Chief, Civil Affairs Division, June 18, 1947, Box 5062, Folder 15, SCAP Records, NA.

100. "Extract from Letter from Mr. Maas," August 8, 1951, attached to letter from Charles Mayer to Donald Nugent, August 16, 1951, Box 5233, Folder 2, SCAP Records, NA.

101. WAR to CINCFE, April 25, 1947, Box 489, Folder 12, SCAP Records, NA.

102. DA (CSCAD EXEC) to SCAP (FOR FOX), February 24, 1949, Box 5072, Folder 2, SCAP Records, NA.

103. Mayer to Maas, May 12, 1949, MPAA General Correspondences, Roll No. 14, Special Collections, MHL.

104. Irving Maas, "Japan: Memorandum of Details of Operation Since Inception," May 13, 1949, MPEA General Correspondences, Roll No. 14, Special Collections, MHL.

105. John G. McCarthy to MPEA foreign managers, May 10, 1949, MPAA General Collections, Roll No. 14, Special Collections, MHL.

106. Crater B. Magruder to MPEA, May 14, 1949, MPAA General Correspondences, Roll No. 14, Special Collections, MHL.

107. MPEA, "Minutes," June 13, 1949, Box 7, Folder 1, Gradwell Sears Papers, United Artists Collection, Wisconsin Center for Film and Theater Research, Madison, Wisconsin (hereafter cited as Sears Papers, WCFTR). According to Charles Mayer, the frozen funds "may exceed $50,000,000." AP Tokyo Service, May 24, 1949, attachment to letter from Irving Maas to MPEA directors, June 2, 1949, Box 7, Folder 5, Sears Papers, WCFTR.

108. MPEA, "Minutes," May 19,1949, Box 7, Folder 5, Sears Papers, WCFTR.

109. *Tokyo shinbun,* July 21, 1949, in Kokuritsu kokkai toshokan, ed., *Dokyumento sengo no nihon: Shinbun, nyūsu ni miru shakaishi daijiten 36* (Tokyo: Ōzorasha, 1997).

110. Hyakutarō Kondō to SCAP, July 1,1949, Box 5072, Folder 2, SCAP Records, NA.

111. American Movie Culture Association to SCAP, June 1, 1949, Box 5072, Folder 2, SCAP Records, NA.

112. MPEA, "Minutes," March 5, 1948, Box 6, Folder 10, Sears Papers, WCFTR; *Motion Picture Herald,* June 25, 1949; *Film Daily,* August 2, 1949.

113. *Film Daily,* August 2, 1949.

114. Herbert J. Erlanger to Directors of MPEA, November 10, 1949, Roll no. 14, Special Collections, MHL; Ministry of International Trade and Industry, Contract No. JI 40358, n.d., Box 7508, Folder 19, SCAP Records, NA.

115. *Motion Picture Herald,* August 6, 1949.

116. MPEA, "Minutes," August 2, 1949, Box 7, Folder 5, Sears Papers, WCFTR; *Motion Picture Herald,* August 6, 1949.

117. MPEA, "Minutes," August 2, 1951, Box 2, Folder 3, Files on the Motion Picture Export Association, WCFTR.

118. Nugent to Mayer, October 4, 1951, Box 5088, Folder 15, SCAP Records, NA.

5. Fountains of Culture

1. *Eiga no tomo,* February 1947, back cover.

2. Terry Cooney, *Balancing Acts: American Thought and Culture in the 1930s* (New York: Twayne, 1995), 106. On "culture," see Raymond Williams, *Keywords: A Vocabulary of Culture and Society,* rev. ed. (New York: Oxford University Press, 1983), 87–93. On *bunka,* see Nishikawa Nagao, *Kokkyō no koekata: Kokumin kokka ron josetsu, zōho* (Tokyo: Heibonsha, 2001), esp. 222–70; and Nishikawa Nagao, *Chikyū jidai no minzoku = bunka riron: Datsu "kokumin bunka" no tameni* (Tokyo: Shinyōsha, 1995), esp. 46–107.

3. On Hollywood as a manifestation of an "American" national identity, see Lary May, *The Big Tomorrow: Hollywood and the Politics of the American Way* (Chicago: University of Chicago Press, 2000), esp. 1–7.

4. See, for example, Sakata Minoru, "Nihongata kindai seikatsu yōshiki no seiritsu," in *Zoku Shōwa bunka, 1945–1989,* ed. Minami Hiroshi (Tokyo Keisō shobō, 1990), 7–32.

5. *Eiga geijutsu,* August 1949, 28; *MPEA News,* 10, n.d., 4.

6. Charles Mayer to Don Brown, March 6, 1947, Box 7494, Folder 22, SCAP Records, NA.

7. A. J. Rehe to CMPE, "License to Engage in Business in Japan," May 26, 1947, Box 7494, Folder 22, SCAP Records, NA.

8. Donald Nugent to Office of C-in-C (Col Adams), October 12, 1951, Box 5088, Folder 15, SCAP Records, NA; *Film Daily,* May 1, 1946; *Film Daily,* May 6, 1946.

9. Sasaki Tetsuo, *Sanpunkan no sagishi: Yokokuhen jinsei* (Tokyo: Pandorasha, 2000), 67–73.

10. Sasaki, *Sanpunkan no sagishi,* 60–69; telephone interview with Yamada Noboru, September 15, 2000.

11. CMPE, "M.P.E.A.-Japan," June 1, 1947, 1, Hidano Atsushi Collection, Tokyo (hereafter cited as Hidano Collection).

12. Mayer to Nugent, August 8, 1950, Box 5081, CIE(B)-08391, Records of the Supreme Commander for the Allied Powers, National Diet Library, Tokyo (hereafter cited as SCAP Records, NDL); *MPEA News* 54 (March/April 1950), 3; Mayer to Nugent, October 16, 1950, Box 5081, CIE(B)-08388, SCAP Records, NDL.

13. Mayer to G. P. Waller, 1951, Box 7494, Folder 22, SCAP Records, NA.

14. MPEA minutes, September 29, 1948, Box 7, Folder 1, Sears Papers, WCFTR.

15. CMPE, "M.P.E.A.-Japan," 1, Hidano Collection.

16. Lease form of Kanesaka Building, July 30, 1946, "Japan—MPA Lease, etc." folder, Warner Bros. Archives, University of Southern California.

17. Arch Reeve, "News Release, Wednesday, March 29, 1950," "MPAA International Committee 1955" folder, MPAA General Correspondence, MHL; *Shinsō,* December 20, 1950, 29.

18. *MPEA News,* 53 (February 1, 1950), 8.

19. *MPEA News,* 20, n.d., 1; telephone interview with Okazaki Eiichirō, September 23, 2000; *MPEA News,* 53 (February 1, 1950), 8.

20. *MPEA News,* 20, n.d., 1; telephone interview with Yamada Noboru, September 15, 2000.

21. CMPE, "M.P.E.A. Japan," 7, Hidano Collection.

22. CMPE, "M.P.E.A. Japan," 45, Hidano Collection.

23. *Eiga no tomo,* February 1951, 91; *MPEA News,* 24, 4; Sasaki Tetsuo, *"Sanpunkan no sagishi" ga kataru ginmaku no uragawa* (Tokyo: Gendai shokan, 2006).

24. *Eiga no tomo,* April 1966, 219–20.

25. *Sentoraru nyūsu* 2, n.d., 3.

26. "Critics Criticize Criticism," *Nippon Times,* ca. November 1, 1949, Box 5171, Folder 11, SCAP Records, NA.

27. *Kinema junpō,* August 15, 1956, 94.

28. *MPEA News* 45 (June 1, 1950), 1; *Hollywood Reporter,* March 21, 1950, 1, 4.

29. *MPEA News* reported that one lecture event took place in a private home around a Japanese fireplace (*irori*). See *MPEA News* 28 (February 1, 1948), 4.

30. *Nihon bunka tsūshin,* March 5, 1949, 2; *Hollywood Reporter,* March 21, 1950, 1, 4; *Nihon bunka tsūshin,* March 5, 1949, 2.

31. Mayer to Waller, May 23, 1951, Box 7494, Folder 22, SCAP Records, NA.

32. *MPEA News,* 10, n.d., 4. On the collection of scientific data, see *MPEA News* 24 (October 1, 1948), 4; *MPEA News* 53 (February 1, 1950), 8.

33. *MPEA News* 43 (April 5, 1950), 1.

34. *Sentoraru nyūsu* 3, n.d., 1; *Sentoraru nyūsu* 7, n.d., 4; *MPEA News* 10, n.d., 4; *MPEA News* 16, n.d., 2; *MPEA News* 18, n.d., 4; *MPEA News* 28 (February 1, 1949), 4.

35. *Eiga no tomo,* September 1949, back cover.

36. *Eiga no tomo,* March 1949, back cover.

37. *Kinema junpō,* March 1, 1947, back cover.

38. *Eiga no tomo,* December 1949, back cover.

39. *Eiga no tomo,* May 1950, back cover.

40. *Eiga to supōtsu,* June 15, 1948, 3; *MPEA News* 47, 1.

41. *MPEA News* 23 (September 1, 1948), 4.

42. *Hollywood,* January 1948, 19.

43. *Kinema junpō,* June 1, 1946, back cover.

44. *MPEA News* 46 (July 1, 1950), 5.

45. *Nihon bunka tsūshin,* March 5, 1949, 2; *Hollywood Reporter,* March 21, 1950, 1, 4.

46. *MPEA News* 45 (June 1, 1950), 1. This department was originally the Lecture Department, which appears to have existed within the larger Publicity Department.

47. MGM's *Tales of Manhattan* (1942) was road-showed at the Nihon gekijō in Tokyo in August 1946. But this screening appears to have been an ad hoc event. *Kinema junpō,* November 1, 1946, 41.

48. *Kinema junpō,* April 1, 1947, 37; *Nihon bunka tsūshin,* March 14, 1947, 2.

49. *Kinema junpō,* May 1, 1947, 37; Subaru kōgyō kabushiki gaisha, *Subaru-za no ayumi: 40 nen shōshi* (Tokyo: Subaru kōgyō kabushiki gaisha, 1987), 9–11, 83.

50. *Sentoraru nyūsu* 6, n.d., 1.

51. David Bordwell, *Narration in the Fiction Film* (Madison: University of Wisconsin Press, 1985), 157–58.

52. *Sentoraru nyūsu* 5, n.d., 2.

53. *Kinema junpō,* April 1, 1947, back cover; *Screen* 4, back cover.

54. *Sentoraru nyūsu* 4, n.d., 2.

55. E. Taylor Atkins, *Blue Nippon: Authenticating Jazz in Japan* (Durham: Duke University Press, 2001), 165–95; Mike Molasky, *Sengo nihon no jazu bunka: Eiga, bungaku, angura* (Tokyo: Seidosha, 2005), 33–134.

56. *Sentoraru nyūsu* 4, n.d., 3.

57. *Sentoraru nyūsu* 5, n.d., 2.

58. Mayer to Nugent, September 30, 1948, Box 5066, Folder 2, SCAP Records, NA; Mayer to Nugent, July 27, 1950, CIE(B)-08391, SCAP Records, NDL. On a related discussion, see Jennifer Fay, *Theaters of Occupation: Hollywood and the Reeducation of Postwar Germany* (Minneapolis: University of Minnesota Press, 2008), 139–41.

59. *Kinema junpō,* April 1, 1947, back cover.

60. *Kinema junpō,* April 1, 1947, back cover.

61. *Kinema junpō,* April 1, 1947, back cover; *Eiga no tomo,* April 1947, back cover.

62. *MPEA Weekly* (featuring *Rhapsody in Blue*), n.d.; *Sentoraru nyūsu* 5, n.d., 2.

63. Balio, *Grand Design,* 235–55.

64. *Kokusai eiga shinbun,* September 1934, 126; *Kokusai eiga shinbun,* October 1934, 5.

65. Kōtō gekijō, *Little Women* program, December 27, 1949, 1; *Kinema junpō,* February 15, 1950, 75; *Kinema junpō,* March 1, 1950, 61.

66. CMPE, *Little Women* press sheet.

67. CMPE, *Little Women* press sheet.

68. CMPE, *Little Women* press sheet.

69. CMPE, *Little Women* press sheet.

70. CMPE, *Little Women* press sheet.

71. CMPE, *Little Women* press sheet.

72. CMPE, *Little Women* press sheet.

73. *MPEA News* 41 (February 1, 1950), 1; *MPEA News* 43 (April 5, 1950), 5; *MPEA News* 42 (March 1, 1950), 6.

74. *MPEA News* 42 (March 1, 1950), 6.

75. CMPE, *Little Women* press sheet.

76. CMPE, *Little Women* press sheet.

77. *Eiga no tomo,* January 1950, back cover.

78. *MPEA News* 41 (February 1, 1950), 5.

79. *MPEA News* 42 (March 1, 1950), 5.

80. *MPEA News* 39 (December 1, 1949), 2; CMPE, *Little Women* press sheet.

81. CMPE, *Little Women* press sheet; *MPEA News* 39 (December 1, 1949), 2.

82. Daniel Walker Howe, "American Victorianism as Culture," *American Quarterly* 27:5 (December 1975): 507–32.

83. Technicolor impressed many viewers at a time when it was a rarity. See, for example, a critic's review of *Little Women* in *Nishi nihon shinbun,* January 4, 1950, 4.

84. CMPE, *Little Women* press sheet.

85. Barbara Welter, "The Cult of True Womanhood, 1820–1860," *American Quarterly* 18:2 (Summer 1966): 151–74.

86. Karen Halttunen, "The Domestic Drama of Louisa May Alcott," *Feminist Studies* 10:2 (Summer 1984): 233–54. Also see Karen Halttunen, *Confidence Men and Painted Women: A Study of Middle-Class Culture in America, 1830–1870* (New Haven: Yale University Press, 1986); June Howard, "What is Sentimentality?" *American Literary History* 11:1 (1999): 63–81.

87. Robyn McCallum, "The Present Reshaping the Past Reshaping the Present: Film Versions of *Little Women,*" *The Lion and the Unicorn* 24:1 (2000): 81–96.

88. CMPE, *Little Women* press sheet. Elaine Tyler May, *Homeward Bound: American Families in the Cold War Era,* rev. ed. (New York: Basic Books, 1999).

89. *Sentoraru nyūsu* 1, n.d., 1.

90. *Sentoraru nyūsu* 1, n.d., 1.
91. *MPEA News* 34 (July 1, 1949), 1–3.
92. *Sentoraru nyūsu* 6, n.d., 4.
93. *Kinema junpō,* September 1, 1949, 40; Ginza zensenza and Teatoru Shibuya, *Union Pacific* program; *Nagasaki minyū,* July 5, 1947, 4.
94. CMPE, *The Kansan* press sheet.
95. Frederick Jackson Turner, "The Significance of the Frontier in American History," in *Frederick Jackson Turner: Wisconsin's Historian of the Frontier,* ed. Martin Ridge (Madison: State Historical Society of Wisconsin, 1986), 26–47; also see Patricia Nelson Limerick, *Legacy of Conquest: The Unbroken Past of the American West* (New York: W. W. Norton, 1987), esp. 17–32.
96. CMPE, *Union Pacific* press sheet.
97. CMPE, *Union Pacific* press sheet.
98. CMPE, *Union Pacific* press sheet.
99. Richard Slotkin, *Gunfighter Nation: The Myth of the Frontier in Twentieth-Century America* (New York: HarperPerennial, 1992), 286–87.
100. CMPE, *Union Pacific* press sheet.
101. See, for example, Andrew Spicer, *Film Noir* (New York: Longman, 2002), 229.
102. *Kinema junpō,* April 15, 1950, 101.
103. CMPE, *Cry of the City* press sheet.
104. CMPE, *Cry of the City* press sheet.
105. *MPEA News* 41 (February 1, 1950), 3.
106. CMPE, *Cry of the City* press sheet.
107. CMPE, *Cry of the City* press sheet.
108. CMPE, *Cry of the City* press sheet.
109. CMPE, *Cry of the City* press sheet.
110. CMPE, *Cry of the City* press sheet.
111. CMPE, *Cry of the City* press sheet.

6. Presenting Culture

1. *Film Daily,* July 19, 1950, 6.
2. *MPEA News* 14, n.d., 1.
3. *MPEA News* 47 (August 1, 1950), 5, 6.
4. *Film Daily,* July 19, 1950, 6.
5. High, *Imperial Screen,* 489–91, 496–99; Jiji tsūshinsha, *Eiga geinō nenkan 1947 nendoban* (Tokyo: Jiji tsūshinsha, 1946), 56.
6. Sashō Shōzaburō, "Memo of Negotiations Rregarding [*sic*] Showing of Central Motion Pictures," September 14, 1946, Box 8618, Folder 11, SCAP Records, NA.
7. "Shuwarutsu seimei to sono hankyō," *Kōgyō Herarudo,* October 15, 1946, 3. This article was suppressed by the Civil Censorship Detachment. See Gordon Prange Collection, University of Maryland–College Park.
8. Sashō, "Memo of Negotiations Rregarding [*sic*] Showing of Central Motion Pictures," September 14, 1946, Box 8618, Folder 11, SCAP Records, NA.
9. *Film Daily,* October 16, 1946.
10. Nikkatsu kabushiki gaisha, ed., *Nikkatsu 50 nenshi* (Tokyo: Nikkatsu kabushiki gaisha, 1962), 57–58.
11. CCD Memorandum, May 13, 1947, Box 8617, Folder 40, SCAP Records, NA.
12. *Kinema junpō,* August 10, 1946, 41.

13. CMPE noted that American movies were being shown in 60 percent of Japanese cities. See *Sentoraru nyūsu,* 4, n.d., 4.

14. CCD Memorandum, May 13, 1947, Box 8617, Folder 40, SCAP Records, NA.

15. Jiji tsūshin sha, *Eiga geinō nenkan 1947 nendo ban* (Tokyo: Jiji tsūshinsha, 1947), 58–9.

16. *Nihon eiga,* June 1937, 63.

17. Balio, *Grand Design,* 210. In addition to employing this "fifty-fifty" system, the CMPE required exhibitors to pay for ads, posters, and other publicity expenses.

18. CCD Memorandum, May 13, 1947, Box 8617, Folder 40, SCAP Records, NA. On Nikkatsu's profits, see Jiji tsūshinsha, *Eiga geinō nenkan 1947 nendoban,* 57; "Yearly Agreement" with Shinseikan (Tokyo), May 23, 1946 to May 22, 1947, Box 7475, Folder 3, SCAP Records, NA; "Yearly agreement between Nikkatsu Kabushiki Kaisha and Central Motion Picture Exchange," Box 8438, Folder 5, SCAP Records, NA.

19. *Asahi shinbun,* November 3, 1946, 3.

20. *Sentoraru nyūsu,* 2, n.d., 1.

21. *Nihon bunka tsūshin,* April 24, 1947, 3.

22. MPEA, "Minutes of a Special Meeting of the Board of Directors of Motion Picture Export Association, Inc.," September 29, 1948, Box 7, Folder 1, Sears Papers, WCFTR.

23. *MPEA Newsletter* 4:12 (December 1949): 4–5.

24. *MPEA News* 8, n.d., 4; *MPEA News* 15, n.d., 4; *MPEA News* 21, n.d., 4.

25. *MPEA News* 8, n.d., 1.

26. *Kinema junpō,* October 15, 1948, 41.

27. *Nihon bunka tsūshin,* February 20, 1947, 3.

28. *MPEA News* 22 (July 1948), 1.

29. *Sentoraru nyūsu* 4, n.d., 1.

30. *MPEA News* 10, n.d., 1.

31. *Sentoraru nyūsu* 5, n.d., 1.

32. *Sentoraru nyūsu* 3, n.d., 1; *MPEA News* 21, n.d., 4; *MPEA News* 52 (January 1, 1950), 1.

33. *MPEA News* 24 (October 1, 1948), 4; *MPEA News* 25 (November 1, 1948), 4.

34. *Sentoraru nyūsu* 2, n.d., 1; *Sentoraru nyūsu* 3, n.d., 2; *MPEA News* 10, n.d., 4.

35. *Sentoraru nyūsu* 4, n.d., 1; *Sentoraru nyūsu* 6, n.d., 1.

36. *Sentoraru nyūsu* 7, n.d., 4. CMPE-Nagoya agent Komaki Toshiharu recalls that he specifically instructed local exhibitors in person to implement this strategy. Interview with Komaki, September 26, 1999, Kamakura, Japan.

37. *MPEA News* 21, n.d., 4.

38. *Sentoraru nyūsu* 2, n.d., 1; interview with Komaki Toshiharu, September 26, 1999, Kamakura, Japan.

39. *Nihon bunka tsūshin* April 24, 1947, 3.

40. *Sentoraru nyūsu* 4, n.d., 1.

41. *MPEA News* 28 (January 1949), 1.

42. Jiji tsūshinsha, *Eiga nenkan 1950nen,* 52; *MPEA News* 14, n.d., 1.

43. *Kinema junpō,* December 1, 1947, 37; *Nihon bunka tsūshin* 346, October 25, 1947, 1.

44. *Zenkoku eigakan shinbun,* October 15, 1947, 2.

45. *Kinema junpō,* August 15, 1955, 39–47.

46. Sennichimae sentoraru kaikan, a second-run theater in Osaka, was a case in point. This theater had caught the CMPE's attention because of its publicity efforts and management. After its renovation in early 1949, the CMPE "promoted" the venue to first-run. *MPEA News* 39 (December 1, 1949), 4.

47. *MPEA News* 38 (November 5, 1949), 1.

48. *MPEA News* 18, n.d., 1; *MPEA News* 17, n.d., 1; *MPEA News* 47 (August 1, 1950), 6; *MPEA News* 27 (January 1, 1949), 4; *Rengō tsūshin,* November 13, 1949.

49. *MPEA News* 17, n.d., 1.

50. CMPE, "Sales Policy," Box 7475, Folder 1, SCAP Records, NA.

51. *Motion Picture Herald,* July 19, 1947, 52.

52. *Variety,* April 4 1951, 13.

53. Kinema junpōsha, ed., *Kinema junpō eiga 40nen zen kiroku* (Tokyo: Kinema junpōsha, 1986), 12.

54. *Nihon bunka tsūshin,* April 24, 1947, 3.

55. *Eiga engeki shinbun,* March 1947, 6. *Nihon bunka tsūshin,* August 26, 1947, 3; *Nihon bunka tsūshin,* December 26, 1947, 1.

56. Kodama Kazuo, "Natsukashi no Subaru-za," *Subaru-za no ayumi: 40 nenshi,* ed. Subaru Enterprises (Tokyo: Subaru Enterprises, 1986), 22.

57. CMPE, "M.P.E.A. Japan," June 1, 1947, 14, Hidano Collection.

58. *Kinema junpō,* December 1, 1950, 28.

59. *Kinema junpō,* October 1, 1949, 24–25.

60. Subaru kōgyō kabushiki gaisha, *Subaru kōgyō 50 nenshi* (Tokyo: Subaru Enterprises, 1997), 13. Also see Civil Intelligence Section and Civil Censorship Detachment, "Special Report," May 9, 1947, Box 8662, Folder 26, SCAP Records, NA.

61. Subaru kōgyō kabushiki gaisha, *Subaru kōgyō 50 nenshi,* 139.

62. The word *za* means "to sit down." It is a common word used in the names of stage theaters and movie houses.

63. Subaru kōgyō kabushiki gaisha, *Subaru kōgyō 50 nenshi,* 13. *Rengō tsūshin eiga geinō kaisetsu,* January 11, 1948, 1.

64. Subaru kōgyō kabushiki gaisha, *Subaru kōgyō 50 nenshi,* 16–17.

65. Subaru kōgyō kabushiki gaisha, *Subaru kōgyō 50 nenshi,* 139.

66. *Kinema junpō,* August 15, 1955, 40.

67. *Kinema junpō gyōkai tokuhō,* September 21, 1948, 2–3.

68. *MPEA News* 16, n.d., 1.

69. For a history of movie programs in Japan, see Makino Mamoru, "'Bunka toshiteno eiga no dokyumentēshon': bunken, posutā, puromaido nado," in *Eiga seitan 100nen hakurankai,* ed. Kawasai shimin myūjiamu (Tokyo: Kinema junpōsha, 1995), esp. 138–41.

70. *MPEA News* 17, n.d., 1.

71. For more on the Subaru programs, see Hiroshi Kitamura, "'Home of American Movies': The Marunouchi Subaruza and the Making of Hollywood's Audiences in Occupied Tokyo, 1946–9," in *Hollywood Abroad: Audiences and Cultural Exchange,* ed. Richard Maltby and Melvyn Stokes (London: British Film Institute, 2004), 105–7.

72. *Yomiuri shinbun,* December 30, 1946, 2.

73. See, for example, *Subaru Theatre News* 8 (*Gaslight,* June 3, 1947), 32.

74. *Subaru Theatre News* 8 (*Gaslight,* June 3, 1947), 32; *Sentoraru Nyusu* 5 (February 1947), 4.

75. *Kinema junpō gyōkai tokuhō,* June 11, 1949, 2.

76. Telephone interview with Asaoka Hiroshi, September 3, 2000.

77. Dower, *Embracing Defeat,* 148–154.

78. Romance seats were first implemented at Osaka Subaru-za, another theater owned by Subaru Enterprises. These seats first appeared at Marunouchi Subaru-za on November 18, 1947. See *Zenkoku eigakan shinbun,* November 1, 1947, 2; *Subaru Theatre News* 11 (*All This and Heaven Too,* November 1947), 32. On popular response to romance seats, see, for example, *Amerika eiga monogatari,* July 1949; *Kindai eiga* 4:8 (August 1948): 11. On other theaters that adopted romance seats, see *MPEA News* 39 (December 1, 1949), 4.

79. Interview with Ishikawa Hatsutarō, November 19, 1999, Tokyo, Japan.

80. Telephone interview with Asaoka Hiroshi, September 3, 2000. *MPEA News* 28 (February 1, 1949), 1.

81. *Subaru Theater News 8* (*Gaslight,* June 3, 1947).

82. *Zenkoku eigakan shinbun,* April 1, 1948, 3.

83. *Kinema junpō* 65 (September 1, 1949), 40.

84. *Zenkoku eigakan shinbun,* October 1, 1949, 3; *Rengō tsūshin,* September 12, 1949, 2; *Rengō tsūshin,* September 17, 1949, 5–7.

85. Jiji tsūshinsha, ed., *Eiga nenkan 1951* (Tokyo: Jiji tsūshinsha, 1951), 56; *Zenkoku eigakan shinbun,* July 11, 1949, 2; *Kinema junpō,* February 15, 1949, 4. *Kinema junpō,* December 1, 1950, 28–29; *Zenkoku eigakan shinbun,* November 1, 1949, 2; *Zenkoku eigakan shinbun,* November 11, 1949, 3; Jiji tsūshinsha, *Eiga nenkan 1951,* 56.

86. *Zenkoku eigakan shinbun,* May 1, 1948, 4.

87. Nagoyashi, *Shinshū Nagoya shishi, dai 7 kan* (Nagoya: City of Nagoya, 1999), 918–19.

88. Itō, *Nagoya eigashi,* 77.

89. CMPE, "M.P.E.A. Japan," 26, Hidano Collection.

90. *MPEA News* 35 (August 1, 1949), 1.

91. *Zenkoku eigakan shinbun,* May 1, 1948, 4.

92. Charles Mayer to Don Brown, November 17, 1947, Box 5062, Folder 15, SCAP Records, NA.

93. State-za, *State-za puroguramu 79* (*The Man from Colorado*); *Zenkoku eigakan shinbun,* May 1, 1948, 4.

94. *Tōkai mainichi shinbun,* March 1, 1949, 2.

95. *MPEA News* 35 (August 1, 1949), 1.

96. State-za, *State-za puroguramu 3* (*The Secret Heart*).

97. *MPEA News* 42 (March 1, 1950), 5; *MPEA News* 38 (November 5, 1949), 4.

98. One exception was the State-za, *State-za puroguramu 92* (*Gone with the Wind*).

99. *MPEA News* 41 (February 1, 1950), 5. State-za organized a minidisplay of Mexican artifacts, for example, during the screenings of *Treasure of the Sierra Madre. MPEA News* 36 (September 1, 1949), 4.

100. *Chubu nihon shinbun,* April 17, 1950, 2.

101. *MPEA News* 38 (November 5, 1949), 4.

102. *MPEA News* 38 (November 5, 1949), 4.

103. *Chubu nihon shinbun,* August 22, 1950, 4.

104. *Tōkai mainichi shinbun,* August 11, 1949, 2.

105. State-za, *State-za puroguramu 50* (*Captain China*); *MPEA News* 48 (September 5, 1950), 5.

106. State-za, *State-za puroguramu 31* (*California*).

107. *Zenkoku eigakan shinbun,* November 4, 1950, 2.

108. *MPEA News* 38 (November 5, 1949), 4.

109. State-za, *State-za puroguramu 3* (*The Secret Heart*).

110. *MPEA News* 38 (November 5, 1949), 4.

111. *Zenkoku eigakan shinbun,* November 4, 1952, 2.

112. *MPEA News* 36 (September 1, 1949), 4.

113. *MPEA News* 38 (November 5, 1949), 1.

114. Itō, *Shinema yoruhiru kaiko: Nagoya eigashi 8 mm kara 70 mm made* (Nagoya: privately printed, 1994), 168–70, 174–75.

115. Hiroshimashi, Nagasakishi genbaku saigaishi henshū iinkai, ed., *Genbaku saigai Hiroshima Nagasaki* (Tokyo: Iwanami bunko, 1985), esp. 1–59.

116. *Nagasaki shinbun,* October 24, 1945, 2; *Nagasaki shinbun,* October 25, 1945, 2; *Nagasaki shinbun,* November 1, 1945, 2; *Nagasaki shinbun,* November 9, 1945, 2.

117. CMPE, "M.P.E.A.," 36, Hidano Collection.
118. *Yūkan taimuzu,* January 1, 1950, 4; *Yūkan taimuzu,* October 9, 1950, 2.
119. *Yūkan taimuzu,* January 1, 1950, 4; *Yūkan taimuzu,* October 9, 1950, 2.
120. *Nagasaki shinbun,* April 4, 1946, 2; CMPE, "M.P.E.A.," 38, Hidano Collection. The Nagasaki Central Theater burned down. The first CMPE films appeared at the Fujikan, at Tōhō Theater, but in early June, the newly built Nagasaki Central Theater earned the right to showcase Hollywood films. See *Nagasaki shinbun,* April 4, 1946, 2; *Nagasaki shinbun,* April 25, 1946, 2; *Nagasaki shinbun,* June 2, 1946, 2; *Nagasaki shinbun,* June 6, 1946, 1. The deadly fire struck on November 15, 1947. See *Minyū,* November 16, 1947, 2; *Nagasaki nichinichi shinbun,* November 16, 1947, 2. *Minyū,* October 4, 1949, 2.
121. Nōma Yoshihiro, *Fukuoka Hakata eiga hyakunen* (Fukuoka: Imamura shoten san kurie-ito, 2003), 103–4, 115–18.
122. *MPEA News* 14, n.d., 4.
123. Jiji tsūshinsha, *Eiga nenkan: 1950nen,* 228.
124. *Minyū,* July 9, 1947, 2; *Minyū,* August 1, 1947, 1; *Minyū,* October 29, 1947, 1; *Nagasaki nichinichi shinbun,* November 16, 1947, 2; *Minyū,* November 19, 1947, 2; *Minyū,* January 1, 1948, 3; *Minyū,* January 21, 1948, 2; *Minyū,* February 10, 1948, 2; *Minyū,* February 18, 1948, 2.
125. *Minyū,* March 4, 1948, 2; *Minyū,* March 10, 1948, 2.
126. Jiji tsūshinsha, *Eiga nenkan 1950nen,* 218.
127. *MPEA News* 14, n.d., 4.
128. Satō Tadao, *Nihon eigashi,* vol. 2 (Tokyo: Iwanami shoten, 1995), 295.
129. *Minyu,* January 10, 1949, 2.
130. *Minyu,* May 30, 1949, 2.
131. *Yūkan taimuzu,* January 1, 1950, 4.
132. Interview with Aijima Masato, December 10, 2000.
133. *Minyū,* September 20, 1948, 1; *Minyū,* December 30, 1948, 2; *Minyū,* December 30, 1949, 2; *Minyū,* January 1, 1950, 3; *Minyū,* September 20, 1949, 1; *Minyū,* October 11, 1949, 2; *Minyū,* October 18, 1949, 2; *Minyū,* November 1, 1949, 2; *Minyū,* November 15, 1949, 2; *Minyū,* January 8, 1950, 2; *Minyū,* January 10, 1950, 2; *Minyū,* January 24, 1950, 2; *Minyū,* December 12, 1949, 2; *Minyū,* December 16, 1949, 2; *Minyū,* December 20, 1949, 2; *Minyū,* January 17, 1950, 2.
134. *Minyū,* February 19, 1950, 2; *Minyū,* February 28, 1950, 2; *Minyū,* March 7, 1950, 2; *Minyū,* March 14, 1950, 2; *Minyū,* April 3, 1950, 2.
135. *Minyū,* February 21, 1950, 2.
136. *Minyū,* March 14, 1950, 2.
137. *Minyū,* February 28, 1950, 2.
138. *Minyū,* March 28, 1950, 2.
139. Interview with Aijima Masato, January 18, 2007, Nagasaki.
140. *Yūkan Nagasaki taimuzu,* February 25, 1950, 2; *Minyū,* February 18, 1950, 2. *Minyū,* May 12, 1950, 1; *Yūkan Nagasaki taimuzu,* May 3, 1950, 2.
141. *Minyū,* December 12, 1951, 2.
142. Telephone interview with Aijima Masato, December 10, 2000.
143. Telephone interview with Aijima Masato, December 10, 2000.
144. *Yūkan Nagasaki taimuzu,* July 20, 1950, 2.
145. Telephone interview with Aijima Masato, December 10, 2000.
146. *Minyū,* November 8, 1950, 2.
147. *Minyū,* January 19, 1951, 3; *Minyū,* January 20, 1951, 2; *Minyū,* February 17, 1951, 3; *Minyū,* February 23, 1951, 3; *Minyū,* March 9, 1951, 3.
148. See, for example, *Daiichi wīkurī* 3, n.d.; *Daiichi wīkurī* 7, n.d.

149. *Ningen keisei,* October 1948, 44.

150. *Eiga nenkan* 1952, 96.

151. Charles Mayer to G. P. Waller, May 23, 1951, Box 7494, Folder 22, SCAP Records, NA.

7. Seeking Enlightenment

1. *MPEA News Release,* July 27, 1949, Special Collections, MHL.

2. I use the phrase "culture elite" to distinguish, but not exclude, this circle of individuals from "intellectuals" as defined in a narrow sense. The phrase "culture elites," as used here, is analogous to the Japanese word *bunkajin.* The English-language phrase owes to Peter Decherney, *Hollywood and the Culture Elite: How the Movies Became American* (New York: Columbia University Press, 2005). Decherney's "culture elite" primarily signify college professors, museum curators, philanthropists, and government bureaucrats.

3. In this chapter, those who belonged to the "culture elite" were official members of AMCA and/or its predecessor, the Committee for the Instruction and Appreciation of American Cinema.

4. On the "organic" function of intellectuals and social groups, see Terry Eagleton, *Scholars and Rebels in Nineteenth-Century Ireland* (Malden, MA: Blackwell, 1999); Antonio Gramsci, *Selections from the Prison Notebooks of Antonio Gramsci,* ed., Quintin Hoare and Geoffrey Nowell Smith (New York: International Publishers, 1971), esp. 5–23.

5. Makino Mamoru, ed., *Fukkokuban kinema record* (Tokyo: Kokusho kankōkai, 2002).

6. Iijima Tadashi et al. eds., *Eiga nenkan 1936nen* (Tokyo: Daiichi shobō, 1936), 30–32.

7. See, for example, *Kinema junpō,* January 1, 1927, 77–82; *Kinema junpō,* February 21, 1927, 20–21; *Kinema junpō,* May 11, 1928, 31; *Kinema junpō,* October 21, 1928, 41.

8. See, for example, *Kinema Junpō,* February 1, 1927, 32–33; *Kinema Junpō,* July 1, 1927, 23.

9. Aaron Gerow, "Tatakau kankyaku: Daitōa kyōeiken no nihon eiga to juyō no mondai," *Gendai shisō* 30:9 (July 2002): 141.

10. Aaron Gerow, "*Miyato Musashi* to senjichū no kankyaku," in *Eiga kantoku Mizoguchi Kenji,* ed. Yomota Inuhiko (Tokyo: Shinyōsha, 1999), esp. 237–46.

11. Iijima Tadashi, *Eiga bunka no kenkyū* (Tokyo: Shinchōsha, 1939), 46–47.

12. Hazumi Tsuneo, *Eiga to minzoku* (Tokyo: Eiga nihonsha, 1942), 265; *Eiga no tomo,* December 1940, 126; *Eiga no tomo,* November 1940, 80.

13. Hazumi, *Eiga to minzoku,* 10. The quote comes from an article titled "War and Cinema," originally published September 1940.

14. Tsumura Hideo, *Eiga seisakuron* (Tokyo: Chūō kōronsha, 1943), 442. The quote is from an article originally published December 29, 1941, three weeks after Pearl Harbor.

15. Iwasaki Akira, *Gendai nihon no eiga* (Tokyo: Chūō kōronsha, 1958), 11, 25.

16. *Kinema junpō,* July 1, 1948, 11.

17. Tsumura Hideo, *Konnichi no eiga* (Tokyo: Kaname shobō, 1950), 2.

18. Iijima Tadashi, *Eiga kanshō dokuhon* (Tokyo: Ōbunsha, 1948), 170–71.

19. Futaba Jūzaburo, *Amerika eiga* (Tokyo: Meikyokudō, 1950), 25.

20. *Kinema junpō,* March 1, 1946, 26.

21. Harry Slott, "Motion Picture Critics' Role in the Democratization of Japanese Motion Pictures," Box 5305, Folder 8, SCAP Records, NA.

22. *MPEA News* 1, 1.

23. *MPEA News* 1, 1.

24. *Hollywood Reporter,* September 12, 1946, 11; *Film Daily,* September 10, 1946, 11.

25. *Sentoraru nyūsu* 1, n.d., 1; *Sentoraru nyūsu* 3, n.d., 4.
26. *Amerika eiga bunka* 1, 1.
27. *Amerika eiga bunka* 1, 2.
28. *Amerika eiga bunka* 1, 1.
29. *Amerika eiga bunka* 3 (December 1, 1947), 2.
30. *MPEA News* 45 (June 1, 1950), 1.
31. *America eiga bunka* 1, 2.
32. *MPEA News* 17, n.d., 4.
33. See, for example, *Zenkoku eigakan shinbun,* April 1, 1948, 3.
34. *Kudamatsu A.M.C.A. News* is available at the Gordon Prange Collection, University of Maryland–College Park.
35. American Movie Culture Association to Supreme Commander for the Allied Powers, June 1, 1949, Box 5072, Folder 2, SCAP Records, NA.
36. Phone interview with Asaoka Hiroshi, October 3, 2000.
37. *MPEA News* 32 (May 1, 1949), 4; *Eiga no tomo,* August 1950, 73. *Eiga no tomo,* May 1951, 94; *MPEA News* 18, n.d., 4; *MPEA News* 52 (January 1, 1950), 6.
38. *MPEA News* 22, n.d., 4.
39. Interview with Komaki Toshiharu, November 22, 1999, Kamakura, Japan. On "Fountain of Words," see Wada Shinken, ed., *Hanashi no izumi* (Tokyo: Aoyama shoten 1947).
40. *MPEA News* 52, 6.
41. AMCA, ed., *Eiga no kisetsu* (Tokyo: Amerika eiga bunka kyōkai, 1949), 47.
42. *Junkan Amerika eiga* 23 (December 1, 1948), 1; *Junkan Amerika eiga* 27 (April 1, 1949), 1; *MPEA News* 31 (April 15, 1949), 2.
43. *Junkan Amerika eiga* 27, 1.
44. *Junkan Amerika eiga* 27, 1.
45. Nakano Gorō, *Keishō* (Tokyo: Kizanbō, 1943), 17–18; Nakano Gorō, *Sokoku ni kaeru* (Tokyo: Shin kigensha, 1943).
46. Nakano, *Keishō,* 17–18.
47. Nakano Gorō, *Tekioku Amerika no sensō senden* (Tokyo: Shin taiyōsha, 1945), 80, 95.
48. Nakano Gorō, *Kakute gyokusai seri: Haisen no rekishi* (Tokyo: Nihon kōhōsha, 1948), 2, 3.
49. Nakano Gorō, *Amerika ni manabu* (Tokyo: Nihon kōhōsha, 1949), 21–22.
50. Nakano Gorō, *Amerika zakkichō* (Tokyo: Shichisei shoin, 1947), 53.
51. Nakano, *Amerika zakkichō,* 65.
52. AMCA, *Eiga no kisetsu,* 171–72.
53. Nakano, *Amerika zakkichō,* 57.
54. Nakano, *Amerika zakkichō,* 119.
55. AMCA, *Eiga no kisetsu,* 174.
56. Nakano Gorō, *Demokurashi no benkyō* (Tokyo: Meguro shoten, 1946).
57. AMCA, *Eiga no kisetsu,* 175.
58. *Amerika eiga bunka* 3 (December 1, 1947), 1.
59. AMCA, *Eiga no kisetsu,* 193–201.
60. Nakano, *Amerika zakkichō,* 124.
61. AMCA, *Eiga no kisetsu,* 179; Nakano, *Amerika zakkichō,* 60.
62. Nakano, *Amerika ni manabu,* 142–48.
63. Nakano, *Kakute gyokusai seri* (Tokyo: Nihon kōhōsha, 1948).
64. This quote comes from Nakano's later article on war films. See Nakano Gorō, "Sensō eiga no shijitsusei to gorakusei," *Gan,* November 1958, 126–37.
65. Nakano, *Kakute gyokusai seri,* 2; Nakano Gorō, *Kimi wa dainiji sekaitaisen o shitte iruka: Kyōkasho dewa manabanai sensō no sugao* (Tokyo: Kojinsha, 1993); Martin Kadin, *Zerosen: Nihon*

kaigun no eikō, trans. Katoyama Kōtaro (Tokyo: Sankei shinbunsha shuppankyoku, 1971). This translation was supervised by Nakano. Also see *Asahi shinbun,* evening edition, June 15, 1966, 7.

66. Honda Akira, *Geijutsu to shakai* (Tokyo: Kawade shobō, 1941); Honda Akira, *Kandō to hihyō* (Tokyo: Sakuhinsha, 1938).

67. Honda Akira, *Ichi chishikijin no kokuhaku* (Tokyo: Fuju shoin, 1948), 141.

68. Honda Akira, *Seishun no kensetsu: Wakai hito ni hanashikakeru* (Tokyo: Akita shoten, 1966), 50.

69. Honda Akira, *Shidōsha: Kono hito o miyo* (Tokyo: Kōbunsha, 1955), 43, 79.

70. Honda Akira, *Kodoku no bungakusha* (Tokyo: Yakumo shoten, 1947), 30–31.

71. *Eiga no tomo,* November 1940, 76.

72. Honda, *Shidōsha,* 62–3, 77–80.

73. *Eiga no tomo,* October 1950, 33.

74. *Eiga no tomo,* October 1950, 32.

75. AMCA, *Eiga no kisetsu,* 34.

76. AMCA, *Eiga no kisetsu,* 34–43.

77. *Junkan Amerika eiga* 23 (December 1, 1948), 3; *Junkan Amerika eiga* 33 (October 1, 1949), 2.

78. *Junkan Amerika eiga* 23 (December 1, 1948), 3.

79. *Junkan Amerika eiga* 23 (December 1, 1948), 3.

80. Honda, *Seishun to hyūmanizumu* (Tokyo: Akebono shobō, 1948), 55–56.

81. High, *Imperial Screen,* 217.

82. AMCA, *Eiga no kisetsu,* 31.

83. AMCA, *Eiga no kisetsu,* 29–30.

84. AMCA, *Eiga no kisetsu,* 29.

85. Honda, *Seishun to hyūmanizumu,* 55–56.

86. AMCA, *Eiga no kisetsu,* 31.

87. Honda, *Seishun to hyūmanizumu,* 152–54.

88. Honda, *Seishun to hyūmanizumu,* 163, 125–39.

89. Honda, *Shidōsha,* 134.

90. Honda, *Shidōsha;* Honda, *Seishun no kensetsu;* Honda Akira, *Idai na jikini: Warera ikani ikubekika* (Tokyo: Hokushindō, 1957).

91. Honda, *Seishun no kensetsu,* 148–80; Honda, *Idai na jikini,* 7–16.

92. *Asahi shinbun,* April 9, 1958, 6.

93. See the Library of Congress website for additional information. http://www.loc.gov/rr/asian/JapanTeam.html (accessed May 12, 2007).

94. Shiho Sakanishi, *Kyogen: Comic Interludes of Japan* (Boston: Marshall Jones Company, 1938); Shiho Sakanishi, *Japanese Folk-Plays: The Ink-Smeared Lady and Other Kyogen* (Rutland, VT: Charles E. Tuttle, 1960); Sachio Ito, *Songs of a Cowherd,* trans. Shiho Sakanishi (Boston: Marshall Jones, 1936).

95. "Sakanishi Shiho san" henshū sewani kai, ed., *Sakanishi Shiho san* (Tokyo: Kokusai bunka kaikan, 1977), 20.

96. *Washington Post,* January 17, 1976, E4.

97. "Sakanishi Shiho san" henshū sewani kai, *Sakanishi Shiho san,* 114–30.

98. "Sakanishi Shiho san" henshū sewani kai, *Sakanishi Shiho san,* 311.

99. "Sakanishi Shiho san" henshū sewani kai, *Sakanishi Shiho san,* 181, 156–57, 207.

100. "Sakanishi Shiho san" henshū sewani kai, *Sakanishi Shiho san,* 201.

101. AMCA, *Eiga no kisetsu,* 272.

102. AMCA, *Eiga no kisetsu,* 272; *Junkan Amerika eiga,* 27 (April 1, 1949), 2.

103. AMCA, *Eiga no kisetsu,* 274.

104. Sakanishi Shiho, *Minshushugi wa seikatsu no nakani* (Tokyo: Ie no hikari bunko, 1947) 1.

105. *Junkan Amerika eiga* 33 (October 1, 1949), 2.

106. AMCA, *Eiga no kisetsu,* 260.

107. AMCA, *Eiga no kisetsu,* 261.

108. AMCA, *Eiga no kisetsu,* 274; Sakanishi, *Minshushugi wa seikatsu no nakani,* 161–63.

109. AMCA, *Eiga no kisetsu,* 273.

110. *Junkan Amerika eiga* 27 (April 1, 1949), 2.

111. AMCA, *Eiga no kisetsu,* 273.

112. Sakanishi Shiho, *Josei to kyōyō: Renai, shakai, gakusei* (Tokyo: Kokudosha, 1949), 176.

113. Sakanishi, *Josei to kyōyō,* 172.

114. Sakanishi, *Minshushugi wa kodomo no toki kara* (Tokyo: Minshu kyōiku kyōkai, 1961), 67.

115. Sakanishi, *Josei to kyōyō,* 174, 173.

116. Sakanishi, *Josei to kyōyō,* 174.

117. Sakanishi, *Josei to kyōyō,* 173.

118. *Junkan Amerika eiga* 33 (October 1, 1949), 2.

119. *Junkan Amerika eiga* 29 (June 1, 1949), 3.

120. *Junkan Amerika eiga* 33 (October 1, 1949), 2.

121. Sakanishi Shiho, *Minshu shakai ni okeru shimin* (Tokyo: Minshu kyōiku kyōkai, 1965), 19.

122. Sakanishi, *Minshu shakai ni okeru shimin,* 25, 22–31.

123. Sakanishi remained supportive of Hollywood in the 1950s and 1960s. At the Congressional Hearings of the Committee on Foreign Affairs in 1963, Robert J. Corkery of the Motion Picture Export Association quoted the following remarks by Sakanishi: "By and large, American feature motion pictures seem to me to reflect American attitudes, principles, and the American way of life… American pictures, for example, entertain and amuse. But after the good time is over, they leave the audience with something to think about." *Winning the Cold War: The U.S. Ideological Offensive,* Hearings before the Subcommittee on International Organizations and Movements of the Committee on Foreign Affairs, 88th Cong., 1st session, September 11–13, 1963 (Washington, DC: U.S. Government Printing Office, 1963), 567.

124. *MPEA News* 50 (November 5, 1950), 1.

125. *MPEA News Release,* July 27 1949, MPAA Collection, Roll 14, Special Collections, MHL.

126. "Statement of Eric Johnston, President of the Motion Picture Association of America and Motion Picture Export Association of America," Overseas Information Programs of the United States, March 6, 1953, Box 7, Folder 87, Eric Johnston Collection, Eastern Washington State Historical Society, Spokane, Washington.

8. Choosing America

1. *Eiga no tomo,* May 1948, 20.

2. Evidence indicates that *Eiga no tomo* occasionally suffered from the Civil Censorship Detachment's censorship practices. For example, in an article titled "A Short History of American Films," censors detected a passage that identified "sexual immorality, sensational costumes and reckless desire for investment[s]" as "peculiar to America." Censors enforced deletion of this passage due to its "criticism of U.S." CCD, "News Matter or Table of Contents," translated September 27, 1946. This memo concerns *Eiga no tomo,* October 1946, 32. See *Eiga no tomo* microfiche in Gordon Prange Collection, University of Maryland–College Park.

3. Dower, *Embracing Defeat,* 148–67, 180–200.

4. "The Motion Picture Producers' Association Report," January 28, 1947, Box 5278, Folder 5, SCAP Records, NA.

5. Silverberg, *Erotic Grotesque Nonsense,* 108–42.

6. One of the magazine's editors later noted that the military would essentially order the magazine to write in support of the country's war endeavors. See Ōguro Toyoji, *Eiga to tomoni 50nen* (Kōchi: Kōchi shinbunsha, 1981), 116–17.

7. *Eiga no tomo,* December 1937, 57. *Eiga no tomo,* January 1941, 59.

8. *Eiga no tomo,* December 1940, 126; *Eiga no tomo,* November 1940, 80.

9. Ōguro, *Eiga to tomoni 50nen,* 145–46.

10. *Eiga no tomo,* August 1946, 34.

11. *Eiga no tomo,* April 1946, 34.

12. *Eiga no tomo,* June 1946, 32–33; *Eiga no tomo,* May 1947, 13.

13. *Eiga no tomo,* November 1947, 12.

14. *Eiga no tomo,* August 1946, 34.

15. Komori Kazuko, *Sutā dokuhon* (Tokyo: Jitsubunkan, 1951).

16. *Eiga no tomo,* October 1948, 30.

17. *Eiga no tomo,* August 1946, 8.

18. *Eiga no tomo,* December 1950, 32–33; *Eiga no tomo,* January 1951, 42–43.

19. *Eiga no tomo,* August 1952, 7.

20. Dower, *Embracing Defeat,* 172–74, 188.

21. *Eiga no tomo,* April 1946, 18–19.

22. *Eiga no tomo,* December 1948, 18–19; *Eiga no tomo,* February 1949, 22–23; *Eiga no tomo,* June 1949, 27; *Eiga no tomo,* August 1949, 26–27.

23. *Eiga no tomo,* April 1950, 65; *Eiga no tomo,* April 1951, 78–79; *Eiga no tomo,* September 1949, 20–22.

24. *Eiga no tomo,* October 1950, 32–33.

25. *Eiga no tomo,* July 1947, 15.

26. *Eiga no tomo,* October 1946, 10.

27. *Eiga no tomo,* January 1948, 27; *Eiga no tomo,* January 1949, 15; *Eiga no tomo,* April 1949, 23; *Eiga no tomo,* June 1950, 40.

28. Yodogawa Nagaharu, "*Eiga no tomo,* editorial notes September 1949," in *Yodogawa Nagaharu shūsei, vol. 4,* ed. Hazumi Arihiro (Tokyo: Haga shoten, 1987), 127.

29. Yodogawa Nagaharu, *Eiga to tomoni ayunda waga hanshōki* (Tokyo: Kindai eigasha, 1973), 52.

30. For some of his recollections about his work at United Artists, see Yodogawa Nagaharu, *Yodogawa Nagaharu jiden, jō* (Tokyo: Chuo kōronsha, 1988), 225–34.

31. *Eiga no tomo,* January 1940, 66–70; *Eiga no tomo,* April 1940, 90–92; *Eiga no tomo,* August 1940, 113–15. Also see *Eiga no tomo,* December 1940, 110–11.

32. *Sentoraru nyūsu* 5, n.d., 4; *Sentoraru nyūsu* 6, n.d., 4.

33. Tsukuda Yoshinori, *Yodogawa Nagaharu ga nokoshite kuretakoto: Eiga ga jinsei no gakkō datta* (Tokyo: Kairyūsha, 1999), 10–15.

34. Yodogawa Nagaharu, *Eiga to tomoni ayunda waga hanshōki,* 132.

35. Yodogawa, *Yodogawa Nagaharu jiden, jō* (Tokyo: Chūō kōronsha, 1988), 396.

36. *Eiga no tomo,* September 1947, 21.

37. *Eiga no tomo,* April 1949, 4.

38. *Eiga no tomo,* April 1949, 4, 5.

39. Ōguro, *Eiga to tomoni 50nen,* 149–50.

40. Yodogawa Nagaharu, *Eiga sansaku* (Tokyo: Fuyu shobō, 1950), 235–38.

41. *Eiga no tomo,* May 1931, 136–37.

42. Satō Yūichi, *Waga shi Yodogawa Nagaharu tono 50nen* (Tokyo: Seiryū shuppan, 2000), 76–77.

43. *Eiga no tomo,* July 1948.

44. *Eiga no tomo,* June 1951, 96–97.

45. John Payne (not Wayne) was an actor who became known in Japan for his performances in *Sun Valley Serenade* (1941) and *Remember the Day* (1941), both released by the CMPE.

46. *Eiga no tomo,* February 1947, 6–9.

47. *Eiga no tomo,* April 1950, 83; *Eiga no tomo,* April 1951, 36.

48. Yodogawa Nagaharu, "*Eiga no tomo,* editorial notes April 1948," in *Yodogawa Nagaharu shūsei, vol. 4,* 110.

49. Yodogawa Nagaharu, "*Eiga no tomo,* editorial notes December 1948," in *Yodogawa Nagaharu shūsei, vol. 4,* 113.

50. *Eiga no tomo,* April 1949, 11.

51. *Eiga no tomo,* April 1951, 37.

52. *Eiga no tomo,* April 1951, 37.

53. *Eiga no tomo,* September 1948, 26.

54. *Eiga no tomo,* September 1948, 26.

55. *Eiga no tomo,* February 1949, 25.

56. *Eiga no tomo* December 1948, 24.

57. *Eiga no tomo,* October 1948, 28.

58. *Eiga no tomo,* March 1949, 24.

59. *Eiga no tomo,* December 1948, 24.

60. *Eiga no tomo,* July 1948, 26.

61. *Eiga no tomo,* September 1948, 26.

62. *Eiga no tomo,* January 1949, 29.

63. *Eiga no tomo,* July 1948, 26.

64. *Eiga no tomo,* September 1948, 27.

65. *Eiga no tomo,* October 1948, 28,

66. *Eiga no tomo,* April 1948, 20.

67. *Eiga no tomo,* November 1948, 26.

68. *Eiga no tomo,* April 1952, 105.

69. *Eiga no tomo,* April 1952, 109.

70. *Eiga no tomo,* March 1948, 30.

71. *Eiga no tomo,* March 1948, 29.

72. *Eiga no tomo,* November 1948, 26.

73. *Eiga no tomo,* June 1948, 27.

74. *Eiga no tomo,* June 1948, 27.

75. *Eiga no tomo,* October 1948, 28.

76. *Eiga no tomo,* June 1948, 26.

77. *Eiga no tomo,* June 1948, 26.

78. *Eiga no tomo,* June 1948, 26.

79. *Eiga no tomo,* March 1948, 29.

80. Satō, *Waga shi Yodogawa Nagaharu tono 50nen,* 55–56; *Eiga no tomo,* March 1949, 25.

81. *Eiga no tomo,* October 1948, 31; *Eiga no tomo,* February 1949, 26; *Eiga no tomo,* March 1949, 26.

82. *Eiga no tomo,* November 1949, 44.

83. *Eiga no tomo,* May 1951, 91.

84. *Eiga no tomo,* October 1949, 43.

85. *Eiga no tomo,* February 1950, 64; *Eiga no tomo,* October 1949, 42.

86. *Eiga no tomo,* February 1951, 32; *Eiga no tomo,* October 1951, 112–13.

87. See, for example, *Eiga no tomo,* June 1949, 32; *Eiga no tomo,* August 1949, 34; *Eig a no tomo,* October 1949, 42; *Eiga no tomo,* April 1951, 94; *Eiga no tomo,* May 1951, 90–91.

88. *Eiga no tomo,* April 1952, 128–30; *Eiga no tomo,* March 1952, 128–31.

89. *Eiga no tomo,* September 1952, 111. Also see *Eiga no tomo,* October 1952, 122–25.

90. *Eiga no tomo,* July 1949, 34; *Eiga no tomo,* August 1949, 34; *Eiga no tomo,* November 1949, 44; *Eiga no tomo,* February 1950, 64; *Eiga no tomo,* January 1950, 54.

91. *Eiga no tomo,* February 1951, 32; *Eiga no tomo,* May 1949, 34; *Eiga no tomo,* March 1951, 88; *Eiga no tomo,* February 1950, 64; *Eiga no tomo,* June 1950, 90.

92. *Eiga no tomo,* December 1949, 34; *Eiga no tomo,* January 1950, 54; *Eiga no tomo,* April 1950, 89; *Eiga no tomo,* June 1950, 91.

93. *Eiga no tomo,* February 1950, 64.

94. *Eiga no tomo,* September 1950, 73.

95. *Eiga no tomo,* February 1951, 94.

96. *Eiga no tomo,* December 1949, 34; *Eiga no tomo,* January 1950, 54.

97. *Eiga no tomo,* March 1953, 177.

98. *Eiga no tomo,* February 1950, 64.

99. *Eiga no tomo,* May 1949, 34.

100. *Eiga no tomo,* March 1951, 90.

101. *Eiga no tomo,* May 1950, 73.

102. *Eiga no tomo,* July 1949, 34.

103. *Eiga no tomo,* July 1950, 88.

104. *Eiga no tomo,* June 1950, 91; *Eiga no tomo,* November 1949, 44; *Eiga no tomo,* December 1949, 34.

105. *Eiga no tomo,* October 1949, 42.

106. *Eiga no tomo,* May 1950, 73.

107. *Eiga no tomo,* February 1950, 64.

108. *Eiga no tomo,* May 1950, 72; *Eiga no tomo,* June 1950, 90.

109. *Eiga no tomo,* September 1949, 32.

110. *Eiga no tomo,* October 1949, 43; *Eiga no tomo,* May 1951, 93; *Eiga no tomo,* January 1950, 55; *Eiga no tomo,* October 1951, 113.

111. *Eiga no tomo,* October 1949, 42.

112. Tsurumi Shunsuke, *Senjiki nihon no seishinshi, 1931–1945* (Tokyo: Iwanami Shoten, 1991), 94; also see the Japanese Christmas Museum, http://www.christmasmuseum.jp/ (accessed June 16, 2006).

113. *Eiga no tomo,* March 1950, 64; *Eiga no tomo,* March 1951, 88.

114. *Eiga no tomo,* April 1950, 89.

115. *Eiga no tomo,* April 1950, 90.

116. *Eiga no tomo,* March 1950, 64.

117. *Eiga no tomo,* April 1950, 89.

118. *Eiga no tomo,* March 1950, 65–66.

119. Sakurai Hikaru, "Saikin no eiga sākuru no hanashi," in *Hyakumannin no eiga chishiki,* ed. Nihon eigajin dōmei (Tokyo: Kaihōsha, 1950), 183.

120. *Kinema junpō gyokai tokuhō,* November 21, 1948, 1.

121. Louise Young, *Japan's Total Empire: Manchuria and the Culture of Wartime Imperialism* (Berkeley: University of California Press, 1998), 117, 161–80.

122. Ōsawa, "Sākuru no sengoshi," *Shūdan: Sākuru no sengoshi,* ed. Shīsō no kagaku kinkyūkai (Tokyo: Heibonsha, 1976), 68–92; Takaoka Hiroyuki, "Haisen chokugo no bunka jōkyō to bunka undō," *Nenpō Nihon gendaishi,* vol. 2, *Gendaishi to minshu shugi,* ed. Awaya Kentaro et al. (Tokyo: Azuma shuppan, 1996), esp. 182–93; Takemura Tamio, "Sengo nihon ni

okeru bunkaundō to rekishi ishiji," *Gendai shakai kenkyū* 2 (2001): 15–29, available online at http://www.cs.kyoto-wu.ac.jp/bulletin/2/takemura.pdf (accessed June 18, 2006). The quote comes from Kitagawa Kenzō, *Sengo no shuppatsu: Bunka undō, seinendan, sensō mibōjin* (Tokyo: Aoki Shoten, 2000), 50.

123. See, for example, Yodogawa Nagaharu, *Yodogawa Nagaharu shūsei,* vols. 1–4 (Tokyo: Hoga shokan, 1987).

124. Terebi Asahi, ed., *Eiga wa buraunkan no shiteiseki de: Yodogawa Nagaharu to "Nichiyō yōga" no 20nen* (Tokyo: Terebi Asahi, 1986), 16–19.

125. The official website for Tomo no kai's Tokyo meetings is http://homepage3.nifty.com/cyaoks/movie/tomonoka.htm (accessed January 22, 2006).

Conclusion

1. *Kinema junpō,* November 1, 1951, 51.

2. See, for example, *Variety,* March 21, 1951, 13.

3. See, for example, Hazumi Tsuneo, *Amerika eiga dokuhon* (Tokyo: Tōzai shuppansha, 1947), 1–4; *Ningen keisei,* October 1948, 44; *Hollywood Reporter,* July 10, 1947, 15.

4. *Variety,* November 21, 1951, 3.

5. *Kinema junpō,* September 1, 1951, 18.

6. M. B. Ridgway to Mayer, October 9, 1951, Box 5088, Folder 15, SCAP Records, NA. Ridgway became the Supreme Commander for the Allied Powers in April 1951, after MacArthur was relieved of his command in occupied Japan.

7. Ezra F. Vogel, *Japan's New Middle Class,* 2nd ed. (Berkeley: University of California Press, 1971).

8. Nicholas Evan Sarantakes, *Keystone: The American Occupation of Okinawa and U.S.-Japanese Relations* (College Station: Texas A&M University Press, 2000).

9. William S. Borden, *The Pacific Alliance: United States Foreign Economic Policy and Japanese Trade Recovery, 1947–1955* (Madison: University of Wisconsin Press, 1984), 149–222; Andrew Rotter, *The Path to Vietnam: Origins of the American Commitment to Southeast Asia* (Ithaca: Cornell University Press, 1987).

10. William M. Tsutsui, *Manufacturing Ideology: Scientific Management in Twentieth-Century Japan* (Princeton: Princeton University Press, 1998), esp. 152–235; Kazuo Wada and Takao Shiba, "The Evolution of the 'Japanese Production System': Indigenous Influences and American Impact," in *Americanization and Its Limits: Reworking U.S. Technology and Management in Post-War Europe and Japan,* ed. Jonathan Zeitlin and Gary Herrigel (New York: Oxford University Press, 2000), 316–39.

11. Takeshi Matsuda, *Soft Power and Its Perils: U.S. Cultural Policy in Early Postwar Japan and Permanent Dependency* (Stanford and Washington, DC: Stanford University Press and Woodrow Wilson Center Press, 2007), 161–255.

12. Marilyn Ivy, "Formations of Mass Culture," in *Postwar Japan as History,* ed. Andrew Gordon (Berkeley: University of California Press, 1993), 249.

13. *Sandē mainichi,* March 17, 1957, 20–23.

14. Jiji tsūshinsha, *Eiga nenkan* (Tokyo: Jiji tsūshinsha, 1952), 49; *Kinema junpō,* September 1, 1953, in *Besuto obu kinema junpō, jō: 1950–1966,* ed. Kinema junpōsha (Tokyo: Kinema junpōsha, 1994), 231.

15. Kinema junpōsha, *Nihon eiga zen kiroku,* 12.

16. See, for example, *Kinema junpō,* June 15, 1954, in *Besto obu kinema junpō,* 323.

17. *Kinema junpō,* December 15, 1954, 26; Motion Picture Export Association of America, Inc.–Tokyo, "Brief History of Eric Johnston's Visit to Tokyo from February 25–March

2, 1956," Box 7, Folder 24, Eric Johnston Manuscript Collection, Eastern Washington State Historical Society, Spokane, Washington.

18. *Film Daily,* February 29, 1956, 1.

19. See, for example, *Yūshū eiga,* 20 (March 28, 1955), 1; *Yūshū eiga,* 63 (September 1, 1959), 3.

20. *Los Angeles Times,* May 4, 1956, A30.

21. Kerry Segrave, *American Films Abroad: Hollywood's Domination of the World's Movie Screens* (Jefferson, NC: McFarland, 1997), 215.

22. *Kinema junpō,* March 1, 1960.

23. Izawa Jun, *Eiga toiu kaibutsu* (Tokyo: Gakugei shobō, 1973), 50.

24. Yomota Inuhiko, *Nihon eiga no radikaru na ishi* (Tokyo: Iwanami shoten, 1999).

25. Kinema junpōsha, *Kinema junpo zen kiroku,* 111–12.

26. *New York Times,* November 17, 1988, C25.

27. *Hollywood Reporter,* May 3, 1994, 8.

28. See, for example, Gavan McCormack, *Client State: Japan in the American Embrace* (New York: Verso, 2007).

Bibliography

Archival Sites and Records in the United States

Cinema and Television Library, University of California, Los Angeles, California
Eastern Washington State Historical Society, Spokane, Washington: Eric Johnston Papers
Franklin and Eleanor Roosevelt Institute, Hyde Park, New York: Franklin Roosevelt Papers; Adolf Berle Papers
Harry S. Truman Institute, Independence, Missouri: Dallas C. Halverstadt Papers; Harry S. Truman Papers; W. Kenneth Bunce Papers
Louis B. Mayer Library, American Film Institute, Los Angeles, California
MacArthur Memorial Library, Norfolk, Virginia: Records of the Supreme Commander for the Allied Powers
Margaret Herrick Library, Academy of Motion Picture Arts and Sciences, Los Angeles, California: Press Clippings, General Collections; Mary Pickford Files, Special Collections; Motion Picture Association of America Files, Special Collections; Production Code Administration Files, Special Collections
National Archives and Records Administration, College Park, Maryland: General Records of the Department of State, Record Group 59; Civil Affairs Division, Department of Army, Record Group 165; Records of the Office of War Information, Record Group 208; Records of the Secretary of Defense, Record Group 330; Records of the Supreme Commander for the Allied Powers, Record Group 331
University of Maryland, College Park, Maryland: Gordon Prange Collection
Warner Bros. Archives, School of Cinematic Arts, University of Southern California, Los Angeles, California: Warner Bros. Collection
Wisconsin Center for Film and Theater Research, Madison, Wisconsin: United Artists Collection

Archival Sites and Records in Japan

Aichi Prefectural Library, Nagoya
Film and Culture Association (Eiga bunka kyōkai), Tōhō Studio, Tokyo
Fukuoka Municipal Library, Fukuoka: Hagio Takemi Collection; Nōma Yoshihiro
     Collection
Kamakura Municipal Library, Kamakura
Kawakita Memorial Library, Tokyo
Makino Mamoru Collection, Tokyo (collection transferred to Columbia University)
Nagasaki Municipal Library, Nagasaki
National Diet Library, Tokyo: Records of the Supreme Commander for the Allied
     Powers
National Film Center, National Museum of Modern Art, Tokyo
Ōtani Library, Shochiku Studio, Tokyo
Ōya Sōichi Library, Tokyo
Tsubouchi Memorial Theater Museum, Waseda University, Tokyo

Unpublished Sources

Robert L. Bishop, "The Overseas Branch of the Office of War Information" (PhD diss.,
     University of Wisconsin–Madison, 1966).
Michael McShane Burns, "The Origin and Development of the Division of Cultural
     Relations within the State Department: 1935–1944" (MA thesis, University of North
     Carolina–Chapel Hill, 1968).
Ralph Edgerton, "The Eric Johnston Story," 1979, Spokane Public Library. 36 pages.
Jennifer Fay, "The Business of Cultural Diplomacy: American Film Policy in Occupied
     Germany, 1945–1949" (PhD diss., University of Wisconsin–Madison, 2001).
Itō Shiei, *Shinema yoruhiru kaiko: Nagoya eigashi 8 mm kara 70 mm made* (Nagoya: privately
     printed, 1994).
Joanne Izbicki, "Scorched Cityscapes and Silver Screens: Negotiating Defeat and Democ-
     racy through Cinema in Occupied Japan" (PhD diss., Cornell University, 1997).
Yuji Tosaka, "Hollywood Goes to Tokyo: American Cultural Expansion and Imperial
     Japan, 1918–1941" (PhD diss., Ohio State University, 2003).
Tsukada Yoshinobu and Yamanaka Toshio, "Burūbādo eiga no kiroku, tsuiho" (Tokyo: 1984,
     available at the National Film Center, National Museum of Modern Art, Tokyo).
Tsukada Yoshinobu, "Nyūjōzei to eigakan nyūjō ryōkin no hensen," (Tokyo: 1985, avail-
     able at the National Film Center, National Museum of Modern Art, Tokyo).
Michael David Walsh, "The Internationalism of the American Cinema: The Establish-
     ment of United Artists' Foreign Distribution Operations" (PhD diss., University of
     Wisconsin–Madison, 1998).
Mark H. Woodward, "The Formulation and Implementation of U.S. Feature Film Policy
     in Germany, 1945–1948" (PhD diss., University of Texas at Dallas, 1987).

Government Publications

Coordinator for Inter-American Affairs, *History of the Office of the Coordinator of Inter-American Affairs: Historical Reports on War Administration* (Washington, DC: Government Printing Office, 1947).

Military Situation in the Far East, Hearings to Conduct an Inquiry into the Military Situation in the Far East and the Facts Surrounding the Relief of General of the Army Douglas MacArthur from his Assignment in the Area. U.S. Senate, 82nd Cong., 1st session, Part 1, May 3, 1951 (Washington, DC: U.S. Government Printing Office, 1951).

Postwar Economic Policy and Planning, Hearings before the Special Committee on Postwar Economic Policy and Planning. House of Representatives, 79th Cong., Part 9, December 20, 1946 "Export of Information and Media, both Government and Private." (Washington, DC: U.S. Government Printing Office, 1947).

Winning the Cold War: The U.S. Ideological Offensive, Hearings before the Subcommittee on International Organizations and Movements of the Committee on Foreign Affairs. House of Representatives, 88th Cong., 1st session, September 11–13, 1963 (Washington, DC: U.S. Government Printing Office, 1963).

General Headquarters, Supreme Commander for the Allied Powers, *Summation No. 1: Non-Military Activities in Japan and Korea for the Months of September–October 1945,* 159.

"Western Europe in the Wake of World War II: As Seen by a Group of American Motion Picture Industry Executives Visiting the European and Mediterranean Theatres of Operation as Guests of the Military Authorities," 1945, Paley Library, Temple University.

Newspapers and Magazines

Japanese

AMCA kaihō
Amerika eiga
Amerika eiga bunka
Amerika eiga monogatari
Asahi shinbun
Chubu nihon shinbun
Eiga engeki shinbun
Eiga geinō shinbun
Eiga hyōron
Eiga no tomo
Eiga nyūsu
Eiga to butai
Eiga to supōtsu (Nigata)
Eiga sekai
Hibiya gekijō nyūsu

Junkan Amerika eiga
Kindai eiga
Kinema junpō
Kinema junpō gyokai tokuho
Kōgyō herarudo
Kokusai eiga shinbun
Kudamatsu A.M.C.A. nyūsu
MPEA News
MPEA Weekly
Nagasaki minyū
Nagasaki nichinichi shinbun
Nagasaki shinbun
Nihon bunka tsūshin
Nihon eiga
Ningen keisei

Nishi nihon shinbun
Rengō tsūshin eiga geinō ban
Screen
Sekai
Sentoraru nyūsu
Shinsō
Subaru Theatre News
State-za puroguramu
Tōhō Studio
Tokai mainichi shinbun
Tokyo eiga shinbun
Yomiuri shinbun
Yūkan taimuzu (Nagasaki)
Yūshū eiga
Zenkoku eigakan shinbun

English

CI&E Bulletin
Film Daily

Film Daily Yearbook
Film Quarterly
Foreign Commerce Weekly
Harvard Business Review
Hollywood Reporter
Life
Los Angeles Times
Motion Picture Herald
Motion Picture Letter
MPEA Newsletter
New York Times
New York Herald Tribune
Newsweek
Nippon Times
Progress
Stars and Stripes
Variety
Wall Street Journal
Washington Post

Interviews

Aijima Masato (Nagasaki daiichi kokusai gekijō, exhibitor), December 10, 2000, Madison, WI (phone)
Akiyama Shigeru (NCC), November 23, 1999, Tokyo
Amata Ihei (Subaru Kōgyō, exhibitor) with Amata Shigeko, September 4, 2000, Madison, WI (phone)
Aoki Kimiko (Subaru Kōgyō, exhibitor), February 26, 2001, Madison, WI (phone)
Asaishi Iwao (CMPE-Tokyo), May 30, 2000, Madison, WI (phone)
Asaoka Hiroshi (Subaru Kōgyō, exhibitor), September 3, 2000, Madison, WI (phone); October 2, 2000, Madison, WI (phone); November 20, 2000, Madison, WI (phone); January 20, 2001, Fujisawa
Paul Fehlen (CMPE-Tokyo), June 28, 2000, Madison, WI (phone)
Fujino Zenpei (CMPE-Fukuoka), November 19, 2000, Madison, WI (phone)
Hidano Atsushi and Rei (CMPE-Tokyo), November 8, 1999, Tokyo
Hino Kōichi, December 28, 1999, Kamakura (phone)
Ishikawa Hatsutarō (Subaru Kōgyō, exhibitor), December 6, 1999, Tokyo
Izaki Susumu (CMPE-Tokyo), December 17, 1999, Kamakura (phone); September 5, 2000, Madison, WI (phone)
Kagawa Yoshikage (CMPE-Osaka), October 3, 2000, Madison, WI (phone)
Kamishima Kimi (Tetrasha), November 24, 1999, Tokyo
Kaneko Yaeko (Subaru Kōgyō, exhibitor), March 4, 2001, Madison, WI (phone)
Kodama Kazuo (CMPE-Tokyo), December 14, 1999, Tokyo

Koike Akira, October 27, 1999, Tokyo

Komaki Toshiharu (CIE, CMPE-Nagoya), November 22, 1999, Kamakura

Kurosaki Hiroshi (CMPE-Sapporo), September 12, 2000, Madison, WI (phone)

Kushida Takeshi (Asahikawa kokumin gekijō, exhibitor), March 16, 2001, Madison, WI (phone)

Miyake Toyoko (Kurashiki sanyūkan, exhibitor), July 9, 2002, Madison, WI (phone)

Murai Hōshō (CMPE-Tokyo), January 3, 2000, Tokyo (phone)

Nakatsuka Takateru (CMPE-Tokyo), September 4, 2000, Madison, WI (phone)

Noto Setsuo (Tōhō), November 25, 1999, Tokyo

Ogata Mochimitsu (Dokuritsu eiga), October 6, 2000, Madison, WI (phone)

Ōi Makoto (CMPE-Tokyo), December 6, 1999, Kawasaki

Oikawa Shirō (CMPE-Tokyo) with Tetsuo Sasaki, November 16, 1999, Tokyo

Okazaki Eiichirō (CMPE-Osaka), September 23, 2000, Madison, WI (phone)

Ōsawa Shūhei (CMPE-Tokyo), May 27, 2000, Madison, WI (phone)

Donald Richie (film critic), October 22, 1999, Tokyo

Sagisu Tomio (CMPE-Tokyo), May 28, 2000, Madison, WI (phone)

Sakai Haruo (CMPE-Tokyo), December 31, 1999, Tokyo

Sakakibara Yoshiko (Subaru Kōgyō, exhibitor), February 22, 2001, Madison, WI (phone)

Sasaki Tetsuo (CMPE-Tokyo), November 2, 1999, Tokyo

Shibata Harumichi (CCD, CMPE-Fukuoka), April 11, 2001, Amherst, MA (phone)

Takahara Gorō (CMPE-Fukuoka), November 18, 2000, Madison, WI (phone)

Terashima Ryūichi (CMPE-Tokyo), September 2, 2000, Madison, WI (phone)

Togawa Naoki (film critic), November 19, 1999, Tokyo

Tsuruhara Tarō (CMPE-Fukuoka), October 12, 2000, Madison, WI (phone)

Ushiroda Suminari (CMPE-Tokyo), June 11, 2000, Madison, WI (phone)

Catherine Wu (RKO-Japan), June 26, 2000, Madison, WI (phone)

Yamada Noboru (CMPE-Sapporo), September 15, 2000, Madison, WI (phone)

Film Databases

Allcinema: Movie and DVD Database. http://www.allcinema.net/prog/index2.php.

American Film Institute, ed., *The American Film Institute Catalog of Motion Pictures Produced in the United States.* 6 vols. (Berkeley: University of California Press, 1989). Also see online version at http://afi.chadwyck.com/home.

The Internet Movie Database. http://www.imdb.com.

Kinema junpō dētabēsu. http://www.walkerplus.com/movie/kinejun/.

Nash, Jay Robert. 1985. *The Motion Picture Guide,* 12 vols. Chicago: Cinebooks, Inc.

Articles and Chapters of Books in English

Allen, Robert C. 1998. "From Exhibition to Reception: Reflections on the Audience in Film History." In *Screen Histories: A Screen Reader,* edited by Annette Kuhn and Jackie Stacey, 13–21. Oxford: Oxford University Press.

Anderson, Robert. 1986. "The Motion Picture Patents Company: A Reevaluation." In *The American Film Industry,* rev. ed., edited by Tino Balio, 133–52. Madison: University of Wisconsin Press, 1986.

Boehling, Rebecca. 1999. "The Role of Culture in American Relations with Europe: The Case of the United States's Occupation of Germany." *Diplomatic History* 23, no. 1: 57–69.

Cohen, Warren I. and Nancy Bernkopf Tucker. "America in Asian Eyes." *American Historical Review* 111, no. 4: 1092–1119.

Delamoir, Jeannette. 2004. "Louise Lovely, Bluebird Photoplays, and the Star System." *Moving Image* 4, no. 2: 64–85.

Edgerton, Ralph A. 1989. "Hometown Boy Makes Good: The Eric Johnston Story." *Pacific Northwesterner* 33, no. 4: 55–64.

Fujiki, Hidaki. 2006. "*Benshi* as Stars: The Irony of the Popularity and Respectability of Voice Performers in Japanese Cinema." *Cinema Journal* 45, no. 2: 68–84.

Gerteis, Christopher. 2007. "The Erotic and the Vulgar: Visual Culture and Organized Labor's Critique of U.S. Hegemony in Occupied Japan." *Critical Asian Studies* 39, no. 1: 3–34.

Gienow-Hecht, Jessica C. E. 2004. "Cultural Transfer." In *Explaining the History of American Foreign Relations,* 2nd ed., edited by Michael Hogan and Thomas Paterson, 257–78. New York: Cambridge University Press.

———. 2006. "Always Blame the Americans: Anti-Americanism in Europe in the Twentieth Century." *American Historical Review* 111, no. 4: 1067–91.

Glancy, H. Mark. 1992. "MGM Film Grosses, 1924–1948: The Eddie Mannix Ledger." *Historical Journal of Film, Radio, and Television* 12, no. 2: 127–44.

Golden, Nathan D. 1936. "Review of Foreign Markets during 1936." Washington, DC: U.S. Department of Commerce.

Grandin, Greg. 2006. "Americanism and Anti-Americanism in the Americas." *American Historical Review* 111, no. 4: 1042–1066.

Halttunen, Karen. 1984. "The Domestic Drama of Louisa May Alcott." *Feminist Studies* 10, no. 2: 233–54.

Hays, Will H. 1942. "The Motion Picture in a World at War: Twentieth Anniversary Report to the Motion Picture Producers and Distributors of America, Inc." MPPDA pamphlet.

High, Peter B. 1984. "The Dawn of Cinema in Japan." *Journal of Contemporary History* 19, no. 1, 23–57.

Hogan, Michael. 1991. "Corporatism." In *Explaining the History of American Foreign Relations,* edited by Hogan and Thomas Paterson, 226–36. New York: Cambridge University Press.

Howard, June. 1999. "What Is Sentimentality?" *American Literary History* 11, no. 1: 63–81.

Howe, Daniel Walker. 1975. "American Victorianism as Culture." *American Quarterly* 27, no. 5: 507–32.

Kepley, Vance Jr. 1996. "The First 'Perestroika': Soviet Cinema under the First Five-Year Plan." *Cinema Journal* 35, no. 4: 31–53.

Komatsu, Hiroshi. 1992. "Some Characteristics of Japanese Cinema before World War I." In *Reframing Japanese Cinema: Authorship, Genre, History,* edited by Arthur Nolletti Jr. and David Desser, 229–58. Bloomington: Indiana University Press.

——. 2005. "The Foundation of Modernism: Japanese Cinema in the Year 1927." *Film History* 17: 363–75.

Laemmle, Carl. 1927. "The Business of Motion Pictures." *Saturday Evening Post* 200 (August 27): 10–11, and (September 3): 18–19, reprinted in *The American Film Industry,* edited by Tino Balio, 153–68. Madison: University of Wisconsin Press, 1976.

Lears, T. J. Jackson. 1995. "The Concept of Cultural Hegemony: Problems and Possibilities." *American Historical Review* 90, no. 3: 567–93.

Marotti, William. 2009. "Japan 1968: The Performance of Violence and the Theater of Protest." *American Historical Review* 114, no. 3: 97–135

Mayo, Marlene J. 1980. "Psychological Disarmament: American Wartime Planning for the Education and Re-education of Defeated Japan, 1943–1945." In *The Occupation of Japan: Educational and Social Reform,* edited by Thomas W. Burkman, 21–140. Norfolk, VA: MacArthur Foundation.

——. 1984. "American Wartime Planning for Occupied Japan: The Role of the Experts." In *Americans as Proconsuls: United States Military Government in Germany and Japan, 1944–1952,"* edited by Robert Wolfe, 3–51. Carbondale: Southern Illinois University Press.

McCallum, Robyn. 2000. "The Present Reshaping the Past Reshaping the Present: Film Versions of *Little Women." The Lion and the Unicorn* 24, no. 1: 81–96.

McCormick, Thomas. 1982. "Drift or Mastery? A Corporatist Synthesis for American Diplomatic History." *Reviews in American History* 10: 318–30.

Miller, Toby. 2000. "Hollywood and the World." In *American Cinema and Hollywood: Critical Approaches,* edited by John Hill and Pamela Church Gibson, 145–55. Oxford: Oxford University Press.

Ohmer, Susan. 1999. "The Science of Pleasure: George Gallup and Audience Research in Hollywood." In *Identifying Hollywood's Audiences: Cultural Identity and the Movies,* edited by Melvyn Stokes and Richard Maltby, 61–80. London: British Film Institute.

Short, K. R. M. "Hollywood Fights Anti-Semitism, 1940–1945." In *Film and Radio Propaganda in World War II,* edited by K. R. M. Short, 146–72. Knoxville: University of Tennessee Press.

Swann, Paul. 1991. "The Little State Department: Hollywood and the State Department in the Postwar World." *American Studies International* 29, no. 1: 2–19.

Tsuchiya, Yuka. 2002. "Imagined America in Occupied Japan: (Re)-Educational Films Shown by the U.S. Occupation Forces to the Japanese." *Japanese Journal of American Studies* 13: 193–213.

Turner, Frederick Jackson. 1893. "The Significance of the Frontier in American History." In *Frederick Jackson Turner: Wisconsin's Historian of the Frontier,* edited by Martin Ridge, 26–47. Madison: State Historical Society of Wisconsin, 1986.

Wada, Kazuo, and Takao Shiba. 2000. "The Evolution of the 'Japanese Production System': Indigenous Influences and American Impact." In *Americanization and Its Limits: Reworking U.S. Technology and Management in Post-War Europe and Japan,* edited by Jonathan Zeitlin and Gary Herrigel, 316–39. New York: Oxford University Press.

Welter, Barbara. 1966. "The Cult of True Womanhood, 1820–1860." *American Quarterly* 18, no. 2: 151–74.

Vaughn, Stephen. 2005. "The Devil's Advocate: Will H. Hays and the Campaign to Make Movies Respectable." *Indiana Magazine of History* 101, no. 2: 125–52.

Wilson, Theodore A. 2000. "Selling America via the Silver Screen? Efforts to Manage the Projection of American Culture Abroad, 1942–1947." In *"Here, There, and Everywhere": The Foreign Politics of American Popular Culture,* edited by Reinhold Wagnleitner and Elaine Tyler May, 83–99. Hanover, NH: University Press of New England.

Yoshimi, Shunya. 2000. "Consuming 'America': From Symbol to System." In *Consumption in Asia: Lifestyles and Identities,* edited by Chua Beng-Huat, 219–238. New York: Routledge.

Young, Louise. 1999. "Marketing the Modern: Department Stores, Consumer Culture, and the New Middle Class in Interwar Japan." *International Labor and Working-Class History* 55: 52–70.

Books in English

Abel, Richard. 1999. *The Red Rooster Scare: Making Cinema American, 1900–1910.* Berkeley: University of California Press.

Anderson, Joseph and Donald Richie. 1982. *The Japanese Film: Art and Industry.* Exp. ed. Princeton: Princeton University Press.

Atkins, E. Taylor. 2001. *Blue Nippon: Authenticating Jazz in Japan.* Durham: Duke University Press.

Balio, Tino. 1976. *United Artists: The Company Built by the Stars.* Madison: University of Wisconsin Press.

———. 1993. *Grand Design: Hollywood as a Modern Business Enterprise, 1930–1939.* Berkeley: University of California Press.

Balio, Tino, ed. 1985. *The American Film Industry.* Rev. ed. Madison: University of Wisconsin Press,.

———. 1990. *Hollywood in the Age of Television.* Boston: Unwin Hyman.

Barbas, Samantha. 2001. *Movie Crazy: Fans, Stars, and the Cult of Celebrity.* New York: Palgrave.

Barnouw, Erik. 1990. *Tube of Plenty: The Evolution of American Television.* 2nd rev. ed. New York: Oxford University Press.

Baskett, Michael. 2008. *The Attractive Empire: Transnational Film Culture in Imperial Japan.* Honolulu: University of Hawaii Press.

Beasley, W. G. 1987. *Japanese Imperialism, 1894–1945.* Oxford: Clarendon.

Bender, Thomas, ed. 2002. *Rethinking American History in a Global Age.* Berkeley: University of California Press.

Bernardi, Joanne. 2001. *Writing in Light: The Silent Scenario and the Japanese Pure Film Movement.* Detroit: Wayne State University Press.

Birdwell, Michael E. 1999. *Celluloid Soldiers: Warner Bros.'s Campaign against Nazism.* New York: New York University Press.

Black, Gregory D. 1994. *Hollywood Censored: Morality Codes, Catholics, and the Movies.* 1994. New York: Cambridge University Press.

Blum, John Morton. 1976. *V was for Victory: Politics and American Culture during World War II.* New York: Harcourt Brace.

Borden, William S. 1984. *The Pacific Alliance: United States Foreign Economic Policy and Japanese Trade Recovery, 1947–1955.* Madison: University of Wisconsin Press.

Bordwell, David. 1985. *Narration in the Fiction Film.* Madison: University of Wisconsin Press.

———. 1988. *Ozu and the Poetics of Cinema.* Princeton: Princeton University Press.

———. 2005. *Figures Traced in Light: On Cinematic Staging.* Berkeley: University of California Press.

Bordwell, David, Janet Staiger, and Kristin Thompson. 1985. *The Classical Hollywood Cinema: Film Style and Mode of Production to 1960.* New York: Columbia University Press.

Bowser, Eileen. 1990. *The Transformation of Cinema, 1907–1915.* Berkley: University of California Press.

Braw, Monica. 1991. *The Atomic Bomb Suppressed: American Censorship in Occupied Japan.* New York: M. E. Sharpe.

Brazinsky, Gregg. 2007. *Nation Building in South Korea: Koreans, Americans, and the Making of a Democracy.* Chapel Hill: University of North Carolina Press.

Capra, Frank. 1971. *The Name above the Title.* New York: MacMillan.

Ceplair, Larry, and Steven Englund. 1979. *The Inquisition in Hollywood: Politics in the Film Community, 1930–1960.* Berkeley: University of California Press.

Cochran, Sherman. 2000. *Encountering Chinese Networks: Western, Japanese, and Chinese Corporations in China, 1880–1937.* Berkeley: University of California Press.

Cohen, Theodore. 1987. *Remaking Japan: The American Occupation as New Deal.* New York: Free Press.

Cooney, Terry. 1995. *Balancing Acts: American Thought and Culture in the 1930s.* New York: Twayne Publishers.

Costigliola, Frank. 1984. *Awkward Dominion: American Political, Economic, and Cultural Relations with Europe, 1919–1933.* Ithaca: Cornell University Press, 1984.

Culbert, David, ed. 1990. *Film Propaganda in America: A Documentary History.* Vol. 2 of *World War II: Part 1.* New York: Greenwood Press.

Decherney, Peter. 2005. *Hollywood and the Culture Elite: How the Movies Became American.* New York: Columbia University Press.

DeCordova, Richard. 1990. *Picture Personalities: The Emergence of the Star System in America.* Urbana: University of Illinois Press.

De Grazia, Victoria. 2005. *Irresistible Empire: America's Advance through Twentieth-Century Europe.* Cambridge: Harvard University Press.

Denning, Michael. 1997. *The Cultural Front: The Laboring of American Culture in the Twentieth Century.* New York: Verso.

Doherty, Thomas. 1993. *Projections of War: Hollywood, American Culture, and World War II.* New York: Columbia University Press.

———. 1999. *Pre-Code Hollywood: Sex, Immorality, and Insurrection in American Cinema 1930–1934.* New York: Columbia University Press.

Dower, John W. 1986. *War without Mercy: Race and Power in the Pacific War.* New York: Pantheon.

———. 1993. *Japan in War and Peace: Selected Essays.* New York: New Press.

———. 1999. *Embracing Defeat: Japan in the Wake of World War II.* New York: W. W. Norton and New Press.

Dym, Jeffrey A. 2003. *Benshi, Japanese Silent Film Narrators, and Their Forgotten Narrative Art of Setsumei.* Lewiston, NY: Edwin Mellen Press.

Eagleton, Terry. 1999. *Scholars and Rebels in Nineteenth-Century Ireland.* Malden, MA: Blackwell.

Edgerton, Gary R. 2007. *The Columbia History of American Television.* New York: Columbia University Press.

Fay, Jennifer. 2008. *Theaters of Occupation: Hollywood and the Reeducation of Postwar Germany.* Minneapolis: University of Minnesota Press.

Fehrenbach, Heide. 1995. *Cinema in Democratizing Germany: Reconstructing National Identity after Hitler.* Chapel Hill: University of North Carolina Press.

Fehrenbach, Heide, and Uta G. Poiger, eds. 2000. *Transactions, Transgressions, Transformations: American Culture in Western Europe and Japan.* New York: Berghahn Books.

Fiske, John. 1988. *Understanding Popular Culture.* New York: Routledge.

Frank, Richard B. 1999. *Downfall: The End of the Imperial Japanese Empire.* New York: Random House.

Gaddis, John Lewis. 1982. *Strategies of Containment: A Critical Appraisal of Postwar American National Security Policy.* New York: Oxford University Press.

Galbraith, Stuart, IV. 2001. *The Emperor and the Wolf: The Lives and Films of Akira Kurosawa and Toshiro Mifune.* New York: Faber and Faber.

Gienow-Hecht, Jessica C. E. 1999. *Transmission Impossible: American Journalism and Cultural Diplomacy in Postwar Germany, 1945–1955.* Baton Rouge: Louisiana State University Press.

Giovacchini, Saverio. 2001. *Hollywood Modernism: Film and Politics in the Age of the New Deal.* Philadelphia: Temple University Press.

Glancy, H. Mark. 1999. *When Hollywood Loved Britain: The Hollywood 'British' Film 1939–1945.* Manchester, UK: Manchester University Press.

Gluck, Carol. 1985. *Japan's Modern Myths: Ideology in the Late Meiji Period.* Princeton: Princeton University Press.

Gobat, Michel. 2005. *Confronting the American Dream: Nicaragua under U.S. Imperial Rule.* Chapel Hill: University of North Carolina Press.

Gordon, Andrew. 1991. *Labor and Imperial Democracy in Prewar Japan.* Berkeley: University of California Press.

Gomery, Douglas. 1992. *Shared Pleasures: A History of Movie Presentation in the United States.* Madison: University of Wisconsin Press.

———. 2005. *The Hollywood Studio System: A History.* London: British Film Institute.

Gordon, Andrew, ed. 1993. *Postwar Japan as History.* Berkeley: University of California Press.

Guback, Thomas. 1969. *The International Film Industry: Western Europe and America since 1945.* Bloomington: Indiana University Press.

Halttunen, Karen. 1986. *Confidence-Men and Painted Women: A Study of Middle-Class Culture in America, 1830–1870.* New Haven: Yale University Press.

Hasegawa, Tsuyoshi. 2005. *Racing the Enemy: Stalin, Truman, and the Surrender of Japan.* Cambridge: Harvard University Press.

Hawley, Ellis W. 1979. *The Great War and the Search for a Modern Order: A History of the American People and Their Institutions, 1917–1933.* New York: St. Martin's Press.

Hays, Will H. 1955. *The Memoirs of Will H. Hays.* New York: Doubleday.

Hearden, Patrick. 1987. *Roosevelt Confronts Hitler: America's Entry into World War II.* Dekalb: Northern Illinois University Press.

High, Peter B. 2003. *The Imperial Screen: Japanese Film Culture in the Fifteen Years' War, 1931–1945.* Madison: University of Wisconsin Press.

Higson, Andrew, and Richard Maltby, eds. 1999. *"Film Europe" and "Film America": Cinema, Commerce, and Cultural Exchange 1920–1939.* Exeter, UK: University of Exeter Press.

Hirano, Kyōko. 1992. *Mr. Smith Goes to Tokyo: Japanese Cinema under the American Occupation, 1945–1952.* Washington, DC: Smithsonian Institute Press.

Hixson, Walter L. 1997. *Parting the Curtain: Propaganda, Culture, and the Cold War, 1945–1961.* New York: St. Martin's Griffen.

Hoare, Quintin, and Geoffrey Nowell Smith, eds. 1971. *Selections from the Prison Notebooks of Antonio Gramsci.* New York: International Publishers.

Inoue, Kyōko. 1991. *MacArthur's Japanese Constitution: A Linguistic and Cultural Study of Its Making.* Chicago: University of Chicago Press.

Itō, Sachio. 1936. *Songs of a Cowherd.* Trans. Shiho Sakanishi. Boston: Marshall Jones.

Jacobs, Lea. 1991. *The Wages of Sin: Censorship and the Fallen Woman Film, 1928–1942.* Madison: University of Wisconsin Press.

James, Dorris Clayton. 1970. *The Years of MacArthur.* 3 vols. Boston: Houghton Mifflin.

Jansen, Marius B. 2000. *The Making of Modern Japan.* Cambridge: Harvard University Press.

Jarvie, Ian. 1992. *Hollywood's Overseas Campaign: The North Atlantic Movie Trade, 1920–1950.* New York: Cambridge University Press.

Jenkins, Henry. 1992. *Textual Poachers: Television Fans and Participatory Culture.* New York: Routledge.

———. 2006. *Convergence Culture: Where the Old and New Media Collide.* New York: New York University Press.

Kasza, Gregory J. 1988. *The State and the Mass Media in Japan, 1918–1945.* Berkeley: University of California Press.

Katzenstein, Peter J., and Robert O. Keohane, eds. 2007. *Anti-Americanism in World Politics.* Ithaca: Cornell University Press.

Kawai, Kazuo. 1960. *Japan's American Interlude.* Chicago: University of Chicago Press.

Kenez, Peter. 1985. *The Birth of the Propaganda State: Soviet Methods of Mass Mobilization, 1917–1929.* New York: Cambridge University Press.

Kirihara, Donald. 1992. *Patterns of Time: Mizoguchi and the 1930s.* Madison: University of Wisconsin Press.

Klein, Christina. 2004. *Cold War Orientalism: Asia in the Middlebrow Imagination, 1945–1961.* Berkeley: University of California Press.

Koikari, Mire. 2008. *Pedagogy of Democracy: Feminism and the Cold War in the U.S. Occupation of Japan.* Philadelphia: Temple University Press.

Koppes, Clayton, and Gregory Black. 1987. *Hollywood Goes to War: How Politics, Profits, and Propaganda Shaped World War II.* Berkeley: University of California Press.

Koszarski, Richard. 1990. *An Evening's Entertainment: The Age of the Silent Feature Pictures, 1915–1928.* Berkeley: University of California Press.

Koshiro, Yukiko. 1999. *Trans-Pacific Racisms and the U.S. Occupation of Japan.* New York: Columbia University Press.

Kramer, Paul. 2006. *The Blood of Government: Race, Empire, the United States, and the Philippines.* Chapel Hill: University of North Carolina Press.

Kuisel, Richard. 1993. *Seducing the French: The Dilemma of Americanization.* Berkeley: University of California Press.

Kushner, Barak. 2006. *The Thought War: Japanese Imperial Propaganda.* Honolulu: University of Hawaii Press.

Laclau, Ernesto, and Chantal Mouffe. *Hegemony and Socialist Strategy.* 2nd. ed. New York: Verso.

LaFeber, Walter. 1997. *The Clash: U.S.-Japanese Relations throughout History.* New York: W. W. Norton.

———. 1998. *The New Empire: An Interpretation of American Expansion, 1860–1898.* 35th anniv. ed. Ithaca: Cornell University Press.

Lifton, Robert Jay, and Greg Mitchell. 1995. *Hiroshima in America: Fifty Years of Denial.* New York: G. P. Putnum's Sons.

Limerick, Patricia Nelson. 1987. *Legacy of Conquest: The Unbroken Past of the American West.* New York: W. W. Norton.

Le Fanu, Mark. 2005. *Mizoguchi and Japan.* London: British Film Institute.

MacArthur, Douglas. 1964. *Reminiscences.* New York: McGraw-Hill.

Matsuda, Takeshi. 2007. *Soft Power and Its Perils: U.S. Cultural Policy in Early Postwar Japan and Permanent Diplomacy.* Stanford and Washington, DC: Stanford University Press and Woodrow Wilson Center Press.

McPherson, Alan. 2003. *Yankee No! Anti-Americanism in U.S.–Latin American Relations.* Cambridge: Harvard University Press.

Maltby, Richard. 2003. *Hollywood Cinema.* 2nd. ed. Malden, MA: Blackwell.

Maltby, Richard, and Melvyn Stokes, eds. 2004. *Hollywood Abroad: Audiences and Cultural Exchange.* London: British Film Institute.

Manela, Erez. 2007. *The Wilsonian Moment: Self-Determination and the International Origins of Anticolonial Nationalism.* New York: Cambridge University Press.

McCormack, Gavan. 2007. *Client State: Japan in the American Embrace.* New York: Verso.

McCormick, Thomas J. 1967. *The China Market: America's Quest for Informal Empire, 1893–1901.* Chicago: Ivan Dee.

———. 1995. *America's Half-Century: United States Foreign Policy in the Cold War and After.* 2nd ed. Baltimore: Johns Hopkins Press.

Manchester, William. 1978. *American Caesar: Douglas MacArthur, 1880–1964*. Boston: Little, Brown and Company.

Marchand, Roland. 1985. *Advertising the American Dream: Making Way for Modernity, 1920–1940*. Berkeley: University of California Press.

May, Elaine Tyler. 1999. *Homeward Bound: American Families in the Cold War Era*. Rev. ed. New York: Basic Books.

May, Lary. 2000. *The Big Tomorrow: Hollywood and the Politics of the American Way*. Chicago: University of Chicago Press.

Miller, Toby, Nitin Govil, John McMurria, Richard Maxwell, and Ting Wang. 2005. *Global Hollywood 2*. London: British Film Institute.

Miyoshi, Masao, and H. D. Harootunian, eds. 1993. *Japan in the World*. Durham: Duke University Press.

Moore, Joe. 1983. *Japanese Workers and the Struggle for Power, 1945–1947*. Madison: University of Wisconsin Press.

Morris-Suzuki, Tessa. 1998. *Re-Inventing Japan: Time, Space, Nation*. New York: M. E. Sharpe.

Myers, James M. 1998. *The Bureau of Motion Pictures and Its Influence on Film Content during World War II: The Reasons for Its Failure*. Lewiston, NY: Edwin Mellen Press.

Neale, Steve. 2000. *Genre and Hollywood*. New York: Routledge.

Neu, Charles E. 1987. *The Troubled Encounter: The United States and Japan*. Malabar, FL: Robert Krieger.

Ninkovich, Frank. 1981. *The Diplomacy of Ideas: U.S. Foreign Policy and Cultural Relations, 1938–1950*. New York: Cambridge University Press.

Nishi, Toshio. 1982. *Unconditional Democracy: Education and Politics in Occupied Japan, 1945–1952*. Stanford: Hoover Institution Press.

Okamoto, Shirō. 2001. *The Man Who Saved Kabuki: Faubion Bowers and Theatre Censorship in Occupied Japan*. Trans. Samuel Leiter. Honolulu: University of Hawaii Press.

Paddock, Alfred H. Jr. 1982. *U.S. Army Special Warfare: Its Origins*. Washington, DC: National Defense University Press.

Pells, Richard. 1997. *Not Like Us: How Europeans Have Loved, Hated, and Transformed American Culture since World War II*. New York: Basic Books.

Poiger, Uta G. 2000. *Jazz, Rock, and Rebels: Cold War Politics and American Culture in a Divided Germany*. Berkeley: University of California Press.

Prince, Stephen. 1999. *The Warrior's Camera: The Cinema of Akira Kurosawa*. Rev. and ex. ed. Princeton: Princeton University Press.

Rosenberg, Emily. 1982. *Spreading the American Dream: American Economic and Cultural Expansion 1890–1945*. New York: Hill and Wang.

Rotter, Andrew. 1987. *The Path to Vietnam: Origins of the American Commitment to Southeast Asia*. Ithaca: Cornell University Press.

Rydell, Robert W., and Rob Kroes. 2005. *Buffalo Bill in Bologna: The Americanization of the World, 1869–1922*. Chicago: University of Chicago Press.

Sakanishi, Shiho. 1938. *Kyogen: Comic Interludes of Japan*. Boston: Marshall Jones.

———. 1960. *Japanese Folk-Plays: The Ink-Smeared Lady and Other Kyogen*. Rutland, VT: Charles E. Tuttle.

Sand, Jordan. 2003. *House and Home in Modern Japan: Architecture, Domestic Space, and Bourgeois Culture, 1880–1930.* Cambridge: Harvard University Press.

Sarantakes, Nicholas Evan. 2000. *Keystone: The American Occupation of Okinawa and U.S.-Japanese Relations.* College Station: Texas A&M University Press.

Sato, Barbara. 2003. *The New Japanese Woman: Modernity, Media, and Women in Interwar Japan.* Durham: Duke University Press.

Schaller, Michael. 1985. *The American Occupation of Japan: The Origins of the Cold War in Asia.* New York: Oxford University Press.

———. 1989. *Douglas MacArthur: The Far Eastern General.* New York: Oxford University Press.

Schatz, Thomas. 2001. *Boom and Bust: Hollywood and the 1940s.* Berkeley: University of California Press.

Schonberger, Howard B. 1989. *Aftermath of War: Americans and the Remaking of Japan, 1945–1952.* Kent, OH: Kent State University Press.

Segrave, Kerry. 1997. *American Films Abroad: Hollywood's Domination of the World's Movie Screens.* Jefferson, NC: McFarland.

Sherry, Michael S. 1987. *The Rise of American Air Power: The Creation of Armageddon.* New Haven: Yale University Press.

Shibusawa, Naoko. 2006. *America's Geisha Ally: Reimagining the Japanese Enemy.* Cambridge: Harvard University Press.

Shull, Michael S., and David Edward Wilt. 1996. *Hollywood War Films, 1937–1945: An Exhaustive Filmography of American Feature-Length Motion Pictures Relating to World War II.* Jefferson, NC: McFarland.

Silverberg, Miriam. 2006. *Erotic Grotesque Nonsense: The Mass Culture of Japanese Modern Times.* Berkeley: University of California Press.

Simpson, Bradley R. 2008. *Economists with Guns: Authoritarian Development and U.S.-Indonesian Relations, 1960–1968.* Stanford: Stanford University Press.

Slotkin, Richard. 1992. *Gunfighter Nation: The Myth of the Frontier in Twentieth-Century America.* New York: HarperPerennial.

Smith, Thomas C. 1955. *Political Change and Industrial Development in Japan: Government Enterprise, 1868–1880.* Palo Alto: Stanford University Press.

Spector, Ronald H. 1985. *Eagle against the Sun: The American War with Japan.* New York: Free Press.

Spicer, Andrew. 2002. *Film Noir.* New York: Longman.

Storey, John. 2003. *Inventing Popular Culture.* Malden, MA: Blackwell.

Sugita, Yoneyuki. 2003. *Pitfall or Panacea: The Irony of U.S. Power in Occupied Japan, 1945–1952.* New York: Routledge.

Swann, Paul. 1987. *The Hollywood Feature Film in Postwar Britain.* London: Croom Helm.

Takemae, Eiji. 2002. *Inside GHQ: The Allied Occupation of Japan and Its Legacy.* New York: Continuum.

Thompson, Kristin. 1985. *Exporting Entertainment: America in the World Film Market 1907–1934.* London: British Film Institute.

Thomson, Charles A. H. 1948. *Overseas Information Service of the United States Government.* Washington, DC: Brookings Institution.

Trumpbour, John. 2002. *Selling Hollywood to the World: U.S. and European Struggles for Mastery of the Global Film Industry, 1920–1950*. New York: Cambridge University Press.

Tsutsui, William M. 1998. *Manufacturing Ideology: Scientific Management in Twentieth-Century Japan*. Princeton: Princeton University Press.

Ulff-Møller, Jens. 2001. *Hollywood's Film Wars with France: Film-Trade Diplomacy and the Emergency of the French Film Quota Policy*. Rochester, NY: University of Rochester Press.

Unger, J. Marshall. 1996. *Literacy and Script Reform in Occupied Japan: Reading between the Lines*. New York: Oxford University Press.

Usabel, Gaizka S. de. 1982. *The High Noon of American Films in Latin America*. Ann Arbor, MI: UMI Research Press.

Vasey, Ruth. 1987. *The World According to Hollywood 1918–1939*. Madison: University of Wisconsin Press.

Vogel, Ezra F. 1971. *Japan's New Middle Class*. 2nd ed. Berkeley: University of California Press.

Wagnleitner, Reinhold. 1994. *Coca-Colonization and the Cold War: The Cultural Mission of the United States in Austria after the Second World War*. Chapel Hill: University of North Carolina Press.

Wagnleitner, Reinhold, and Elaine Tyler May, eds. *"Here, There, and Everywhere": The Foreign Politics of American Popular Culture*. Hanover, NH: University Press of New England.

Wakabayashi, Bob Tadashi, ed. 1998. *Modern Japanese Thought*. New York: Cambridge University Press.

Watson, James L., ed. 1997. *Golden Arches East: McDonald's in East Asia*. Stanford: Stanford University Press.

Weigley, Russell F. 1973. *The American Way of War: A History of United States Military Strategy and Policy*. Bloomington: Indiana University Press.

Welch, David. 1993. *The Third Reich: Politics and Propaganda*. New York: Routeledge.

Wheeler, Leigh Ann. 2004. *Against Obscenity: Reform and the Politics of Womanhood in America, 1873–1935*. Baltimore: Johns Hopkins University Press.

Williams, Raymond. 1983. *Keywords: A Vocabulary of Culture and Society*. Rev. ed. New York: Oxford University Press.

Williams, William Appleman. 1972. *The Tragedy of American Diplomacy*. New York: W. W. Norton.

Winkler, Allan M. 1978. *The Politics of Propaganda: The Office of War Information, 1942–1945*. New Haven: Yale University Press.

Wittner, Lawrence S. 1993. *One World or None: A History of the World Nuclear Disarmament Movement through 1953*. Stanford: Stanford University Press.

Yamamura, Kozo, ed. 1997. *The Economic Emergence of Modern Japan*. New York: Cambridge University Press.

Yoshimoto, Mitsuhiro. 2000. *Kurosawa: Film Studies and Japanese Cinema*. Durham: Duke University Press.

Young, Louise. 1998. *Japan's Total Empire: Manchuria and the Culture of Wartime Imperialism*. Berkeley: University of California Press.

Zunz, Oliver. 1998. *Why the American Century?* Chicago: University of Chicago Press.

Articles and Chapters of Books in Japanese

Deguchi Fumihito. 1991. "Nani ga hakujin konpurekkusu wo umidashitaka." In *Nihon eiga to modanizumu 1920–1930*, edited by Iwamoto Kenji, 104–23. Tokyo: Riburo pōto.

Fukuda Kizō. 1975a. "Eiga tōitsu kenetsu no naiyō to mondai: eiga tōsei ni kansuru kenkyū 2." *Seikei daigaku bungaku kiyō* 11: 46–55.

———. 1975b. "Taishōki ni okeru eiga tōsei jokyo, sono ichi." *Seikei daigaku bungakubu kiyō* 10: 51–65.

Gerow, Aaron. 1997. "Jigoma to eiga no 'hakken': Nihon eiga gensetsushi josetsu." *Eizōgaku* 58: 34–50.

———. 1999. "*Miyamoto Musashi* to senjichū no kankyaku." In *Eiga kantoku Mizoguchi Kenji*, edited by Yomota Inuhiko, 226–50. Tokyo: Shinyōsha.

———. 2002. "Tatakau kankyaku: Daitōa kyōeiken to nihon eiga no juyō no mondai." *Gendai shisō* 30, no. 9: 136–49.

Hase Masato. 1994. "Kenetsu no tanjō: taishōki no keisatsu to katsudō shashin." *Eizōgaku* 53: 124–38.

Katō Atsuko. 2004. "Taishu goraku kara eiga kokusaku e." In *Media shi o manabu hitono tameni*, edited by Ariyama Teruo, 208–31. Kyoto: Sekai shisōsha.

Makino Mamoru. 1995. "'Bunka toshiteno eiga no dokyumenteshon': Bunken, posutā, puromaido nado." In *Eiga seitan 100nen hakurankai*, edited by Kawasai shimin myūjiamu, 136–42. Tokyo: Kinema junpōsha.

Nakano Gorō. 1958. "Sensō eiga no shijitsusei to gorakusei." *Gan:* 126–37.

Okudaira Yasuhiro. 1986. "Eiga to kokka tōsei." In *Sensō to nihon eiga*. Tokyo: Iwanami shoten: 238–49.

Ōsawa Shinichirō. 1976. "Sākuru no sengoshi." In *Shūdan: Sākuru no sengoshi*, edited by Shīsō no kagaku kinkyūkai, 68–92. Tokyo: Heibonsha.

Shimizu Akira. 1972. "20.9.22 kara 23.8.19 made: Senryōka no eigakai no kiroku." *Firumu sentā* 7: 9–10.

Takaoka Hiroyuki. 1996. "Haisenchokugo no bunka jōkyō to bunka undō." In *Gendaishi to minshushugi*. Vol. 2 of *Nenpo nihon gendaishi*, edited by Awaya Kentarō, 182–93. Tokyo: Azuma shuppan.

Takemura Tamio. 2001. "Sengo nihon ni okeru bunka undō to rekishi ishiji." *Gendai shakai kenkyū* 2: 15–29. http://www.cs.kyoto-wu.ac.jp/bulletin/2/takemura.pdf (accessed June 18, 2006).

Books in Japanese

Amano Shōko. 2005. *"Tsukiai" no sengoshi: Sākuru, nettowaku no hiraku chihei*. Tokyo: Yoshikawa kōbunkan.

America eiga bunka kyōkai, ed. 1949. *Eiga no kisetsu* Tokyo: America eiga bunka kyōkai.

Ariyama Teruo. 1996. *Senryōshi media kenkyū: jiyū to tōsei, 1945 nen*. Tokyo: Kashiwa shobō.

Etō Jun. 1994. *Tozasareta gengo kūkan: Senryōgun no kenetsu to sengo nihon*. Tokyo: Bungei shunjūsha.

Fujiki Hideaki. 2007. *Zōshoku suru perusona: Eiga sutādamu no seiritsu to nihon kindai.* Nagoya: Nagoya University Press.

Fujitake Akira and Yamamoto Akira, eds. 1994. *Nihon no masu komyunikēshon* 3rd ed. Tokyo: NHK Books.

Fukuokashi Kōgyō kyōkai, ed. 2003. *Hakata: Gekijō 50 nen no ayumi II.* Fukuoka: Gen shobō.

Futaba Jūzaburo. 1950. *Amerika eiga.* Tokyo: Meikyokudō.

Hazumi Arihiro, ed. 1987. *Yodogawa Nagaharu shūsei.* Vols. 1–4. Tokyo: Haga shoten.

Hazumi Tsuneo. 1942. *Eiga to minzoku.* Tokyo: Eiga nihonsha.

———. 1947. *Amerika eiga dokuhon.* Tokyo: Tōzai shuppansha.

High, Peter B. 1995. *Teikoku no ginmaku: 15nen sensō to nihon eiga.* Nagoya: Nagoya University Press.

Hirata Tetsuo. 2002. *Reddo pāji no shiteki kenkyū.* Tokyo: Shin nihon shuppansha.

Hiroshimashi, Nagasakishi genbaku saigaishi henshū iinkai, ed. 1985. *Genbaku saigai Hiroshima Nagasaki.* Tokyo: Iwanami bunko.

Honda Akira. 1938. *Kandō to hihyō.* Tokyo: Sakuhinsha.

———. 1941. *Geijutsu to shakai.* Tokyo: Kawade shobō.

———. 1947. *Kodoku no bungakusha.* Tokyo: Yakumo shoten.

———. 1948a. *Ichi chishikijin no kokuhaku.* Tokyo: Fuju shoin.

———. 1948b. *Seishun to hyūmanizumu.* Tokyo: Akebono shobō.

———. 1955. *Shidōsha: Kono hito wo miyo.* Tokyo: Kōbunsha.

———. 1957. *Idai na jikini: Warera ikani ikubekika.* Tokyo: Hokushindō.

———. 1966. *Seishun no kensetsu: Wakai hito ni hanashikakeru.* Tokyo: Akita shoten.

Hori Makoto, and Kanba Toshio. 1946. *Minshu shugi no rekishi.* Tokyo: Aiikusha.

———. 1946. *Minshu shugi no shomondai.* Tokyo: Aiikusha.

———. 1949. *Minshu shgi no riron.* Tokyo: Aiikusha.

Hosoiri Tōtaro. 1947a. *Amerika bunka no seichō.* Tokyo: Aoyama shoin.

———1947b. *Gendai Amerika dokuhon.* Tokyo: Kobarutosha.

Iijima Tadashi. 1939. *Eiga bunka no kenkyū.* Tokyo: Shinchōsha.

———. 1948. *Eiga kanshō dokuhon.* Tokyo: Ōbunsha.

Izawa Jun. 1973. *Eiga toiu kaibutsu.* Tokyo: Gakugei shobō.

Inoue Masao. 2007. *Bunka to tōsō: Tōhō sōgi, 1946–1948.* Tokyo: Shinyōsha.

Itō Shiei. *Nagoya eigashi: 8 mm kara 70 mm made.* 1980. Nagoya: Ukai insatsu.

Iwasaki Akira. 1958. *Gendai nihon no eiga.* Tokyo: Chūō kōronsha.

Jiji tsūshinsha. 1947. *Eiga geinō nenkan 1947 nendoban.* Tokyo: Jiji tsūshinsha.

———. 1949. *Eiga nenkan 1950.* Tokyo: Jiji tsūshinsha.

Kadin, Martin. 1971. *Zerosen: Nihon kaigun no eikō.* Trans. Katoyama Kōtarō, supervised by Nakano Gōrō. Tokyo: Sankei shinbunsha shuppankyoku.

Kamishima Kimi. 1995. *Jimaku shikakenin ichidaiki: Kamishima Kimi jiden.* Tokyo: Pandora.

Katō Atsuko. 2003. *Sōdōin taisei to eiga.* Tokyo: Shinyōsha.

Kinema junpōsha, ed. 1986. *Kinema junpō eiga 40nen zen kiroku.* Tokyo: Kinema junpōsha.

Kitagawa Kenzō. 2000. *Sengo no shuppatsu: Bunka undō, seinendan, sensō mibōjin.* Tokyo: Aoki shoten.

Kodama Kazuo. 1974. *Yabunirami eigashi: Sengo no kiroku 1945–1972.* Tokyo: Yomiuri shinbunsha.

Kokuritsu kokkai toshokan, ed. 1997. *Dokyumento sengo no nihon: Shinbun, nyūsu ni miru shakaishi daijiten 36*. Tokyo: Ōzorasha.

Kokusai eiga tsūshinsha, ed. 1925. *Nihon eiga jigyō sōran, Taishō 15 nendoban*. Tokyo: Kokusai eiga tsūshinsha.

———. 1927. *Nihon eiga jigyō sōran, Shōwa 2 nendoban*. Tokyo: Kokusai eiga tsūshinsha.

———. 1928. *Nihon eiga jigyō sōran, Shōwa 3–4 nendoban*. Tokyo: Kokusai eiga tsūshinsha.

———. 1930. *Nihon eiga jigyō sōran, Shōwa 5 nendoban*. Tokyo: Kokusai eiga tsūshinsha.

———. 1934. *Nihon eiga jigyō sōran, Shōwa 9 nendoban*. Tokyo: Kokusai eiga tsūshinsha.

Komori Kazuko. 1951. *Sutā dokuhon*. Tokyo: Jitsubunkan.

Kurosawa Akira. 2001. *Gama no abura no yōna mono*. Rpr. ed. Tokyo: Iwanami shoten.

Makino Mamoru. 2003. *Nihon eiga kenetsushi*. Tokyo: Pandorasha.

Makino Mamoru, ed. 2002. *Fukkokuban kinema record*. 3 vols. Tokyo: Kokusho kankōkai.

Matsuura Sōzō. 1974. *Senryōka no genron danatsu zōho ketteiban*. Tokyo: Gendai jānarizumu kenkyūkai.

Molasky, Mike. 2005. *Sengo nihon no jazu bunka: Eiga, bungaku, angura*. Tokyo: Seidosha.

Minami Hiroshi, and Shakai shinri kenkyūjo. 1990. *Zoku showa bunka 1945–1989*. Tokyo: Keisō shobō.

Nagai Hiroshi. 1949. *Nagasaki no kane*. Tokyo: Hibiya shuppansha, 1949.

Nagoyashi. 1999. *Shinshu Nagoya shishi, dai 7 kan*. Nagoya: Nagoyashi.

Nakano Gorō. 1943a. *Keishō*. Tokyo: Kizanbō.

———. 1943b. *Sokoku ni kaeru*. Tokyo: Shin kigensha.

———. 1945. *Tekikoku Amerika no sensō senden*. Tokyo: Shin taiyōsha.

———. 1946. *Demokurashī no benkyō*. Tokyo: Meguro shoten.

———. 1947. *Amerika zakkichō*. Tokyo: Shichisei shoin.

———. 1948. *Kakute gyokusai seri: haisen no rekishi*. Tokyo: Nihon kōhōsha.

———. 1949. *Amerika ni manabu*. Tokyo: Nihon kōhōsha.

———. 1993. *Kimi ha dainiji sekai taisen o shitte iruka: Kyōkasho dewa manabanai senōo no sugao*. Tokyo: Kojinsha.

Nakazato Kaizan. 1995. *Daibosatsu tōge*. 20 vols. Tokyo: Chikuma shobō.

Nanbu Keinosuke. 1956. *Eiga sendensen*. Tokyo: Dōbunkan.

Nikkatsu kabushiki gaisha, ed. 1962. *Nikkatsu 50 nenshi*. Tokyo: Nikkatsu kabushiki gaisha.

Nishikawa Nagao. 1995. *Chikyū jidai no minzoku = bunka riron: Datsu "kokumin bunka" no tameni*. Tokyo: Shinyōsha.

———. 2001. *Kokkyō no koekata: Kokumin kokkaron josetsu, zōho*. Tokyo: Heibonsha.

Nōma Yoshihiro. 2003. *Fukuoka Hakata eiga hyakunen*. Fukuoka: Imamura shoten san kurieito.

Ōguro Toyouji. 1981. *Eiga to tomoni 50nen*. Kochi: Kochi shinbunsha, 1981.

Sakanishi Shiho. 1947. *Minshushugi wa seikatsu no nakani*. Tokyo: Ie no hikari bunko.

———. 1949. *Josei to kyōyō: Renai, shakai, gakusei*. Tokyo: Kokudosha.

———. 1961. *Minshushugi wa kodomono toki kara*. Tokyo: Minshu kyoiku kyōkai.

———. 1965. *Minshu shakai ni okeru shimin*. Tokyo: Minshu kyōiku kyōkai.

"Sakanishi Shiho san" henshū sewani kai, ed. 1977. *Sakanishi Shiho san*. Tokyo: Kokusai bunka kaikan.

Sasaki Tetsuo. 2000. *Sanpunkan no sagishi: Yokokuhen jinsei*. Tokyo: Pandorasha.

———. 2006. *"Sanpunkan no sagishi" ga kataru ginmaku no uragawa.* Tokyo: Gendai shokan.

Satō Tadao. 1995. *Nihon eigashi.* Vols. 1–4. Tokyo: Iwanama shoten.

Satō Takumi. 2002. *"Kingu" no jidai: Kokumin taishū zasshi no kōkyōsei.* Tokyo: Iwanami shoten.

Satō Yūichi. 2000. *Waga shi Yodogawa Nagaharu tono 50nen.* Tokyo: Seiryū shuppan.

Shindō Kaneto. 1983. *Tsuihōsha tachi: Eiga no reddo pāji.* Tokyo: Iwanami shoten.

———. 1994. *Shindō Kaneto no sokuseki.Vol. 4* Tokyo: Iwanami shoten.

———. 2005. *Genbaku o toru.* Tokyo: Shin nihon shuppansha.

Shōchiku eiga kabushiki gaisha. 1964. *Shōchiku 70 nenshi.* Tokyo: Shōchiku eiga kabushiki gaisha.

Sodei Rinjirō. 1986. *Senryō shita mono sareta mono.* Tokyo: Simul Press.

Subaru Kōgyō kabushiki gaisha. 1987. *Subaru-za no ayumi: 40 nen shōshi.* Tokyo: Subaru Kōgyō kabushiki gaisha.

———. 1997. *Subaru Kōgyō 50 nenshi.* Tokyo: Subaru kōgyō.

Suzuki Sadami. 2005. *Nihon no bunka nashonarizumu.* Tokyo: Heibonsha.

Takemae Eiji. 1982. *GHQ.* Tokyo: Iwanami shoten.

Takemura Tamio. 2004. *Taishō bunka: Teikoku no yūtopia.* Tokyo: Sangensha.

Tanaka Junichirō. 1963. *Nihon eiga hattatsushi.* Vols. 1–5. Tokyo: Chūō kōronsha.

Tanikawa Takeshi. 2002. *Amerika eiga to senryō seisaku.* Kyoto: Kyoto daigaku shuppankai.

Terebi Asahi, ed. 1986. *Eiga ha buraunkan no shiteiseki de: Yodogawa Nagaharu to "Nichiyo yoga" no 20nen.* Tokyo: Terebi Asahi.

Tsukuda Yoshinori. 1999. *Yodogawa Nagaharu ga nokoshite kuretakoto: Eiga ga jinsei no gakko data.* Tokyo: Kairyūsha.

Tsumura Hideo. 1943. *Eiga seisakuron.* Tokyo: Chūō kōronsha.

———. 1950. *Konnichi no eiga.* Tokyo: Kaname shobō.

Tsurumi Shunsuke. 1991. *Senjiki nihon no seishinshi, 1931–1945.* Tokyo: Iwanami shoten.

———. 1991. *Sengo nihon no taishū bunkashi 1945–1980.* Tokyo: Iwanami shoten.

Uekusa Keinosuke. 1985. *Waga seishun no Kurosawa Akira.* Tokyo: Bunshun bunko.

Wada Shinken, ed. 1947. *Hanashi no izumi.* Tokyo: Aoyama Shoten.

Yamada Taichi, Saitō Masao, Tanaka Kōgi, Miyagawa Shōji, Yoshida Takeshi, and Watanabe Yutaka, eds. 1995. *Hito wa taisetsu na kotomo wasurete shimaukara: Shōchiku Ōfuna satsueijo monogatari.* Tokyo: Magazine House.

Yamamoto Kikuo. 1982. *Nihon eiga ni okeru gaikoku eiga no eikyō.* Tokyo: Waseda University Press.

Yamamoto Taketoshi. 1996. *Senryōki media bunseki.* Tokyo: Hosei University Press.

Yodogawa Nagaharu. 1950. *Eiga sansaku.* Tokyo: Fuyu shobō.

———. 1973. *Eiga to tomoni ayunda waga hanshōki.* Tokyo: Kindai eigasha.

———. 1980. *Boku no kyōkasho wa eiga datta.* Tokyo: Popurasha.

———. 1988. *Yodogawa Nagaharu jiden.* 2 vols. Tokyo: Chūō kōronsha.

Yomota Inuhiko. 1999. *Nihon eiga no radikaru na ishi.* Tokyo: Iwanami shoten.

———. 2000. *Nihon eiga 100 nenshi.* Tokyo: Shūeisha.

Yoshimi Shunya. 1987. *Toshi no doramaturugī: Tokyo, sakariba no shakaishi.* Tokyo: Kobundo.

———. 2007. *Shinbei to hanbei: Sengo nihon no seijiteki muishiki.* Tokyo: Iwanami shoten.

Acknowledgments

My first words of gratitude go to my mentors at the University of Wisconsin–Madison. I wish to thank Paul S. Boyer, whose sage advice, warm presence, and characteristic good humor have inspired the creation of this book. I am also indebted to Tom McCormick, David Bordwell, Jeremi Suri, Louise Young, and Brett Sheehan who offered countless feedback and encouragement. Other teachers and friends in Madison have helped me as well. I am grateful to Tino Balio, Teresa Becker, Jeffrey and Katie Carté Engel, Jen Fay, David Herzberg, Vance Kepley Jr., Eric Morser, Patrick Jones, Mike Rawson, and Chris Wells. Fujiki Hideaki tirelessly commented on my writings and shared his boundless knowledge of Japanese cinema. I am also deeply appreciative of Sandy Heitzkey, Jim Schlender, Jane Williams, and the late Judy Cochran, who steered me through the bureaucratic ocean of higher education.

Other friends, colleagues, and teachers have supported this book along the way. I would like to thank Robert C. Allen, Robert Angel, Dirk Bonker, Peter Decherney, Chris Endy, Brian Etheridge, Steve Fuchs, Kathy Fuller-Seeley, Hirano Kyōko, Walter Hixson, Kristin Hoganson, Chris Jespersen, Matt Loayza, Hosoya Masahiro, Lary May, Toby Miller, Miyao Daisuke, Richard Pells, Emily Rosenberg, Maureen Shanahan, Walter Skya, Brian Yecies, and Tosaka Yūji. Richard Maltby, Melvyn Stokes, and Jeffrey Engel patiently guided my early research toward publication. In a pivotal moment, colleagues at the Social Science Research Council's Japan studies workshop gave me a much needed energy boost. Many others have listened to my presentations and given pointed feedback. I owe a heartfelt thanks to the panelists and audiences whom I encountered at the American Historical Association, American Studies Association, Carleton College, James Madison University, Johns Hopkins University ("Pairing Empires: Britain and America" Conference), Nagoya University, Society for Cinema and Media Studies, Society for Historians of American Foreign Relations, University College London ("American Cinema and Everyday Life" Conference), University of Wisconsin–Madison, and Yale University ("Lives and Consequences: The Local Impact of the Cold War" Conference).

Portions of chapter 6 were previously published in slightly different form as Hiroshi Kitamura, "'Home of American Movies': The Marunouchi Subaruza and the Making of Hollywood's Audiences in Occupied Tokyo, 1946–9," in *Hollywood Abroad: Audiences and Cultural Exchange,* edited by Richard Maltby and Melvyn Stokes (London: British Film Institute, 2004), 99–120, reproduced here with permission of Palgrave Macmillan; and Hiroshi Kitamura, "Exhibition and Entertainment: Hollywood and the American Reconstruction of Defeated Japan," in *The Local Consequences of the Global Cold War,* edited by Jeffrey A. Engel (Washington, DC, and Stanford: Woodrow Wilson Center and Stanford University Press, 2007), 33–56, reproduced here with permission of Woodrow Wilson Center Press. I gratefully acknowledge the publishers for allowing me to use the material.

In addition, this book would not have been completed without generous financial support. Scholarships and grants from the College of William and Mary, Franklin and Eleanor Roosevelt Institute, Society for Historians of American Foreign Relations, Toyota Foundation, Harry S. Truman Library Institute, and the University of Wisconsin–Madison have been invaluable.

No less helpful were the librarians and archivists who navigated me through the mounds of primary and secondary sources. I especially wish to thank Liz Safly and Dennis Bilger at the Harry S. Truman Library; Amy Wasserstrom at the University of Maryland–College Park; Barbara Hall at the Academy of Motion Picture Arts and Sciences; Ned Comstock and Noelle Carter at the University of Southern California; and Jim Zobel at the MacArthur Memorial Library.

During a pair of research trips to Washington, DC, Bob and Toyoko Miyashiro opened their cozy living space and allowed me to complete my hectic (and chaotic) research schedule. Connie and Bill Gillen have given me comfort via countless meals and good company.

Research in Japan was far more exciting and far less frustrating because of the kind help of many people. Murakami Hisanobu, Ishikawa Toshiharu, and Hirata Itsue at Tōhō Studio's Film and Culture Association generously opened the doors to their precious repository. Makino Mamoru shared with me his vast knowledge and private archive. Mizobuchi Kumiko painstakingly assisted my newspaper research in Nagoya. I particularly treasure the opportunity to have met and interviewed film critics, Hollywood employees, exhibitors, and other contemporaries who made history in occupied Japan. Their first-hand accounts were invaluable. Many thanks to them all, especially Aijima Masato, Asaoka Hiroshi, Hidano Atsushi, Komaki Toshiharu, Ōi Makoto, Oikawa Shirō, Donald Richie, Sasaki Tetsuo, and Yamada Noboru.

In addition, friends and colleagues in two educational institutions have been invaluable allies. At SUNY–Oswego, Frank Byrne, Doug Deal, Jean Dittmar, Leo Hernandez, Gwen Kay, Mark Kulikowski, Chris Mack, Ming-te Pan, Tim Thurber, and Gerry Forbes have supported my research in full. I owe unpayable debts to my friends and colleagues at the College of William and Mary. Rachel DiNitto, Eric Han, Arthur Knight, and Karin Wulf ably read and critiqued portions of my manuscript; Ismail Abdalla, Jim Allegro, Tim Barnard, Tuska Benes, Gail Bossenga, Chandos Brown, Craig Canning, Gail Conner, Fred Corney, Ed Crapol, Phil Daileader, Mel Ely, Andy Fisher, Maureen Fitzgerald, Betty Flanigan, Chris Grasso, Cindy Hahamovitch, Dale Hoak, Ron Hoffman, LuAnn Homza, Laurie Koloski, Kris Lane, Paul Mapp, Jim McCord, Charlie McGovern, Leisa Meyer, Scott Nelson, Kim Phillips, Ed Pratt (now at Florida Atlantic University), Abdul-Karim Rafeq, Ron Schechter, Carol Sheriff, Roz Stearns, Jim Whittenburg, and Chitralekha Zutshi helped me in more ways than one.

Cornell University Press has been a publisher that I have always held in high esteem. It is an honor to have my book included in the "United States in the World" series. Alison Kallett (now at Princeton University Press), Michael Mc-Gandy, Ange Romeo-Hall, and Emily Zoss have patiently guided me from start to finish. Katy Meigs's careful copyediting saved me from numerous errors. The three anonymous reviewers aided me with words of wisdom and sharp insight. Kate Mertes created a superb index. I am out of words to thank the two series editors. Paul Kramer has been a model scholar and teacher to me since my days in graduate school. His advice has always been upbeat, encouraging, and inspiring. Mark Bradley has read and commented on every single page of my manuscript, line by line. Among other things, he has taught me that good histories are written with heart.

My closing words of thanks go to family. My wife Aiko has been with me since the most challenging of times in graduate school. It is impossible to put to words what she has meant to me. Our daughter Erica joined our world during the late stages of writing this book. She is an inspiration who continues to enrich our lives. Finally, I would like to gratefully acknowledge my late father Takao Kitamura and my mother Mitsuyo Kitamura for their love and support. This book would not have existed without their countless sacrifices to make my overseas studies a reality. I genuinely appreciate what they have given me throughout my life.

HIROSHI KITAMURA

Williamsburg, Virginia, May 2009

Index

Page numbers in *italics* indicate illustrative material. For specific movies, please see the separate Index of Films.

Cotten, Joseph, 167
culture elites and American movies, 134–54;
AMCA (*See* American Movie Culture
Association); defined, 219n2–3; film critics
(*See* film critics and criticism in Japan);
Japanese versus American movies, attitudes
toward, 136–37, 139, 148, 181–82; at Marunouchi Subaru-za (Tokyo) events, 124–25
"cultures of defeat," 52–53

Daiei, 17, 43, 45, 49, 58, 129, 130, 180, 182
Daiichi kokusai gekijō or DKG (Nagasaki), 120,
128–33
de Wolf, Francis Colt, 27
DeMille, Cecil B., 104, 106, 108
democracy, American, Japanese interest in.
See Americanization
Disney, Walt, 24, 132
distribution and exhibition of films in Japan,
112–33; "bicycling" prints between theaters,
115; at end of occupation, 178; fees, raising
of, 115; financial arrangements, dissatis-
faction with, 64, *84*, 84–85; during and
immediately after WWII, 113–15; marketing
practices, 116–18, *117*, 123, 131–32; prewar
government regulation of, 17; quality improvement techniques, 118–19; reformation
of exhibition practices, 115–18; responses of
exhibitors to Hollywood dictates, 119–20;
road-show system, 122–23, 126–27; studio
ownership, 45; as urban affair, 191n44. *See
also* film theaters
Dower, John W., x, 52
Durbin, Deanna, 22, 126, 158

Edison, Thomas A., and Edison Company, 3, 7
education and self-improvement: AMCA,
as aim of, 135, 140–41, 145–46, 148–49,
151–52; *Eiga no tomo* and, 160–61, 163, 168,
170; English, learning, 93, 160, 172
Eiga geijutsu, 135, 157
Eiga hyōron, 135, 157
Eiga nenkan, 44, 45, 115
Eiga no tomo and fan culture, 155–76; after end
of occupation, 176, 182; AMCA compared,
174; censorship of, 222n2; content and
coverage, 158–61, *159,* 163–65; cultural
activities sponsored by, 174–76; educational
aspects of, 160–61, 163, 168, 170; Honda's
and Nakano's articles for, 147–48, 160–61;
on marketing of Hollywood films, 87, *88,*

95; occupation powers, endorsed by, 156,
157–58, 162–63; origins and postwar rebirth
of, 157–58; polls and surveys, use of, 164–65;
pro-American bias of, 156, 157–58, 160–61,
167–69, 175–76; reader demographics,
161, 163–65, *166;* reader participation ad
response, 163–70; Tomo no kai (Meeting
of friends), 156, *162,* 169–74; Yodogawa
Nagaharu's editorship of, 156, 161–63, *162,*
165, 171–72, 176
Eihai (Shadan hōjin eiga haikyūsha), 17
Eito Toshio, 139
elites. *See* culture elites and American movies
English, learning, 93, 160, 172
"enlightenment campaign" to spread American
values and ideals, ix–xi, 112–13, 177–78. *See
also* Japan's postwar Americanization, role of
Hollywood in
European cinema, xi, 3, 6, 7, 66, 93, 120, 130
exhibition of films. *See* distribution and exhibition of films in Japan

fan culture. *See Eiga no tomo* and fan culture
"feudalism," American concern with, 31,
34–36, 46, 50, 51, 57, 60, 73, 74, *74,* 149
film. *See* European cinema; Hollywood; Japanese
film industry
film critics and criticism in Japan: under Allied
occupation, 138; AMCA and, 139, 141–42;
before, during, and immediately after WWII,
135–38; CMPE control of, 93; Hollywood's
approach to, 138–39
The Film Daily, 6, 112
Film Law (Japan, 1939), 16–17, 18, 35
film theaters: awards and prizes for, 119; competition, encouraging ("good movies to good
theaters" policy), 118; Daiichi kokusai gekijō
or DKG (Nagasaki), 120, 128–33; Denki-
kan (Matsumoto), 155; first-run and second-run
venues, 92–93, 118–19; health and hygiene
issues, 116; Hibiya eiga gekijō (Tokyo), 11;
Hōgaku-za (Tokyo), 114; Kitano gekijō
(Osaka), *181;* Kokusai eiga gekijō (Fukuoka), 129; Marunouchi Subaru-za (Tokyo),
120–25, *122,* 126, 127, 130, 132; Meiga-za
(Tokyo), 122; Musashino-kan (Tokyo), 11;
Nagasaki Central Theater, 129, 218n120;
number at end of WWII, 114; Orion-za
(Tokyo), 122; seating arrangements, 118,
123–24, 127–28, 131, 218n78; Sekai-kan
(Fukuoka), 11; Sennichimae sentoraru kaikan

industry under Allied occupation); culture elites's attitudes toward, 136–37, 139, 148, 181–82; distribution and exhibition business (*See* distribution and exhibition of films in Japan); independent studios, 44, 45; marketing for Hollywood films denigrating, 90; monopoly investigations of, 45; organized labor in, 45, 46, 47, 48; postwar challenges faced by, 43–45; postwar rebuilding of, 33–38, 47; prewar government regulation of, 15–17, 34; prewar vibrancy of, 2, 6–8, 12–15; wartime collaborators in, 44–45

Japanese names, treatment of, xiv

Japan's postwar Americanization, role of Hollywood in, ix–xiv; after end of occupation, 177–83; censorship (*See entries at censorship*); cinema campaign encouraged by Allied occupation, ix–xi, 22–23; culture elites, 134–54 (*See also* culture elites and American movies); distribution and exhibition of films, 112–33 (*See also* distribution and exhibition of films in Japan); *Eiga no tomo* and fan culture, 155–76 (*See also Eiga no tomo* and fan culture); "enlightenment campaign," ix–xi, 112–13, 177–78; historical background (*See* prewar relationship between Japan and Hollywood; wartime, Hollywood in); marketing of U.S. films in Japan, 87–111 (*See also* marketing of Hollywood in occupied Japan); privileging and institutionalization of Hollywood film trade, 38–41, 66, 67; rebuilding of Japanese film industry, 33–38, 47

jazz portrayed as white music in *Rhapsody in Blue*, 98–100

Jiji tsūshin, 157

Johnson, E. Bruce, 12

Johnston, Eric Alva, 28–29, 83, 85, 154, 181

jun eiga undō or pure film movement, 13

kabuki, 8, 12, 57

Kaeriyama Norimasa, 13

Kamei Fumio, 148

Kanesaka Building, 92, 211n16

Kataoka Chiezō, 61

Katayama Tetsu, 140

Kawakami Hajime, 147

Kenny, Elizabeth, 149–50

Kikuta Kazuo, 139

Kinema junpō, 57, 93, 94–95, 114, 135, 157, 178

Kinetoscope, 7, 12

Kinugasa Teinosuke, 13, 180

Kōgyō herarudo, 63–64

Kokusai eiga shinbun, 1, 12, 14, 58

Komaki Toshiharu, 215n36

Korean War, 112, 178

Kotani, Henry, 13

Kubo Hisaji, 19–20

Kudamatsu A.M.C.A. News, 140

kumi, 13

Kurihara Sumiko, 13

Kurihara, Thomas, 13

Kurosawa Akira, 49, 50, 51, 52, 53, 72, 180

kyodatsu condition, 30, 147–48

labor unions in Japanese film industry, 45, 46, 47, 48

Laemmle, Carl, 3

Latin America: Hollywood cinema in, 6, 197n29; Japanese releases of films from, 66

Lawson, John Howard, 69

Leonowens, Anna, 77, 117–18, 149–50

LeRoy, Mervyn, 103, 104

Levant, Oscar, 97, 98

Lincoln, Abraham, 77–78, 105

"Little State Department." *See* Motion Picture Export Association

Little Three studios (U.S.), 5, 28

Lumière brothers, 7

Maas, Irving A., 83–84, 112, 118, 178

MacArthur, Douglas, 31, 32, *80*, 81, 134–35, 178. *See also* Allied occupation of Japan

MacLeish, Archibald, 25

Magruder, Carter B., 84–85

Maltby, Richard, 10

Manchurian Incident (1931), 16, 54

Manet, Edouard, 118

Manila Massacre (1945), 55

Marco Polo Bridge Incident (1937), 18

marketing of Hollywood in occupied Japan, 87–111; actors, publicity about, 93; after end of occupation, 177–78, 180–82; *bunka* (culture), American films portrayed as, 87–90, 94–96; CMPE as business institution, 90–94; *Cry of the City*, case study of, 108–11; film critics, control of, 93; by film distributors and exhibitors, 116–18, *117*, 123, 131–32; first-run and second-run film theaters, 92–93; genre-based promotions, 94–95; Japanese cinema, denigration of, 90; *Little Women*, case study of, 100–104, 111; MPEA seal, use of, 87, *88*, 119; program

Index of Films